Conflicting
Missions?

Conflicting Missions?

Teachers Unions and Educational Reform

TOM LOVELESS

Editor

BROOKINGS INSTITUTION PRESS
Washington, D.C.

Copyright © 2000
THE BROOKINGS INSTITUTION
1775 Massachusetts Avenue, N.W., Washington, D.C. 20036
www.brookings.edu

Library of Congress Cataloging-in-Publication data
Conflicting missions? : teachers unions and educational reform /
Tom Loveless, editor.
    p.   cm.
Includes bibliographical references and index.
ISBN 0-8157-5304-7 (cloth : alk. paper)
ISBN 0-8157-5303-9 (pbk. : alk. paper)
    1. Teachers' unions—United States. 2. Educational change—United
States. I. Title: Teachers unions and educational reform. II. Loveless,
Tom, 1954–
LB2844.53.U62 C66 2000   00-008614
331.88'113711'00973—dc21   CIP

9 8 7 6 5 4 3 2 1
The paper used in this publication meets minimum requirements of the
American National Standard for Information Sciences—Permanence of Paper
for Printed Library Materials: ANSI Z39.48-1984.

Typeset in Adobe Garamond

Composition by R. Lynn Rivenbark
Macon, Georgia

Printed by R. R. Donnelley and Sons
Harrisonburg, Virginia

Contents

Conflicting Missions?

TOM LOVELESS

Introduction

A SK PEOPLE WHETHER teachers unions are good or bad for education
and you are likely to receive a wide variety of opinions. A 1998
Gallup Poll asked whether teachers unions helped, hurt, or made no difference in the quality of education in U.S. public schools. Twenty-seven
percent responded that unions helped, 26 percent that they hurt, and
37 percent that they made no difference (10 percent said they did not
know).[1] Two popular 1997 books offered dramatically opposing answers to
this question. In *United Mind Workers*, Charles Kerchner, Julia E. Koppich,
and Joseph G. Weeres portray teachers unions as an integral part of the
quest to improve American education. Myron Lieberman's *The Teacher
Unions,* on the other hand, depicts them as irredeemable supporters of the
status quo, intractable and politically powerful enemies of reform.[2]

These two books joined a surprisingly small body of literature evaluating the impact of teachers unions on American education. Although

1. Lowell C. Rose and Alec M. Gallup, "The Thirteith Annual Phi Delta Kappa/Gallup Poll of
the Public's Attitudes toward the Public Schools," *Phi Delta Kappan* 80, 1 (September 1998): 41–56.
2. Charles Taylor Kerchner, Julia E. Koppich, and Joseph G. Weeres, *United Mind Workers:
Unions and Teaching in the Knowledge Society* (Jossey-Bass, 1997); Myron Lieberman, *The Teacher
Unions: How the NEA and AFT Sabatoge Reform and Hold Students, Parents, Teachers, and Taxpayers
Hostage to Bureaucracy* (Free Press, 1997).

teachers unions were first organized in the nineteenth century, and collective bargaining has been a fact of life in most communities since the 1960s, a serious gap exists between what we think we know about teachers unions and what we really know. Aspiring to close that gap, the Program on Education Policy and Governance at Harvard University invited approximately eighty scholars for a two-day conference on the topic of teachers unions and educational reform, held September 25–26, 1998. Paul Peterson and I organized the meeting, and funding was provided by the John M. Olin Foundation and the A. Alfred Taubman Center for State and Local Government at the John F. Kennedy School of Government. We solicited papers from researchers representing a broad array of disciplinary backgrounds and methodological approaches and invited union leaders and some of the unions' harshest critics to the conference. We asked each author to inventory what is known about the impact of teachers unions on educational reform; to analyze the quality of that knowledge, paying particular attention to ambiguities in the research; and to identify questions on which future investigations would be fruitful. The papers were everything we hoped for—provocative, engaging, and informative—and the ensuing discussions were both lively and thought provoking.

The papers from the conference are presented as the chapters of this book. In examining the relationship of teachers unions and educational reform, the authors approach the subject from several directions. They ask whether unions affect educational productivity, most notably in terms of an impact on student achievement. They analyze how teachers unions function as professional organizations concerned with the occupation of teaching, as institutional actors defending interests within a bureaucratic system of education, and as political actors wielding influence on legislation and elections. Taken as a whole, these varying perspectives do not provide readers with a simple answer to the question of whether unions help or hurt educational reform. But the book does illustrate the many dimensions of the teachers unions' role in American education and offers a well-balanced, comprehensive analysis of the unions' controversial relationship with education reform.

In the first chapter, Susan Moore Johnson and Susan M Kardos of Harvard University show that the way teachers unions bargain has evolved over time. Industrial style bargaining prevailed for most of this century, with wages and work conditions subject to contentious negotiations between teachers and management. Beginning in the 1980s, reform-style bargaining gained a foothold in local labor negotiations. Drawing on eleven districts from a national sample, Johnson and Kardos compare pre-1986 contracts and contracts from the 1990s. Unions' influence on school reform varies from school district to school district. Johnson and Kardos discover that contracts negotiated with reform bargaining were able to advance educational reform, while contracts produced by industrial bargaining were not. Johnson and Kardos urge an enlarged role for reform-style bargaining as a means of harnessing the power of teachers unions to the improvement of teaching as a profession—and to education reform more generally.

A hotly debated topic is the effect of teachers unions on educational quality—whether schools are better or worse off because of collective bargaining. Joe A. Stone of the University of Oregon surveys the evidence pertaining to teachers unions' impact on four aspects of schools: (1) teacher pay and benefits, finding that collective bargaining tends to increase both; (2) schools as workplaces, finding that collective bargaining "standardizes" work conditions, lowers student-teacher ratios, and provides protections against job loss for teachers; (3) the total cost of instruction, finding that costs increase 8 to 15 percent under unionization; and (4) student achievement, finding that the effects of collective bargaining are mixed and, whether positive or negative, are small. Stone concludes that the widespread suspicion that teachers unions have increased the costs of public schooling is true, but the equally widespread belief that they have depressed student achievement is false. He also highlights questions where additional evidence is needed and pinpoints topics that future researchers of educational productivity should tackle.

Dale Ballou of the University of Massachusetts and Michael Podgursky of the University of Missouri are also concerned with unions' influence on the profession of teaching. They are critical of proposed changes in regulating the teaching profession, especially the idea of shifting control over training and licensure from state agencies to professional boards. Ballou and Podgursky argue that there is scant evidence that such professional self-regulation would enhance teacher quality or school performance. The leading organization that currently accredits teacher training institutions, the National Council for Accreditation of Teacher Education (NCATE), would see its power increase under professional boards. Both national teachers unions—the American Federation of Teachers (AFT) and the National Education Association (NEA)—play a leading role in NCATE. Ballou and Podgursky show that NCATE accreditation focuses on teaching processes rather than outcomes, restricts the supply of would-be teachers, and is unrelated to producing high-quality teachers. Professional self-regulation would increase the power of teachers unions and organizations such as NCATE, Ballou and Podgursky conclude, but it would not improve American schooling.

Howard Fuller of Marquette University, George Mitchell, and Michael Hartmann examine the influence of teachers unions on the quality of education in one city: Milwaukee, Wisconsin. They describe Milwaukee's collective bargaining agreements from World War II to the 1990s. They identify when Milwaukee's contracts first adopted specific, well-known elements of teacher contracts—for example, in 1944, the single salary schedule (paying teachers with the same degrees and years of experience an equivalent amount regardless of effectiveness), and in the 1960s, restrictions on the definition of a "teacher day." Fuller, Mitchell, and Hartmann find that, instead of educational quality, Milwaukee's teacher contracts have primarily addressed compensation, job security, and working conditions since teachers unionized. The Milwaukee contract grew from 18 pages in 1964 to 174 pages in 1992, but boosting schools' performance cannot be found in these documents—an unfortunate omission given the steady decline in educational quality that Milwaukee schools have suffered during the same time period.

James Cibulka of the University of Maryland examines the political opposition of teachers unions to school choice. The national teachers unions publicly and adamantly oppose vouchers, providing students with public funds to attend private schools. But Cibulka shows that the NEA's position on choice is not monolithic. Its stance on other forms of school choice, such as charter schools, has been less rigid and more accepting over time. Cibulka also notes that local affiliates hold varying positions on charters and that some of the affiliates have changed their stance in response to local political realities. Cibulka explains these nuances in the NEA's position on choice using two analytical perspectives. The institutional perspective views the NEA as an interest group pursuing goals in an institutional arena teeming with competing interests. The regime perspective spotlights how NEA's leaders accommodate internal pressures for change, leading the union to strategically alter its stance on major issues. Like other institutions, the NEA's political positions emerge in response to both external and internal forces.

William Lowe Boyd of Pennsylvania State University and David N. Plank and Gary Sykes of Michigan State University also analyze teachers unions as political actors, focusing on the state teachers' organizations in

Michigan and Pennsylvania. The two unions experienced political success in the 1980s, followed by failure and decline in the 1990s. The election of strong Republican governors, John Engler in Michigan and Tom Ridge in Pennsylvania, reflected voter unhappiness with the educational status quo. The two governors championed sweeping education reforms that included expanded parental choice of schooling and stronger academic standards—proposals the teachers unions opposed. The unions launched a strong counterattack. They vehemently fought any Republican proposal for reform, urged increased funding as the solution to education's woes, and painted reformers as enemies of public education. This strategy failed politically, allowing the unions' opponents to brand them as obstacles to reform. Boyd, Plank, and Sykes conclude by discussing the teachers unions' political future and where the political battles over choice and standards are likely to proceed.

Maris A. Vinovskis of the University of Michigan examines the history of education research conducted by teachers unions. This in-house research has fulfilled two purposes. One is to keep members abreast of important developments in the field. The nineteenth-century NEA issued numerous reports and a few, such as that of the Committee of Ten on Secondary School Studies in 1893, were influential in guiding the direction of American education. In the late twentieth century, Al Shanker and the AFT similarly used research reports to mobilize union members and the public behind standards-based reforms.

The second purpose of union-sponsored research is to promote higher teacher salaries, increased benefits, and better working conditions. In the early twentieth century, the NEA's Research Division gathered data on school finance that local members could use to argue for increased funding in their districts. More recently, NEA studies have included an investigation of the working conditions of educational support personnel and an analysis of the health and pension needs of retired teachers. Vinovskis explores the tensions these activities have created, particularly as related to the independence of in-house researchers from the unions' other organizational units. He also reviews the unions' dealings with the bureau in charge of federally funded research (currently the Office of Educational Research and Improvement in the Department of Education) and concludes that unions could play a strong role in improving education research overall.

Bruce S. Cooper of Fordham University provides a comparative analysis of teachers unions, looking at how teachers unions have adapted to political changes internationally. Examining teachers unions in fifteen nations, Cooper finds that four characteristics influence unions' core operation: (1) the source of funding for the nation's educational system (whether revenues come from national or regional governments); (2) the locus of political control (if school systems are governed by federal, state, or local authorities); (3) political affiliations (whether the teachers union is associated with a national labor organization or national Labor party); and (4) professional rights and responsibilities (the extent to which unions reinforce the classical mission of teaching as an educative endeavor). Cooper finds that these four characteristics have shaped the history of collective bargaining for teachers in each country. He also discusses the future of teacher unionism internationally in light of recent experiments with privatization and parental choice.

Charles Taylor Kerchner and Julia E. Koppich of Claremont Graduate University revisit some of the issues explored by Johnson and Kardos in the book's first chapter and ask whether teachers unions can successfully organize in support of quality teaching and standards for students. Drawing on the experiences of five unions—Minneapolis, Minnesota; Rochester, New York; Columbus, Ohio; Cincinnati, Ohio; and Seattle, Washington—Kerchner and Koppich conclude that unionization devoted to quality is possible but difficult. Obstacles arise from the culture of teaching, the ideologies of teacher unionism and school administration, the limited organizational capacity of teachers unions to promote a quality agenda, and elements of public policy that allow but do not encourage reform. The industrial organizational principles of yesterday's teachers unions are now outmoded and a hindrance to effective reform. Kerchner and Koppich conclude by calling for labor laws that would reorient teacher unions toward principles of craft, artistic, and professional excellence.

Ideologues who are searching for unequivocal evidence that teachers unions either wear halos from heaven or horns from hell will not find what they are looking for in this volume. But readers who want to discover how complex and interesting teachers unions are and the influence—both positive and negative—they wield in the national effort to improve America's schools will find this book a useful starting point for their endeavors.

1

SUSAN MOORE JOHNSON
SUSAN M KARDOS

Reform Bargaining and Its Promise for School Improvement

A s school reformers work intently to repair or rethink public education in the United States, there are conflicting calls to eliminate or to expand the influence of teachers unions. Those opposing collective bargaining and unions typically contend that teacher contracts unduly regulate schools and unwisely constrain teachers' best professional efforts. Those endorsing a broader role for unions stress that teachers must play a key part in school improvement, and they point to the early successes of progressive unions in districts such as Rochester or Cincinnati.[1]

Given the current demands of school reform, should the role of unions be enlarged or diminished? In answering this question, it is important to consider both what is known about teacher unionism as well as what is known about the demands of school improvement. Unless the direction of union activity is consistent with the best educational practices, creating a greater role for collective bargaining would be unwise. Yet if unions can work to effect constructive change and if collective bargaining can provide a forum where systematic and sustainable progress can be achieved, there is good reason to further support and invest in this policy and process.

---

1. For those opposing unions see Lieberman (1993), Wise (1979); for those favoring the broader role see Kerchner, Koppich, and Weeres (1997), Rosow and Zager (1989).

7

Many in the United States believe that teachers unions have moved uniformly, powerfully, and steadily during the past thirty years to control public education. In fact, as this chapter will show, the influence of teachers unions has been uneven—strong in some districts, weak in others—and the progress of union gains has been irregular over time. Despite researchers' early predictions that all districts would eventually have uniform contracts, replete with provisions favoring labor over management, most districts never adopted such contracts and the unions' seemingly inexorable progress in securing greater rights and protections for teachers stalled unexpectedly in the mid-1970s. An analysis of a national sample of contracts currently in effect reveals that, rather than becoming more alike over time, negotiated agreements are now more varied in substance and style than ever before.

In large part this variation is the result of two distinctly different approaches to educational bargaining. The first, *industrial bargaining,* emerged in the 1960s when teachers won the right to organize and negotiate about wages, hours, and working conditions. The states modeled their public-sector labor laws directly on the 1935 National Labor Relations Act, which regulates private-sector labor practices. As a result, legislation written with the needs of industry in mind ultimately defined the character of labor practices in education. Conventional industrial bargaining, with its ritualized pattern of demands, rebuffs, and concessions, was prominent in all districts until the 1980s and persists in many today.

However, in the mid-1980s, union leaders and school administrators in a small number of districts across the country experimented with a second approach to negotiations, that of *reform bargaining.* By recognizing their shared interests in working collaboratively for change, union leaders and administrators in these flagship districts moved beyond the adversarial process of the past and devised new ways to resolve their differences and to improve their schools. Some of the contract changes they made (such as moderating the force of seniority-based transfers) seemed modest on the surface, but they had far-reaching, positive effects in schools. Other changes, such as introducing peer review for teachers, were dramatic innovations that challenged basic union principles and advanced the interests of better teaching.

There have been, as well, two very different approaches to schooling in this century. One, the *factory model,* which emerged from the Efficiency Movement of the 1920s and became the standard in most large, urban districts, endures today in many places.[2] In this approach district officials strive to effectively manage the operation of large, uniform schools, while teachers serve as workers in a production-line process, delivering standardized education to students.

Although a second approach, the *professional model,* has existed in various settings throughout the century, it gained prominence in many places during the "second wave" of school reform that began in 1986. This approach recognizes that schools must be responsive to their students and communities and that the individual school's need for autonomy and flexibility should take precedence over the school district's pursuit of order and uniformity. Rather than functioning like factory laborers whose work can be preplanned by managerial experts, teachers in schools that promote a professional model are encouraged to regularly assess their teaching and make professional decisions based on the needs of their students or their schools.

Many researchers and analysts have concluded that the factory model of schooling does not work.[3] This line of research demonstrates that important decisions about how best to organize teaching and learning must be made at the school site rather than at the district office. Moreover, these researchers conclude that to prepare students for success in today's (and tomorrow's) society, teachers cannot deliver information and demand its rote mastery but must draw from a rich repertoire of instructional strategies that develop students' technical, analytic, and social skills. Teachers must approach their work as a craft or profession rather than as routine labor, and schools must be organized to encourage them to do so.[4]

While industrial bargaining enabled teachers in factory-model schools to gain some measure of control in their workplace and garner much-needed resources for public education, it failed to change schooling for students in any fundamental way. Industrial bargaining defines participants as adversaries, favors uniform work rules for all teachers and schools, and deals with teachers as if they are interchangeable laborers. By contrast, reform bargainers began with the assumption that union leaders and school administrators shared a genuine interest in making schools better. They recognized the wisdom of minimizing rules and maximizing flexibility for

2. Callahan (1962); Tyack (1974); Darling-Hammond (1997).
3. Callahan (1962); Darling-Hammond (1997); Fullan (1991); Hill, Pierce, and Guthrie (1997); Meier (1995); Murnane and Levy (1996).
4. Kerchner and Mitchell (1988); Darling-Hammond (1997); Johnson (1990).

schools, and they regarded teachers as individuals and professionals. While industrial bargaining falls short of what is needed to truly improve schools, reform bargaining offers considerable promise. As this discussion shows, however, the course of progress to real school reform through collective bargaining is neither obvious nor assured.

This chapter explores both the shortcomings of industrial bargaining and the promise of reform bargaining. The tenets of industrial bargaining and their problematic legacy for public education are considered first. Then we appraise the first decade of collective bargaining in schools, a period marked by industrial-style negotiations and agreements. The practices and outcomes of industrial bargaining are contrasted with those of reform bargaining. Next, we analyze current contracts and compare them with agreements from the same districts fifteen or twenty years ago. Finally, we reconsider the role of collective bargaining in school reform and conclude with recommendations for policy and practice.

Industrial Unionism and the Needs of Schools

Central to the process of industrial bargaining are three assumptions that were transported directly from industry to education in the 1960s and that defined its profile from the start. First is the belief that the interests of labor and management are at odds, that in a world of scarce resources one side's gain is the other's loss. Kerchner and Koppich see this opposition as a key feature of industrial unionism in schools as well: "Industrial unionism assumes permanent adversaries. It organizes around vigorous representation of the differences between teachers and managers."[5]

Second is the belief that standardized practice is desirable, that uniform operations across an organization make for better, more efficient, management; greater control over products; and more certain enforcement of company policy and union work rules. In education, teachers unions seek to establish through their bargaining the standards and regulations that apply equally to all schools in a district.

Third is the assumption that similarly skilled workers are interchangeable and should be treated alike. This tenet holds that employees with similar qualifications are members of industrywide classifications and that their identity as members of these generic groups takes precedence over dis-

5. Kerchner and Koppich (1993, p. 15).

Figure 1-1. *Industrial Bargaining*

The Principles of Industrial Bargaining	The Factory Model of Schooling
Interests of labor and management are at odds.	Administrators set policy and teachers comply.
Standardized practice is desirable.	Instruction is delivered uniformly to large groups of students.
Similarly skilled workers are interchangeable and should be treated alike.	Teaching force is undifferentiated.

tinctions about them as individuals with unique strengths or needs. In industry this means that certain tasks are restricted to particular types of workers, but those who qualify for the role can be reassigned to any comparable work setting in the company. In education, as Kerchner, Koppich, and Weeres explain, this means that teachers' roles are undifferentiated and all teachers are to be treated uniformly: "Union power is threatened when the boundaries of existing job classifications are breached and when schools provide different treatment to teachers of the same classification. Thus unions have historically opposed differentiation among teachers in pay and privilege."[6] These three assumptions—labor-management opposition, the value of standardized practice, and the generic treatment of workers— underlie the character of industrial unionism, which is at the historical core of teacher unionism (see figure 1-1).

What might once have been functional for factories is now widely understood to be dysfunctional for schools.[7] There is increasing evidence that teachers and administrators share a deep interest in devising educational approaches that will effectively educate young people. And, while efficient operations are as important to public schooling as they are to good companies, standardized practice enforced by a large bureaucracy or union stifles innovation and discourages educators from responding to the varied

6. Kerchner, Koppich, and Weeres (1997, p. 39).
7. Darling-Hammond (1997); Elmore, Peterson, and McCarthey (1996); Meier (1995); Sizer (1992).

needs of students, schools, and communities. Further, although individual teachers bring different repertoires of skills and experiences to their jobs, the potential of this variety is often lost when teachers are assigned to restricted roles and treated like interchangeable components in an impersonal school machine. Given the differences between yesterday's factories and today's schooling needs, one could dismiss collective bargaining out of hand, arguing that it is an outmoded industrial process that might have helped teachers gain basic workers' rights and fair wages in the factory-model schools of the past but that cannot adapt to current demands for responsive schools and responsible teachers.

However, the history of collective bargaining in public education is neither simple nor static. What began as an industrial process producing uniform work rules has proven to be far more varied and responsive than many critics realize. Collective bargaining can lead to either restrictive or adaptive policy; it can lead to stale responses or creative solutions to pressing problems. Two researchers, who studied educational labor relations over fifteen years, concluded: "Our research and that of others . . . clearly indicate that the collective bargaining process and the resulting contract can serve either as an efficient vehicle for shaping and implementing new approaches to teacher professionalism . . . or as a major hindrance to reform." In the ten years since the publication of McDonnell and Pascal's report, experience with school reform has reinforced that conclusion.[8]

During the first decade of collective bargaining in education, teacher contracts closely mirrored those in industry. For example, contracts spelled out the rights of management, set forth standardized pay scales, secured seniority-based layoffs, defined teachers' in-school work responsibilities, and established grievance procedures. Although the process of industrial bargaining was often rigid, scripted, and sometimes led to disruptive strikes, it served as a workable mechanism by which unionized teachers could pursue certain compelling objectives, such as curbing administrative abuse and favoritism, defining reasonable expectations for their work, and establishing evenhanded procedures for evaluation. One urban principal, commenting in 1980 on the extent and detail of the local contract, explained why it was necessary: "The thickness, the scope, of this phone book of a contract is, in my view, an indictment of how administrators ran their schools in the past."[9]

8. McDonnell and Pascal (1988, p. 54).
9. Johnson (1983, p. 108).

Mixed Effects of Negotiated Provisions

It was the errors and excesses of that past that organized teachers sought to change with their industrial approaches to bargaining. Between the mid-1960s and mid-1970s, teachers unions relied on collective bargaining to secure many contract provisions that were favorable to their interests and benefited students indirectly, such as securing smaller classes or time for teachers to prepare for classes. But frequently those gains were accompanied by unintended consequences. Too often the new job rules that ensured reasonable expectations and fair treatment also unwisely restricted what teachers could be asked to do, led to inappropriate teaching assignments, made it unreasonably difficult to dismiss incompetent teachers, or restricted teachers' role in policymaking to the union's activity at the bargaining table. Several illustrations of these mixed effects are discussed below.

WHAT TEACHERS COULD BE ASKED TO DO. In establishing explicit hours and responsibilities for teachers' work, the early, industrial-style contracts effectively limited unreasonable demands that administrators might make on teachers and their time. For example, McDonnell and Pascal found that, by 1975, 34 percent of the 155 district contracts they studied set the maximum size of teachers' classes. Johnson found that teachers in the six districts of a national sample had bargained shorter in-school work days and fewer nonteaching responsibilities. In some cases, where responsibilities had been unreasonable and the school staff stretched too thin, that kind of union gain was a good thing for teachers and for students; but in others it was problematic. For example, it seemed sensible not to require teachers to teach subjects for which they had no preparation or to use time designated for classroom preparation standing on bathroom duty. It was only fair to guarantee teachers a half-hour of duty-free time to eat their lunch. It did not seem sensible, though, that teachers' work time could be prescribed to the minute or that they might be expected to meet with parents only twice a year. Often contracts, particularly those in large, urban districts, defined teachers' responsibilities narrowly and minimally, thus making teaching more like labor and less like a profession.[10]

HOW TEACHERS WOULD BE ASSIGNED. Although collective negotiations had no effect on hiring, for that right continued to be the prerogative of

---

10. McDonnell and Pascal (1979, p. 11); Johnson (1983); Kerchner and Mitchell (1988).

management in all school districts, decisions about layoffs, transfers, and often even promotions were frequently regulated by contract; seniority became the most common criterion used to make those decisions. Perry found that, over time, seniority played a greater role in promotion and layoffs in the nine districts he studied; it was the sole criterion for layoffs in six districts. Johnson found that seniority within certification areas determined layoffs in four of six districts of her sample and, unlike many other provisions, seniority layoff and transfer rights were virtually always enforced.[11]

Seniority, an objective measure that is relatively easy to use as a criterion in making hard employment decisions, assures that layoffs and transfers are not subject to patronage or favoritism. Despite this strength, seniority is often inappropriate for deciding who will teach in a particular grade, program, or subject, especially when no distinctions can be made about the unique qualifications of individuals or the particular needs of programs. During times of severe enrollment declines in the 1980s, seniority-based transfer procedures repeatedly allowed more experienced teachers to displace, or "bump," less experienced but highly qualified teachers, thus repeatedly decimating the staffs of many innovative programs. Sometimes the consequences were absurd, as in the case of a kindergarten teacher whose generic state certificate allowed her to bump a high school physics teacher even though she had never studied the subject. Some local districts carefully negotiated contract provisions to avoid such outcomes. For example, in Michigan, where state law rather than local contracts designated seniority as the sole layoff criterion, a district contract specified that teachers had to hold a major or minor in any subject they sought to teach. In studying the district, Johnson, Nelson, and Potter concluded that "no physics teacher, however junior in the science department, would be laid off unless there was another qualified physics teacher to fill the position."[12]

In many cases, however, the effects of seniority-based decisions were not carefully anticipated or moderated. In 1980 a midwestern principal anticipated serious problems: "I'm very concerned over this thing of seniority transfers, and I see somewhere down the road that seniority is coming into full blossom. I can anticipate the time when I'm not able to interview teachers if I have a vacancy in the building. Instead, the seniority list will

11. Perry (1979) and Johnson (1983).
12. Johnson, Nelson, and Potter (1985, p. 82).

determine who goes here and who leaves my building."[13] This principal's fears subsequently were realized in many large, urban districts. Ironically, it was often teachers who were most disturbed by the effects of their own union's success.

HOW TEACHERS WOULD BE EVALUATED. Many local contracts mandated evaluation procedures by the mid-1970s. For example, McDonnell and Pascal found that 42 percent of the 151 contracts they studied in 1970 specified procedures by which teachers could respond formally to administrators' evaluation; 77 percent of the same districts did so by 1980. Similarly, in 1980 Johnson found that four of six districts studied included procedures for observing and evaluating teachers; the remaining two incorporated similar requirements into board policies. Typically these negotiated rules called for tightly prescribed observations and evaluations by principals and department heads. Nontenured teachers received annual ratings, while their tenured colleagues were observed and evaluated every two or three years. Often administrators had to give advanced warning that they would observe a class and, if they decided to rate either a nontenured or tenured teacher negatively, had to suggest strategies for improvement and offer a chance for reassessment. Many contracts also imposed time limits on the process. For example, Johnson found in one district that principals could not assign unsatisfactory ratings unless they gave teachers written reports within five days of the observation. Another contract required that any teacher receiving an unsatisfactory rating "must have been observed at least once a quarter for not less than twenty (20) minutes."

These evaluation procedures, which were intended to curtail capricious and arbitrary assessments—which had been all too common—usually succeeded in doing just that. Sometimes, however, the procedures also made it excessively difficult to dismiss incompetent teachers, an effect that principals often lamented. For example, the forty principals whom Johnson interviewed disagreed about whether their district's procedures were "unreasonably burdensome." One said the process was "so difficult that it tends to make us not want to go through it as much as we might or should." Others, however, thought that the procedures were "warranted and workable." All principals agreed, however, that dismissing weak teachers took time, minimally two years.[14]

13. Johnson (1983, p. 80).
14. McDonnell and Pascall (1988, p. 61); Johnson (1983, esp. pp. 118–19, 120–21).

By law, unions must represent teachers whose procedural rights are violated, particularly if decisions made in that process threaten their jobs.
Notably, unions have a "duty of fair representation" and can be sued if they
defend teachers in a perfunctory manner.[15] Over the past thirty years this
legal obligation, combined with strong state tenure laws, complex evaluation procedures, and administrators' lack of preparation to evaluate teaching, has meant that poor teachers often retained their jobs.

Teachers who had witnessed administrative abuse in the past often saw
great need for evenhanded approaches to evaluation, and they endorsed
exacting procedures. Others, however, agreed with public critics and found
the presence of "deadwood" peers in their schools so troubling that they
wished their unions would bargain a more streamlined dismissal process or
represent weak teachers less vigorously. One teacher from an urban district
in Johnson's 1983 study said, "The Federation claims that they want to
enhance the teaching profession. I believe that if they can identify a teacher
who abuses the teaching profession, then there ought to be a kind of
understanding between the administration and the Federation that the
teacher deserves only minimal defense." A principal in another district
agreed: "They no longer should have to defend the riff-raff." Jessup, who
studied unionism in three small districts between the mid-1960s and late
1970s, found that one union had decided its role was "to protect teachers'
right to due process—but not to protect incompetent teachers"; another
took a hard line, vigorously defending any teacher whose competence was
challenged.[16]

WHAT INFLUENCE TEACHERS COULD HAVE ON POLICY AND PRACTICE.
Prior to collective bargaining, school boards and administrators were the
ones who prescribed policy and practice, while teachers were expected to
comply with district directives, use the chosen texts, and teach the designated curriculum. While individual teachers could always decide how to
teach when they closed the classroom door, that professional space was not
inviolable. At the extreme, administrators could change the report card
grades that teachers assigned.

---

15. "This doctrine, which originated with U.S. Supreme Court decisions about railroad unions'
discrimination against black workers [*Steele* v. *Louisville and Nashville Railroad Company,* 323 U.S. 192,
65 Sup Ct. 226, 89 L.Ed. 173 (1944)], requires that the union must 'act for and not against those
whom it represents.'" See Johnson (1983, p. 124).

16. Johnson (1983, pp. 125, 151); Jessup (1985, p. 79).

Collective bargaining explicitly changed the way in which certain policies and practices—those affecting wages, hours, and working conditions—were set and, in doing so, constrained the discretion of management to run schools as they liked. Critics of collective bargaining contend that labor laws granted teachers far too much control over educational policy. Yet, for most teachers, that influence could only be exerted by their elected representatives at the bargaining table. Few local unions won the right for teachers to play a decisive role in policymaking once the contract was signed, although teachers often were granted advisory roles in decisions affecting instruction, such as textbook selection.

McDonnell and Pascal found that 31 percent of the 151 contracts they studied allowed teachers to participate in curricular decisions. Eberts and Stone identified similar language in 39 percent of the New York state contracts of their research sample. Finch and Nagel found that 35 percent of the Connecticut contracts they studied included advisory roles for teachers. Researchers virtually always found that teachers were to advise, not decide. What influence they actually exercised depended on how receptive and responsive their principals and superintendents were.[17]

Therefore, industrial bargaining yielded mixed effects for teachers and their schools. Teachers gained assurances of a fairer and more reasonable work environment, yet their contracts often contributed to a narrow definition of their roles and responsibilities, limiting not only what they could be required to do but also what they would be allowed and encouraged to do. Contracts routinely ensured equity, but also reinforced the notion that all teachers were similarly skilled and, therefore, interchangeable, no matter what they had to offer. And, although they sat down to bargain collectively every few years, administrators and teachers continued to occupy separate domains of the policy space—managers set policy and teachers sometimes advised, though more often they simply complied—thus ensuring that teachers' professional judgment would not widely influence the policy that determined school practice.

Standardized Schooling

There was one far-reaching consequence of industrial bargaining in education that had been predicted by analysts but was largely unanticipated by

---

17. McDonnell and Pascal (1979); Eberts and Stone (1984); Finch and Nagel (1984).

teachers and principals: the standardization of schooling. Because contracts were negotiated districtwide, in keeping with the industrial model of companywide bargaining, their provisions were meant to apply equally to all school sites.

It was always apparent that unions favored standardized labor practice, but during the first decade of collective bargaining in education it became clear that many superintendents did as well: "School superintendents often come to value teachers unions because they not only stabilize but also formalize administration." Collective bargaining, often criticized for undermining management, in fact, reinforced district bureaucracy and centralized school administration. Whether school superintendents were assigning teachers to schools, reviewing requests for personal leave, or monitoring principals' supervision of staff, they could call upon the authority of negotiated regulations to ensure compliance. Kerchner and Mitchell conclude, "Managers often find that the new rules work in their favor and proceed to use them aggressively."[18]

By all accounts collective bargaining for teachers meant more standardized schools, leaving principals with less latitude to run their schools. Not only could they not tell teachers what to do, but uniform, districtwide rules limited their management options and thus reduced their schools' responsiveness and independence. In one of the earliest studies of union effects, Perry and Wildman concluded that "negotiations on 'working conditions' in the schools have to some extent substituted centralized decision-making for decentralized decision-making on the management side. School principals *have* lost significant discretion in this process." McDonnell and Pascal contended: "There is no question that collective bargaining has made the principal's job more difficult." Yet these researchers concluded, as Johnson and Jessup subsequently did, that effective school leaders need not be hamstrung by negotiated rules:

> Truly effective principals usually accept collective bargaining and use the contract both to manage their building more systematically and to increase teacher participation in school decisionmaking. Less effective principals may view the contract as an obstacle to a well-run school and then use it as an excuse for poor management.[19]

18. Kerchner and Mitchell (1988, pp. 31, 190).
19. Perry and Wildman (1970, p. 214); McDonnell and Pascal (1979, p. 83); Jessup (1985); extract from Johnson (1983, p. 81).

Teachers and principals share an interest in making their schools work well, and often that shared interest prevailed even when the detail of written labor agreements became problematic. Therefore, effective principals could encourage teachers to be flexible about some matters—meeting times, covering recess, taking an extra student in class—and gradually win their support, thus ensuring that the school worked well and students were effectively served. But on other matters—seniority-based layoff and transfer rules, or class-size caps that protected jobs—there was no room for compromise and standardized practices prevailed. Furthermore, in some districts, union members in one school could file grievances about alleged violations of the contract in another school, and the threat of such a grievance sometimes diverted a principal and teachers from fashioning sensible exceptions to unwise contractual restrictions.[20]

Reaching the Limits of Usefulness

In retrospect, what was not apparent to researchers at the time has now become clear. By the late 1970s this industrial model of unionism had nearly reached the limits of its usefulness in education. In many districts the approach had enabled organized teachers to set reasonable boundaries for their work, establish useful procedures for making staffing decisions once fraught with patronage, and ensure important protections that kept good teachers teaching. In others, however, industrial bargaining led to lower expectations for teachers, rule-driven school management for principals, and uninspired school practices for too many. Industrial bargaining was good for setting rules and dividing resources, but of little use in addressing the many educational challenges that educators faced, such as reorganizing school schedules, supporting interdisciplinary teaching, effectively integrating students with special needs into regular classrooms, or engaging parents more actively in the education of their children.

During the first decade of bargaining, researchers who analyzed contracts predicted that unions would make steady gains until, eventually, all contracts would look alike. Like the general public, these researchers assumed that all local teachers unions had the same goals in negotiations, that districts across the country bargained about the same set of issues, and that eventually they would adopt essentially the same contract provisions. In short, negotiated agreements would become ever stronger and more

20. Johnson (1983).

alike. In 1979 McDonnell and Pascal analyzed the 1970 and 1975 contracts from a national sample of 151 districts and reported that there was a "convergence of collective bargaining outcomes over time. As more and more school systems follow the lead of flagship districts, there is less variation among individual contracts." In 1984 Goldschmidt and Stuart analyzed eighty local contracts and compared them with contracts studied by McDonnell and Pascal ten years earlier. Based on these comparisons, they concluded that the extent of bargaining over noncompensation items increased over time. Perry was the only researcher who before 1980 noted the slackened pace of union gains. Returning to nine of the twenty-four districts he and Wildman had studied in 1970, Perry found that, although class size was bargained about in all of them, the unions had "made relatively little concrete progress in achieving definite, enforceable limits on class size or in reducing those limits where they exist."[21]

The predicted convergence, in fact, never happened. Subsequent analyses of union contracts revealed that, with the exception of layoff and transfer provisions, collective bargaining did little from 1975 to 1985 to reduce teachers' obligations, further standardize practice, or extend job protections. When McDonnell and Pascal returned to their original sample of districts and analyzed agreements through 1985, they discovered that "[w]ith relatively few exceptions, the improvements in working conditions unions had attained by 1975 were not enhanced in the 1980 and 1985 contracts." Their study showed "quite conclusively that there are real limits on what teachers can obtain through the traditional collective bargaining process. Not only did the rate of gain for our sample slow in the 1980s as compared with the previous decade, but a majority of unions still cannot obtain key provisions such as strong class size limits, curbs on teachers having to teach outside their fields, and clear criteria for involuntary transfers." Similarly Jessup's longitudinal analysis of three small districts revealed that the "strongest" contract of the group was "essentially the same" in 1979 as in 1973. Further, Johnson, Nelson, and Potter, who studied a national sample of 155 contracts in 1985, concluded that "collective bargaining agreements are neither as comprehensive nor prescriptive as some might believe. Many do not address key staffing issues. [And] although many contract provisions are intended to advance teacher interests, the contracts reviewed were not simply lists of union privileges. Much contract

---

21. McDonnell and Pascal (1979, p. 31); Goldschmidt and Stuart (1984); Perry (1979, p. 13).

language about staffing specifies the prerogatives of management." Empirical research does not support the conventional belief that collective bargaining produces ever "stronger" union privileges and protections for teachers.[22]

There is, therefore, convincing evidence that what seemed to be a steady pace of union gains came to a virtual halt by the end of the1970s, yet there is only speculation about why this occurred. One explanation is that management, who had been unprepared for early bargaining and often made unwise concessions to union demands, started to encounter the consequences of careless negotiation and resisted further union gains. Another related explanation is that declining enrollments and budget cuts in the1970s led to much more cautious, conservative negotiations by administrators and school boards. Jessup explains how hard times strengthened the hand of management in the districts she studied:

> At first, union leaders believed they could simply postpone negotiations on the unacceptable issues into future years, regarding collective bargaining as a long-term process in which each contract would represent a step forward. As the 1970s progressed, however, this possibility receded. The atmosphere of economic crisis, heightened by local tax revolts and declining student enrollments, led boards not to be more expansive, but to cut back on school financing. The atmosphere of public criticism and distrust led them to try to tighten, not loosen, controls over teachers. These situations pressed all three unions into far more defensive positions during the 1970s so that protection of existing staff positions and the contract took priority.[23]

During this period in many districts, deadlocked negotiations and subsequent union "give-backs" were common.

In addition to these two explanations of the slowed pace of union gains, a third deserves attention. There is evidence that teachers, themselves, started to see the limits of industrial bargaining and to resent the inflexibility it sometimes imposed on them and their schools.[24] There can be no doubt that teachers appreciated their union's success in winning better wages, defining reasonable boundaries on their in-school responsibilities,

22. McDonnell and Pascal (1979, pp. vi, 52); Jessup (1985); Johnson, Nelson, and Potter (1985, p. i).

23. McDonnell and Pascal (1988); for quotation see Jessup (1985, p. 196).

24. Johnson (1983).

and gaining assurances of fair treatment. Yet teachers also recognized that the realities of their schools were different from the realities of the factories. Children were not undifferentiated raw materials, and good schooling should not be an impersonal process of mass production. Despite having similar credentials, all teachers were not the same, and seniority was not an invariably sound criterion for deciding who would teach where. In the view of many teachers, individual schools needed to retain (or regain) the capacity to make important decisions for themselves about how best to organize instruction and use the resources they had (time, money, and expertise) to support that instruction.

School Reform Brings New Approaches to Bargaining

With the publication of *A Nation at Risk,* the political context of both public education and collective bargaining abruptly changed.[25] Schools and teachers, widely ignored by the public, suddenly were surveyed and found to be lacking. Critics predicted that the shortcomings of schools would compromise the country's economic security, and teachers became easy targets of blame. Many state legislatures took the lead in responding to this report's disturbing alarm.

State-Initiated Reforms

During the so-called first wave of reform (1983–86), which came as a response to *A Nation at Risk,* individual states set out to change teachers by monitoring and assessing their practices or offering state money to fund local programs that would identify and reward meritorious teachers and schools. Since these state reforms would affect some teachers' wages and working conditions, they were subject to local negotiation, and as local districts bargained about their impact, the scope of negotiations gradually increased to include explicit discussion of instructional policy, long assumed to be the exclusive province of management. For example, a plan to implement performance-based pay typically involved discussions of curriculum and testing. Over the next few years the state-initiated reforms changed the substance of what labor and management saw to be appropri-

25. National Commission on Excellence in Education (1983).

ate topics for negotiation. In some districts the prospect of getting more money or protecting the district from outside meddlers fostered a collaborative spirit among many who had always assumed that the people on the other side of the bargaining table were their enemies.

McDonnell and Pascal studied the role of teachers unions in such reforms and found that between 1983 and 1986 local union officials and their teachers sought to gain "material benefits (i.e., higher salaries, restrictions on class size, etc.)" rather than pursue "strategies aimed at enhancing teacher professionalism (e.g., performance-based compensation, increased teacher participation in school-site decisionmaking)." And when local union leaders advocated professional reforms, "many rank-and-file teachers reacted with skepticism and even hostility." McDonnell and Pascal found that California's Mentor Teacher Program "was implemented in most districts as a classic pork barrel, with benefits allocated as broadly as possible and on criteria other than strict merit." In Pennsylvania unions sought to "accommodate" the state's reforms and "mitigate" the perceived negative effects on teachers of local curricular reforms triggered by state legislation.

Similarly, Johnson, Potter, and Nelson found that major state initiatives in California and Florida had redirected local bargaining in the two districts under study. The local union in California initially resisted merit pay but eventually acceded to a carefully fashioned plan that would sidestep the very initiatives that California legislators had hoped to achieve. One local union official explained, "We wanted input into the policy and the selection process. We wanted to help manage the process of the program. We wanted to protect our members." Pitner and Goldschmidt, who analyzed contracts and documents regarding California's Mentor Teacher Program in the state's eleven largest districts, also found that the program had been "shaped through bargaining to reflect more closely the teachers union goals of deference to seniority."

In Florida, where legislators passed a merit program intended to promote healthy competition by rewarding outstanding schools, the union and management of a large county district devised plans to secure state funds without imposing competition that might divide the staff or pit schools against each other. Many in the district thought that these state-sponsored programs would eventually disappear because of limited funding or faulty implementation. In the meantime, union leaders and school officials tried to garner the funds while protecting their schools from adverse effects. They did not see themselves as participants in school reform. As the union's executive director explained: "What we're doing here is a whole lot of damage control."[26]

Although the rhetoric of the day was reform, local teachers widely saw the reforming legislators as ignorant outsiders offering money in exchange for ill-advised concessions. Often unions undermined the state policies during implementation, complying superficially while continuing business as usual. Yet there were far-reaching, unexpected effects. Labor and management, accustomed to highlighting their disagreements, discovered new reasons to cooperate as they explored how best to secure state funds without undermining their current programs. Inadvertently, through their new reform agenda, state officials reshaped both the scope and tenor of local bargaining practices.

Home-Grown Reform

While most local districts' attention was captured by the agendas of state legislators, key leaders in a few local districts began to review their own policies and practices, undistracted by the demands of state mandates or the lure of state money. These reformers began to acknowledge publicly what many had privately understood: teachers' interests and management's interests were not necessarily at odds. Often the process of adversarial bargaining, pitting teachers against administrators in ritualized dissembling and bullying, undermined the possibility of collaborative work once the contract was signed. The dissension and disappointment caused by public blame and militant job actions damaged working relationships and dimmed the public's view of local educators. Some who had experienced the cost of such combat began to moderate its effects. In some places union and school officials recognized that they would have to experiment with new approaches in order to find their way to better schools. In 1981 negotiators in Toledo signed a contract that "pledged the parties to begin a program of teacher evaluation"; that program eventually would engage teachers in assessing their peers, a practice that most unions vehemently opposed. After publication of *A Nation at Risk* in 1983, the teachers union president and superintendent in Miami-Dade County, Florida, met regularly about reform. In Rochester, superintendent Peter McWalters and union president Adam Urbanski recognized that industrial bargaining had

---

26. McDonnell and Pascal (1988, pp. viii, 42, 45); Johnson, Potter, and Nelson (1985); Pitner and Goldschmidt (1987, pp. 5, 58).

mixed effects on their schools, and they began to search for a better approach to unionism and schooling. Urbanski said, "It was clear we needed a change in kind, not just a change in degree. We had reached the point where not taking risks was a greater risk than taking risks."[27]

In a large urban district dubbed East Port by Johnson, Nelson, and Potter, labor and management agreed in 1982 to modify several contract provisions that had excessively favored teachers and shortchanged children. Relying on conventional bargaining practices, East Port's negotiators reached a settlement that included union concessions "most would never have anticipated three years before." They eliminated sequential bumping, prohibited assigning teachers to program areas where they had not recently demonstrated competence, added an "excellent" rating category to recognize exemplary teachers, extended the school year, required that teachers attend extra meetings, and granted principals the right to choose from among the three most senior applicants for voluntary and involuntary transfers. Despite the many give-backs in this settlement, the union president called it "fair," and a district official said it was "a giant step toward professionalism in the teaching ranks. There's no way that one could perceive this as a management-imposed agreement." Yet the participants recognized that conventional bargaining practices could take them no further. The superintendent spoke about the need for a new relationship—"We're in the same leaky lifeboat together"—while the union president asserted publicly: "The animosity which characterized labor/management relations last summer and fall must give way to a spirit of professional cooperation. To improve the quality of education, to restore public confidence in the school system, and to secure adequate funding for public education, such cooperation is not only desirable, it is vital." A union representative observed that the "union is attempting to change its approach to unionism. I think we realize that unionism, as we have known it in the sixties and seventies, is gone by the boards."[28]

When negotiators entertained new possibilities and experimented with practices unprecedented in educational bargaining, collaboration often emerged. McDonnell and Pascal point out that such risk taking was possible only because teachers had already attained "traditional bread-and-butter items that regulate teachers' basic working conditions (e.g., length of working day, class size)." These researchers conclude that such basic guarantees serve as "enabling conditions that unions must attain before they

27. Gallagher (1977, p. 158); Phillips (1993, p. 120); Koppich (1993, p. 141).
28. Johnson, Nelson, and Potter (1985, pp. 65, 66, 67, 68).

can move on to questions of professional autonomy and full participation." In their view, industrial unionism had been a necessary precursor to the professional unionism that some districts subsequently undertook.[29]

This attention to locally initiated change was augmented in 1986 when two influential publications, *A Nation Prepared* and *Tomorrow's Teachers,* started what would come to be called the "second wave" of school reform. The authors of these reports proposed approaches to reform that were fundamentally different from those the states had feverishly introduced just a few years before. Teachers, they argued, should be the agents rather than the objects of school reform. *A Nation Prepared* called for a "profession of well-educated teachers prepared to assume new powers and responsibilities to redesign schools for the future." *Tomorrow's Teachers* warned against continuing "to attempt educational reform by telling teachers what to do rather than empowering them to do what is necessary."[30]

Suddenly local districts that had been exploring new labor-management approaches quietly found they had a special license to empower teachers. In Miami-Dade County, the superintendent and union president "talked about the whole professionalization movement that came out of Carnegie" and agreed to add to the contract a task force on the professionalization of teaching. Later that year at the convention of the American Federation of Teachers (AFT), president Albert Shanker urged local union leaders to experiment with reforms at the local level, and many seized the opportunity to do so. Cincinnati union president Tom Mooney, who had already introduced in his district a union campaign called "Bargaining for Better Schools," explained that Shanker's authorization enabled him to promote his reform agenda among the rank-and-file: "The AFT gave us the sanction internally. That makes the stuff easier to sell."[31]

COLLABORATIVE APPROACHES TO BARGAINING. In devising new reforms, local districts found that they first had to invent new approaches to negotiation. Conventional bargaining, with its dissembling, distrust, and deceit, could never create conditions that would inspire teachers and administrators to work on hard problems together. Moreover, the split-the-difference settlements that typically emerge from bartering were hardly the kind of creative solutions that schools needed. Therefore, the parties in

---

29. McDonnell and Pascal (1988, p. ix).
30. Carnegie Forum on Education and the Economy (1986, p. 2); Holmes Group (1986, p. 61).
31. Provenzo (1989, pp. 150–51); Johnson (1989, p. 128).

these flagship districts began to experiment with collaborative bargaining practices, variously called "win-win negotiations" or "principled bargaining."[32] Rather than exchanging demands and counteroffers across the table, negotiators sat side-by-side in labor-management task forces, seeking solutions to challenging problems. Since union leaders and administrators in districts such as Miami and Rochester were long-time professional colleagues who had committed themselves to working together, their new experiments were further supported by personal candor, a readiness to try new things, and an underlying trust in each other's good intentions.

The detailed accounts of these districts' efforts, the difficulties they encountered, and the reforms they devised are instructive, even inspiring, although perhaps overly optimistic about the outcomes.[33] What is certain, however, is that the scope of bargaining, still technically restricted in many states to issues of wages, hours, and working conditions, had in practice greatly expanded beyond those formal limits. Local negotiators dealt with a wide range of issues, including teachers' role and responsibilities, professional accountability, curriculum reform, staff development, administrative practice, and parental involvement. Educational policy was at the center, rather than the margins, of their attention.

In some local districts, this shift from industrial unionism to "professional unionism" led to contract provisions that directly challenged the three tenets of industrial unionism: adversarial labor-management relations, standardized practice, and generic roles for employees (see figure 1-2).[34] Examples of these new approaches will be discussed briefly.

JOINT COMMITTEES PROMOTE LABOR-MANAGEMENT COOPERATION. Recognizing that the challenges of reform could not be met simply by negotiating and signing a contract, many districts instituted joint labor-management committees to promote ongoing, collaborative problem solving. Kerchner and Koppich report that such committees were "universal [among these reforming districts], although their configuration and mission var[ied] markedly." In Cincinnati, where there were at least thirty-seven such committees, administrators joined union-appointed teachers in equal numbers to "address a variety of issues, including curriculum reform, textbook selection, staff development, Chapter I . . . planning, and the

32. Fisher and Ury (1981).
33. Kerchner and Koppich (1993); Rosow and Zager (1989).
34. Kerchner and Caufman (1993).

Figure 1-2. *Reform Bargaining*

Tenets of *Reform Bargaining*	*Reform Model* *of Schooling*
Management and labor share interests and collaborate.	Teachers and administrators hold joint responsibility for schooling.
Flexibility and site-based discretion are built into contract.	Governance and instruction are school based.
Varied roles and status are recognized.	Teachers participate as mentors, curriculum experts, and peer reviewers.

school calendar." One of the most successful of these joint committees in Cincinnati, the Teacher Allocation Committee, monitored enrollments and then assigned teachers from a surplus pool in order to reduce class size in overcrowded grades and schools. "The district agreed to leave decisions solely in the hands of this joint labor-management committee. The union agreed not to grieve the committee's decisions." In the past, class size would have been bargained contentiously and then enforced class-by-class and school-by-school, seldom solving the class-size problem and rarely using resources creatively or efficiently. By creating a joint committee that would assess ever-changing needs and carefully assign surplus teachers, labor and management acknowledged and acted on their shared interest in staffing the schools as wisely as possible. They also recognized the need to continue their collaboration long after the contract was signed.[35]

PEER REVIEW AND CAREER LADDERS CHALLENGE TEACHERS' GENERIC ROLES. Industrial bargaining reinforces the generic definition of teachers' roles. Although some teachers have earned more academic degrees than their peers and may be paid better salaries as a result of that education, their jobs, in fact, are much the same from the first day of employment to the last. There were two reforms introduced by several of these flagship dis-

35. Kerchner and Koppich (1993, p. 11). For Cincinnati see King (1993, p. 73).

tricts that fundamentally changed that uniform conception of teachers' roles. Peer review, first developed in Toledo, identifies a small number of accomplished teachers who advise and assess both beginning teachers and experienced teachers judged to be in need of assistance. Peer review typically is overseen by a joint labor-management committee that selects the consulting teachers and weighs their recommendations for reappointment or dismissal. In Toledo, Cincinnati, and Rochester, this approach has won support among teachers because the peer reviewers bring expertise to the task and make a genuine effort to help. Remarkably, the process has led to considerably more dismissals of incompetent teachers than administrators accomplished before the program began.

Several of these districts also introduced the basic elements of a career ladder with promotional steps that signaled individuals' increasing skill and rewarded them for assuming new responsibilities. Rochester's Career in Teaching Program created a four-step ladder that included new intern teachers, provisional resident teachers, tenured professional teachers, and competitively selected lead teachers. Lead teachers take on roles as mentors, peer reviewers, staff developers, curriculum designers, or adjunct instructors at local colleges or universities. Similarly, Cincinnati introduced a Career in Teaching Program that was inspired, union president Mooney reports, by ideas from *A Nation Prepared*. In Cincinnati, as in Rochester, a joint committee was "formed to oversee the assessment process, credential lead teachers, and recommend additional roles and responsibilities for lead teachers."[36] In these districts, therefore, teachers were recognized and compensated for having attained different levels of competence and for exercising different kinds of responsibilities.

DECENTRALIZATION AND SCHOOL-BASED MANAGEMENT MODERATE STANDARDIZATION. Many reforming districts instituted some form of school-based management after 1986. Where in the past the policies of the district office and union contract applied equally to all schools, this decentralized approach to governance was designed to empower local schools to hire staff, allocate the budget, select their instructional programs, and seek waivers from union or district requirements. The point of this reform was to ensure that local schools could adapt their practices to meet the needs of their students.

36. For Rochester see Koppich (1993, pp. 144, 145); for Cincinnati see King (1993, pp. 71, 72).

Educators in Miami-Dade County had been working on these ideas since 1973, even though school-based management was not approved as a pilot program until 1986. The next year thirty-two schools participated in this experiment, and most had requested and received waivers from particular provisions of the contract. Provenzo observes that "despite all the hoopla" about innovation in Miami-Dade, "one does get the sense that a number of very important changes are taking place—ones that have the potential to be not only long lasting but of national importance." According to Phillips, by 1993 school-based management had been instituted in more than 160 schools and had served as a model for similar initiatives across the country. Every school that successfully won control of its budget or gained the right to regulate class size despite contract language stood as a challenge to union and bureaucratic pursuit of standardized practice.[37]

Current Contracts Reveal Different Approaches

When Rosow and Zager, and Kerchner and Koppich, set out to study districts engaged in developing labor-management alliances that explored the possibilities of professional unionism, the researchers planned to document what worked, and thus focused on reformers and districts at the forefront of this new movement. The fact that four chapters in their two books describe events in the same districts indicates that researchers had few such districts to choose from at the time.

As we took up this issue of reform bargaining a decade later, we wondered what might be found among a more representative sample of districts. Had more districts subsequently experimented with professional unionism and, if so, would their contracts include provisions contrary to the tenets of industrial unionism? We collected the current contracts of eleven districts from two samples previously studied by Johnson and her colleagues and compared them with earlier contracts from 1979–80 (the first sample) or 1984–85 (the second sample). Although both samples were small—the first included six districts and the second included five—they had been deliberately selected to represent the range of negotiating districts in the United States. These eleven districts provide valuable infor-

37. Provenzo (1989, pp. 156–57); Phillips (1993, p. 122).

mation about how local districts have responded to the possibilities of professional unionism.[38]

Before we began this current contract analysis, we recognized that there is inevitably a difference between negotiated policy and actual practice. Implementing contract language requires more than good intentions, for changes—particularly the kinds of changes advanced by reform bargainers—call for new attitudes and approaches from everyone involved. Not only must principals and teachers who have had no part in negotiating the agreement behave in new ways, but school boards must fund the changes and central office administrators must develop new procedures to support them. Meanwhile, secretaries and administrative staff must make the new approaches work day to day. Often, therefore, contracts promise more than they can possibly deliver. Any effort to truly understand whether and how these school districts are implementing negotiated reforms, and if these reforms are connected to student outcomes, would require extensive field work. However, there is still much to learn from comparing contracts before and after 1986. We can discover whether or not these districts moved beyond the conventions of adversarial bargaining and adopted provisions more consistent with the needs of schools and the goals of professional unionism. The fact that these provisions had been adopted represents a type of labor-management collaboration that is critical to, and promising for, school improvement.

Wider Variation Exists among Contracts Today

This analysis revealed that today even more variation exists among contracts than in 1988 when McDonnell and Pascal declared that collective bargaining agreements had not "converged." The current sample of eleven districts includes several that we call "reform contracts," because the parties have redefined labor-management relationships and ambitiously negotiated about a wide range of topics. Those districts have adopted contract

38. The first sample (Johnson, 1983) consisted of six districts ranging in size from 850 to 240,000 students. There were urban, suburban, and rural districts located in four regions of the country. Three were affiliated with the National Education Association, three with the AFT, and they provided variation in labor histories, contract strength, and current labor relations. The second sample (Johnson, Nelson, and Potter, 1985) of five districts had been selected for field work from a stratified, random sample of 155 districts in eleven states. We deliberately selected these districts for their diversity on a number of variables—region, size, labor history, contract, and union affiliation.

provisions that are consistent with the needs of school reform. They are distinctive in their clearly stated purpose and collaborative tone; they espouse shared responsibility for school improvement, encourage experimentation, and provide much-needed flexibility for schools and teachers.

By contrast, there are "industrial contracts" in this group that are scarcely different from those negotiated in the 1970s. Their provisions assume that labor and management have opposing interests, that standardization is a virtue, and that teachers' roles should be restricted to instructing and supervising students. We were surprised to see that the few changes that had been made in these industrial contracts during the past fifteen or twenty years usually favored management rather than the union.

Finally, we found a third group of contracts that we labeled "modified-industrial." They lack the coherence and clearly stated purpose of the reform contracts, yet they include several new provisions that suggest the possibility of labor-management cooperation or expanded roles for teachers. The tremendous variation apparent in this sample of eleven contracts illustrates once again that negotiations can produce remarkably different outcomes depending on a district's needs and priorities, its labor-management history and relationships, and its leadership.

REFORM CONTRACTS. There were three districts with contracts we judged to be reform agreements in that, through their various provisions, they recognize the shared interests of labor and management; affirm the importance of flexible, nonstandardized practice; and define differentiated, professional roles for teachers. One district (Metropolis) had been studied in 1979–80, and two (Citrus County and East Port) had been part of the 1985 study. Notably, these are the three largest districts in the current sample of eleven. Their earlier contracts had been industrial in tone and rule, emphasizing teachers' rights and protections, setting forth elaborate districtwide procedures for seniority-based staffing and disregarding the needs of individual schools. They typified most people's notion of excessively restrictive union agreements.

Today, in a remarkable departure from what might be expected, the contracts of these same districts suggest a different stance. For example, the East Port agreement begins with a preamble, "A Shared Commitment to Educational Achievement," in which the partners dedicate themselves "to doing better" and explicitly acknowledge that a prior contract was "also intended to promote change" but "accomplished less than was hoped." Lessons learned from that experience are, the preamble states, reflected in the new agreement, though the signers acknowledge that the intended outcomes will not follow automatically from signing the agreement:

> Change will not come of its own accord; it requires intensive, carefully planned, and skillfully executed implementation. Strong, consistent leadership and widespread training is needed to transform the traditional labor-management culture. To achieve real educational improvement, the parties and the community will have to work together collaboratively.

The preamble further explicitly affirms the importance of school-based decisionmaking, flexibility, professional development, parent involvement, and "accountability for quality and performance." It describes the adversarial labor relationship of the past and candidly acknowledges the challenges the district faces to "overcome vestiges of a litigious and suspicious culture focused on work rules, hierarchical power and resistance to change by both parties."[39]

In support of this spirit of collaboration and shared responsibility, the East Port contract includes provisions to establish an extensive professional development center and to create a Mentor Teacher Program administered by a joint labor-management committee. The contract sets forth a detailed plan for school-based management and shared decisionmaking, giving school site councils broad powers over curriculum design, budgeting, and staffing. Changes in specific provisions also signal the parties' recognition that individual schools need to handle their own affairs. For example, they explicitly give schools the right to decide how best to allocate time in a longer school day. More boldly, the East Port contract creates an experimental in-district charter program where selected schools operate free of both union and district regulations.

The Metropolis agreement includes new language that differs markedly from its 1980 contract. While the old contract specified emphatically what a teacher "shall" and "shall not" be required to do, the new agreement more broadly assigns responsibility for improvement. For example, it states:

> The Federation and the School District recognize that neither teaching nor learning can flourish in a disorderly, disruptive environment. Therefore, there is a need to become more pro-active in determining

39. Johnson, Nelson, and Potter (1985).

the cause of discipline problems as well as to isolate the distraction from the teaching and learning of the classroom.

The contract establishes a joint committee to study discipline and safety and to create schools throughout the district for students "whose behavior interferes with the teaching/learning process."

Throughout the current Metropolis contract, guiding language explains the relationship between good schooling and the stated expectations for teachers' performance, such as: "The orderly planned opening of the school day is essential to the full and effective utilization of instructional time. Consequently, teachers should be in their classrooms at the contractual time and should remain in the classroom until all students are dismissed." Exemplary Metropolis teachers, like those in East Port, can assume new roles that reach beyond their classrooms by serving as peer reviewers or administering that program as members of the joint Peer Intervention Panel.

Once an extremely bureaucratized district that revered standardized practice, Metropolis, through its contract, has ventured to give more autonomy to schools and programs within schools. Where in 1980 Metropolis principals had to informally convince teachers to depart from particular negotiated rules, today the contract provides for more flexibility and variation. For example, the staff and principal of an individual school or program may "jointly develop an Experimental School Improvement Plan which may require modifications of provisions of this Agreement, including but not limited to, class size, teacher rosters, teacher, student and administrator evaluations, grading, scheduling or trade-offs." All management powers are not relinquished, however. The contract states the superintendent's right to "reconstitute an academically distressed school" by dissolving and reopening it with newly assigned (or reassigned) teachers and administrators.

Although Citrus County, the third district with a reform contract, was characterized as once having had "the most contentious educational labor relationship in the state," its contract was never quite as detailed or restrictive as those of East Port or Metropolis. Basic working conditions, essentially set by 1974, still form the core of today's agreement, but they are supplemented with programs and initiatives found in other reforming districts. For example, the contract outlines a school-based management program and encourages individual schools to devise approaches that will achieve greater instructional success: "The parties agree that local school and professional staff will be empowered to identify ways of improving the educational process and to determine alterations to this agreement necessary to implement those improvements."

The Citrus County contract includes no provision for teachers to evaluate their peers or to move up a career ladder, but it does establish for them a role in policymaking that is more than advisory. The parties agree, for example, that teachers "should continue to be a major source of development and innovations in improving the educational programs carried on in the schools" and "that it is important for the professional staff to participate in the overall coordination of studies, projects, and other activities directed toward the development, improvement, and implementation of such programs, toward the evaluation of existing programs, toward the devising, testing and introduction of new programs, and toward research in pertinent and educationally related areas."[40] Thus, the contract affirms teachers' expertise and their readiness to do more than deliver the district's curriculum.

Therefore, each of these three contracts redefines the labor-management relationship, expands the role of teachers, and provides for varied, flexible practices within the schools. The parties express confidence in the promise of a collaborative relationship, declare their shared interest in providing better instruction, and acknowledge their interdependence in making daily progress. The contracts still contain basic guarantees of teachers' working conditions—in-school work hours, duty-free lunch, restricted meeting obligations, evaluation procedures—but there is less focus on minimal job requirements and there are fewer practices prescribed in detail than in the past.

INDUSTRIAL CONTRACTS. In marked contrast to the three reform agreements that rejected industrial conventions and introduced new roles and programs, five contracts were distinctly industrial in tone, form, and content. Three of these districts—Mill City, Northwood, and Vista—come from the 1980 sample and two—Harbor Mills and Midland Heights—from the 1985 sample. While, in this study, the reform districts are all large, the districts with industrial contracts are relatively small, ranging in size from 1,000 to 15,000 students. The districts are very different demographically—two wealthy suburbs, a large rural area, and two poor cities.

40. The preceding quotations are from Johnson, Nelson, and Potter (1985).

These industrial-style contracts are, overall, shorter and less detailed than the agreements that incorporate reforms. Unlike the reform agreements, these documents are formal and legalistic in tone, specifying rather narrowly what can, cannot, and must be done by the various parties. While the reform agreements explicitly consider the particular needs and programs of the district, these industrial contracts include a great deal of boilerplate language, making them sound much like one another. They set forth procedures for layoffs and transfers, class size limits, preparation time, and teaching loads, with little allowance for school-based decisionmaking.

These districts' contracts continue to define teachers' roles narrowly and specify their responsibilities in surprising detail. For example, the Midland Heights contract lists the ways in which the teacher's in-service day "may be used"—"to attend an assignment-related conference, workshop or to make a school visitation"—and requires teachers to document how they eventually use the time. Teachers in the Vista district are expected to sponsor one student organization or be a member of one building level committee. In Mill City, principals still can change teachers' report card grades "in unusual cases." Northwood teachers "may be asked by the Administration to cover for an absent colleague during assigned preparation time," but the contract also states that teachers "may decline such requests." In Harbor Mills, the contract spells out precisely what constitutes an "unexcused absence": "A teacher who is absent before and after a school holiday is presumed to be absent for the holiday for the same reason as she is absent for the school days, unless excused by the Superintendent of Schools after presentation of a physician's certificate of legitimate incapacity of the teacher."

Notably, most of the changes that were apparent in the current contracts favored management over labor, contradicting once again the belief that unions gain ever-stronger contracts over the years. Whereas the old Vista contract included a section called "Rights and Responsibilities," the new one is titled "Recognition of Responsibilities and Rights," shifting the emphasis, if only symbolically, from the limitations on teachers' obligations to expectations for their practice. In 1980 the contract said that teachers should be consulted about their preferred subject or grade level assignments and that the principal "shall then develop a schedule based upon consideration of the teacher's stated preference, professional preparation, and teaching experience and qualifications." The current contract strengthens the principal's authority in this process by stating, "The principal shall develop the master schedule and make teacher assignments using input from department chairpersons and teachers." The changes in the Vista contract are few, but those that have been made offer evidence that management has reasserted formal authority.

Changes in the Northwood contract seemed to include concessions to both labor and management and to suggest a process more of bartering than collaborative problem solving. In the current contract, seniority is not included as a criterion for voluntary or involuntary transfers, but teachers did win the right to "present [their] input to the principal regarding the effects of the involuntary transfer upon the students and staff," be given the reason for the transfer "providing time permits," and object in writing to the superintendent. All these are very modest gains by the union, if indeed they are gains at all.

Therefore, with the exception of layoff and transfer provisions added in response to the enrollment declines that hit many districts in the early 1980s, almost half of the contracts in this sample have remained virtually unchanged over the last fifteen or twenty years. Although the contracts were not hostile or contentious in tone, they were formal and prescriptive. Basic working conditions had been established long ago, and what adjustments in those provisions did occur appear to have shifted the balance of authority toward management.

MODIFIED INDUSTRIAL CONTRACTS. Contracts from three remaining districts—Canyon Unified, Shady Heights, and Plantville—contained new elements of reform that seem to have been appended to the old agreements without changing their overall purpose or character. From simply reading the documents, it is impossible to know whether these additions are the first steps of a new labor-management relationship or simply freestanding changes that will have little effect on larger labor or schooling practices.

The most progressive of these modified-industrial contracts is Canyon Unified's, which establishes joint labor-management committees to evaluate the applications of teachers seeking assignments that are partially outside their field of certification. Another provision creates a joint committee to approve teachers' applications for new program development money. There is a pilot program for site-based decisionmaking allowing individual schools to adopt practices contrary to the contract, although that program is not explained in any detail. Responding to a state initiative, the district provides for the appointment of *professional growth advisors*, who work as mentor teachers. Although this might suggest the teachers' roles have been expanded, the contract also allows individuals to resign from the district while holding these positions; elsewhere the agreement states that "unit members shall not be assigned to participate in the evaluation of other unit members." The contract also reveals some ambivalence about the labor-management relationship. It emphasizes the parties' shared responsibility for instructional improvement, an objective that "can be more readily achieved by a willingness on the part of both parties to assist all unit members, but especially less experienced unit members, in improving their professional skills." This collaborative spirit, however, is quickly undercut by a subsequent statement cautioning that this provision is not subject to the grievance process.

In Shady Heights, too, the recent contract assigns some measure of new professional power to teachers. Where the 1980 agreement prescribed in detail how time should be used on early release days, the current agreement assigns this to a planning committee that includes teachers; final proposals require approval by the administration and the union. A joint labor-management committee is charged with reviewing current report cards if, and when, they are to be revised. In choosing department heads, two teachers now are part of a five-member selection committee, and seniority, which once was decisive in the department head's appointment, now is only one criterion to be considered.

Of the three districts with modified-industrial contracts, Plantville provides the least evidence of reform. It establishes joint committees to oversee minicourses and to study "the problem of curriculum continuity on days of excessive pupil absences." It also requires that a committee of six, including two teachers, approve any plan requiring narrative report cards.

Although it is possible that these modified-industrial contracts are the precursors of more ambitious reform agreements, that does not seem likely. There is some evidence of broader, more collaborative ideas, but the contracts remain essentially industrial in style and detail. The changes seem only superficial adjustments to an otherwise adversarial, rule-bound way of doing business.

Limits of Industrial Bargaining and the Potential of Reform Bargaining

There is remarkable variation in collective bargaining agreements today. Some open the way for better schools by affirming labor and management's commitment to work together, establishing structures that make joint responsibility truly possible, guaranteeing the right of individual schools to manage their own affairs, and engaging teachers as professionals in the process of educational improvement. In stark contrast, there are other contracts that heighten distinctions between labor and management (subordinating the former to the latter), establish uniform practices districtwide, and specify in precise terms the rights and obligations of all teachers and administrators. This second group of contracts, industrial in form and content, is far more likely to inhibit than to advance school reform.

In this array of contracts, both the limits of industrial bargaining and the potential of reform bargaining can be discerned. For, if a district retains and reinforces rigid distinctions between labor and management, it will not likely open discussions about a wide range of issues, including how to reconcile assurances about teachers' working conditions with anticipated reforms. By restricting the flexibility of individual schools and imposing detailed rules that apply to all schools, a district is likely to prevent those schools from adopting creative approaches that would serve children better. If a district narrowly limits teachers' roles and prescribes what they must do or not do, it will surely discourage professional initiative and forfeit the chance to draw upon the full range of teachers' commitments and expertise. By contrast, a district engaged in reform bargaining can consider a wide range of related issues and fashion coherent, consistent approaches to school reform. It can carefully discern which decisions affect the well-being of the whole district and, therefore, must be centralized, while delegating decisions about school-based practice to the schools, where they belong. Reform bargaining can encourage teachers to think expansively about both what they currently do and what they might do in their work.

Looking Ahead

We return, therefore, to the original question: What role should unions and collective bargaining play in school reform? There are several options. First, of course, policymakers might settle for the status quo. Alternatively, collective bargaining could be eliminated entirely, a strategy that seems increasingly plausible, given the growth of charter schools and popularity of vouchers. Third, public schools could deliberately expand the role of collective bargaining in reform by adopting a collaborative approach to negotiations and keeping school improvement at the center of their deliberations.

Maintain the Status Quo

For a small number of enterprising districts already engaged in reform bargaining, steadily following their current course will likely lead to productive change. However, in most districts, where industrial bargaining is the norm, continuing business as usual will only serve to reinforce problematic distinctions between labor and management and minimize teachers' engagement in change. As we saw in contracts from Harbor Mills, Northwood, and Mill City, many districts now routinely use negotiations solely to reach agreement on wages and benefits, while provisions addressing non-compensation items carry over without review from one contract to the next. Administrators in such districts may be so discouraged by the negative, stagnant character of conventional bargaining that, if they decide to promote change, they do so entirely outside the bargaining process, without regard to the contract or the union and without much chance of systematic or substantial reform. In some districts where politics and favoritism have historically held sway, teachers might well interpret district officials' efforts to reform schooling by sidestepping negotiations as an effort to divide them from their union or undermine the rights that their contracts protect; in response, teachers may actively or passively resist reform. If, on the other hand, teachers see good intentions and competence in such administrative action and thus choose to take an active role in shaping reforms, progress is possible. However, since many initiatives that are central to instructional change (peer review, career ladders, or school-based management) inevitably affect how teachers' work is organized or how their time is used, those proposals would ultimately reach the bargaining table anyway. There, the outmoded process of industrial bargaining would be of little use in helping the parties craft creative, locally appropriate changes. Many administrators today may never venture to recommend far-reaching reforms in teachers' work because they know that such proposals would be subject to negotiation, and they realize that the conventional bargaining practices used in their districts are not up to the difficult task of reform.

The force of institutional inertia and the lack of leadership by administrators and union officials will probably mean that most districts will settle for the status quo. However, this failure to choose a more challenging option is not as benign as it might seem. For relying on the status quo over time can only increase differences that already exist between the educational practices of reforming districts and those of stagnating districts. For children, those differences mean inequity in public education.

Eliminate Collective Bargaining

Some who call for an end to collective bargaining likely start from the assumption that administrators really do know best how to reform education, and they proceed to conclude that schools will improve once management reasserts its right to regulate the work of teachers. However, there is no evidence to support the notion that administrators know how to revitalize schools. Other advocates of this position may start from a different place and assume that teachers and administrators already see the need to work together as professionals and will collaborate naturally once the restrictions of bargaining and contracts are removed. This belief is apparent in the considerable enthusiasm about the potential of charter schools to engage teachers as professionals and equals in a new approach to public education. Yet, it is not clear what the outcome of this movement will be. Possibly, charter schools could simply recreate the educational factory-model of the past, where administrators make all decisions about the school's organization and teachers either withdraw to the privacy of their classrooms or leave education for jobs in more rewarding workplaces. Early research by Johnson and Landman suggests that the opportunity to work in charter schools will not diminish good teachers' interest in securing basic assurances about their work.[41] A study of teachers' work in such deregulated schools revealed that, union or no union, these teachers sought to have reasonable boundaries placed on what they could be expected to do. They also wanted to establish their role in policymaking and to ensure a means by which they could voice complaints and resolve disputes. Individual schools may address and settle these issues informally, but a few instances of administrative excess or abuse will likely provoke teachers to insist that their needs be formally addressed. One possibility, of course, is that they will exercise their rights to organize as a union and bargain collectively.

Enlarge the Role of Collective Bargaining

Considerable evidence supports the third option—enlarging the role of collective bargaining in school reform. The analysis of past research and

41. Johnson and Landman (2000).

current contract data presented here documents our confidence about the promise that reform bargaining has for school improvement, although those who pursue this course cannot ignore the substantial challenge in implementing such change. Rather than creating obstacles to improvement, collective bargaining can provide a legitimate, collaborative process for discussing educational challenges, exploring options for improvement, and tailoring strategies to meet local needs and realities.

First, reform bargaining requires that the parties embrace a broad range of issues, for it is virtually impossible to truly change schools with a series of minor, isolated adjustments. Changes in one practice inevitably require changes in others. If discussions are limited to the traditional topics of wages, hours, and working conditions, participants will never face the important challenges about teachers' professional roles, school organization, and instructional practice.

Second, both labor and management must acknowledge their shared stake in improving education and adopt a collaborative approach to negotiation, one that encourages candor and creative determination, demonstrates a readiness to rethink long-held beliefs, and expresses a willingness to make needed, sometimes unpopular, concessions.

Third, to ensure that their professional judgment shapes decisions and practices, a broad group of teachers—not simply the inner circle of regulars—must offer advice about contract deliberations from the start, and there must be a variety of key roles for these teachers to assume once the contract has been signed (for example, as members of joint committees or participants in peer review).

Fourth, in negotiating and administering a contract, the needs of individual schools must be kept at the center of these deliberations so that these schools gain the flexibility they need to make reform work for their students and communities. In the past, far too many contract provisions have been geared to uniform application rather than school-by-school adaptation. Kerchner, Koppich, and Weeres recommend that districts replace the "all-inclusive districtwide contract" with two documents—a "slender central agreement" that sets forth broad principles and district structures, and a series of "compacts" negotiated at the school sites that lay out the details for a range of school-level practices.[42] There is much to recommend this approach. However, reformers who underestimate the challenges of implementation or seek to introduce such change hastily will

42. Kerchner, Koppich, and Weeres (1997, p. 104).

inevitably stumble. Research on program implementation reveals the wisdom of gradual adoption. Schools might initially bargain about a small list of provisions, such as preparation time or professional development, and once they become practiced in establishing school-based policy take on more challenging issues, such as the school schedule, tracking, or differentiated staffing.

Achieving the conditions that would support reform bargaining requires far more than simply having both sides agree to a new approach, for the context in which public schools operate regularly imperils the stability of cooperative labor relationships. Many local reformers who had set out to bargain collaboratively discovered that precarious norms about teamwork collapsed when budget cuts threatened teachers' pay raises or job security.[43]

Moreover, a signed contract, no matter how progressive, is only a beginning. That both labor and management endorse printed words by no means ensures that participants will carry out the commitments they have signed. In every district there is inevitably a gap between what the contract allows and what actually transpires. When practice falls short of what a contract permits or promises, participants and observers often are cynical about whether the parties ever truly intended to make it work. In reality, there were likely good intentions at the start. However, most districts that engage in ambitious reform discover that they do not have the organizational capacity needed to transform practice rapidly. They can look to other districts for new models of teaching and administration, but each time they introduce a new program they must develop the skills, procedures, and relationships needed to make it work. A district that adopts an induction program for new teachers will soon discover that most teachers do not yet know how to mentor their peers. A district that introduces decentralized budgeting will find that school-site councils do not intuitively understand how to allocate resources. A district that encourages individual schools to reconfigure their use of instructional time may find that principals are not practiced in constructing flexible teaching schedules. A district that seeks to transform the role of a personnel office in hiring new teachers will find that central office administrators do not immediately see the many ways that they might support a school's decision to recruit its own staff. Developing such capacity takes both time and "steady work."[44] Increased capacity will not be enough without consistent, strong leadership

---

43. Johnson, Nelson, and Potter (1985).
44. Elmore and McLaughlin (1988).

in support of reform from the superintendent and union president. It is informative but sobering to see how many of the advances in flagship districts grew out of long-term professional and personal relationships between the leaders of labor and management. Trust is not built easily and can be lost with the departure of key reformers. The arrival of an autocratic superintendent or the election of an antagonistic union leader can suddenly set back the pace of change. However, the longer that a district works at reform and the more that many participants are invested in its outcomes, the less likely it will be that individuals can enter the scene and dismantle accomplishments.

With increased focus on instructional standards and accountability, superintendents and school boards are likely to feel pressure to recentralize districts and reassert managerial authority. In the short run, a superintendent may conclude that exacting greater compliance from principals and teachers is the best response to the public's demands for quick results. However, school districts will not achieve high levels of instructional success by prescribing detailed practices for classrooms or for schools. In fact, the new higher standards for learning demand adaptive, creative teaching, not restrictive, assembly-line treatment of students. Uniform schooling is not good schooling. We have already learned that lesson but perhaps not taken it to heart.

Therefore, of these options—maintaining the status quo, eliminating collective bargaining, or expanding the role of reform bargaining—we make a case for choosing the third, although we do so with caution. This approach would encourage comprehensive discussions, informed by the judgments of both administrators and teachers. Moreover, reform bargaining has the greatest potential for achieving systemic change, thus ensuring comparable opportunities for all students. However, achieving these benefits requires far more than simply making a choice and installing a program. Learning new approaches to collaboration, changing ingrained attitudes about one's adversaries, and reconsidering beliefs about what is possible all call for courage, imagination, and resolve. Changing central office procedures, building capacity for decisionmaking in the schools, preparing expert teachers to assume supervisory roles, and developing principals' confidence as educational leaders all take time, a tolerance for failure, and a determination to get things right. The work is surely hard, but the stakes are high, and reform bargaining still offers the best promise for success.

References

Callahan, Raymond E. 1962. *Education and the Cult of Efficiency.* University of Chicago Press.

Carnegie Forum on Education and the Economy. 1986. *A Nation Prepared: Teachers for the 21st Century.* New York.

Darling-Hammond, Linda. 1997. *The Right to Learn: A Blueprint for Creating Schools That Work.* Jossey-Bass.

Eberts, R. A., and J. A. Stone. 1984. *Unions and the Public Schools: The Effect of Collective Bargaining on American Education.* Lexington.

Elmore, Richard F., and Milbrey Wallin McLaughlin. 1988. "Steady Work: Policy, Practice, and the Reform of American Education." Bound report. Santa Monica, Calif.: RAND.

Elmore, Richard F., Penelope Peterson, and Sarah J. McCarthey. 1996. *Restructuring in the Classroom: Teaching, Learning, and School Organization.* Jossey-Bass.

Finch, M., and T. W. Nagel. 1984. "Collective Bargaining and the Public Schools: Reassessing Labor Policy in an Era of Reform." *Wisconsin Law Review* (6): 1580–70.

Fisher, Roger, and William Ury. 1981. *Getting to Yes: Reaching Agreement without Giving In.* Houghton-Mifflin.

Fullan, Michael G. 1991. *The New Meaning of Educational Change.* Teachers College Press.

Gallagher, D. G. 1977. "Teacher Bargaining and School District Expenditures." *Industrial Relations* (17): 231–37.

Goldschmidt, Steven, and Leland Stuart. 1984. "The Extent of Educational Policy Bargaining and its Impacts on School System Adaptability." Eugene, Oregon: Center for Educational Policy and Management.

Hill, Paul T., Lawrence C. Pierce, and James W. Guthrie. 1997. *Reinventing Public Education: How Contracting Can Transform America's Schools.* University of Chicago Press.

Holmes Group. 1986. *Tomorrow's Teachers.* Lansing, Mich.

Jessup, Dorothy K. 1985. *Teachers, Unions, and Change: A Comparative Study.* Praeger.

Johnson, Susan Moore. 1983. *Teacher Unions in Schools.* Temple University Press.

———. 1989. "Bargaining for Better Schools: Reshaping Education in the Cincinnati Public Schools." In *Allies in Educational Reform: How Teachers, Unions, and Administrators Can Join Forces for Better Schools,* edited by J. M. Rosow and R. Zager, 124–145. Jossey-Bass.

———. 1990. *Teachers at Work: Achieving Excellence in Our Schools.* Basic Books.

Johnson, Susan Moore, and Jonathan L. Landman. 2000. "Sometimes Bureaucracy Has Its Charms: Teachers' Experiences in Deregulated Schools." *Teachers College Record* 102, 1 (February): 85–124.

Johnson, Susan Moore, Niall C. Nelson, and Jacqueline Potter. 1985. *Teacher Unions, School Staffing, and Reform.* Harvard University Press.

Kerchner, Charles Taylor, and Krista Caufman. 1993. "Building the Airplane While It's Rolling Down the Runway." In *A Union of Professionals: Labor Relations and Educational Reform,* edited by C. T. Kerchner and J. E. Koppich, 1–24. Teachers College Press.

Kerchner, Charles Taylor, and Julia E. Koppich. 1993. *A Union of Professionals: Labor Relations and Educational Reform.* Teachers College Press.

Kerchner, Charles Taylor, Julia E. Koppich, and Joseph G. Weeres. 1997. *United Mind Workers: Unions and Teaching in the Knowledge Society.* Jossey-Bass.

Kerchner, Charles Taylor, and Douglas E. Mitchell. 1988. *The Changing Idea of a Teachers' Union.* Teachers College Press.

King, Byron. 1993. "Cincinnati: Betting on an Unfinished Season." In *A Union of Professionals: Labor Relations and Educational Reform,* edited by C. T. Kerchner and J. E. Koppich, 61–78. Teachers College Press.

Koppich, Julia E. 1993. "Rochester: The Rocky Road to Reform." In *A Union of Professionals: Labor Relations and Educational Reform,* edited by C. T. Kerchner and J. E. Koppich, 136–57. Teachers College Press.

Lieberman, Myron. 1993. *Public Education: An Autopsy.* Harvard University Press.

McDonnell, Lorraine, and Anthony Pascal. 1979. "Organized Teachers in American Schools." Santa Monica, Calif.: RAND.

———. 1988. "Teacher Unions and Educational Reform." Santa Monica, Calif.: Center for Policy Research in Education, RAND.

Meier, Deborah. 1995. *The Power of Their Ideas: Lessons from America and a Small School in Harlem.* Beacon Press.

Murnane, Richard J., and Frank Levy. 1996. *Teaching the New Basic Skills: Principles for Educating Children to Thrive in a Changing Economy.* Free Press.

National Commission on Excellence in Education. 1983. *A Nation at Risk: The Imperative for Educational Reform.*

Perry, C. R. 1979. "Teacher Bargaining: The Experience in Nine Systems." *Industrial and Labor Relations Review* (33): 3–17.

Perry, C. R., and W. A. Wildman. 1970. *The Impact of Negotiations in Public Education: The Evidence from the Schools.* Worthington, Ohio: Charles A. Jones.

Phillips, LeRae. 1993. "Miami: After the Hype." In *A Union of Professionals: Labor Relations and Educational Reform,* edited by C. T. Kerchner and J. E. Koppich, 116–35. Teachers College Press.

Pitner, Nancy, and Stuart Goldschmidt. 1987. "Bargaining over School Reform: California's Teacher Mentor Program." Paper presented at the annual meeting of the American Educational Research Association, Washington, D.C., April.

Provenzo, Eugene F. 1989. "School-Based Management and Shared Decision Making in the Dade County Public Schools." In *Allies in Educational Reform: How Teachers, Unions, and Administrators Can Join Forces for Better Schools,* edited by J. M. Rosow and R. Zager, 146–63. Jossey-Bass.

Rosow, J. M., and R. Zager, eds. 1989. *Allies in Educational Reform: How Teachers, Unions, and Administrators Can Join Forces for Better Schools.* Jossey-Bass.

Sizer, Theodore R. 1992. *Horace's School: Redesigning the American High School.* Houghton-Mifflin.

Tyack, David. 1974. *The One Best System: A History of American Urban Education.* Harvard University Press.

Wise, Arthur E. 1979. *Legislated Learning: The Bureaucratization of the American Classroom.* University of California Press.

2

JOE A. STONE

Collective Bargaining and Public Schools

> Never before in recent history have the public schools been subjected to such savage criticism for failing to meet the nation's educational needs.[1]

FAILURE STALKS THE HALLS of many public schools. At least, that is the implication of a series of recent studies, beginning prominently with *Politics, Markets and America's Schools* by John E. Chubb and Terry M. Moe. This perceived failure and the suspected culprits have been a prominent part of the debate over public schools for at least the last decade or so. The stream of studies that followed Chubb and Moe includes, among others, *Making Schools Work* by Eric Hanushek and others; *Holding Schools Accountable,* edited by Helen F. Ladd; and *Does Money Matter?* by Gary Burtless.[2] Throughout the debate, unions have often been at or near the center of controversy, with recent evidence provided by Caroline Hoxby that teachers unions increase costs while reducing student achievement via increased high school dropout rates.

The author is indebted to Thomas Kane, David Figlio, Tom Loveless, anonymous referees, and Randy Eberts for helpful comments and suggestions.

1. Chubb and Moe (1990, p. 1).
2. Hanushek and others (1994); Ladd (1996); and Burtless (1996).

Is this true? Are unions a culprit in the failures, or perceived failures, of public schools? What evidence is available to assess this conclusion, or on the broad range of possible effects of collective bargaining—from teacher pay to student achievement? To what extent is the evidence consistent or reliable? What additional evidence is required to resolve key questions? My objective here is to evaluate the answers to these questions. Other studies of collective bargaining in public schools focus on related, but clearly different questions regarding the institutional context, evolution, and operation of collective bargaining in public schools. Two early examples of this research genre are *Teacher Unions in Schools* by Susan Moore Johnson and *The Changing Idea of a Teachers' Union* by Charles Taylor Kerchner and Douglas Mitchell.[3]

To begin, suppose there was no *direct* evidence whatsoever on the influence of collective bargaining on public schools; instead, all that was known were the *indirect* implications from the effects of unions elsewhere, whether in private industry or other parts of the public sector (for example, the typical effects reviewed in the classic *What Do Unions Do?* by Richard B. Freeman and James L. Medoff). What would be predicted, based only on this indirect evidence, about the effects of collective bargaining on public schools? This question is a powerful lens through which to examine the anticipated effects of collective bargaining on public schools.

Relying on this approach, I survey evidence of the effects of collective bargaining on (1) teacher pay and benefits, where collective bargaining tends to increase both in other sectors; (2) schools as a workplace, where collective bargaining typically has myriad effects, including improved working conditions, a more regulated or "standardized" workplace, and greater protection against loss of employment; (3) total cost of instruction, where unionized firms typically have higher costs of production; and (4) perhaps most important, individual student achievement, where the effects of collective bargaining on "productivity" in other sectors are mixed and often small, whether positive or negative. A final section summarizes key conclusions and speculates on evidence required to resolve some of the important questions.

Teacher Pay and Benefits

"More" is the famous answer Samuel Gompers gave to the question, "What do unions want?" That is, unions and the members they represent

---

3. Johnson (1984); Kerchner and Mitchell (1988).

typically want higher pay and better fringe benefits. Evidence suggests that unions tend to succeed in these objectives, in that pay and fringe benefits for union workers almost universally exceed those for comparable nonunion workers. The magnitude of this differential, though, is highly variable from one setting to another, but for pay is typically at least 8 to 10 percent for identical workers and probably substantially larger for fringe benefits.[4] If teachers unions are like other unions, predictions would be for at least modestly higher pay and better fringe benefits from successful collective bargaining.

Teacher Pay

Ideally, to study the effects of collective bargaining on teacher pay one would like to be able to randomly assign teachers with exactly the same attributes to school districts, which have also been randomly assigned to either union or nonunion status. Of course, no actual study can replicate this ideal. Instead, studies attempt to control for as many attributes of teachers and districts as possible, while estimating the union-nonunion pay differential. In some studies, instrumental variable (IV) estimates are employed in an attempt to account for the fact that union status is not actually randomly assigned (for example, causality might be reversed, in that low wages or inferior working conditions might induce unionization) or for other factors, including potential measurement error.

One of the first detailed studies of the union pay premium for teachers was the study by William H. Baugh and Joe A. Stone based on data for individual teachers in the Current Population Survey.[5] By matching teachers in the survey in adjacent years, they are able to estimate a union pay premium by using a "fixed-effects" estimator for individual teachers, which estimates the wage change associated with a change in union status for the *same* individual teacher. The estimated union pay premium in this case is significantly positive, about 12 percent. That is, this result indicates that teachers in a district where they are covered by a collective bargaining contract earn 12 percent more than teachers in a district where they are not covered. Note that this is roughly the same as, if slightly higher than, the union pay premium (8–10 percent) found in other contexts and reported earlier. The IV estimate, based upon geographic variables, is also not significantly different,

4. Freeman and Medoff (1984, pp. 47, 66–68).
5. Baugh and Stone (1982).

revealing little evidence of bias arising from the nonrandom nature of union status or measurement error. Estimates without individual fixed-effects are typically higher, however, suggesting that unionized teachers may have unobserved attributes associated with higher pay.

A second, more aggregate study, by Morris M. Kleiner and Daniel L. Petree, relies on state data for average teacher salaries from 1972 to 1982 and an estimator with fixed state effects. The dependent variable is the logarithm of the average teachers' salary in the state and the key union variable is the percentage of teachers covered by a collective bargaining contract.[6] The estimated union pay premium in this case is just 1 percent and statistically insignificant, as reported in table 2-1, though the estimate without state fixed effects is significantly positive at 7 percent. Again, though, the Kleiner-Petree study employs more aggregate data, with fewer controls for individual teacher and district characteristics.

A recent study of pay for unionized teachers by Caroline Minter Hoxby employs Census of Governments data for school districts for the years 1970, 1980, and 1990, matched along with other data, to estimate the union pay premium for teachers in districts with a collective bargaining agreement where at least 50 percent of teachers are members. Hoxby's specification controls for district, time, and district-specific time fixed effects. The estimated union pay premium in this case is significantly positive at 5.1 percent. The IV estimate, based on state collective bargaining laws as instruments, is virtually identical, at 5.0 percent. The Hoxby study has more detailed controls than the Kleiner-Petree study, but fewer than the Baugh-Stone study, and yields an estimate roughly between the two, below 12 percent but above 1 percent.[7]

Fringe Benefits

As in other settings for collective bargaining, evidence on the union pay premium is more extensive than on the fringe-benefit premium. Typically,

---

6. Kleiner and Petree (1988) also present estimates based upon union membership as the measure of collective bargaining status, but contract status is typically preferred as the better indicator.

7. With data that extend through 1990 and a specification that emphasizes "late" changes in union status, the pay differentials associated with these changes may be small because one would expect districts with the largest potential pay differences to organize first. Also, the spillover effects from previously organized districts may be a factor. Zwerling and Thomason (1995), for example, find that the spillover effects of collective bargaining in public schools may even be larger than the direct effects, at least more recently after the vast majority of districts are already organized.

though, the fringe-benefit premium is almost always larger than the pay premium. Eberts and Stone present direct evidence of the effect of collective bargaining on fringe benefits for teachers.[8] They construct a measure of the extent of collective bargaining based upon a hierarchy of contract items established by a Guttman-scale analysis. In this approach, the number of items in the contract consistent with Guttman scaling can be interpreted as an indicator of the extent and power of the union contract.

Based upon detailed contract data for New York public schools in 1976–77, Eberts and Stone estimate a significantly positive effect for the number of contract items on fringe benefits for teachers, an effect substantially larger than the corresponding effect on salaries. This result corresponds to evidence on the effect of collective bargaining on fringe benefits in other sectors, but is based upon data for only one state.

Schools as a Workplace

Unions tend to affect the workplace in a variety of subtle ways. These changes are in part an effort to improve working conditions, but often are an attempt to "standardize" the workplace so that employers have less discretion in dealing with individual workers or to protect workers from loss of employment, particularly as pay and fringe benefits rise. Many of these more diverse changes in the workplace are also surveyed by Freeman and Medoff.

Working Conditions

While there are few controlled studies of the effects of collective bargaining on the working conditions for teachers, three studies offer some evidence, as summarized in table 2-2. Eberts and Stone use nationally representative data from the Sustaining Effects Survey of elementary schools to examine both the amount of paid preparation time and the student-teacher ratio.[9] They find that the paid time teachers have to prepare for their duties is about 4 percent greater for unionized teachers, and that the student-teacher ratio is nearly 12 percent lower. Kleiner and Petree rely on state-level data and find that the student-teacher ratio decreases by about 7 percent (or

8. Eberts and Stone (1984, p. 146).
9. Eberts and Stone (1984).

Table 2-1. *Collective Bargaining and Teacher Pay*

Study	Year	Data	Unit of observation	Specification	Estimated premium (percent)[a]	Comment
Baugh and Stone	1982	Current Population Survey, 1977–78	Individual teacher	Individual fixed effects, ordinary least squares	12.0 (4.7)	Instrumental variable not significantly different
Kleiner and Petree	1988	State, 1972 to 1982	State	State fixed effects, ordinary least squares	1.0 (1.0)	Seven percent estimated without fixed effects
Hoxby	1996	Census of Governments 1972, 1982, 1992 matched to other data	School district	District, time, and district-time fixed effects, ordinary least squares	5.1 (0.8)	Instrumental variable not significantly different

a. Standard errors in parentheses. Dependent variable in each study is the logarithm of annual teacher salary.

Table 2-2. *Collective Bargaining and Working Conditions*

				Working condition differentials (percent)		
Study	*Year*	*Data*	*Unit of observation*	*Paid preparation time*	*Student-teacher ratio*	*Comment*
Eberts and Stone	1984	Sustaining Effects Survey, 1978	Individual teacher/ student	4.0*	–12.0*	Mean difference by school
Kleiner and Petree	1988	State, 1972 to 1982	State	n.a.	–7.0*	Mean difference by state
Hoxby	1996	Census of Governments 1972, 1982, 1992 matched to other data	School district	n.a.	–6.0* –9.0*	Mean difference by district Instrumental variable

* Significant at the 5 percent level or better.
n.a. Not available.

1.48 students with a hypothetical student-teacher ratio of 20) if the percentage of districts with a collective bargaining agreement increases from zero to 100 percent. Hoxby's study relies upon district-level data and a differences-in-differences specification and finds that the student-teacher ratio decreases by about 6 percent (or 1.1 students). Hoxby's IV estimate is even more negative, and the student-teacher ratio decreases by about 9 percent (or 1.7 students).[10] This evidence from three divergent studies, while limited in scope, is roughly consistent and suggests that teachers in unionized districts have greater paid time to prepare for their duties and fewer students to teach and supervise.[11]

Workplace Standardization

Collective bargaining usually brings greater "regulation" of the workplace, in part to reduce the discretion of employers over individual workers, as well as to reduce the variation in working environments. Is this true for teachers? Eberts and Stone provide evidence from districts in New York that specific items typical to union contracts (for example, class-size provisions) lead to greater reliance on traditional classroom organization, as compared to other types of instructional modes.[12]

This "standardizing" effect of collective bargaining is confirmed in greater detail by Eberts and Stone in national data for fourth-grade students in the Sustaining Effects Survey. They find that unionized districts are less likely to rely on a variety of specialized instructional modes.[13] As compared to students studying mathematics in nonunion districts, students in union districts on average spend 42 percent less time with a specialist, 62 percent less time with an aide, 26 percent less time with a tutor, and 68 percent less time in independent, programmed study. It appears that teachers in unionized districts are more likely to teach in a standard classroom setting, relying much less on specialized instructional modes. Laura M. Argys and Daniel I. Rees recently have found that low- and high-ability students are in larger classes in union schools, even with the overall student-teacher ratio held constant. As we will later see, this type of standardization appears to have substantial consequences for the lower and

10. Eberts and Stone (1984); Kleiner and Petree (1988, p. 316); Hoxby (1996, p. 695).

11. In a related study, Eberts (1984) also finds evidence of a decrease in the student-teacher ratio in unionized districts.

12. Eberts and Stone (1984).

13. Eberts and Stone (1984, pp. 149, 156).

upper tails of the student population, in ways that are different from those for average students.

Employment Protection

Unions and their members are also interested in protecting employment, both from temporary downturns in the need for their services and from the employer's incentive to reduce employment as the costs of union pay and fringe benefits rise.[14] The evidence presented earlier on student-teacher ratios is pertinent here. Even in the face of higher pay and more costly fringe benefits, unionized districts employ more rather than fewer teachers per student. Why? Contract clauses tend to protect teachers from employment loss in unionized districts, especially limitations on class size and reduction-in-force (RIF) provisions. Eberts and Stone find in data for New York districts that both class size and RIF provisions, by boosting employment above what it would otherwise be, tend to significantly increase employment and the total cost of instruction.[15]

Cost of Instruction

The effects surveyed thus far—increased pay, better fringe benefits, improved working conditions, a more regulated, standardized workplace, and protections against loss of employment—typically lead to higher total costs of production in unionized settings.[16] Is this conclusion true for school districts or are there compensating effects that tend to offset the pressure for higher costs? Conceivably, for example, the higher pay and benefits, better working conditions, and more secure employment might attract more able teachers and offset, at least partially, the higher costs with better teaching and improved student performance.

The first studies of collective bargaining and district costs are based on limited samples of districts and few controls for differences in student characteristics and other factors. Not surprisingly, estimates from these studies

---

14. Employment restrictions are also usually required to enforce economically efficient contracts that lie on a Pareto-efficient contract curve, as in McDonald and Solow (1981).

15. Eberts and Stone (1984, pp. 143–44).

16. In some industries, researchers have found lower total costs of production at very large scales of integrated operations, for example, Allen (1987) in construction and Wilson et al. (1995) in sawmills.

conflict. Daniel G. Gallagher estimates that operating budgets in unionized districts are 9 percent higher than in nonunionized districts, yet
William C. Hall and Norman Carroll, as well as Jay G. Chambers, find no
difference.[17] Eberts and Stone provide an early study based on detailed
data.[18] They rely on data from two separate, nationally representative surveys (the Sustaining Effects Survey for elementary schools and High School
and Beyond), both of which contain detailed controls for individual students, including student achievement and other key factors. Estimates
from the Sustaining Effects Survey, as summarized in table 2-3, indicate
that unionized districts spend about 15 percent more to achieve the same
level of student performance, while estimates from the High School and
Beyond survey indicate that unionized districts spend about 8 percent
more.[19]

Two other studies summarized in table 2-3 provide similar evidence.
Kleiner and Petree find based on state-level data that *nonwage* district
expenditures rise by $158 (roughly 12 percent) as the proportion of teach-
ers covered by collective bargaining contracts rises from 0 to 100 percent.
They do not present estimates for total expenditures. Hoxby relies on
district-level data and IV differences-in-differences estimator as the preferred specification. In that specification, union districts appear to spend
about 12 percent more than nonunion districts with the same characteristics. So, despite the relatively small union pay premium Hoxby finds, the
overall effect on costs is essentially the same as in the Eberts-Stone and
Kleiner-Petree studies.

Productivity: Effects on Student Achievement

The question that has attracted the most attention, by far, is the extent to
which unions influence actual student achievement. On this question indirect evidence drawn from collective bargaining in other settings is mixed.
In some industries, unionized workers appear to be more productive, in
others less—but often any differences are modest, especially in the most
controlled studies.[20] After reviewing the evidence on student achievement,

17. Gallagher (1979); Hall and Carroll (1975); Carroll (1973); and Chambers (1977).
18. Eberts and Stone (1986).
19. Instrumental variation estimation in both cases tends to yield somewhat higher cost differentials.
20. Studies of the effect of collective bargaining on productivity include Pencavel (1977) for British
coal fields, Clark (1980a, 1980b) for cement producers, Ehrenberg et al. (1983) for municipal libraries,

I argue that much of the value of the current evidence on productivity comes not from the answer to the question of whether or not the overall effect of collective bargaining on student achievement is positive or negative, but from the more detailed ways in which teachers unions appear to influence the effectiveness of particular aspects of schools.

Student Achievement

As with other aspects of collective bargaining, the ideal experiment for analyzing student achievement would randomly assign students to schools that are also randomly assigned to union or nonunion status. The best approximations to this unattainable ideal involve extensive control variables for both student and school attributes, as well as controls for the nonrandom assignment of students and schools. Despite the numerous studies of collective bargaining and student achievement, even good approximations to the ideal have been difficult to achieve.

Seven studies of student achievement are summarized in table 2-4. Eberts and Stone use detailed student, teacher, and school data from the Sustaining Effects Survey of elementary schools to examine the average performance of fourth-grade students in mathematics.[21] (The distribution of achievement differentials across students is also important, but for now I focus only on evidence for average student achievement.) Based upon detailed controls, including a "pretest" score from the beginning of the year, Eberts and Stone find that students in districts with a collective bargaining contract score roughly 1 percent higher on a standardized mathematics examination toward the end of the year, or about 3.3 percent higher as a percentage of the average gain from the pretest to the posttest. This effect is small, but significantly positive.

In a similar study based on the High School and Beyond Survey, Milkman examines the average performance of twelfth-grade high school students on a standardized test of mathematics, with their score on a similar tenth-grade test as a control variable.[22] Over the two-year period from

---

Allen (1986) for school and office construction, and Mitchell and Stone (1992) for western U.S. sawmills.

21. Eberts and Stone (1987). Researchers often concentrate on student performance in mathematics because schools appear to be relatively more important for mathematics than for reading, where family differences appear to play a larger role and where raw differentials are typically smaller (see Madaus et al., 1979).

22. Milkman (1987).

Table 2-3. *Collective Bargaining and Total Cost of Instruction*

Study	Year	Data	Unit of observation	Total cost differential (percent)[a]	Comment
Eberts and Stone	1982	Sustaining Effects Survey, 1978	School district	15.0 (5.02)	Ordinary least squares with student achievement controls
		High School and Beyond, 1982	School district	8.0 (3.43)	Ordinary least squares with student achievement controls
Kleiner and Petree[b]	1988	State, 1972 to 1982	State	12.0 (3.09)	Ordinary least squares without student achievement controls, nonwage costs only
Hoxby	1996	Census of Governments 1972, 1982, 1992 matched to other data	School district	12.3 (3.31)	Instrumental variable without student achievement controls, but with fixed district, time, and district-time effects

a. Standard errors in parentheses. Dependent variable is either total expenditures per student or total expenditures, with student enrollments as a control variable. The measures of union status are the same as in table 2-1.

b. The Kleiner-Petree estimate is for nonwage costs only.

Table 2-4. *Collective Bargaining and Measures of Student Achievement*

Study	Year	Data	Unit of observation	Specification	Estimated differential (percent)	Comment
Eberts and Stone	1987	Sustaining Effects Survey, 1977–78	Individual student	Math test score, with pretest, ordinary least squares	1.0*	Of average score, 3.3 percent of gain
Milkman	1987	High School and Beyond, 1982	Individual student	12th grade math score with 10th grade score, ordinary least squares	2.0*	Of average score, over two years
	1997	High School and Beyond, 1982	Individual minority students	12th grade math score with 10th grade score, ordinary least squares	1.4*	Of average score, over two years
Kleiner and Petree	1988	State, 1972 to 1982	State	SAT and ACT scores, with state fixed effects, ordinary least squares	6–8*	Few detailed student controls
				Graduation rates, with state fixed effects, ordinary least squares	4.4*	Few detailed student controls
Grimes and Register	1990	NAEE data for TEL,[a] 1987–88	Individual student	TEL score with SAT score, ordinary least squares	1.9*	With detailed student controls
Argys and Rees	1995	NELS, 1988[a]	Individual student	10th grade math score with 8th grade score, ordinary least squares	1.3*	Of average score, over two years
Nelson and Rosen	1996	State, 1995	State	SAT score with no state fixed effects, ordinary least squares	4.5*	No fixed effect, more controls than Kleiner-Petree
Hoxby	1996	Census of Governments 1972, 1982, 1992 matched to other data	School district	Drop-out rate with district, time, and district-time effects, instrumental variable	2.3*	Increases drop-out rate

* Significant at the 5 percent level or better.

a. NAEE, National Assessment of Economic Education; TEL, Test of Economic Literacy; NELS, National Education Longitudinal Study.

the sophomore to senior years, Milkman finds that students in union districts score about 2 percent higher than students in nonunion districts, which is roughly the same magnitude as the 1 percent gain found over one year by Eberts and Stone for fourth-grade students. In a follow-up study, Milkman uses the same approach to examine average student achievement for minority students and finds that minority students in districts with a collective bargaining contract score about 1.4 percent higher than minority students in districts without a contract.[23]

Kleiner and Petree use aggregate state data, with few individual or school variables, to estimate a model with fixed state effects. They find that SAT and ACT scores are on average 6 to 8 percent higher in states where every teacher is covered by a collective bargaining contract, as compared to states where no teacher is covered. With the same data and a similar specification, Kleiner and Petree find that graduation rates are 4.4 percent higher for states where every teacher is covered by a contract. The aggregate nature of the data and the paucity of detailed controls, though, should lend caution to the estimates.

In perhaps the most specific study, Grimes and Register use data on the Test of Economic Literacy (TEL) taken by high school students and reported in the National Assessment of Economic Education (NAEE). With extensive student, curricula, and school controls—including even the student's SAT score—the authors find in their most detailed specification that students in schools covered by a collective bargaining contract score on average 1.9 percent higher on the TEL, as reported in table 2-4. With the SAT score included as a covariate, their estimate appears to be a conservative one.[24]

Echoing the findings of Eberts-Stone and Milkman, Argys and Rees also find a positive effect of unions on mathematics performance. Based on the National Educational Longitudinal Study of 1988 (NELS), they examine the performance of tenth-grade high school students on a standardized test of mathematics, with their score on a similar eight-grade test as a control variable. Over the two-year period from the eighth to tenth grades, Argys and Rees find that students in union districts score on average 1.3 percent higher than in a nonunion district, or roughly the same difference Milkman found for the two-year period from the sophomore to senior year (and also roughly consistent with the difference Eberts-Stone found over a one-year period for fourth-grade students).

23. Milkman (1997).
24. Grimes and Register (1990).

Nelson and Rosen have repeated a study of aggregate state data similar to the Kleiner-Petree study. They do not include fixed state effects, but do include more detailed student controls. Students in states where more than 90 percent of teachers are in districts with a collective bargaining contract score on average 4.5 percent higher on the SAT than students in states where fewer than 50 percent of teachers are covered by a contract. Again, the aggregate nature of the analysis lends caution to the estimate.[25]

The most recent detailed study is by Hoxby (1996), who uses district-level data and a specification that includes district, time, and district-specific time trends to examine high school drop-out rates. Hoxby's preferred specification also employs instrumental variables to account for potential correlations between contract status and the error term. Hoxby's measure of unionization, as before, is the presence of a collective bargaining contract where at least 50 percent of the teachers are also members of the union. In the preferred specification, Hoxby finds that collective bargaining increases the high school drop-out rate by 2.3 percent and therefore infers that unionization reduces student achievement. In addition, Hoxby explores whether or not the effects of collective bargaining are strengthened by a concentrated local market structure for school districts. Based on a Herfindahl measure of school-district concentration, she finds that increases in the drop-out rate associated with collective bargaining are significantly larger in areas with little interdistrict competition. This result seems especially powerful.

Even if one sets aside the studies based on aggregate state data by Kleiner and Petree and Nelson and Rosen, the remaining studies based on individual student data and detailed controls (that is, the Eberts-Stone, Milkman, Grimes-Register, and Argys-Rees studies) yield strikingly consistent evidence of a small but significantly positive effect of collective bargaining on average student achievement. Yet Hoxby's well-controlled study employing instrumental variables with district-level data finds the reverse, that student achievement, measured as the high school drop-out rate, declines with collective bargaining. Which answer is correct?

25. Nelson and Rosen (1996). Another aggregate study, Peltzman (1993), also provides estimates based on state-level data but does not include either state fixed effects (as in Kleiner and Petree, 1988) or detailed student controls (as in Nelson and Rosen, 1996). Peltzman finds a modestly positive effect for National Education Association unionization from 1972 to 1981, but a negative effect for the American Federation of Teachers (AFT). These effects appear more negative in the 1980s, especially for the AFT.

Distribution of Student Achievement

There is, I believe, evidence that these apparently conflicting answers are not necessarily inconsistent. As the starting point of this argument, one can turn to the evidence on the effect of collective bargaining on the *distribution* of student achievement, as compared to the effect on *average* student achievement. In three separate sets of data for individual students, Eberts-Stone, Milkman, and Argys-Rees find significant evidence of an inverted-U shape for the effects of collective bargaining, with positive effects for average students and negative effects for atypical students in the upper- and lower-tails of the distribution. The pattern found by Eberts and Stone for fourth-grade students in mathematics is presented in figure 2-1.[26]

How does this evidence possibly help to reconcile the evidence of positive effects on student achievement with the evidence of negative effects on high school drop-out rates? We know, certainly, that drop-out rates are highly related to student success in schools, and that students in the lower tail of student performance are much more at risk of dropping out. If the effects of collective bargaining tend to reduce the academic success of weak students, then one would also expect an increase in the drop-out rate. Moreover, if the concentration of local school districts exaggerates the inverted-U distribution of achievement differentials (that is, increases both the average and the dispersion of student achievement), as one might reasonably expect, then drop-out rates would also rise even more as weak students do even worse in areas with little interdistrict competition.

Why do the effects of collective bargaining appear to differ across different types of students? At least part of the answer appears to lie in the evidence reviewed earlier on the standardizing effect of collective bargaining on the workplace. In particular, unionized schools are much more likely to rely on traditional classroom instruction and much less on a variety of specialized modes of instruction. This phenomenon likely has two effects for students. First, if one is teaching in a traditional classroom setting, the norm of instruction is most likely to be directed toward the central, or average, student in the classroom. With smaller class sizes aimed at the

---

26. Eberts and Stone (1987); Milkman (1987); Argys and Rees (1995). Milkman (1997) finds complementary evidence for minority students. In schools where minority students are "atypical" (that is, constitute a minority of the student population of the school), the effects of collective bargaining on achievement are negative, by about 1 percent. However, in schools where minority students are "typical" (that is, constitute a majority of the student population of the school), the effects of collective bargaining on achievement are positive, by about 1.8 percent.

Figure 2-1. *Differences between Union and Nonunion Predicted Post-Test Scores*

Difference

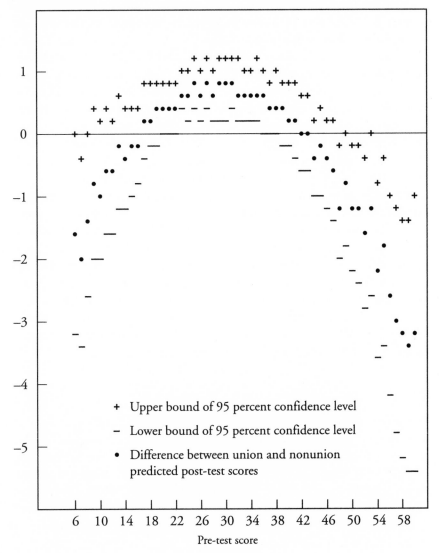

Pre-test score

average student, it is not surprising then that unionized schools tend to do a bit better with average students—whether average is measured in terms of student ability or other factors, such as ethnicity or socioeconomic status. Second, the paucity of specialized modes of instruction means that atypically good or bad students tend to receive less attention for their unique needs than in nonunion schools.[27]

Indeed, Argys and Rees find that low- and high-ability students are taught in larger classes in union schools than in nonunion schools, even if one holds the overall student-teacher ratio in the school constant. Pursuing this difference, they examine the union-nonunion difference in student performance across various ability levels after holding constant the size of the student's class, academic track, and overall class achievement level. With these class characteristics held constant, Argys and Rees find that the low- and high-ability students no longer perform worse in union schools, which suggests that the effect of unionization works, at least to a substantial degree, through these channels.

The linkages between these various pieces of evidence, while plausible, remain only suggestive. It may also be the case that only one of the answers is true, or even that average student achievement increases *because* the high school drop-out rate increases. If most drop-outs are low-achieving students, then increases in the drop-out rate in high school could increase the average level of achievement among graduates. This story, though, would not explain the positive gains found for elementary students or why the gains there appear even larger than for high school students.

The Effectiveness of School Inputs

The larger part of the story of the effect of collective bargaining on student achievement may lie in how unionization alters the effectiveness of particular school inputs or policies, not so much in what the overall effects on student achievement might be, since these appear to be modest regardless of the sign. As a practical matter, collective bargaining will be a prominent feature of public schools in most states over any foreseeable future, and knowledge of how collective bargaining affects student achievement can be helpful in modifying its impact.

27. A number of recent studies appear to demonstrate the potential importance of specialized modes of instruction. Farkas (1993), for example, finds in a study of Dallas schools that, even without altering the basic organization of classroom instruction, the use of hourly paid tutors with selected students is effective in improving student performance, especially among disadvantaged students.

On this issue, evidence from Eberts-Stone, Milkman, and Hoxby is consistent: "Inputs are quite effective in nonunion schools, while unionized schools show the traditional pattern of ineffective inputs."[28] Hoxby notes that a one-student decrease in the student-teacher ratio decreases the drop-out rate by 0.4 percentage points in nonunion schools, with no effect in union schools, and that a 10 percent increase in teacher salaries decreases the drop-out rate by 0.7 percentage points in nonunion schools, again with no effect in union schools. Similarly, Eberts and Stone find that changes in the student-teacher ratio in nonunion schools are about 3.4 times as effective in improving student achievement as in union schools.[29] In addition, changes in instructional time per student are about 2.1 times more effective than in nonunion schools.

How should we interpret these differences? Since we know that student-teacher ratios are smaller in union schools, then it should not be surprising that further reductions are less effective than they would be in nonunion schools. But that may be only part of the answer. Suppose that it makes a difference *how* the student-teacher ratio changes? Does the ratio change by reducing average class sizes for traditional classrooms or by also introducing specialized instructional modes alongside or within traditional classrooms? Based on the evidence we have already seen, reductions in the student-teacher ratio in union districts are more likely to be the former, while reductions in the ratio in nonunion districts are more likely to be the latter. A similar interpretation can be applied to the evidence on the greater effectiveness of instructional time in nonunion schools.

If this interpretation is correct, then part of the ineffectiveness of changes in the student-teacher ratio or instructional time in union schools might be explained by differences in the way instruction is organized in union and nonunion schools.[30] This conclusion seems to offer a more pragmatic (and optimistic?) direction to explore than whether or not the overall effects of collective bargaining are positive or negative, since the overall effect on student achievement appears modest regardless of the sign and also since collective bargaining is unlikely to simply fade away.

28. Hoxby (1996, p. 707).

29. Eberts and Stone (1987). An exception is Argys and Rees (1995), who do not find that the student-teacher ratio is less effective in union districts.

30. The key role of the organization of instruction appears to be reflected in the enhanced role of principals in union schools, where Eberts and Stone (1987, p. 358), for example, find that the principal's leadership in designing and organizing instruction is substantially more effective and critical in union as compared to nonunion schools.

Conclusion

I began with the proposition that the effects of collective bargaining in other sectors present a strong lens through which to examine the effects for public schools. Indeed, as predicted, there is much evidence that collective bargaining in public schools:

—increases teacher pay and fringe benefits,

—improves aspects of the workplace (for example, the amount of preparation time and student-teacher ratios),

—generates a more regulated, standardized workplace, especially with respect to the diversity in instructional modes,

—provides greater security against loss of employment, both through reduction-in-force provisions and limitations on class size, and

—increases the total cost of instruction by between 8 and 15 percent in order to produce a given level of student achievement.

With respect to productivity, or the effect of collective bargaining on student achievement, evidence from other sectors is less clear, since both positive and negative effects are found. To some extent this too is a pattern found for public schools, where collective bargaining appears to

—increase (modestly) *average* student achievement,

—reduce (modestly) achievement for low- and high-ability students, and

—increase (modestly) the high school drop-out rate.

Even the apparently contradictory evidence of an increase in average student achievement and an increase in the high school drop-out rate may be consistent, in that collective bargaining appears to reduce achievement among low-ability students, who are the ones most at risk for dropping out. More direct examination of this potential link would be helpful.

The evidence also suggests that key attributes of instruction (for example, instructional time and student-teacher ratios) are less effective in union schools. An interpretation pursued here is that improvements in instructional time or student-teacher ratios are more likely in union schools to come in the form of modest changes in traditional classroom instruction, as compared to expanded opportunities for specialized instruction tailored to the needs of either low- or high-ability students— whereas the latter are a more prominent feature of nonunion schools. As with the achievement-drop-out link, more direct evidence on this issue would also be insightful, especially with regard to the directions and prospects for the debate over the "new unionism" movement in teacher education.

In the end there is little evidence that collective bargaining has had a deep, pronounced influence in depressing (or increasing) average student achievement. There is much evidence, though, that collective bargaining has had powerful effects on pay, fringe benefits, working conditions, the organization of instruction, and the total costs of schools. Taxpayer criticism of public schools correctly identifies collective bargaining as one of the culprits in the higher costs of schools, but incorrectly identifies it—at least based on the spectrum of evidence currently available—as a culprit in poor student performance, at least for students on average.

References

Allen, Steven G. 1986. "Unionization and Productivity in Office Building and School Construction." *Industrial and Labor Relations Review* 39: 187–201.

———. 1987. "Can Union Labor Ever Cost Less." *Quarterly Journal of Economics* 102: 347–73.

Argys, Laura M., and Daniel I. Rees 1995. "Unionization and School Productivity: A Reexamination." In *Research in Labor Economics*, vol. 14, edited by Solomon Polachek. Greenwich, Conn.: JAI Press.

Baugh, William H., and Joe A. Stone. 1982. "Teachers, Unions, and Wages in the 1970s: Unionism Now Pays." *Industrial and Labor Relations Review* 35: 368–76.

Burtless, Gary, ed. 1996. *Does Money Matter? The Effect of School Resources on Student Achievement and Adult Success.* Washington, D.C.: Brookings.

Carroll, Stephen. 1973. "Analysis of the Educational Personnel System: III. The Demand for Educational Professionalism." Report R-1308-HEW. Santa Monica, Calif.: Rand Corporation.

Chambers, Jay G. 1977. "The Impact of Collective Bargaining for Teachers on Resource Allocation in Public School Districts." *Journal of Urban Economics* 4: 324–39.

Chubb, John E., and Terry M. Moe. 1990. *Politics, Markets, and America's Schools.* Washington, D.C.: Brookings.

Clark, Kim B. 1980a. "Unionization and Productivity: Micro-Econometric Evidence." *Quarterly Journal of Economics* 95: 613–39.

———. 1980b. "Unionization and Productivity: A Case Study." *Industrial and Labor Relations Review* 33: 451–69.

Eberts, Randall W. 1984. "Union Effects on Teacher Productivity." *Industrial and Labor RelationsReview* 37: 346–48.

Eberts, Randall W., and Joe A. Stone. 1984. *Unions and Public Schools: The Effect of Collective Bargaining on American Education.* Lexington Books.

———. 1986. "Teacher Unions and the Cost of Public Education." *Economic Inquiry* 24: 631–44.

——— 1987. "Teachers' Unions and the Productivity of Public Schools." *Industrial and Labor Relations Review* 40: 355–63.

Ehrenberg, Ronald G., Daniel R. Sherman, and Joshua L. Schwartz. 1983. "Unions and Productivity in the Public Sector: A Study of Municipal Libraries." *Industrial and Labor Relations Review* 36: 199–213.

Farkas, George. 1993. "Structuring Tutoring for At Risk Children in the Early Years." *Applied Behavioral Science Review* 1: 69–92.

Freeman, Richard B., and James L. Medoff. 1984. *What Do Unions Do?* Basic Books.

Gallagher, Daniel G. 1979. "Teacher Negotiations, School District Expenditures, and Taxation Levels." *Educational Administration Quarterly* 15: 67–82.

Grimes, Paul W., and Charles A. Register. 1990. "Teachers' Unions and Student Achievement in High School Economics." *Journal of Economic Education* 21: 297–308.

Hall, William C., and Norman Carroll. 1975. "The Effect of Teachers' Organizations on Salaries and Class Size." *Industrial and Labor Relations Review* 28: 834–41.

Hanushek, Eric A., and others. 1994. *Making Schools Work: Improving Performance and Controlling Costs.* Washington, D.C.: Brookings

Hoxby, Caroline Minter. 1996. "How Teachers' Unions Affect Education Production." *Quarterly Journal of Economics* 111: 671–718.

Johnson, Susan Moore. 1984. *Teacher Unions in Schools.* Temple University Press.

Kerchner, Charles Taylor, and Douglas E. Mitchell. 1988. *The Changing Idea of a Teachers' Union.* New York: Falmer Press.

Kleiner, Morris M., and Daniel L. Petree. 1988. "Unionism and Licensing of Public School Teachers: Impact on Wages and Educational Output." In *When Public Sector Workers Unionize,* edited by Richard B. Freeman and Casey Ichniowski. University of Chicago Press.

Ladd, Helen F., ed. 1996. *Holding Schools Accountable: Performance-Based Reform in Education.* Washington, D.C.: Brookings.

Madaus, George F., Thomas Kellaghan, Ernest A. Rakow, and Denis J. King. 1979. "The Sensitivity of Measures of School Effectiveness." *Harvard Educational Review* 49: 207–30.

McDonald, Ian M., and Robert M. Solow. 1981. "Wage Bargaining and Employment." *American Economic Review* 71: 896–908.

Milkman, Martin I. 1987. *Teacher Unions and High School Productivity.* Ph.D. dissertation, University of Oregon.

———. 1997. "Teachers' Unions, Productivity, and Minority Student Achievement." *Journal of Labor Research* 18: 247–50.

Mitchell, Merwin W., and Joe A. Stone. 1992. "Union Effects on Productivity: Evidence from Western U.S. Sawmills." *Industrial and Labor Relations Review* 46: 135–45.

Nelson, F. Howard, and Michael Rosen. 1996. "Are Teachers' Unions Hurting American Education? A State-by-State Analysis of the Impact of Collective Bargaining among Teachers on Student Performance." Technical report. Milwaukee, Wis.: Institute for Wisconsin's Future.

Pelzman, Sam. 1993. "The Political Economy of the Decline of American Public Education." *Journal of Law and Economics* 36: 331–70.

Pencavel, John H. 1977. "The Distribution and Efficiency Effects of Trade Unions in Britain." *British Journal of Industrial Relations* 40: 137–56.

Wilson, Wesley W., with Joe A. Stone and Merwin C. Mitchell. 1995. "Product Selection and Costs in a Partially Unionized Industry." *Journal of Labor Research* 16: 81–95.

Zwerling, Harris L., and Terry Thomason. 1995. "Collective Bargaining and the Determinants of Teachers' Salaries." *Journal of Labor Research* 16: 467–84.

3

DALE BALLOU
MICHAEL PODGURSKY

Gaining Control of Professional Licensing and Advancement

THE TRAINING AND LICENSURE of doctors, lawyers, and many other professionals is largely regulated by organizations of practitioners. To date the regulatory framework for elementary and secondary school teaching has been very different. In most states licensing requirements are set by state education agencies and state boards of education. State agencies also accredit teacher training institutions. While a private accrediting organization, the National Council for Accreditation of Teacher Education (NCATE), has existed since the mid-1950s, fewer than a dozen states mandate NCATE accreditation and the majority of teacher training institutions are not NCATE-accredited.

In the last several years a campaign to put teacher training and licensing on the same professional footing as medicine has gained considerable momentum. Proponents of professionalization want practitioner associations put in charge of the accreditation of teacher education programs and the licensing of public school teachers. Organizations of educators would replace state departments of education and school boards in setting standards for how teachers will be trained, tested, hired, and promoted.

The authors thank Julie Wehling and Jae Ho Chang for their assistance with this research, as well as Caroline Hoxby and Myron Lieberman.

Proponents claim that such measures will upgrade the quality of the work force. Evidence on this point will be examined below. One thing is clear, however. Professionalization would shift power away from elected officials to organizations in a position to promote private producer interests. Hence it is not surprising that professional organizations are often among the most vocal proponents of these forms of labor market regulation.

Teacher Professionalization: An Overview

Advocates of teacher professionalization want to transform teacher training and licensing from a decentralized system with regulatory power centered in state education agencies to a centralized, national system with regulatory power wielded by private education organizations. One of the early statements on this theme was the 1986 report of the Carnegie Task Force on Teaching as a Profession, *A Nation Prepared*. The task force, which included American Federation of Teachers (AFT) president Albert Shanker and National Education Association (NEA) president Mary Futrell, drew an explicit parallel between teaching and medicine.

> In 1910, educator Abraham Flexner transformed medical practice in the United States by insisting on rigorous professional preparation of physicians. Flexner's work, supported by the Carnegie Foundation for the Advancement of Teaching, laid the groundwork for the development of a medical delivery system second to none in the world. That historic Carnegie contribution has paid incalculable benefits to America and its people. We are confident that improvements in the preparation of teachers . . . will prove as significant to the country and its children.[1]

Among the reforms advocated by the task force was the creation of a national organization to certify highly proficient "master" teachers. In the view of the task force, the influence of this national certification board would extend far beyond the relatively small number of nationally certified teachers. The standards developed by the board would play a central role in upgrading professional practice.

1. Carnegie Forum on Education and the Economy (1986, p. 7).

Long before the Board produces its first assessment, its standards will begin to be available as a resource to those shaping teacher education programs and setting standards for graduation. Institutions and those responsible for state program approval should take advantage of Board standards to raise the quality of teacher education.[2]

The Carnegie Foundation proceeded to invest several million dollars to launch the National Board for Professional Teaching Standards (NBPTS) in 1986. This Carnegie investment acted as a magnet for other foundation contributions and eventual federal support.

At the same time the Carnegie task force was preparing its report, an organization of deans of leading schools of education, the Holmes Group, put out its own recommendations for the future of teacher training. Teacher education ought to be a postbaccalaureate program of study (as in the medical and legal professions); classroom study should be followed by an internship in a professional development school (analogous to a teaching hospital) where newly trained teachers would work under the supervision of expert mentor teachers. The recommendations of the Holmes Group were endorsed by other advocates of teacher professionalization, who argued that a large body of research had finally established what effective teachers needed to know and do. This claim was echoed by the accrediting agency, NCATE, which claimed that its newest standards were grounded in a body of scientific research like that supporting medical protocols—hence "knowledge based."

The latest phase of the debate on teacher training and licensing has been dominated by a second Carnegie commission, the National Commission on Teaching and America's Future (NCTAF), established in 1995. Like the earlier Carnegie panel, the NCTAF includes the presidents of the NEA and AFT. Unlike the earlier panel, it also includes the president of NCATE and the president of the newly created NBPTS.

In its 1996 report entitled *What Matters Most: Teaching for America's Future,* the commission charged that public schools employ large numbers of unqualified teachers, largely as a result of inadequate and poorly enforced standards for teacher training and licensing. The commission set out a detailed and ambitious policy agenda to professionalize teaching, transferring regulation of teacher training and licensing from public officials to

2. Carnegie Forum on Education and the Economy (1986, p. 68).

private professional organizations. Key components of this agenda included the following:

—Mandatory accreditation of all teacher training programs by the NCATE,

—Assessment of beginning teachers using instruments developed by the Interstate New Teacher Assessment and Support Consortium (INTASC) as a condition of licensing,

—Certification of 105,000 "master" teachers by the NBPTS, and

—Establishment of independent professional boards in all states to set policies regarding teacher education, testing, licensing, and continuing certification.

Although the commission left many of the details of reform to various councils and professional bodies, *What Matters Most* endorsed the vision of the Holmes Group. The commission applauded states that restructured teacher education as postgraduate or five-year programs and disparaged reforms reducing the amount of preservice training in order to streamline entry into the profession (as in many alternative certification programs). Through the activities of the independent professional boards, NCTAF would close loopholes in the licensing process that permit unlicensed teachers to be hired on waivers ("temporary" and "emergency" certificates) to fill vacancies in districts that have trouble attracting qualified teachers.

Teachers Unions and Professional Self-Regulation

Professional self-regulation concentrates power in organizations of practitioners. As the dominant teacher organizations, the NEA and the AFT have been strong advocates of professionalization. Indeed, their advocacy predates both Carnegie commissions.

NCATE

Before 1954 accreditation of teacher education programs was carried out by the American Association of Colleges of Teacher Education (AACTE). In that year this function was transferred to a newly created organization, the NCATE. From the beginning, the NEA has had a substantial presence within the NCATE, although the implications of its participation changed over time as the NEA developed from a professional association dominated by administrators into a union that represented teachers in collective bargaining and authorized strikes and other work actions.[3]

NCATE accreditation has never played the central role that accreditation plays in such professions as medicine and law. Currently only approximately 500 of the 1300 teacher training programs are NCATE accredited. Advocates of teacher professionalization, including the NEA, would change this. Recent resolutions adopted by the union show how the NEA uses its influence within the education community to promote a central role for NCATE:

> Individuals interested in teaching careers should attend institutions accredited by the National Council for Accreditation of Teacher Education (NCATE). Counselors and advisors should inform students of the advantages of attending NCATE-accredited institutions.

Another resolution on accreditation states that the "National Education Association believes that teacher education programs should be approved at two levels: at the state level through an agency such as a professional standards board and at the national level through the National Council for Accreditation of Teacher Education."[4] Another NEA publication ("The NEA-NCATE Connection") calls on affiliates to promote NCATE accreditation in a variety of ways, including "developing collective bargaining language requiring local school boards to hire only those professionals who have graduated from NCATE-approved institutions.[5]

Although the AFT did not become involved until the late 1980s, both unions are now constituent members of NCATE, providing financial support and helping to shape the council's policy. (The 1997–98 NEA contribution was $366,600; AFT's contribution has not been disclosed). The unions occupy a prominent position in the leadership of the council: the thirty-one-member NCATE executive board includes five persons

---

3. Lieberman (1997).The passage of time has seen steady diminution in state and school board representation in NCATE. The Council of Chief State School officers, the National Association of State Directors of Teacher Education and Certification, and the National School Board Association originally held nine of twenty-one positions on NCATE's governing board (Lieberman 1956). They now account for only one-quarter of these positions (and an even smaller share on the committee that actually makes accreditation decisions). The National School Board Association originally held three of twenty-one seats. It now accounts for just one of twenty-one members of NCATE's executive board.

4. NEA (1997, pp. 292, 324).

5. NEA (undated, p. 1).

appointed by the NEA and two by the AFT, including the president and vice president of each union. Eight individuals appointed by the AFT and the NEA serve on NCATE's thirty-member unit-accrediting board. All on-site visitation teams include a teacher from NCATE's Board of Examiners. The AFT and NEA nominate virtually all these teacher-examiners. In addition, NCATE's procedures allow NEA and AFT state affiliates to appoint representatives as nonvoting members of examination teams.

Independent Professional Boards

Since the 1970s the NEA has lobbied for teacher-dominated professional boards to set policy with respect to teacher education, licensing, professional development, and advanced certification.

> The National Education Association believes that the profession must govern itself. The Association believes that each state should have a professional standards board, composed of a majority of practicing public school teachers.
>
> The professional standards boards should have the exclusive authority to license and to determine criteria for how a national certificate will be recognized for professional educators.

Other NEA policy documents recommend that these teachers be nominated by the "majority teachers' organization" in the state and appointed by the governor.[6] In most states, of course, this organization would be the state NEA affiliate. The union urges that these professional boards align their standards with those of NCATE:

> The Association believes that these boards should apply National Council for Accreditation of Teacher Education (NCATE) standards as a minimum for granting, denying, or withdrawing the approval of teacher preparation programs.[7]

The AFT, on the other hand, has not taken a stand on state professional boards. It appears to be the union's position that uniform standards for the profession should be set nationally rather than by fifty separate state bodies.

6. Rodman (1987).
7. For both quotations see NEA (1997, p. 322).

The first independent professional boards were established in Oregon (1973) and Minnesota (1980). In both cases the local NEA affiliate was the major moving force behind the relevant legislation. After a lull during the 1980s, the pace of enactment has accelerated and there are now fifteen states with independent or semi-independent boards, ten of which have been established since 1990. Eleven states have given these boards full authority to set standards for licensure. In ten states, teachers and administrators constitute a majority of the board members. In six, teachers are in a majority; in one (Georgia), they occupy half the positions. Of the six states with teacher majorities, three have full legal authority for establishing licensure requirements, independent of their state boards of education (Minnesota, Nevada, North Dakota).[8]

There is a clear correlation between union influence and the establishment of a professional board. Of the thirty-four states that have enacted mandatory bargaining laws for teachers, nearly one-fourth (eight) have independent boards with teachers or administrators and teachers in the majority. Of the seven states that permit but do not require districts to bargain with unionized teachers, only one has such a board. Similarly, there is only one professionally controlled board in the nine remaining states that prohibit collective bargaining by teachers unions.

National Board Certification

Both the NEA and AFT have been strong supporters of certification of teachers by the NBPTS since the idea was first given national prominence by Albert Shanker.[9] Union influence on the board is considerable. Board by-laws stipulate that two-thirds of the members will be teachers and that one-third of these teachers "shall be persons who hold, or within the past ten years have held, local, state, or national office in the two national teacher unions." This number is divided equally between the NEA and the AFT and two of the positions are automatically filled by the national

8. In addition to Oregon and California, the following states have professional boards (year enacted): Nevada (1987), California (1988), Iowa (1989), Kentucky (1990), Georgia (1991), Indiana (1992), Wyoming (1993), West Virginia (1995), North Dakota (1995), Hawaii (1995), Oklahoma (1995), Texas (1995), and North Carolina (1996). The dates indicated are those in which the professional board became independent of the state boards of education. In four states (Kentucky, Nevada, North Carolina, and Texas), the state board of education still retains the authority to veto actions of the professional board. NEA (1998, p. 21).

9. The history of this idea and how it led to the formation of the National Board for Professional Teaching Standards is reviewed in Lieberman (1993).

presidents of the unions. The by-laws also require that another one-third of the teachers on the board be office holders from "teacher disciplinary or other specialty associations" (for example, the National Council of Teachers of Mathematics). Finally, these two groups nominate the remaining teachers on the board, who must be persons with "outstanding records of accomplishment but who may not have held office with either a teacher union or with a teachers' disciplinary or other specialty association during the last ten years." Given the number of union members in disciplinary and specialty associations, the NEA and AFT are probably in a position to control, directly or indirectly, a majority of the positions on the board. The board's current president, Barbara Kelley, is an active NEA member.

NEA publications such as *NEA Today* regularly feature articles on national board-certified teachers. Assistance is provided on how to prepare portfolios and other materials required by the board. The unions have pressed for districts to defray the $2,000 application fee charged by the board. They have also obtained state and federal funds for this purpose. They have lobbied and bargained for higher salaries for board-certified teachers.

As its founders envisioned, the influence of the national board extends beyond the certification of master teachers. It is intended that the standards developed by the board be the basis of licensing and accreditation decisions. Supporters of the board appear to believe that professional self-regulation will help ensure that the board's standards are widely adopted.

> The existence of the National Board for Professional Teaching Standards (NBPTS) should be a strong arguing point for independent professional boards in the states. If teaching standards are to be structured in ways that are similar to other professions' standards then having teacher standards boards in all states becomes more compelling. *NBPTS should be working with state teacher boards, not state boards or departments of education.*[10]

Union Interests

Teacher professionalization offers some clear benefits to unions. The activities over which the profession seeks control—accreditation of teacher edu-

---

10. NEA (1998). Emphasis added.

cation programs and teacher licensing—are well-recognized means of restricting supply.

> Whenever a new piece of licensing legislation is passed, it almost always involves the creation of a regulatory board made up of practitioners of the very occupation or profession in question. Thus they are left to 'regulate' themselves and their peers. Licensing boards have frequently had wide latitude in interpreting eligibility requirements, setting fee schedules, preparing examinations, and engaging in other activities that may serve to exclude would-be practitioners.[11]

By limiting the number of practitioners, licensing boards restrict competition and put upward pressure on salaries. This is a strategy that has been followed successfully by many professions, the most notable (and widely emulated) example being physicians. In the first decades of this century the American Medical Association (AMA) pursued a successful campaign to raise licensing requirements for physicians. As state licensing boards began to withhold licenses from doctors who had not graduated from colleges accredited by the AMA, the number of medical schools fell by 45 percent in just ten years, from 155 in 1910 to 85 in 1920.[12] This led to a decline in the number of physicians, reducing what practitioners saw as "overcrowding" in the field. Not coincidentally, doctors' incomes also rose.

There can be no doubt that teachers unions see the professionalization movement as a means to increase salaries. NCTAF is quite explicit about the connection between higher standards for teacher preparation and higher salaries, as the following statements from its 1996 report attest.

> Thousands of children are taught throughout their school careers by a parade of teachers without preparation in the fields they teach, inexperienced beginners with little training and no mentoring, and short-term substitutes trying to cope with constant staff disruptions. . . . Unequal resources and inadequate investments in teacher recruitment are the major problems. Other industrialized countries fund their schools equally and make sure there are qualified teachers for all of them by underwriting teacher preparation and salaries. However,

---

11. Shimberg, Esser, and Kruger (1973).
12. Numbers (1988).

teachers in the United States must go into substantial debt to become prepared for a field that in most states pays less than any other occupation requiring a college degree. . . . In most European and Asian countries, teachers are highly respected, well compensated, and better prepared. . . . Rather than spend money on add-ons and band-aid programs to compensate for the failures of teaching, [these countries] spend their education resources on what matters most: well-trained teachers who work intensively with students and with other teachers to improve teaching and learning.[13]

By raising standards for licensure and closing loopholes that permit districts to hire unlicensed teachers on an emergency basis or as long-term substitutes, professional regulatory bodies will create pressure for states to increase salaries in order to attract a sufficient supply of teachers with the requisite credentials.

By latest count there are 1,363 institutions that train teachers in the United States. If medicine and law are the models for professionalization, it is clear that there are "too many" teacher training institutions. While there are 5.3 teachers for every physician, the ratio of teacher training programs to medical schools is nearly twice as great, at 9.6. Similar discrepancies arise in comparison to dentistry and law. If teacher education programs are required to obtain accreditation from NCATE, we can expect that unions will use their influence within this organization to reduce the number of accredited programs. Recent history shows as much. In the mid-1970s the NEA obtained more power within NCATE's governing bodies and greater representation for teachers on examining teams. The proportion of programs denied accreditation subsequently doubled, from one in ten before 1973 to one in five throughout the rest of the decade.[14]

In addition, the size of teacher education programs would likely shrink should independent professional boards follow the recommendations of the Holmes Group and the NCTAF. At present, teacher education is a lucrative business, bringing in more revenues than colleges spend to train prospective teachers. Classes are frequently taught by adjunct faculty hired at low salaries. In addition, students spend a substantial part of their time

---

13. NCTAF (1996, pp. 16–19).

14. Bureau of Labor Statistics (1998); Tom (1996, p. 14). Whether this is a valid guide to future practice is less clear. In virtually all states NCATE accreditation remains optional. Often programs are not denied accreditation outright, but rather tire of investing the time and effort needed to get off probation. If NCATE accreditation were made mandatory, presumably more would persevere.

in the program off-campus doing student teaching while continuing to pay program fees. Much of this will change if institutions must meet the standards set by NCATE for education faculty and if a year-long internship in a professional development school becomes an essential part of the training prospective teachers receive. The NCTAF estimated in 1996 that the changes it recommended would increase the annual cost of training teachers to more than $7,000 per capita. Such costs will almost certainly reduce enrollments, particularly in programs now disparaged as diploma mills.

Although professional self-regulation creates opportunities for practitioner organizations to reduce the supply of trained personnel, this is not the only way unions stand to benefit from professionalization. As educators, most union leaders and the rank-and-file share a genuine interest in improving public schools. In this respect they are no different from physicians who, as they benefit from the high accreditation and licensing standards promulgated by the AMA, also believe that the public has been well served by these policies. Support for higher standards may also derive from the public perception that unions have shielded incompetent teachers from disciplinary action, for the resulting damage to the unions' image could be avoided if fewer ineffective teachers were hired in the first place. In addition, by taking steps to improve teacher quality, unions enhance the moral case for an increase in salaries. Teacher pay is only partly determined by market forces. To the extent that the public and its elected representatives are swayed by considerations of equity and fair treatment, unions have an easier time making the case that teachers deserve higher salaries when they can point to the high cost of meeting stricter licensure standards.

However, the analogy between teaching and medicine can be drawn too tightly. The AMA's successful campaign to raise the standards for medical training and physician licensure occurred at a time when the organization did not pretend to speak for the entire medical profession of the day, which included homeopaths, mental healers, midwives, and so-called eclectics. On the contrary, the association was avowedly exclusive. By contrast, the NEA and AFT represent many thousands of members who do not meet high standards of intellectual or professional accomplishment, a circumstance that makes it difficult for these organization to promote reform from within the profession. For example, while both the NEA and the AFT endorse more rigorous standards for teacher licensure, the issue is a delicate one for the unions. The stronger the case for improving the quality of new teachers, the more questions it raises about the ability of current practitioners. The recent testing of teachers in Massachusetts illustrates the risk.

Political leaders have been quick to conclude that if a majority of prospective teachers cannot pass the state's basic skills exam, then the current work force is not likely to do much better. Public discussion has moved on to the issue of testing all teachers as a condition for recertification.[15]

This is profoundly threatening to the unions' current membership. The unions have responded with a two-faceted strategy: endorsing rigorous testing for new teachers, while at the same time opposing the testing of current teachers:

> The National Education Association advocates rigorous state standards for entry into the teaching profession. These standards, as established by professional standards boards, shall include high academic performance, field training experience that includes student teaching, and passage of appropriate pedagogical and subject matter tests.

Yet later in the same section:

> The Association urges the elimination of state statutes/regulations that require teachers to renew their licenses. Where such renewal continues to be required, standardized literacy and basic skills tests to determine competency should not be used.[16]

The NEA's position is not novel. It is standard practice for occupations to seek the exemption of current practitioners from changes in licensing requirements.[17] If professional organizations assume control of licensing, we can expect the unions to use their influence within these organizations to shelter current members or at a minimum to ensure that the tests given for license renewal are not difficult. Thus the unions' interest in professional self-regulation is double-edged: to restrict the flow of new entrants, thereby creating upward pressure on salaries, while at the same time protecting incumbents from more demanding relicensure requirements.

---

15. Some states have already ventured down this road. Texas, Georgia, and Arkansas tested veteran teachers in the 1980s and removed those with very low scores from the classroom. Toch (1991). California tests veteran teachers who seek a credential in a different field. New York has begun testing teachers as a condition of moving from probationary to full licenses. Arenson (1998). In North Carolina, recent legislation has authorized the state's department of education to test veteran teachers in low-performing districts. Chaddock (1998).

16. NEA (1997, p. 323).

17. Rottenberg (1962).

Teacher education programs, many of which are quite nonselective in their admissions policies, can be expected to resist a tightening of standards that would discourage many would-be teachers and lower their enrollments.[18] Since these programs are well represented in NCATE, state independent boards, and other professional organizations, prospects for significant strengthening of licensing standards are uncertain, particularly if the unions' interest in reducing the supply of teachers can be accommodated in other ways. Thus coalitions may form within NCATE that lead to a reduction in the number and size of accredited programs on grounds unrelated to academic strength. This is discussed below.

In addition, the NEA is strongly committed to the recruitment of teachers who are members of racial and ethnic minorities. This makes the adoption of rigorous licensure tests problematic, given the gap between scores of blacks and whites. Indeed, union policy on this question has been schizophrenic, with the national organization endorsing rigorous examinations while state affiliates file suits to block teacher examinations on the ground that they have a disparate impact on minorities. While affirmative action solutions may be found satisfying both objectives (for example, setting different standards for racial minorities, as in *Allen* v. *Alabama*), the prospects for such settlements are increasingly uncertain in the current legal climate.

Some of the reforms sought by proponents of teacher professionalization would actually increase teacher supply relative to demand. Both the Holmes Group and the NCTAF seek to reduce high levels of attrition during the early years of teachers' careers by offering new teachers better professional preparation before they are sent to "sink or swim" in the classroom. If successful, such reforms could have a significant impact on teacher labor markets. Studies of teachers' career patterns show that between 40 and 50 percent quit within the first five to seven years of service. Changing the year-to-year retention rate over this period by just 3 percent (say, from 70 percent to 72.1 percent) reduces the number of teaching vacancies by approximately 15 percent.[19] However, because this makes it

---

18. It might be doubted that enrollments in teacher education would fall. After all, the unions' objective is not to create lasting shortages, but to see temporary shortages alleviated by an increase in salaries, drawing enough capable persons into teaching to satisfy demand. On this view the number of teachers would not change, only their level of ability. However, this scenario is unrealistic. There is a significant oversupply of teachers in the labor market today, as there has been for the past twenty years. See Feistritzer (1998). If shortages are to lead to a rise in teacher pay, this glut must be removed, implying a fall in teacher education enrollments.

19. Ballou and Podgursky (1997).

easier for districts to fill their remaining vacancies, salaries are less likely to climb.

Again, it is difficult to foresee what would happen if professional organizations controlled teacher licensing. Such authorities could find other ways to raise the demand for teachers—for example, by requiring new teachers to work in tandem with experienced mentors as long they hold probationary licenses. This kind of featherbedding could more than offset the impact of declining turnover on teacher demand.[20]

Finally, if unions are to successfully follow the model of the AMA, they will need to ensure that school districts facing a shortage of qualified applicants have few options for dealing with the problem besides raising pay. Thus unions can be expected to exercise their influence to block such alternatives as larger classes and substitution of paraprofessionals for teachers. Since shortages will occur in some subject areas before others, stricter licensure standards may also threaten the single salary schedule, as districts seek the flexibility to award higher salaries to teachers of the subjects in shortage without increasing pay across the board.[21] To the extent that unions give ground on this issue, salary increases will be localized and specific to teachers of certain subjects.

Teacher Professionalization and the Quality of Public Education

Advocates of teacher professionalization are unapologetic about the prospect of higher salaries. In their view, the nation has undervalued the services teachers provide and has not spent enough to recruit and retain good teachers. If high standards compel state and local governments to increase teacher salaries, that is only what they ought to have done anyway. In short, proponents of professional self-regulation argue that the reforms they advocate represent a "win-win" solution to some of the nation's educational ills: good for teachers and good for the rest of the country.

20. This is not to deny that team-teaching can be valuable for brand-new teachers. However, by requiring it in all cases and prolonging it, professional boards could turn the policy into one that promotes private over public interests.

21. Approximately 9 percent of school districts now have this flexibility, which usually takes the form of advancing teachers of shortage subjects on the district salary schedule. However, this option does not appear to be widely used by administrators in these systems, and has had little or no impact on recruitment or salaries. Ballou (1998); Ballou and Podgursky (1997).

However, this is only one of the possible outcomes of professionaliza-tion. The consequences of reform depend on the answers to two questions: (1) Will reform along the professionalization model raise teacher quality; and (2) Will it lead to teacher shortages? Since neither of these questions entails the other, there are four possible outcomes, as depicted schemati-cally in figure 3-1. In the upper left-hand cell of the diagram, the answer to both questions is yes. This is reform on the medical model, in which an improvement in the quality of practitioners is accompanied by a decline in their number and an increase in their incomes. If this should happen in education, it could be argued that both teachers and the public have gained. Whether this is correct will depend on the facts of the case: if the improvement in teacher quality is small, it may be that the money spent on higher salaries could be better spent on other educational innovations. Nonetheless, it is at least possible that this outcome would represent the win-win solution envisioned by reformers.

The outlook is still more positive in the lower left-hand cell of figure 3-1: licensure standards rise, but there is no shortage of qualified teachers and therefore no need to raise salaries across the board. This scenario rests on sev-eral optimistic assumptions. First, higher standards improve the training that schools of education provide their students, who in turn graduate from these programs with significantly stronger skills. That is, reform upgrades the cur-rent applicant pool to meet the demand for better teachers. Second, declin-ing turnover reduces the demand for teachers, offsetting any tendency for higher standards to lower the number of qualified applicants. Third, the sta-tus of the teaching profession rises, attracting better teachers. Fourth, the uniform salary schedule gives way to differentiated pay, which allows dis-tricts to target funds to the relatively small number of fields in which short-ages appear. This is the best outcome from the standpoint of the public, but it also offers something to teachers unions, which benefit from improve-ments in teacher quality even when shortages do not appear, as explained above.

The worst outcome for the public is depicted in the upper right-hand cell: shortages without improvement in teacher quality. In this scenario, teacher training takes longer and becomes more costly, but teachers are no better. Despite the claims about the profession's "emerging knowledge base," schools of education either do not know how to prepare more effec-tive teachers or endorse misguided theories of pedagogy for ideological rea-sons. At the same time, protracted training discourages many individuals of

Figure 3-1. *Outcomes of Reform*

Does reforming professional standards raise teacher quality?

	Yes	No
Yes	**Medical model:** Shortages of qualified teachers drive up salaries.	Training is longer and more costly, but teachers are no better on average. Teacher tests are not rigorous; authentic assessments are an elastic yardstick. Education schools close for reasons unrelated to quality (for example, costs); enrollments decline.
No	Education schools improve training; teachers meet higher standards Turnover falls. Higher stature of profession attracts candidates. Uniform salary schedule gives way to differentiated pay. Teacher salaries may increase via the political process.	**Political opposition blocks reforms:** National Council for Accreditation of Teacher Education fails to close programs. Cheaper, quicker routes to certification retain their market niche. Teacher tests are not rigorous. Alternative certification survives.

Does reform produce shortages?

ability from pursuing teaching careers, offsetting whatever limited gains might be achieved by reforming the curricula of teacher education programs. Some schools of education, pressured to meet expensive accreditation standards that have little to do with teacher quality, reduce their enrollments or close outright. The result is a win-lose outcome. The decline in teacher supply puts upward pressure on salaries, benefiting union members. But the public loses, paying more for teachers who are no better than at present.

The final scenario, in the lower right-hand corner, represents the failure of reform to take hold, largely as the result of political opposition. As a result, matters remain substantially as they are. This may well be the outcome of present reform efforts. While union rhetoric expresses strong support for stricter licensing standards for new teachers, it is questionable how far unions will go in this direction, given the risks to incumbent members, the opposition of teacher education programs, and the impact on minority recruitment. In addition, the available evidence on the professionalization of accreditation and teacher assessment (reviewed below) fails to demonstrate that either of these functions is performed better by professionally controlled boards than by public authorities.

Our greater concern, however, is that the outcome of reform will be the win-lose scenario depicted in the upper-right cell of figure 3-1. Professional self-regulation almost invariably poses the risk that practitioner-regulators will use their power to promote private interests at the public's expense. This is a concern even when self-regulation has raised standards for practice, as in the case of medicine. It is still more likely in the case of education.

Most regulated professions are dominated by private practitioners selling their services to the public. For example, in the medical profession, doctors contract directly with patients or with hospitals and clinics that indirectly represent patients' interests. As a result, market competition exerts considerable pressure to ensure that the standards for licensure and for the accreditation of professional schools are valid. If they are insufficient in this respect, other credentials will emerge under market pressure. Indeed, precisely these circumstances characterize the market for physicians' services. In addition to state licensure, most physicians seek certification from medical specialty boards. Licensure is required to practice; certification is not. The latter arose because hospitals and clinics sought stronger evidence of professional competence in medical specialties than a license alone provided.[22]

22. This is not the only reason that the analogy between teaching and medical practice, so often drawn by proponents of professionalization, breaks down. The central argument for medical licensing is that there exists a deep and complex body of clinical knowledge that is well beyond the grasp of the typical consumer, thus making the latter vulnerable to incompetent practitioners. The existence of a vigorous, and largely unregulated, private market for schooling suggests that many consumers are capable of making informed choices. In addition, parents do not purchase directly the services of teachers. Rather, teachers are hired by professional administrators. The question then is whether self-regulation by the teaching profession represents the best possible method for disciplining wayward administrators, a dubious proposition. For further discussion of this issue see Ballou and Podgursky (1998a, b).

These pressures are much weaker in public education. The quasi-monopoly enjoyed by public schools means they are virtually assured of students no matter how poorly they perform. Deprived of the opportunity to express their preferences in the market, the public lacks the countervailing power to check producer interests through the political process, which is dominated by industry insiders. Unions, which are better organized than the public at large, often determine the outcome of school board elections. They are regularly rated among the most powerful lobbyists at the state level.[23] Together with the schools of education, they exert a powerful influence on educational policy.

By conferring additional authority on practitioner organizations, teacher professionalization exacerbates this imbalance between private and public interests in public education. This power might be used to improve the performance of public schools, but a review of the evidence in several key areas of reform suggests that it probably will not.

Accreditation

While the immediate focus of accreditation is program quality, its ultimate value depends on the information it conveys about the graduates of accredited programs. Accreditation is meaningless if the graduates of accredited programs routinely lack the skills needed to function effectively in the classroom. Yet it is not apparent that NCATE, the private accreditation agency supported by the unions, is successful by this criterion.

Although NCATE stipulates that programs recruit candidates "who demonstrate potential for professional success," it does not require any particular admissions test or specify a passing score. Criteria for successful completion are just as vague. NCATE standards require that institutions ensure the competency of their graduates before recommending them for licensure, but competency is left undefined. Instead, NCATE indicates that a program can meet this standard by assessing graduates "through the use of multiple sources of data such as a culminating experience, portfolios, interviews, videotaped and observed performance in schools, standardized tests, and course grades."[24] This is a requirement that program administrators use various methods of assessment, not that graduates be held to any particular standard of achievement.

23. Lieberman (1997).
24. National Council for the Accreditation of Teacher Education (1997, p. 23).

By available objective measures, there is virtually no relationship between NCATE accreditation and the quality of newly trained teachers.[25] We begin by looking at state-level data on the results of teacher licensing examinations.[26] Figure 3-2 depicts pass rates for graduates of teacher training institutions in Missouri.[27] Each bar on the chart represents an institution. As figure 3-2 shows, NCATE schools are to be found at the top, middle, and bottom of the distribution. Indeed, the poorest performing institution in the state, as measured by licensing pass rates, is NCATE-accredited.

Figure 3-3 displays results for teacher licensing examinations recently administered in Massachusetts. (To improve comparability of results, the scores on the Communications and Literacy Skills test taken by all students in each program are used.) As in Missouri, NCATE-accredited programs

25. After this chapter was written, the Educational Testing Service released a study of scores on the Praxis II teacher licensing examination that appears to contradict this conclusion. ETS (1999). Ninety-one percent of the examinees from colleges with NCATE-accredited programs passed, compared to just 83 percent from nonaccredited institutions. Whether this actually demonstrates any superiority of NCATE-approved teacher education programs remains open to doubt, however. Fourteen percent of the Praxis II test takers never enrolled in a teacher training program. The ETS researchers assigned test takers to NCATE categories based on the college they attended, not whether they were actually in a teacher training program. The never-enrolled group has a lower pass rate (74 percent) as compared to candidates currently enrolled in a teacher training program (91 percent). Thus, both the NCATE and non-NCATE samples contain unreported proportions of individuals who were never enrolled in any type of teacher training program. However, it is likely that the non-NCATE population will have a proportionately larger share of the never enrolled group, since test takers who graduated from colleges without a teacher training program will always be classified as "non-NCATE."

Differences in pass rates are affected by the mix of tests taken by graduates as well as the state in which the tests are taken. For example, a student in North Carolina, where NCATE accreditation is mandatory, can pass the Praxis II elementary exam with a score of 153, whereas the minimum passing score is 164 in Pennsylvania, where roughly 40 percent graduate from NCATE programs. The pass rates also depend on the exam taken, ranging from 91 percent on elementary education down to 76 percent on math and 75 percent on social studies. Although the ETS researchers could have clarified this matter by reporting mean NCATE/non-NCATE test scores for the major Praxis II exams or by disaggregating the results by state, they elected not to do so.

26. The list of NCATE-accredited colleges suggests that politics are more important than educational quality in determining whether a school is accredited. Where governors have lent their support to the professionalization movement, teacher education programs have sought and obtained accreditation. In North Carolina, whose governor, James Hunt, chaired both the NCTAF and National Board, every college offering teacher education has obtained NCATE accreditation. In Arkansas, all but two have it. By contrast, New York has 103 state-accredited programs but in 1997 only three had been approved by NCATE.

27. We eliminated a small number of records with out-of-state institutions or for which the institution code was missing. When a test taker repeated the same test more than once, only the first test score is used in the analysis. The classification of institutions was based on the May 1997 list of accredited programs obtained from NCATE.

Figure 3-2. *Pass Rates on National Teacher Exams by Program: Missouri*[a]

Pass rate (percent)

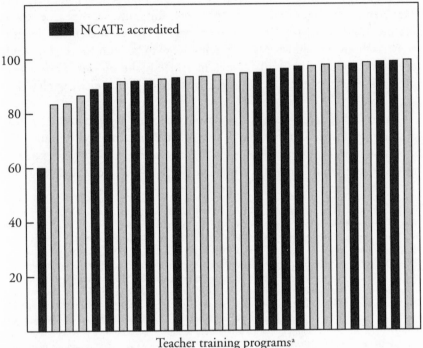

Teacher training programs[a]

a. All exams, 1994–95 to 1996–97; programs administering at least 150 tests.

are not concentrated at the upper end of the distribution (although one rates second highest), and performance at four of the seven accredited institutions was distinctly mediocre.

Further evidence on NCATE standards comes from Pennsylvania, where there are large numbers of both accredited and nonaccredited programs. Since the state would not release test scores by institution, the (smoothed) distribution of test scores for all teachers seeking elementary certification between 1994 and 1997 is plotted in figure 3-4. There is no substantial difference between the two distributions. Figure 3-5 presents the same information for Missouri. In this case scores from NCATE-accredited programs are distinctly inferior. Compared to the non-NCATE

Figure 3-3. *Pass Rates by Teacher Training Program: Massachusetts*[a]

Pass rates (percent)

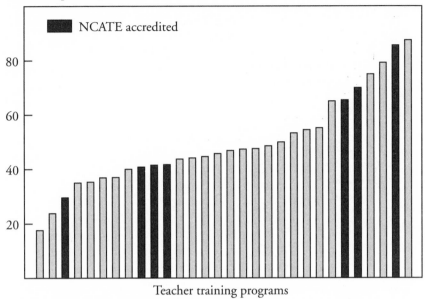

Teacher training programs

Source: Massachusetts State Department of Education.
a. Pass rates for Communications and Literacy Skills Test. All programs with at least 15 test takers.

distribution, there are fewer programs in the center of the distribution and more in the left-hand tail, creating a bulge of NCATE test takers among the lowest scores.

In summary, NCATE regularly accredits institutions with very low admissions standards, a signal failing given the widespread recognition that academic ability among education majors is alarmingly low. Nor is it apparent that graduates of NCATE-accredited institutions are superior by other indicators. For example, the NCTAF has claimed that NCATE accreditation helps ensure that teachers receive instruction in state-of-the-art pedagogical methods. According to the NCTAF, graduates of NCATE-accredited programs will be better prepared for the challenges of the classroom and suffer less attrition during the early years of their careers. They will exhibit a higher degree of professionalism in their relations with students and colleagues.

Figure 3-4. *Distribution of National Teacher Exam Elementary Education Test Scores: Pennsylvania*[a]

Frequency

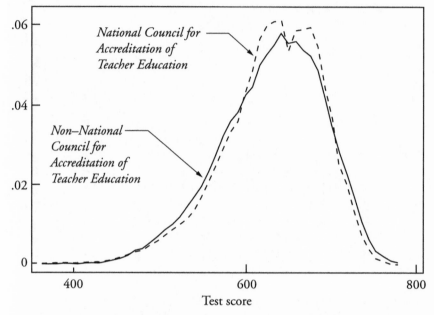

Test score

Source: Pennsylvania Department of Education.
a. Elementary Education NTE scores for 8,223 NCATE and 11,436 non-NCATE test takers for academic years 1994–95 to 1996–97.

These claims can be tested using data from two surveys conducted by the Department of Education. By most measures there is little difference between graduates of accredited and nonaccredited programs.[28] Virtually identical percentages sought teaching jobs after graduating (table 3-1). Of those who obtained a job, a substantial majority (80 percent in both groups) expressed no regret at having chosen teaching as a career, saying they would make the same choice again. More than 50 percent of both groups intended to spend their entire careers as teachers. Fewer than 25 percent (and more NCATE than non-NCATE graduates) indicated that they sometimes felt it was a waste of time to do their best in the class-

---

28. Because NCATE accreditation procedures changed in 1987, the sample was restricted to individuals who graduated in 1990 or later and who began teaching no earlier than 1992.

Figure 3-5. *Distribution of National Teacher Exam Elementary Education Test Scores: Missouri*[a]

Frequency

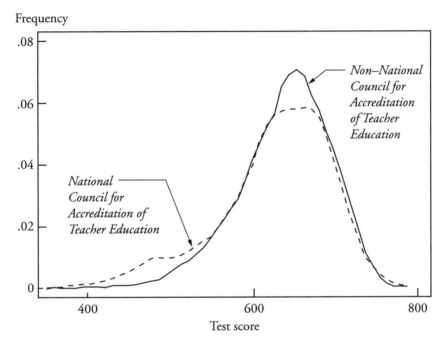

Test score

Source: Missouri Department of Elementary and Secondary Education.

a. Elementary Education NTE scores for 3,756 NCATE and 2,723 non-NCATE test takers for academic years 1993–94 to 1996–97.

room. NCATE teachers spent somewhat more time during the week preceding the survey on instruction-related activities outside school (preparing lessons, grading papers, and so on). However, the difference between the two groups was not significant at conventional levels. A slightly larger proportion of NCATE teachers moonlighted during the school year, but again the difference was not statistically significant.

In short, there is little evidence that teachers trained in NCATE-accredited schools conduct themselves more professionally, are more likely to continue teaching, or experience more satisfaction with their career choice. Perhaps more revealing, there is no evidence that those hiring new teachers think so either. The percentage of non-NCATE applicants who found a teaching job was as high as among NCATE applicants. The jobs they obtained paid as well.

Table 3-1. *Comparison between Teachers Accredited and Not Accredited by the New National Council for Accreditation of Teacher Education (NCATE)*

Percent unless otherwise noted

Indicator	Accredited by NCATE	Not accredited by NCATE
Applied for a teaching job[a]	92.0	90.0
"Certainly" or "probably" would become a teacher, if given the chance to start over again[b]	80.2	79.7
Plan to spend full career as teacher[b]	58.6	58.4
Sometimes feel it is a waste of time to do a good job[b]	24.4	18.9
Time spent after school on lesson preparation, grading, parent conferences (hours in the most recent week)[b]	10.4	9.7
Moonlight in a nonteaching job during the school year[b]	13.2	12
Received an offer, conditional on having applied[a]	82.0	84.0
Mean teaching salary[a]	$19,843	$20,076

Sources: (a) Baccalaureate and Beyond Longitudinal Study, First Follow-Up, 1993–94 (sample restricted to certified teachers); (b) Schools and Staffing Survey, 1993–94 (sample restricted to persons who earned their bachelor's degrees in 1990 or later and who started teaching no earlier than 1992).

Teacher Assessment

Proponents of professionalization call for teachers to pass tests of basic skills, subject matter, and pedagogical knowledge before they are licensed. The first two are fairly straightforward. The third has proven problematic, and it is here that professionalization is said to offer the greatest benefit.

Standardized tests of pedagogical knowledge have come under a great deal of criticism. Because so many teaching decisions are highly context-specific, test items regularly fail to assess examinees' knowledge in a meaningful way. Either the situation is so simplified that context is relatively unimportant—but then the answer is obvious—or important contextual facts are omitted and the correct answer is unclear. Proponents of teacher professionalization, concerned about the triviality and irrelevance of these examinations, have argued the need for "authentic assessments" based more directly on classroom conditions. With this goal in mind, the NBPTS has issued standards on what effective teachers know and do. The work of translating these standards, which are very general, into performance-based assessments has been taken up by the Interstate New Teacher Assessment and Support Consortium (INTASC). These assessments take the form of portfolios, videotaped simulations and other exercises in laboratory settings, and classroom observations.

It is naive to suppose that performance-based assessments have become popular solely because they correct defects in traditional standardized tests. Assessment instruments like portfolios answer to a host of other fashionable concerns, such as the desire for prospective teachers to become "active discoverers and producers of their own knowledge base."[29] Such assessments are also significantly less threatening to examinees. Standards are fuzzy; there is the comforting thought that there is no one "right answer"; allowances can be made for different cultural perspectives (an implicit form of race-norming); and teachers are likely to be given the opportunity to portray themselves in the best possible light by choosing the materials for their portfolios or the lessons they will be observed teaching. Finally, proponents see performance-based assessments as the essence of professional self-regulation. The relationship between interns and doctors furnishes the model: expert practitioners judge the performance of novices in light of standards that reflect professional consensus on best practices. Authentic assessment of teachers is, by its very nature, something that only teachers are (allegedly) competent to carry out.

Authentic assessment is not without problems, however. It is time-consuming and expensive. There are doubts about the objectivity of evaluators and the reliability of their ratings. Little is known about the predictive validity of these types of assessments and whether they are superior in this regard to more traditional ways of testing teachers.[30]

In addition, the language of the national board standards is extremely general, as the following examples show:

—Teachers use a variety of methods and materials to promote individual development, meaningful learning and social cooperation.

29. Barton and Collins (1993).

30. The National Board for Professional Teaching Standards, which has promulgated standards for the purpose of conducting performance-based assessments, has undertaken no studies of predictive validity.

—Teachers use their knowledge of child development and their relationships with children and families to understand children as individuals and to plan in response to their unique needs and potentials.
—Accomplished teachers create a caring, inclusive and challenging environment in which students actively learn.[31]

One reason for this level of generality is the lack of agreement among professionals on many pedagogical issues. The board's standards were developed by committees through a consensus-building process. This was facilitated by rising above controversial questions to a statement of general principles from which few would dissent. However, another reason for the lack of specificity is surely the very problem that confronts the makers of standardized teacher tests: good teaching decisions depend greatly on context. More specific standards might be overly prescriptive.

The question is what happens when evaluators attempt to judge particular teachers in light of standards like these. A pilot project undertaken in Maine to develop a new system for licensure of beginning teachers serves as a good example. The goal was to replace transcript-based licensing (ascertaining whether the student completed the right courses) with one based on demonstrated competency. Following the lead of the NBPTS and INTASC, teacher educators participating in the pilot project established standards for what a beginning K–12 teacher should know and be able to do.[32]

Supervisors of student teachers were then asked to write observations that would indicate whether these standards had been met. Several of these assessments were published in a report to the state board of education. As the following excerpts show, supervisors found it difficult to fit their observations into the framework of the standards. Often the connection between the standard and the teacher's actions was slight. Fairly trivial actions were accepted as evidence that the standard was met. Supervisors tended to write about things they liked even if the behavior was unrelated to the standard in question. In some cases they grasped for something that seemed to apply, however tangentially.

31. NBPTS (1996).
32. "A number of states have redesigned teaching standards and created partnerships with universities and schools to incorporate the new standards into preparation and professional development programs. . . . Maine also developed *new standards for teacher licensing* that are based on the INTASC standards and tied to Maine's Learning Results for Children. Eight colleges are developing and piloting performance-based assessments of the standards." Darling-Hammond (1997, p. 41, emphasis in original).

For example, the following report was submitted to show a student teacher had met Standard VIII: Understands and uses a variety of formal and informal assessment strategies to evaluate and support the development of the learner.[33]

> The setting for this description is an art classroom in an urban high school in southern Maine. At the beginning of class, "Janice," an Art Education intern . . . hands out a media literacy "pop quiz" consisting of a magazine advertisement and a blank sheet of paper to pairs of students as they settle in at their tables. She directs their attention to questions written on the board: "Before you get started on your masks, work with your partner to answer these questions. They relate to the lesson on advertising. Put the finished papers here on my desk." This quiz is a test of knowledge gained in a previous media literacy lesson.

All this teacher has done is administer a pop quiz on material covered earlier. There is only one assessment strategy in evidence here, not a variety, and nothing to indicate that the quiz was particularly well-constructed or contributed to student learning, as stipulated by the standard. Students were allowed to prepare answers in pairs, suggesting this teacher was trained to use cooperative learning, a pedagogical method currently in fashion. But if the pop quiz was intended as an assessment rather than merely a learning experience, her judgment is questionable. Even staunch proponents of cooperative learning stress the importance of maintaining individual student accountability.

The following report was offered to show a student teacher met Standard I: Demonstrates a knowledge of the central concepts, tools of inquiry, and structures of the discipline(s) she or he teaches.

> Student teacher, J.N., taught science, specifically five microganisms (sic), to a heterogeneous grade 5/6. She included in her instruction guidelines: "scientific" journaling (sic), (emphasis on precision, accuracy of drawing and writing), how to share materials in a manner that respects both the things themselves and the people using them, and several opportunities to work with five self-selected and interested *first grade partners* (emphasis in original). J.N. developed an

---

33. All excerpts are from State of Maine Advisory Committee on Results-Based Initial Certification of Teachers (1997).

equitable and innovative rubric including clear guidelines for group work, clearly defined outcomes for the two and one-half hour laboratory which used microscopes, slides, live one celled organisms, and an electron microscope that J.N. had obtained from her own home school district through a successful co-authored grant application. Using a previously developed learning style profile of the class, J.N. made sure that every student had an opportunity to succeed based on lesson objectives that she developed from a wide variety of assessed student strengths.

The writer is clearly impressed with the performance of this student teacher and, indeed, this may have been an excellent lesson. But the things that have impressed the supervisor have little to do with the standard, which concerns mastery of subject matter. Instead, the supervisor focuses on teaching methods (how clear the instructions were, how the students worked cooperatively in groups, how all students had a chance to succeed) and the materials used in the lesson. The only part of this description that relates to the standard is the second sentence, where the supervisor remarks that J.N. instructed the students on the importance of keeping precise, accurate records in scientific work.

The following submission pertains to Standard II: Demonstrates the ability to integrate other disciplines, their concepts, tools of inquiry, and structures of other disciplines with the discipline she or he teaches.

Student teacher, G.H., taught social studies to an eighth grade class, developed in concert with his mentor teacher, a unit on immigration. G.H. asked students to design and illustrate family shields . . . of the countries from which the students were traveling to the U.S. Students researched their countries of origin, presented oral reports on their reasons for leaving, wove together fact and fiction into powerful stories of courage and pride in who they were. G.H. feels that eighth graders, particularly, grow from imagining themselves to be what they may not yet be in reality; for example, one day students were creating their visas. A boy barely 5'2" described himself as a 6'4" 229 lb Russian from the Ukraine. G.H. also has begun an inventory of what motivates these students and which of the multiple intelligences (proposed and described by Howard Gardner and his team) best fits their emerging intellectual and social strengths. Linked to those multiple intelligences inventories G.H. has produced a list of choice opportunities for each student to use in developing and presenting knowledge of their (sic) "native" culture.

In addition, immigrants/students kept a journal of the events of their journey. In the journal they answered teacher-generated questions about conditions of passage, problems and dilemmas encountered, and joys and sorrows witnessed and lived through.

Apparently the writer believes the student teacher has met Standard II because he has integrated art (designing shields) and fiction writing (stories, journals) into the teaching of social studies. These may have been sound teaching devices, but their relation to the standard is not clear, as neither appears to be a concept or "tool of inquiry" from another discipline. For example, were any literary concepts introduced? Did the teacher even check student journals for grammar, punctuation, and style? Successful integration of methods from other disciplines also requires that they not be overused. But this question slips between the cracks in this report: we cannot tell if the teacher relied too much on student-produced art and fiction at the expense of more conventional materials.

Some of the supervisor's remarks hint at priorities that other educators might question. The supervisor is evidently impressed with the teacher's sensitivity to student self-esteem. Many psychologists and psychometricians have not found Gardner's thesis on multiple intelligences plausible.[34] That it is even mentioned in this report suggests the supervisor does not appreciate the distinction between integrating the study of different disciplines and turning to another discipline (educational psychology) for suggestions on pedagogy.

The comments on these reports are not meant to disparage the performance of these new teachers or the conscientious effort of supervisors to carry out the task they were given. Rather, this discussion is intended to bring out two things: how hard it is to make standards like those of the NBPTS the basis for meaningful performance assessments, and how difficult it is for outsiders reading these reports to ascertain whether teachers had truly demonstrated the desired competency. Supervisors had trouble determining the kind of teaching behavior to which each standard applied. There was no yardstick to measure whether a standard had been met. If the supervisor could identify something that seemed to fall under the right

---

34. A penetrating critique of the Gardner thesis and its implications for pedagogy is offered by Klein (1997).

heading, that was good enough. Ultimately, supervisors used the standards as a very loose framework for describing things the student teachers did that the supervisors liked. As a result, procedures of this kind are only too likely to reproduce the flaws of the present educational system. Teachers who use trendy pedagogical techniques will be applauded. Ideological biases will enter supervisors' assessments and influence licensing decisions.

There is no reason to think that this is an isolated example, somehow atypical of performance-based assessments under professional self-regulation. Standards were patterned on those of INTASC and the NBPTS; evaluations were carried out by experienced teachers. Given the generality of the standards, much depends on how these guidelines are interpreted, the perceptiveness and professional judgment brought to the supervisory task, and the ability to convey in writing a full picture of the candidate's strengths and weaknesses. Authentic assessments therefore tend to reproduce the strengths and weaknesses of one generation of teachers in the next. It is not evident that the information they provide is any better than that obtained from more traditional forms of evaluation, including observations conducted in schools by administrators and department chairs and the feedback, formal and informal, that supervisors of student teachers have always provided.

To summarize, there is little credible evidence that professional self-regulation significantly improves program accreditation or teacher assessment. Professional control has not stopped NCATE from accrediting weak programs of teacher education. Both NCATE and the NBPTS have issued vague standards that afford little basis for improving accountability. This is not the end of the matter, however. If policymakers cannot improve the nation's schools, they should at least take as their motto: first do no harm. Unfortunately, teacher professionalization would turn over to educators regulatory powers that can be used in ways that will impede efforts to improve the nation's schools.[35]

35. As a result, it would be better simply to pay teachers more than to put teachers and teacher educators in a position to use the regulatory process to achieve the same end; it would cost no more, and it would spare the public the collateral damage. This is, of course, the conventional economic conclusion about the inefficiency of occupational licensing. In the usual case, however, there is no obvious way for practitioners to effect a transfer of wealth from the public (except, perhaps, for farmers). Thus occupations seek regulatory powers to accomplish what they could not by simply asking for the money.

This is not, however, the situation in public education. Teachers are public employees. They are not only free to ask for more money, it is expected that they will do so, offering whatever arguments and data they can muster showing that higher salaries will be in the public interest. In short, this is a sector of the economy where for once the more efficient solution, a simple income transfer, is readily available.

Resource-Based Accreditation

If NCATE accreditation were required of all teacher education programs, the costs of compliance could drive small programs in liberal arts colleges from the market. These costs are of two kinds: the direct costs of the accreditation process and the indirect costs of correcting "weaknesses" identified by NCATE. Both can be considerable. Complaints about the amount of paperwork and the lengthy and time-consuming process of preparing documentation for NCATE are common.[36] However, it is probably the second category that is more threatening to liberal arts colleges that train small numbers of teachers. In such institutions, educational methods courses are often taught by adjunct faculty with no responsibilities for research. There may be no department of education, only a set of courses staffed by faculty from other departments (for example, psychology). Such programs may well have difficulty meeting NCATE standards for the qualifications and responsibilities of a professional education faculty.

In the past, faced with the opposition of liberal arts colleges and other smaller institutions, NCATE has backed off proposals to require minimum faculty-student ratios or expenditures per student of accredited programs.[37] Whether it would continue to accommodate these programs if accreditation became mandatory is unknown. In any case, the absence of hard and fast standards does not prevent resources from being a factor in an accreditation decision. Organizations like the Holmes Group and the NCTAF have called for substantially higher per-pupil expenditures in teacher preparation. If examining teams from NCATE come to share the outlook of these organizations, programs that are not prepared to spend heavily on teacher education will be in jeopardy.

One issue that has received little attention concerns the conflict of interest when unions participate in NCATE while at the same time representing faculty in the institutions applying for accreditation. The NEA has 78,000 members in higher education. The AFT has roughly 90,000 members in higher education, with 32,000 in New York state alone. These unionized faculty are concentrated in states with the most permissive bargaining laws and in state colleges with large education programs. In California, for example, all twenty-three of the state colleges are organized by the California Faculty Association, an NEA-affiliate. These unionized campuses

36. Tom (1996).
37. Tom (1996).

account for twelve of the thirteen NCATE-accredited teacher training programs in the state.

This creates a conflict of interest for union representatives who serve on NCATE's governance bodies and examining teams, particularly if accreditation becomes mandatory and programs that are not approved by NCATE are forced to close down. NEA and AFT members may use their influence within NCATE to protect the jobs of faculty in colleges with union contracts. Of course, this bias need not be explicit. It might take the form of union support for accreditation criteria that favor large public-sector affiliates (which are already unionized or more readily organized) over nonunion competitors (for example, private sector liberal arts colleges). Accreditation criteria that require large, fixed investments will be met more easily by large programs in state universities and colleges, as will NCATE standards that limit the use of nonregular or adjunct faculty in teacher education.[38]

Prolonged Preservice Training

When colleges lose (or drop) their teacher education programs, students find it more difficult to become teachers. This is particularly true of graduates of liberal arts programs, who do not know when they begin college that they will decide to teach and who therefore do not choose a college with this goal in mind. However, this may be the least of the barriers that teacher professionalization places in the way of prospective teachers. Much more significant may be the impact on career decisions if proponents of professionalization have their way and teacher education becomes a protracted multiyear program. Such changes will deter some individuals from pursuing teaching careers. Of course, if those deterred should not have become teachers in the first place, this will be of little concern. But there is no reason to expect such a happy outcome.

Protracted preservice training will deter individuals already in the work force who are contemplating career changes. The practical experience and maturity of many of these individuals make them attractive candidates for teaching. Precisely for these reasons many states have adopted alternative certification routes that waive standard requirements for certification, facil-

---

38. This highlights one more important difference between teaching and other professions. Professional associations such as the AMA or ABA, which accredit training programs, do not engage in collective bargaining in higher education.

itating the entry of such persons into the profession. Proponents of teacher professionalization (including the unions) oppose such programs, and professional self-regulation would almost surely mean their demise or transformation into something that would no longer serve the original purpose. For example, the model of alternative certification supported by the NCTAF would have career-changers spend a year in a master's program before they begin to teach. There is no question that this would deter many if not most of the individuals who now enter through alternate routes. Prospective teachers working outside education have cited traditional licensing requirements more often than any other explanation for not seeking a teaching position. Time and expense are the usual reasons given for why they do not apply to traditional teacher education programs.[39]

Career-changers are not the only prospective teachers who will be deterred if professionalization raises the cost of acquiring a license. Undergraduates in some majors (for example, the sciences) find it difficult to fit additional education courses into demanding course schedules. More generally, raising the requirements for teacher education will deter students who are wavering between teaching and other careers, since any increase in the requirements for a teaching license will have an obvious opportunity cost: less time for courses that make them more marketable should they pursue other options. These reforms would therefore tend to screen out (by their own choice) prospective teachers with the interest and ability to pursue other careers, leaving the applicant pool to those who never thought of themselves as anything but teachers. This would have precisely the opposite effect of other policies that are intended to improve the quality of the teaching pool (for example, raising teacher salaries). Higher pay is intended to attract capable persons who are wavering between two careers by tipping the balance in favor of education. By contrast, raising entry barriers discourages those who have attractive options.

Prolonged preservice training also discourages individuals who want to try teaching before making a lifelong commitment to it or who enter in the

---

39. Feistritzer (1992). More than 1,000 persons in the work force who had expressed an interest in alternative certification were surveyed. Of those who had not become teachers, 34 percent "did not want to go back to college to take requisite courses to meet requirements for teaching credentials." To this should be added the 27 percent who said they "could not find/get into an alternative teacher certification program." Since survey participants could give more than one answer, the total must be reduced by the percentage of overlapping responses (not reported). Licensing requirements were probably also responsible for deterring some of the additional 12 percent who said that it was "too much trouble to find out what was required to become a teacher," and the 15 percent who selected "too much red tape," though these responses may also show that initial interest was not very strong.

expectation that after several years they will be ready to move on. Since attrition from teaching rises with academic ability, more capable students will, on average, anticipate having fewer years in which to amortize their investment in a credential that has no value outside the teaching profession. The result is that promising students turn elsewhere.

> In a society with abundant opportunities for talented college graduates and a tradition of labor market mobility, it will never be possible to persuade two million of them to teach their whole lives. Public rhetoric that implies personal failure when a teacher leaves the classroom after successfully teaching for a number of years may deter many of them from ever setting foot in a classroom.[40]

According to a consortium of teacher educators from sixteen of the most prestigious colleges and universities in the northeast, terminating undergraduate programs in education and replacing them with postbaccalaureate programs would significantly reduce the number of students entering teaching from selective liberal arts colleges. The consortium therefore opposed the recommendations of the Holmes Group, stating that "we must maintain certification options for students desiring to teach directly upon graduation."[41]

Proponents of teacher professionalization respond to such concerns by pointing to the example of doctors, who spend far more years in study and internships than would teachers under the proposed reforms. Yet high entry requirements do not deter interested and qualified persons from pursuing careers in medicine. Why should this be feared in education?

The foregoing discussion has discussed some of the reasons. Attrition from teaching (unlike medicine) is high and is highest among those who were the most capable in college and who are likely to have the most attractive options outside education. The testimony of numerous beginning teachers reminds us that teaching is what economists call an "experience good"—it is hard to know whether one will like it without trying it. High entry barriers will discourage many persons from finding out whether teaching is for them.

40. Murnane and others (1991).
41. Olson (1987).

Further evidence on this point comes from Teach for America (TFA), an alternate route program that places liberal arts graduates without education course work in public school systems that face a shortage of conventionally prepared applicants. One of the attractions of this program for new graduates is the prospect of teaching without first spending a year or two taking professional education courses. When asked what they would have done had they not joined TFA, only 22 percent of participants who arrived for summer training in 1997 indicated that they would have entered teaching through traditional teacher education.[42] No doubt this percentage would have been still lower if teacher education were the longer and more costly program of study envisioned by the Holmes Group.

Although Teach for America members initially enlist for only two years, many remain in teaching after the enlistment period ends. Of the 784 former members who responded to a 1998 alumni survey, 53 percent were employed in education, the great majority as classroom teachers.[43] These data should not be taken to imply that half of all TFA volunteers make their careers as teachers. There is almost certainly some sampling bias in these responses: alumni who have remained active in education are probably more likely to respond to mail from TFA than those who have lost interest in teaching and gone on to other careers. Nonetheless, it is clearly wrong to assume that volunteers' involvement in teaching is invariably of short duration. Rather, this evidence shows the importance of giving talented persons an opportunity to experience teaching without putting high barriers to entry in their way.

Even so, the medical analogy might apply if there were persuasive evidence that prolonged preservice training is essential to teaching performance. But the evidence is not strong.

> Significant additions to what teacher candidates should know and be able to do before embarking on a career in education not only [have] large economic costs, but there is reason to question whether students can learn and effectively transfer to practice all or even much of the pedagogical knowledge and skills that would be taught in

---

42. Personal communication from Rebecca Berreras of Teach for America, January 28, 1998.

43. Personal communication from John Darby, director of research and development for Teach for America.

extended programs. Considerable evidence exists that experienced teachers think differently about their work than do novices. . . . Teachers may learn some things best, such as cooperative learning strategies, once they have an experiential base upon which to build.[44]

Instead, there is convincing evidence that the nation needs teachers with greater intellectual capacity, even if this means they have not completed a prescribed sequence of education courses. The response of administrators who have hired TFA members has been extremely positive. Three-quarters of the principals responding to a 1997 survey rated TFA instructors superior to other beginning teachers.[45] Almost two-thirds rated them above average in comparison to all faculty, including veteran teachers. Almost nine of ten indicated they would hire a TFA instructor again. Responses on parent and student surveys were also very positive.

The example of private schools is also instructive. These schools operate in a competitive marketplace and have a clear incentive to hire the best teachers available. Many employ unlicensed instructors with no prior education course work. Although most Catholic school teachers are certified, barely half the teachers in other private schools are.[46] The proportion of unlicensed teachers is particularly high among nonsectarian schools, which cannot depend on religious instruction to attract customers but must compete primarily on the basis of educational quality. By hiring unlicensed teachers, these schools have increased the proportion of faculty who graduated from selective colleges and universities.

Credentialism

School districts are able to stretch the size of their work forces by giving teachers classes outside their main assignment areas. This practice has been severely criticized by advocates of teacher professionalization, in some cases justly so. Unions have also resisted this practice, recognizing that flexible assignment policies give districts an option for dealing with shortages that, in the absence of this alternative, might force them to raise salaries.

Unfortunately, this can easily lead to a situation in which the credential becomes more important than the teacher's actual skills. For example, the

44. Evertson, Hawley, and Zlotnik (1985, p. 7).
45. Kane, Parsons and Associates (1997).
46. Ballou and Podgursky (1997).

NCTAF recommends that all secondary school mathematics teachers have at least a college minor in mathematics. The National Council of Teachers of Mathematics, which belongs to NCATE and is responsible for approving the mathematics curriculum of teacher educator programs, goes further, recommending the "equivalent of a college major" for all math teachers in grades 9–12. If these recommendations became requirements and the requirements were strictly enforced, a good deal of administrative flexibility would be lost. Fifty-five percent of the students taking general math in grades 7–12 are taught by instructors who have less than a minor in the subject. This does not mean they are poor teachers; a background in college mathematics is not needed to teach general math, which requires no mathematical skills above arithmetic. In fact, the same could be said for most of the high school mathematics curriculum. The study of mathematics at the collegiate level encompasses topics that an instructor would never be called on to teach to high school students. Mathematics majors are often frustrated teaching subjects like elementary algebra to students far less adept in mathematics than themselves. Teachers with backgrounds in the humanities or social sciences might well be superior teachers of these subjects, provided they know the mathematics content. This could be ascertained by a subject matter exam, a simpler and more cost-effective screening mechanism than the requirement that anyone teaching a mathematics course have completed six or seven college courses in the subject.

Ironically, professional self-regulation will promote a credentialism that runs counter to the larger goals proponents of professionalization have set. In 1986 the Carnegie Forum on Education and the Economy articulated a vision of a profession marked by deep intellectual curiosity and ambition.

> Teachers should have a good grasp of the ways in which all kinds of physical and social systems work; a feeling for what data are and the uses to which they can be put, an ability to help students see patterns of meaning where others see only confusion. . . . They must be able to learn all the time, as the knowledge required to do their work twists and turns with new challenges and the progress of science and technology. . . . We are describing people of substantial intellectual accomplishment.[47]

47. Carnegie Forum on Education and the Economy (1986, p. 25).

The irony, of course, is that people of substantial intellectual accomplishment can teach many school subjects if they have the interest to do so. When public education succeeds in attracting the kinds of teachers described in this passage, the last thing it ought to do is stifle their curiosity and creativity. If an English teacher develops over the years a love of history and has the other attributes mentioned by the Carnegie forum, there is reason to expect he or she would make an excellent history instructor. Yet these will be the kinds of choices that professionalization will take away, replacing them with a numbing emphasis on credentials.

Conclusion

A campaign is underway to professionalize teaching—to give private organizations of educators the same control over professional training and credentials exercised by practitioners in occupations like medicine and law. Functions now performed by state agencies, such as the accreditation of teacher education programs and establishing the requirements for licensure to teach in public schools, would be taken over by the NCATE and independent boards made up of teachers, teacher educators, and school administrators.

The major teachers unions, the NEA and the AFT, have a leading role in NCATE. The NEA has also been a strong advocate of the formation of independent professional boards, anticipating that such boards will be more responsive to their members' needs than the state agencies that have performed these regulatory functions until now. The activities of NCATE and the independent boards—accreditation of teacher education programs and control of teacher licensing—are well-recognized means of restricting the supply of would-be teachers and creating pressures for states and districts to raise salaries in order to recruit enough qualified applicants. Indeed, supporters of teacher professionalization are unapologetic about this prospect, arguing that the nation needs to pay more to obtain better teachers.

On closer analysis, however, there is little reason to expect that professional self-regulation will improve teacher quality. NCATE standards focus on process rather than outcomes. They do not ensure that the graduates of accredited institutions meet minimum standards of competency; indeed, NCATE has accredited programs with extremely low admissions standards.

Professional self-regulation would also bring with it greater reliance on authentic or performance-based assessments to determine who should be licensed. These assessments are unproven; as our examination of one pilot program based on standards developed by INTASC shows, there are scant grounds for supposing they would be superior to traditional ways of evaluating teachers.

In addition, there are signs that professional self-regulation will be used to restrict teacher supply in ways that impede efforts to recruit better teachers. Among them are costly accreditation standards that make it prohibitively expensive for small liberal arts colleges to continue to train teachers, prolonged preservice training that deters too many capable students and mature career-changers from entering teaching, and an excessive credentialism that restricts administrative flexibility as well as teachers' opportunities for professional growth.

Public education in the United States is a regulated monopoly. The vast majority of parents have their children enrolled in public schools. In most school districts, parents have little or no choice of schools or teachers within schools. While it is possible to exercise choice via private schooling or residential relocation, these are costly options. Unlike medicine or other professional service markets, consumers also lack the protection provided by antitrust law or malpractice lawsuits. The monopolistic structure of this product market, combined with the fact that well-organized state affiliates of the NEA and AFT bargain with thousands of fragmented local school districts, confers a great deal of economic power on the teachers unions. Professional self-regulation would increase significantly this bargaining power, giving unions market power not enjoyed by producers or unions in any major industry in our economy.

References

Arenson, Karen W. 1998. "Jobs at Risk, Teachers Are Studying Again to Pass Tests." *New York Times* (January 17).

Ballou, Dale. 1998. "The Condition of Urban School Finance: Efficient Resource Allocation in Urban Schools." In *Selected Papers in School Finance, 1996,* edited by William Fowler. Washington D.C.: U.S. Department of Education, Office of Educational Research and Improvement, pp. 65–83.

Ballou, Dale, and Michael Podgursky. 1997. *Teacher Pay and Teacher Quality.* Kalamazoo Mich.: W. E. Upjohn Institute.

————. 1998a. "The Case against Teacher Licensing." *Public Interest* (Summer).

————. 1998b. "Teacher Training and Licensure: A Layman's Guide to the Teacher Quality Debate." In *Better Teachers, Better Schools,* edited by Marci Kanstoroom and Chester E. Finn Jr., 31–82. Washington, D.C.: Fordham Foundation.

Barton, James, and Angelo Collins. 1993. "Portfolios in Teacher Education." *Journal of Teacher Education* 44 (May–June): 200–09.

Bureau of Labor Statistics, U.S. Department of Labor. 1998. *Occupational Outlook Handbook, 1998–99 Edition.* Bulletin 2500. Government Printing Office.

Carnegie Forum on Education and the Economy. 1986. *A National Prepared: Teachers for the 21st Century.* New York: Carnegie Corporation.

Chaddock, Gail Russell. 1998. "Change of Pace: The Good News about Teaching." *Christian Science Monitor* (July 14), B1.

Darling-Hammond, Linda. 1997. *Doing What Matters Most: Investing in Quality Teaching.* N.Y.: National Commission on Teaching and America's Future.

Educational Testing Service. 1999. *The Academic Quality of Prospective Teachers: The Impact of Admissions and Licensure Testing.* Princeton, N.J.

Evertson, Carolyn M., Willis D. Hawley, and Marilyn Zlotnik. 1985. "Making a Difference in Educational Quality through Teacher Education." *Journal of Teacher Education* 36 (May–June): 2–12.

Feistritzer, C. Emily. 1992. *Who Wants to Teach?* Washington D.C.: National Center for Education Information.

————. 1998. "The Truth behind the 'Teacher Shortage.'" *Wall Street Journal* (January 28), A-18.

Kane, Parsons, and associates. 1997. *A Survey of Principals, Parents and Students in School Districts with Teach for America Corps Members.* New York.

Klein, Perry. 1997. "Multiplying the Problems of Intelligence by Eight: A Critique of Gardner's Theory." *Canadian Journal of Education* 22 (4): 377–94.

Lieberman, Myron. 1956. *Education as a Profession.* Prentice-Hall.

————. 1993. "Take the $25 Million and Run: The Case of the National Board for Professional Teaching Standards." *Government Union Review* 11 (1): 1–23.

————. 1997. *The Teacher Unions.* Free Press.

Murnane, Richard J., et al. 1991. *Who Will Teach? Policies That Matter.* Harvard University Press.

National Board for Professional Teaching Standards (NBPTS). 1996. *National Board Certification Portfolio Sampler, 1996–1997.*

National Commission on Teaching and America's Future. 1996. *What Matters Most: Teaching for America's Future.*

National Council for the Accreditation of Teacher Education. 1997. *Standards, Procedures, and Policies for the Accreditation of Professional Education Units.* Washington, D.C.

National Education Association. 1997. *Handbook, 1997–98.* Washington, D.C.

————. 1998. *Independent Professional Teacher Standards Boards: An Overview of Activities for Establishing Independent Professional Standards Boards.* Washington, D.C.

————. Undated pamphlet. *The NEA-NCATE Connection.* Washington, D.C.

Numbers, Ronald L. 1988. "The Fall and Rise of the American Medical Profession." In *The Professions in American History,* edited by Nathan O. Hatch, 51–72. University of Notre Dame Press.

Olson, Lynn. 1987. "Group Says Reforms May Dissuade Some from Career in Teaching." *Education Week* (March 18).

Rodman, Blake. 1987. "NEA Pursues Plan to Establish Teacher-Controlled State Boards." *Education Week* (April 29).

Rottenberg, Simon. 1962. "The Economics of Occupational Licensing." *National Bureau of Economic Research, Aspects of Labor Economics*. Princeton University Press.

Shimberg, Benjamin, Barbara F. Esser, and Daniel H. Kruger. 1973. *Occupational Licensing: Practices and Policies*. Washington, D.C.: Public Affairs Press.

State of Maine Advisory Committee on Results-Based Initial Certification of Teachers. 1997. *Final Report to the State Board of Education and the Commissioner of Education*. September.

Toch, Thomas. 1991. *In the Name of Excellence*. Oxford University Press.

Tom, Alvin R. 1996. "External Influences on Teacher Education Programs: National Accreditation and State Certification." In *Currents of Reform in Preservice Teacher Education*, edited by Ken Zeichner, Susan Melnick, and Mary Louise Gomez, 11–29. Teachers College Press.

4

HOWARD L. FULLER
GEORGE A. MITCHELL
MICHAEL E. HARTMANN

Collective Bargaining in Milwaukee Public Schools

W HEN AMERICAN PUBLIC school teachers began to bargain collectively in the early 1960s, many observers expected that increased compensation and changed working conditions would foster improved academic achievement. To test this, we analyzed the educational impact of bargaining in the Milwaukee Public Schools (MPS) between 1964 and 1996.[1] While teachers achieved most contractual objectives they identified, hoped-for gains in academic achievement did not follow. Instead, we found:

—Academic achievement among low-income, mostly minority students—the majority of MPS's enrollment—remained at unacceptable levels.

—Morale among many teachers was low.

—Relations between the union and the district were often acrimonious and educationally counterproductive.

1. This chapter primarily reflects a yearlong study of the contract between Milwaukee Public Schools (MPS) and the Milwaukee Teachers' Education Association (MTEA). See Howard Fuller, George Mitchell, and Michael Hartmann, "The Milwaukee Public Schools' Teacher Union Contract—Its History, Content, and Impact on Education," Report 97-1, Institute for the Transformation of Learning, Marquette University, October 1997, p. 94. The study was sponsored by a grant from the Helen Bader Foundation, Inc. All errors are the responsibility of the authors.

An advisory committee convened on several occasions to offer us suggestions and comments on drafts. Its members had diverse backgrounds and policy perspectives; several differ with us on various educational policy issues. The members of the committee, and their affiliations at that time, were David

Rather than improving educational conditions, our research suggests that the net impact of bargaining in Milwaukee was negative.

We presented our findings to officials of MPS and the Milwaukee Teachers' Education Association (MTEA). Neither disputed the factual accuracy of our data, nor did they assert that bargaining has had a positive educational impact in Milwaukee.[2]

The MTEA has made several proposals it believes would enhance achievement. These include reducing the student-teacher ratio, increasing overall spending, and hiring teachers' aides. Also, the teachers' contract, in a section on "Teaching Conditions and Educational Improvements," includes provisions that teachers deem important in regard to school climate and students' achievement, including: exceptional education class sizes, building security and discipline, reimbursement for in-service training and

---

Lucey, an attorney and former member of the Milwaukee School Board; Jeanette Mitchell, program officer-education, Helen Bader Foundation, a former member and president of the Milwaukee School Board; Grace Thomsen, a faculty member at MPS's South Division High School; Jan Johnson, an acting assistant principal and faculty member at MPS's Lincoln Center Middle School of the Arts; Tom McGinnity, principal of MPS's Grand Avenue School; and Bob Lowe, professor of education at National Louis University and a cofounder of the Milwaukee educational publication *Rethinking Schools.*

We also received comments and suggestions from Cecilia Rouse, Charles Kerchner, Myron Lieberman, Sammis White, Thomas Kohler, Bob Smith, Delbert Clear, Carolyn Kelley, and John Rury. The Wisconsin Association of School Boards allowed us to review its records. The Milwaukee Public Schools made available substantial information, responded to many questions, and critiqued the factual accuracy of certain materials. Former MPS superintendent Robert Jasna and acting superintendent Barbara Horton designated Ray Nemoir and Myra Vachon as primary contacts. Deborah Ford, Chris Toth, Ed Burnette, Himanshu Parikh, and David Kwiatkowski assisted them.

With one exception, the MTEA declined to provide information in response to several written and verbal requests.

2. At the outset of our research, the MTEA's executive director questioned whether we could present an unbiased analysis. This concern reflected the fact that we advocate public policies that are opposed by teachers unions. Also, Fuller's tenure as MPS superintendent was marked by acrimonious relations with the union.

We sought to address such concerns. We met frequently with, and provided review copies of all drafts to, the advisory committee described in note 1. We provided all drafts of our report to MPS and MTEA, asked for their comments and criticism, and offered them space in our final report for unedited rebuttals. Supporting data used in preparing tables and figures were presented to MPS and MTEA for review. MPS provided considerable technical information and factual clarification. MTEA declined to respond.

In September 1998 Adam Urbanski, president of the Rochester Teachers Association, American Federation of Teachers (AFT), told a national conference that our report contained numerous factual errors. He said he based this statement on information provided him by the MTEA. Urbanski said he would provide us with specific erroneous data, but declined subsequent requests to do so. Urbanski later shared our study with the AFT research staff; its resulting critique of our report identified no factual errors.

attendance at university courses, and procedures allowing teachers at a school to initiate a formal investigation if they believe educational conditions are inadequate.

Our review of union newsletters over three decades identified several devoted to the goal of improved academic achievement. Our principal conclusion is that empirical results demonstrate that the union's efforts and those of management have been inadequate.

While these findings are confined to Milwaukee's experience, observations by two national teachers union leaders also suggest that collective bargaining by teachers generally has fallen short of meeting important educational goals. In 1993 the late Albert Shanker, former president of the American Federation of Teachers (AFT), told a conference:

> We're not going to change the way schools function without simultaneously changing the way unions function. . . . As long as there are no consequences if kids or adults don't perform, as long as the discussion is not about education and student outcomes, then we're playing a game as to who has the power. . . . Unless you start with a very heavy emphasis on accountability, not end with it, you'll never get a system with all the other pieces falling into place.[3]

These comments became public in 1997, in a posthumous tribute to Shanker published in *Education Week*. In the same year, the president of the National Education Association (NEA), Robert Chase, speaking to the National Press Club, said:

> For nearly three decades . . . the [NEA] has been a traditional, somewhat narrowly focused union. . . . This narrow, traditional agenda . . . is utterly inadequate to the needs of the future. . . . America's public schools do not exist for teachers and other employees. They do not exist to provide us with job and salaries. Schools do exist for the children—to give students the very best—beginning with a quality teacher in every classroom.

If the status quo persisted, Shanker said, "We will get—and deserve— the end of public education through some sort of privatization scheme if

---

3. "A Tribute to Al Shanker," Pew Forum on Education Reform, special insert in *Education Week*, May 14, 1997.

we don't behave differently." Chase said: "The imperative now facing public education could not be starker: simply put . . . we must revitalize our public schools from within, or they will be dismantled from without."

Why did Shanker and Chase make these statements? The history of collective bargaining in Milwaukee offers answers.

In Milwaukee, teacher bargaining and the resulting contract have a direct, daily impact on school operations and, therefore, on educational outcomes. If bargaining's impact elsewhere is similar, it explains why Shanker and Chase urged a fundamental change. We argue that the most important change involves setting a new purpose—improved academic achievement—for educational bargaining.

In Milwaukee neither management nor labor has used collective bargaining as a primary way to increase academic achievement. Instead, bargaining mostly has been a means for teachers to attain goals that may coincide with, but often stand apart from, educational effectiveness. Much responsibility for this outcome rests with successive failures of Milwaukee's elected school board and administration to use bargaining as a means for presenting and implementing a strategy of improving academic achievement. This management vacuum let the union define the bargaining agenda during the three-plus decades that were studied.

Recent developments hint at the possibility of a change in this relationship. Late in 1998 widespread and largely negative media reaction greeted a new MPS–MTEA contract that substantially improved early retirement benefits and, in the process, created sizable unfunded liabilities. The criticism increased when MPS spurned an independent actuarial assessment of the new contract. A strongly worded editorial in the *Milwaukee Journal Sentinel* declared that the union-dominated school district was not in "safe hands."[4] The widespread negative reaction may have influenced MTEA's

4. The contract that prompted such criticism illustrates many problems that historically have characterized teacher bargaining in Milwaukee.

Throughout the 1997–98 school year MPS and MTEA failed to agree on a new contract. The stalemate continued during the summer of 1998. Two weeks into the 1998–99 school year an agreement resulting from secret negotiations was announced. While it included no apparent progress on major goals identified by the school board in February 1997, the parties held a press conference to describe the agreement as "cutting edge."

In financial terms, the new contract provided (1) pay raises that were "substantially more" than required by state bargaining law (from the September 4, 1998, issue of *The Sharpener*, the MTEA member newsletter) and (2) a major expansion of the district's supplemental early retirement pension plan.

Missing was progress on several goals established by management at the outset of bargaining. For example, in "Milwaukee Board of School Directors and Administration—Bargaining Proposals for 1997–99 MPS/MTEA Contract" (February 13, 1997), MPS listed these key goals: "reassignment of

decision in early 1999 to make a potentially significant concession on the issue of how dominant seniority would be in filling teacher vacancies at some schools.

These developments coincided with a school board election campaign where the alleged domination of the school board by union-supported directors became a major issue. With five of nine board seats contested, and with unprecedented levels of local and national spending, the campaign drew wide media attention as a clash between supporters and opponents of the teachers union. All five candidates supported by the teachers union, including three incumbents, were defeated.[5] Four of the five winners, including former labor organizer and incumbent citywide school director John Gardner, received 60 percent of the vote. Gardner actively supported reform of the collective bargaining process.[6]

It remains to be seen whether Gardner and his colleagues will redirect collective bargaining in Milwaukee to focus more directly on issues of academic achievement. One important test will come in negotiations for the contract beginning in mid-2001. The new board majority must overcome a long tradition in which the responsible parties—both union and management—duck accountability. In a system with limited accountability for academic outcomes, many public school officials have found that it suffices to explain low achievement by citing factors "beyond their control," such as student demographics and alleged inadequate spending.

Other factors also contribute to a cautionary outlook:

—Local union leaders in 1997 openly rejected Chase's thesis about the need and rationale for major change.[7]

---

teachers without regard to seniority as determined by principal"; "excessing of staff in schools will be made by principals without regard to seniority"; more authority "to implement reasonable innovation where the primary purpose is to increase efficiency and effectiveness in MPS"; various health care cost containment measures; changes in auto vandalism insurance; and a doubling, to five hours per month, in time that teachers may be required to attend faculty meetings.

5. Kerry A. White, "Milwaukee Voters Reject Union-Backed Candidates," *Education Week*, April 14, 1999.

6. Milwaukee's pioneering school choice program also was an important issue motivating supporters and opponents of candidates. Gardner is the most visible of several school board members who support the tax-supported program of private choice for low-income parents.

7. Presidents of the four largest NEA affiliates in Wisconsin vigorously disagreed with Chase's 1997 speech. "Your remarks are not only appalling, they ignore the fundamental strength of a union. The very foundation of our union is threatened by those who will capitalize on your remarks as an expression of weakness. . . . Because you were a social studies teacher before you became president of NEA, you should understand the results of appeasement in Eastern Europe in the 30's and 40's. . . . We

—Bargaining is carried out in secret. The public does not understand bargaining's impact on academic outcomes. Secrecy and a general lack of information make bargaining seem peripheral to educational outcomes.

—Milwaukee's news media historically have not provided sustained coverage of collective bargaining or its impact on educational outcomes.[8]

As a first step in addressing these concerns, we proposed in 1997 that MPS and MTEA (1) bargain in public and (2) accept responsibility for negotiating a contract that leads to improvement in student achievement. At the time, neither party showed an interest in these ideas. Some reviewers of our proposal were unenthusiastic; one said a "solution" of open negotiations "is far too tame a medicine to correct the malady."

We continue to believe that open bargaining is a prerequisite, but by no means a guarantee, of meaningful change. Absent open negotiations, the public's main access to information about bargaining will continue to be potentially self-serving explanations of management and labor.

Principal Findings

Between 1964 and 1996 bargaining enabled Milwaukee teachers to reach many stated objectives in areas of compensation, fringe benefits, and contractual working conditions, including: growth in purchasing power; substantial fringe benefits and job security; increased real spending on education; a lower student-teacher ratio; and the hiring of thousands of new aides, ostensibly to let teachers spend more time on educational responsibilities.

However, in the course of achieving such gains, bargaining often worsened relations among teachers, many principals, other system administrators, and the school board. This undermined two prerequisites for effective schools: high teacher job satisfaction and a positive school climate. The situation was exacerbated by a rigid collective bargaining agreement, where

---

are union and we are proud; we stand in solidarity to defend against those who are attempting to destroy us." C. Howard, S. Bringman, M. Remsing, and D. Wiser, letter to Bob Chase, February 20, 1997. These four were presidents, respectively, of teachers unions in Milwaukee, Madison, Green Bay, and Racine. Executive directors of the four unions also were signatories.

8. Coverage of bargaining by the *Milwaukee Journal Sentinel* in 1998 and 1999 included more stories linking contract issues to school effectiveness.

uniform, systemwide rules often conflicted with the school-based autonomy and flexibility that are key ingredients of effective schools.[9]

Finally, the contract's current size—174 pages in 1992–95, compared to 18 pages in 1964—makes it nearly impenetrable. This is made worse by a "contract behind the contract" consisting of about 1,700 memoranda of understanding (MOUs), nearly 300 grievance-arbitration rulings, and various state declaratory rulings.[10]

In the end, the hope that gains in compensation, fringe benefits, job security, and other working conditions might improve academic outcomes has not been realized. Rather, we argue that the negative aspects of collective bargaining contribute to MPS's ranking near the bottom in statewide measures of academic achievement.

Historically, the impact of bargaining and the teachers' contract has been all but absent from the ongoing discussion about urban education reform in Milwaukee and Wisconsin. Unless that changes, we believe the significant and negative impacts of bargaining on educational outcomes will continue.

Why Even Study a Teachers Union Contract?

In Milwaukee, the importance of this question surfaced frequently during 1996 in discussions at Marquette University. The discussions were organized by the Institute for the Transformation of Learning and attended by a wide range of Milwaukee area residents—parents, teachers, school board members, and others. Many said they knew little of the MPS-MTEA contract and its impact on educational outcomes. The sponsor of the discussions—the Helen Bader Foundation, Inc.—subsequently approved our proposal to

9. The school board elected in 1999 recognizes this problem. It hired as a new superintendent a former MPS principal whose record and commitment both reflect a goal of introducing more flexibility into school-based decisions. The first real test for the board and superintendent will come in bargaining for a contract scheduled to begin in mid-2001.

10. For comparison purposes, we reviewed teacher contracts at two prominent private high schools in metropolitan Milwaukee that do not bargain collectively with their faculty. Messmer High School is a central city Catholic school with a student body composed mostly of minority students from moderate and low-income families. It has received widespread recognition for attaining levels of academic achievement that match or exceed those of MPS high schools. Messmer's teacher employment contract is three pages long and is supplemented by a twenty-two-page faculty and staff handbook. The contract for the second school was a single page, supplemented by a sixty-three-page faculty and staff handbook. Officials at the second school requested that it not be identified. The school is generally regarded as a successful institution with a student body focused primarily on preparing for college.

"analyze the . . . teacher union contract [and its] impact on district management and educational effectiveness."

Locally and nationally, we found such research is relatively scarce, perhaps reflecting what labor law expert Thomas C. Kohler calls a "tendency
to regard [collective] bargaining as . . . narrowly concerned with wage rates
and benefits."[11] We believe an opposite conclusion is warranted—at least
with respect to education—because bargaining addresses so many core
issues affecting educational outcomes:

—how teacher qualifications are set,

—how teachers are assigned and transferred,

—how teachers are compensated,

—what a teacher's duties are and how they are evaluated, and

—the relationship between teachers, school administrators, and elected
board members.

Because these issues determine how schools function, many observers
expected that bargaining would improve educational results.[12] Offering a
somewhat different perspective, Wayne Urban, a historian of the American
teacher labor movement, emphasized that teachers organized primarily for
improved wages and working conditions.

> First, teachers organized to pursue material improvements, salaries,
> pensions, tenure, and other benefits and policies which helped raise
> teaching in the cities to the status of a career. Second, through the
> pursuit of salary scales and other policies, teachers sought to insti-
> tutionalize experience, or seniority, as the criterion of success in
> teaching.[13]

In striving to achieve such objectives, Urban observed that many teachers hoped that educational outcomes also would improve, citing a belief
that "reform was needed not only to pay teachers large enough salaries to
live on, but also to give them the security and freedom to do their best
work."

11. Kohler (1995, p. 149). While research on collective bargaining in education is not widespread,
relatively speaking, it is far from nonexistent. Myron Lieberman, Charles Kerchner and colleagues, and
several others have examined the issue extensively. Two recent reports discuss the contents and implications of collective bargaining in Maryland and Michigan. See Liebmann (1998); Munk (1998).

12. See, for example, Doherty and Oberer (1967, pp. 123–25); Seitz (1965–66); Poltrock and Goss
(1993).

13. Urban (1982, p. 22).

Enough time has passed to evaluate the outcome. What kind of contracts resulted? What explains their contents? Have teachers achieved the main goals they identified? What has been the impact of bargaining on educational quality? These are questions to which we sought answers in Milwaukee.

Before Collective Bargaining

Events prior to collective bargaining heavily influenced the bargaining era and resulting contracts. Shanker says that many provisions in teacher contracts might sound "terrible" unless understood by "the context that [they] came from."[14] Milwaukee's historical "context" confirms both Shanker's assessment and Urban's finding that teachers organized for economic goals and seniority rights.[15] This context helps clarify why many contracts we analyzed do not directly address the issue of student achievement.

Researchers Delbert K. Clear and William J. Kritek describe MPS between World Wars I and II as characterized by stability, continuity, and benign paternalism.[16] They cite the following:

—*Authority.* The school board and administration were in charge. Their authority was final and unencumbered by requirements to bargain with teachers. Thus, a "source of stability was the Board's ability to resist the demands of its various employees' groups."

—*Continuity of leadership.* Milton Potter was MPS superintendent for thirty years (1914–43). For twenty-four of those years, Frank Harbach was the powerful secretary-business manager.

—*Teachers: different groups, different agendas.* In the pre-bargaining era, various organizations representing teachers were not unified. One was affiliated with the AFT. Others were associated with the NEA. They "presented different salary proposals [and] it is little wonder that teachers were gener-

14. *Education Week,* May 14, 1997, p. 35.

15. The roots of teacher collective bargaining and organizing date to the late nineteenth century. For Milwaukee, we relied on information primarily from the period after World War I, including: Proceedings of the Milwaukee Board of School Directors, various volumes from 1948 to 1964; Rury and Cassell (1993); Lamers (1974, pp. 64–65). (Robert Lowe, a member of our advisory committee, noted that Lamers [1974] is a so-called house history document); Decision No. 27833–A, from State of Wisconsin Interest Arbitrator Raymond E. McAlpin, November 25, 1994, in a case on MPS's residency requirement for teachers; and teacher salary data provided by MPS.

16. Clear and Kritek (1993, pp. 145–92).

ally ineffective in changing board policies. Moreover . . . the largest of these organizations [used] a strategy of patience rather than stridency."

Potter's 1943 resignation, after twenty-nine years, marked the beginning of major changes in MPS-teacher relations. Festering issues surfaced, issues that two decades later became central to the collective bargaining process. For example:

—*Different teacher salary schedules.* Different groups of teachers (elementary, secondary, and so on) had separate salary schedules.

—*Variable hiring qualifications.* The board and administration could set qualifications that exceeded the minimum requirements for state certification.

—*Merit pay.* MPS used a form of merit-based promotion to determine if teachers at the maximum of their salary division would move to a higher division and receive increased pay. Unlike the provisions of a "single salary schedule" (see below), pay increases were not tied only to a teacher's training or number of years in the system. Instead, other factors were considered, such as: "power in the classroom"; "sympathy and understanding with children"; "industry and resourcefulness"; and "last but not least, growth of pupils as manifested in the handling of subject matter and their reaction to home and school situations."[17]

Teacher organizations opposed the authority, discretion, and lack of uniformity inherent in such policies. As discontent increased, the system began to change. This occurred gradually during the 1940s and 1950s. It accelerated with collective bargaining in the 1960s.

The Single Salary Schedule

A seminal development occurred in 1944, when the Milwaukee board implemented a single salary schedule. Pay under a single salary schedule is determined by two factors: the chronological length of a teacher's service and that teacher's level of educational attainment. Its purpose, according to Shanker, is to foster a system in which teacher pay is not "subject to some individual administrator who can use [teachers] politically or in a discriminatory way."[18] This goal notwithstanding, Shanker essentially concurred

---

17. Clear and Kritek, p. 155, quoting from a 1925 communication from Superintendent Potter to the board. Lowe notes that this merit pay system applied only to high school teachers.

18. *Education Week,* May 14, 1997.

with Allan Odden and Carolyn Kelley, two of several scholars who have identified a fundamental weakness in the single salary schedule system: teachers with the same degree and amount of experience are therefore assumed to be equally qualified.[19] In other words, under a single salary schedule, teachers of different ability but similar education and years of experience get the same pay. This is a form of compensation with no demonstrable relationship to improved academic achievement.[20]

For most teachers, the typical single salary schedule provides for two annual pay adjustments. The first results from negotiated, and often well-publicized, contractual pay increases. The second, often known as a "step increase," automatically arises from a teacher having served an additional year and advancing a step on the salary schedule.[21] Media reports of negotiated salary increases often do not mention the additional step increase. Thus a reported increase of, say, 4 percent, might reflect only half of the actual increase a teacher receives.[22]

Other Key Issues

Many other issues that surfaced in the 1940s later became central to the era of collective bargaining. Several were illustrated in the board's *unilateral* adoption, in 1949, of personnel rules.[23] The topics served almost as an organizational outline for the first collective bargaining resolution in 1964. Major issues—then and today—included
—applications and examination for hiring,
—appointments of probationary and permanent teachers,
—general qualifications of teachers and special teachers' qualifications,
—state certification,
—experience credit (for teaching outside of MPS),
—salaries and pensions,

19. Odden and Kelley (1997).
20. Dale Ballou and Michael Podgursky (1997) summarize other research and analyze the trade-offs inherent in a single salary structure system.
21. Depending on the specific terms of a district's single salary schedule, longevity or step increases typically occur for about the first fifteen years of a teacher's tenure, after which he or she receives only an annual negotiated increase.
22. One reviewer's reaction to our mention of this fact illustrates the sometimes-contentious turn that a discussion of bargaining can produce. This reviewer, a recognized expert, said it was "inflammatory" and thus unwarranted to call attention to the fact that most teachers receive two annual pay increases.
23. MPS Proceedings, November 1, 1949, pp. 224–37.

—assignments to schools and transfers to other assignments,

—notifications of absence and intention to return to service (including tardiness or unexcused absence; absence of more than thirty consecutive school days; absence without leave; sickness absence; absence due to quarantine, fire, or other casualty; absence on account of death; absence due to funeral of a fellow teacher; brief absence; leave and reassignment; leave of absence for illness; maternity leave; professional study leave; duration and curtailment of leaves),

—return after leave of absence; professional study required after absence from teaching service; conventional leave,

—suspensions, discharges, and resignations, and

—evaluation.

Collective bargaining became the vehicle for teachers to change such policies and procedures, matters that the board once had unilaterally decided.

The Contract, and the Contract-behind-the-Contract

In 1959 Wisconsin became one of the first states to establish collective bargaining rights for teachers. Milwaukee teachers did not use the law until 1964, when the MTEA was recognized as the exclusive bargaining agent for teachers. In October 1964 the school board concluded the first round of teacher collective bargaining in MPS history, fundamentally changing the district's relationship with its most important employees.

Collective bargaining led to widespread and systematic changes in the authority and rules by which MPS was governed. It directly involved the union in a wide range of administrative and governance matters that previously were the province of management. Many of these issues involved major policy, while others dwelt on administrative minutiae. One result is a common question asked when board members and administrators consider administrative and policy decisions: *Will the contract allow it?* The mere posing of this question can stall an idea.

The contract's central—and often stifling—importance is illustrated by the following provision: "Where any [MPS] rule or [school board] policy is in conflict with any specific provision of the contract, the contract shall govern."[24]

24. Contract between MPS and MTEA, July 1, 1992, to June 30, 1995, p. 3.

Our judgment of the contract's negative effect on school operations, flexibility, and education reform is influenced by agreement among many researchers and practitioners that school effectiveness is linked to a decentralized approach, where individual schools have more autonomy and accountability. Those conditions are at cross-purposes with districtwide contracts premised on uniformity and consistency, both traditional objectives of collective bargaining.

The contract evolved from an 18-page resolution in 1964 to a 55-page contract in 1968 to a 174-page contract in 1992–95 (see Figure 4-1). The contract's language, and its implementation, go to the heart of determining how a school operates day-to-day.

Qualifications, Assignment, and Seniority

More than any other noneconomic matters, these issues have dominated collective bargaining. Before bargaining, the board and administration could set qualifications for MPS teachers and determined where they would be assigned. With some exceptions, this no longer is so. For example, the 1992–95 contract says:

> In the event the board decides to impose additional qualifications beyond those established by the Wisconsin Department of Public Instruction, the board shall notify the MTEA . . . and meet with the MTEA to discuss whether such qualifications are reasonabl[e]. . . . The board shall grant tuition reimbursement to those teachers presently in assignments who must obtain additional credits as a result of the imposition of qualifications beyond DPI certification.

While the contract nominally "recognizes the superintendent's power to assign teachers unless otherwise limited by this agreement," twelve pages that follow limit the superintendent from assigning all but the newest teachers entering the system. Charles Kerchner describes such provisions, common to many teachers union contracts, as effectively converting a teacher's initial assignment into a "property right."[25] At the beginning of bargaining, the MTEA was clear in defining its view on this issue:

25. Kerchner and others (1997, p. 38).

Figure 4-1. *The Growing Length, in Pages, of the Milwaukee Teachers Union Contract, by Section, 1965, 1968, 1995*

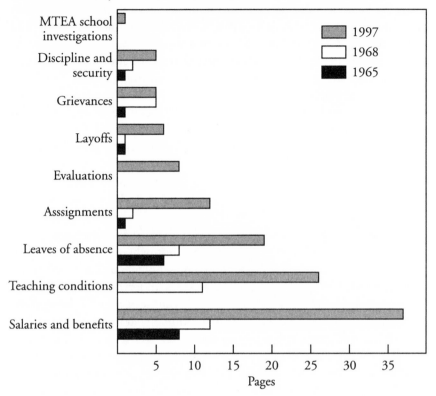

The MTEA believes that the superintendent [has] the right to initially assign teachers [but] a teacher has a right to remain in the building to which he is originally assigned. . . . If the administration sees a need to involuntarily transfer a teacher, then the administration has the burden of proof to establish a . . . need for the transfer and the teacher has a right to have the . . . decision reviewed by an impartial arbitrator.[26]

26. *At Issue,* No. 1 (undated, from the late 1960s), a publication of MTEA.

Duties, Scheduled Work Day, Extra Compensation

Prior to collective bargaining, a six-point, one-page document addressed such issues as length of the school day, teacher preparation time, and duties outside the classroom.[27] The 1962 version stated:

—"Approximately four clock hours per week in addition to the class time day devoted to extracurricular activities and pupil services should be accepted as reasonable and necessary."

—"It is desirable that each teacher be assigned an uninterrupted lunch period . . . if such arrangements can be made."

—"Provision should be made for a daily period for preparation, record keeping and similar curricular activities."

—"Related curricular duties, including attendance at professional meetings, open house, commencement, and similar activities are properly part of the teachers' assignments."

—"A proportionate amount of advisory and supervisory duties, incident to the proper conduct of the school including homeroom advisement responsibilities, are expected to be shared by school faculties."

The brevity and generality of these passages underscore the administration's previous discretion and authority. This authority, and its implementation, was the bane of the union. A major union goal in bargaining was to restrict this authority. It has largely succeeded. Most policies have been replaced by extensive contract provisions that: define the length of the "teacher day"; describe "collateral duties related to . . . teaching functions" that "teachers are required to perform"; and specify activities that are not included in the regular school day. Forty pages of supporting material—compared to four in the mid-1960s—contain salary schedules and rates of additional pay for extracurricular, income-producing activities; teaching all or part of a class when a regular teacher is absent; supervision of pupil transportation before or after the close of the teacher work day; and others. The contract also provides limits for activities that are part of the regular teaching schedule. For example, "all teachers may be required to attend faculty meetings or in service sessions not to exceed two and one-half hours per month. . . . The administration shall notify the teachers of the dates of in service and the expected duration of the in service or faculty meeting at least one week prior . . . if it is to last longer than one hour."

27. "General Policies Respecting Teacher Assignments," Milwaukee Public Schools. Four pages of supplementary schedules defined levels of pay for duties beyond the regular teaching day.

The interpretation and implementation of these provisions have prompted a long history of disputes. The nature of these disputes speak directly to the our focus, which was to assess the impact of bargaining on educational achievement. Several representative examples follow, drawn from various MTEA publications. They illustrate the substance and tenor of the relationship that has characterized the era of collective bargaining.[28]

—In 1976, MTEA building representatives (BRs) "voted unanimously to reject a proposal [for] 'teachers' rap sessions'" on Saturdays to "give teachers an opportunity to discuss human relations problems during [racial] integration of" MPS. BRs "feel teachers are making significant contribution to the integration efforts in Milwaukee Public Schools and it is unreasonable to request that teachers extend their time and energy to weekend programs."

—The same newsletter reported that "it has come to the attention of the MTEA that an elementary school principal [plans to] encourage his staff to participate in three new programs prior to discussion and agreement with the MTEA." The programs included luncheons with parents and students, three PTA programs a year, and a "student activities program on Fridays from 2–3 p.m. in which teachers would supervise students participating in club and hobby activities." The newsletter said "the building committee plans to . . . tell [the principal] that programs of this kind must be agreed to by the MTEA prior to implementation."

—Later in 1976 an arbitrator agreed with a union claim that a "principal's reinstitution of homeroom and a procedure directing homeroom teachers to call parents of absent students" violated the contract. According to the arbitrator, "reinstitution of homeroom without bargaining violated the contract, and that the . . . absent student calling duty is not a collateral duty within the meaning of the contract."

—The same newsletter reported that the board "violated the MTEA contract . . . when it failed to compensate secondary teachers assigned to detention . . . supervision before 8:05 a.m. and after 3:28 p.m." MPS had contended that detention room supervision "was a 'collateral duty' related to teaching" and therefore no extra compensation was required. The MTEA successfully argued that detention room supervision was not a collateral teaching duty and that teachers so assigned should be paid extra.

28. Our full study—see note 1—contains dozens more examples. Our research included a review of more than 450 issues of the MTEA newsletter, *The Sharpener,* between the years 1975 and mid-1997. In addition, other MTEA publications and a large collection of newspaper articles were reviewed. This was supplemented by conversations with teachers, school officials, and union officers.

—In 1976 a grievance was filed to clarify what requirements a teacher was to follow in preparing lesson plans. On at least two occasions—more than a decade later—the MTEA newsletter contained reminders about these guidelines, providing in part that "all teachers prepare lesson plans for their own use. . . . A principal cannot require a [teacher] to submit lesson plans weekly nor on any other periodic basis."

—In March 1983 the MTEA reported that "elementary schools were involved in 'school effectiveness' planning on February 18. Since then some principals have attempted to require teachers to attend additional meetings before and after school to write goals and objectives. The MTEA's position is that writing goals and objectives, curriculum writing, and in service participation before or after school are activities for which teachers should be paid [extra] and that a memorandum of understanding should be negotiated if MPS wishes to ask teachers to perform these services."

—The previous advice followed by two months a separate newsletter dealing with "school effectiveness" planning. The MTEA described meetings it had with MPS regarding "school effectiveness activities on the record/staff planning day" that had been negotiated in the contract and further described in a subsequent memorandum of understanding. According to the newsletter: "The majority of the day is to be set aside for teachers to complete records. The only school effectiveness activity required . . . is the viewing of a 12-minute telecast. . . . Faculties may discuss school effectiveness if they wish. However, such discussions may not exceed a maximum of one hour."

—An amendment to the teacher contract in 1988 illustrates the complexity and level of detail involved in establishing and modifying the length of the teacher work day. State legislation adopted in 1988 added twenty minutes per day to the elementary student instructional day. Below is a partial summary, provided by MTEA, on negotiations to accommodate that increase. *About all that is clear is that providing twenty minutes of additional instruction per day was a low priority.*

There will be a ten-minute increase in the length of the elementary teacher work day [to] provide an additional ten minutes of student instruction, 5 minutes in the morning session and 5 minutes in the afternoon session. In addition . . . 10 minutes of the student lunch period will be designated as a recess period. Under DPI guidelines up to 30 minutes of recess per day may be considered part of the requirement for student instructional time. . . . The 10-minute increase in the teacher day plus the 10-minute recess from the student lunch period will provide the minimum increase of 20 minutes required by state law.

The common thread in such examples is that any tangible connection with issues of educational effectiveness is either nonexistent, marginal, or coincidental. This underscores the fact that the contract itself is not concerned primarily with educational effectiveness. Rather, it is mainly concerned with addressing teacher concerns about compensation, job security, and working conditions that predate the era of collective bargaining.

The Contract-behind-the-Contract

A voluminous collection of documents interprets, amends, or waives contract provisions. Totaling thousands of pages and comprising more than 2,000 documents, they include:
—grievance-arbitration rulings,
—memoranda of understanding, and
—declaratory rulings by the Wisconsin Employment Relations Commission.

Our study both describes these categories and provides a long list of representative examples, illustrating a climate that often is inconsistent with educational flexibility and innovation. The examples illustrate an MPS-MTEA relationship that often stymies risk and experimentation. The contract-behind-the-contract reinforces the rigid system of district governance that has resulted from collective bargaining, all of which relates directly, and adversely, to bargaining's impact on educational operations and outcomes.

Some MTEA and MPS officials say that MOU-type waivers can be used to achieve flexibility. A few examples provide limited support for this view; many others show the opposite effect. In the end, the need for so many waivers itself suggests an incompatibility between the structure of the contract and the goal of school-based autonomy. As Kerchner has pointed out, schools operating under MOUs often are seen as temporary experiments from the norm. Ultimately the volume of MOUs raises a basic question: What is good about a contract that must be routinely amended in the name of so-called education reform?

Box 4-1. *Termination or Resignation of Ineffective Teachers, 1986–97*

Average number of teachers employed per year, 1986–97	5,874
Total number of central office conferences with teachers receiving unsatisfactory evaluations, 1986–97	26
Average number of such conferences per year	2.2
As percentage of all teachers	0.04
Total number of central office conferences resulting in resignations or terminations	18
Average number of such resignations or terminations per year	1.5
As percentage of all teachers	0.03

Teacher Evaluation

A singular failure of the collective bargaining era is that MTEA and MPS have not developed an adequate system to evaluate and assist ineffective teachers and to terminate those who are incompetent. This failure goes to the core of bargaining's adverse impact on educational quality. One aspect of this is summarized in box 4-1, showing that during a twelve-year period, negative evaluations led to an average of only 1.5 terminations a year.

Flaws in the evaluation process have long been recognized. An independent 1985 assessment of personnel practices in MPS (and suburban Milwaukee districts) reported that "non-renewal recommendations for incompetent teachers in the 22 districts [totaled] 18 over a 3-year period."[29] In addition, the study estimated that 121 ineffective teachers resigned or were "counseled out"—about 1 percent of the teaching staff in the twenty-two districts, over a three-year period, for an annual rate of about 0.003 percent. The study found that while three of four principals feel they are able to identify incompetent teachers, the vast majority believe they are not able to act on that knowledge.

The historical lack of action in addressing the problem suggests that it has not been a real priority of either MPS or MTEA. A 1989 report by a joint committee of MTEA and MPS concluded:

29. Backus and others (1985).

Teacher evaluation is . . . a bureaucratic exercise that yields little assistance, but does contribute to the weariness of the teacher. Some teachers receive evaluations without ever having been observed; some are given unsatisfactory evaluations with no offers of assistance, no clear understanding of administrative expectations and no administrative support. There is a wide disparity among principals, supervisors, and teachers regarding factors which should contribute to the teacher's evaluation.[30]

What should be done about this problem? The joint committee suggested another "joint committee . . . to explore possible areas of mutual concern and interest in the evaluation process." In other words: we've studied the problem, we agree it is a problem, let's study the problem again.

A year later, the *Milwaukee Journal* suggested that nothing came even of this mild proposal. It said that MPS "officials say their efforts [to deal with unsatisfactory teachers] are thwarted by a powerful teachers union and a contract loaded with due process protections for teachers and daunting hurdles for principals." One principal said that "if a poor teacher is unwilling to change and doesn't want to go, you have your work cut out for you as a principal." Another said, "It's nearly impossible to get rid of a teacher unless he or she is involved in a criminal act."[31] This article quoted an MPS official describing the "annual dance of the lemons," whereby ineffective teachers are rated "satisfactory" with the understanding that they will not oppose a transfer to a different school.[32]

The MTEA's response to the 1990 article was reported as follows:

James R. Colter, (then) executive director of the teachers union . . . was the only person interviewed . . . who refused to acknowledge that there were incompetent teachers on Milwaukee's rolls. "If there are, it's administration's job to prove it," Colter said. "My job is listen to any person represented by the union and help that individual."

---

30. *MBSD/MTEA Joint Study Committee on Teacher Professionalization,* "Findings and Recommendations," September 22, 1989, p. 8. The summary of the joint study committee was contained in the September 22, 1989, edition of MTEA's *Negotiations Digest.*

31. P. Ahlgren, "Bad Apples: Firing Teachers Is Tough," *Milwaukee Journal,* May 4, 1990. The article said, "Not one of the 1,000 new teachers hired [in the previous five years] has been denied tenure."

32. The persistence of this practice was evident five years later. A March 10, 1995, *Milwaukee Sentinel* article ("Bad MPS Teachers Rotated, Audit Says," by Joe Williams) began: "Bad teachers are often traded from school to school because it is easier for principals to recommend their transfer than to suggest that they be fired, [an MPS] audit . . . revealed."

In bargaining for the 1995–97 contract, potentially significant changes were made in provisions affecting probationary teachers, who previously had almost identical protections as did tenured teachers. The following new language was negotiated:

> The administration shall have the authority to non-renew a first or second year teacher provided it has made reasonable efforts at remediation and that its decision is not arbitrary and capricious . . . the administration shall have the authority to non-renew a third year teacher provided it has made reasonable efforts at remediation and that its decision has a factual and rational basis and is supported by a preponderance of the evidence.

In a public appearance following the adoption of this language, MTEA's executive director said, "We have nothing to gain by protecting incompetence."[33] He stated that "we'll know [soon] whether the new process [for nontenured teachers] is working."

The need for change was clear. Historically, for example, it appears that no probationary teachers were denied tenure during 1985–1989.[34] MPS's Division of Human Resources, responding to a question in 1997 for this study, said: "We expect that during the 1997–98 school year, this [new contract] provision will be used." This turned out not to be the case. In response to a follow-up question, we learned that during all of 1997–98, only "one first year teacher was dismissed" using the new contract provision.[35]

The MTEA executive director, in his 1997 comments, also described a new program for "struggling [tenured] teachers who aren't doing the right thing for the children of MPS. . . . We need to make some decisions about people who aren't doing the job. . . . It's long past time for this action for people who see no alternative but to stay in the profession." The Teacher Evaluation and Mentoring (TEAM) program includes a board of five teachers appointed by the MTEA and four administrators named by MPS. After

33. Sam Carmen, remarks at University of Wisconsin-Milwaukee, January 24, 1997. Author's notes.

34. Ahlgren, May 4, 1990.

35. August 28, 1998, letter to George A. Mitchell from Myra Vachon, executive director, MPS Department of Human Resources.

two years (1996–97 and 1997–98), the cumulative number of referrals to the program totaled 62, less than 1 percent of the district's faculty. Only two had been referred by teachers, even though as a group they are the most directly familiar with examples of inadequate teaching. The remaining 60 referrals were from administrators (49) and self-referrals (11).[36]

Education Spending and Teacher Compensation

We researched progress during collective bargaining on spending and economic objectives identified by the MTEA. For the period 1964–1996, we found that:

—Real per-pupil spending grew 188 percent.

—The ratio of students to teachers declined from about 25:1 to 16:1.

—More than 2,000 paraprofessional aides were hired to assist teachers. In 1964, there were none.

—Career teachers experienced an increase in purchasing power.

—Fringe benefits, which cost about 45 percent of an average teacher's salary, have improved substantially.

Spending

Figure 4-2 shows year-to-year growth in real per-pupil spending from the beginning of collective bargaining through 1996. This near-tripling of real per-pupil spending is at odds with repeated assertions by Milwaukee educators that taxpayers and their elected officials have been unwilling to invest in better schools. The following categories illustrate how much of that investment has been used.

Student-Teacher Ratio

An early goal that teachers identified in collective bargaining was a "specific program for reduction of [the] pupil-teacher ratio." The number of teachers increased 51 percent from 1964 to 1996—a period when enrollment dropped 7 percent. Figure 4-3 illustrates the impact on the student-teacher ratio.

---

36. "Teacher Evaluation and Mentoring Program Cumulative Data, Spring 1998," Milwaukee Public Schools—Milwaukee Teachers' Education Association.

Figure 4-2. *Milwaukee Public School Per-Pupil Spending, 1964–96*

1996 dollars

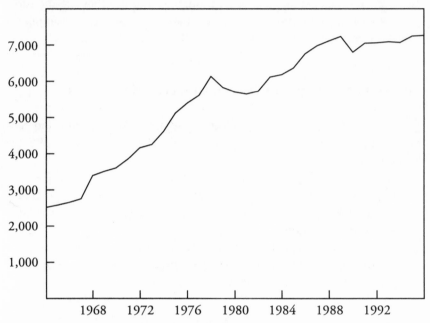

Source: Milwaukee Public Schools and authors' calculations.

Teacher Aides

The initial collective bargaining agreement called for the "hiring of school aides on all levels to relieve teachers of nonprofessional duties." MPS responded aggressively to meet this union bargaining proposal. From the late 1960s to the mid-1990s, the number of teachers grew 37 percent, while the number of teachers' aides grew 333 percent. As a result, the ratio of teachers to teachers' aides declined dramatically, from 9:1 to 3:1.

Salary and Fringe Benefits

From 1964 to 1996 the purchasing power of career teachers grew, as did retirement benefits, medical insurance, and other fringe benefits.[37]

37. We measured changes in purchasing power using the Consumer Price Index—Urban, for Milwaukee, U.S. Department of Labor. Many economists believe the CPI overstates actual changes in

Figure 4-3. *Changes in the Milwaukee Public School Student-Teacher Ratio, 1964–96*

Percent

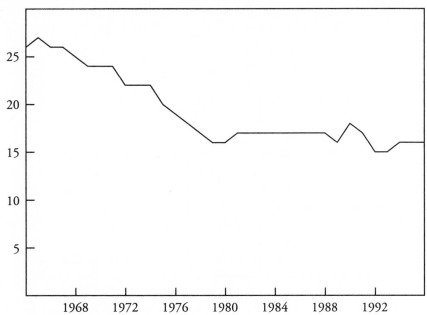

Source: Milwaukee Public Schools.

We tracked the salary of teachers with no prior experience and a bachelor's degree who entered MPS at various times during the period of collective bargaining.[38] Our objective was to measure whether teachers with the minimum required credentials who entered and remained in MPS—career teachers—experienced salary growth that exceeded the rate of inflation, this being a major bargaining goal identified by teachers. In all four scenarios we tested, career teacher salaries grew, in real terms, as shown in table 4-1.

Teachers experienced real salary growth in part due to the previously described, twice-a-year pay increases provided by the single salary schedule.

purchasing power, in which case teacher salaries have grown faster, in real terms, than portrayed in this section.

38. The tracking began in 1964 (the first year of bargaining) and also included 1970, 1980, and 1990.

Table 4-1. *Change in Purchasing Power, Career Teachers in Milwaukee Public Schools Starting in 1964, 1970, 1980, and 1990*
1996 dollars unless otherwise noted

First year of teaching	Starting salary	1996 salary	Percent real growth
1964	26,836	42,820	59.6
1970	31,764	42,820	34.8
1980	21,374	40,095	87.6
1990	26,969	32,089	19.0

Source: Milwaukee Public Schools and authors' calculations.

In years when the negotiated pay increase alone might have been less than the growth in the cost of living, the second pay increase—the step increase—often enabled a teacher's salary to match or exceed the rate of inflation.

Using payroll records for six MPS teachers who retired in 1997, figure 4-4 shows that the number of pay increases they received exceeded the number of years they taught.[39]

One gauge of the magnitude of the MPS teacher salary increases is to compare them to other professionals with similar levels of education. For example:

—Since 1972 teacher salaries have grown slightly faster than those in engineering, accounting, business administration, economics, and other liberal arts fields. Since 1980 teacher salaries have grown more sizably in comparison to computer science graduates.[40]

—Between 1964 and 1996 the real median income of women and, separately, men with at least a bachelor's degree grew 36 percent and 8 percent.[41]

These growth rates are not comparable to those in table 4-1, which account more fully for change in experience. We could not find good data on median teacher salaries for MPS in 1964. A thorough comparison would also include job security and fringe benefits, areas where teachers may have fared better than other professions during this time period.

39. In addition to annual step increases and negotiated pay increases, some of these teachers received pay increases based on additional levels of educational attainment.

40. Odden and Kelley (1997, p. 5, table 1.2, "Beginning Teacher Salaries Compared with Salaries of Other College Graduates").

41. U.S. Bureau of the Census, *Current Population Reports, P60-203, Measuring 50 Years of Economic Change* (http://www.census.gov/hhes/www/income.html).

Figure 4-4. *Years of Teaching versus Number of Pay Increases for Six Milwaukee Public School Teachers with Varying Tenure*

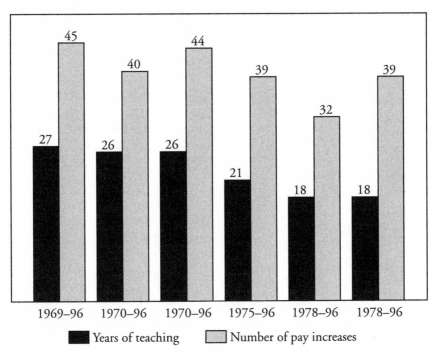

1969–96 1970–96 1970–96 1975–96 1978–96 1978–96

■ Years of teaching   ▢ Number of pay increases

Source: Milwaukee Public Schools.

Fringe Benefits

Fringe benefits for MPS teachers have improved significantly. The overall cost for an average MPS teacher is summarized in table 4-2. In some cases entirely new benefits are now available; in other cases previous benefit levels have grown. The new and enhanced benefits include improved medical insurance while employed by MPS, medical insurance during retirement, early retirement benefits, and other increased retirement benefits.

Medical

The medical, dental, and vision insurance program is one of the better packages available to public or private employees in Wisconsin. With limited exceptions, MPS teachers receive, at no cost to themselves, insurance

Table 4-2. *Salary and Fringe Benefits, Average Milwaukee Public Schools Teacher, 1996–97*

	1996–97 (dollars)	Benefits as a percentage of salary
Average salary	40,978	. . .
Fringe benefits		
Social security and medicare	3,135	7.7
Regular pension	5,491	13.4
Early retirement	716	1.8
Health	8,128	19.8
Dental	649	1.6
Vision	113	0.3
Life	172	0.4
Subtotal benefits	18,404	44.9
Total salary and benefits	59,382	. . .

Source: Milwaukee Public Schools.

that allows them to choose any doctor or hospital. Deductibles and copayments are limited. Teachers may choose from four different insurance programs. Discount programs provide for low prescription drug costs.

Early Retirement

New state and local early retirement benefits enable teachers to retire as early as age fifty-five and receive lifetime pension benefits that are prorated based on payments that would have been received at regular retirement ages.

The 1997–99 MPS-MTEA contract contained substantial increases in the teachers' supplemental early retirement pension program. These increases, combined with prior benefits, create a significant long-term financial commitment for MPS and put the supplemental pension plan in a tenuous financial position. For example, figure 4-5 shows that the MTEA early retirement plan is significantly underfinanced compared with selected other major retirement plans.

The 1997–99 contract continued a pattern of imprudent financial decisions with respect to the early retirement program. Table 4-3 illustrates the steady growth since 1991 in unfunded long-term liabilities.

Figure 4-5. *Assets of Milwaukee Teachers' Education Association's Early Retirement Plan and Other Selected Plans*

Percent of actuarial accrued liability

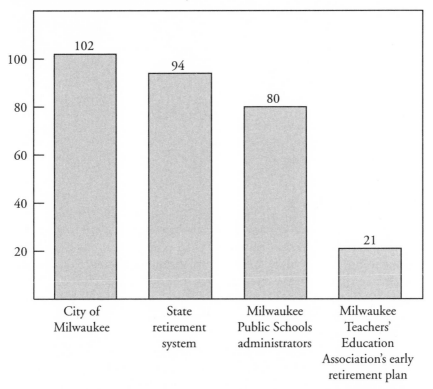

The trends illustrated in table 4-3 effectively put the school district in a "pay-as-you-go" posture with respect to the early retirement program. The resulting unfunded liabilities will have to come from future MPS budgets. Given Wisconsin's overall spending limits on local school districts, the recently approved pension benefits mean that fewer dollars will be available for spending on current educational programs in MPS. When future budget difficulties arise, it can be predicted with some certainty that MPS and MTEA officials will not point to their own actions in creating an unfunded pension plan or in approving some of the largest pay increases in the state of Wisconsin.

Table 4-3. *Changes in Financial Condition, Milwaukee Public Schools–Milwaukee Teachers' Education Association's Supplemental Early Retirement Pension Plan, 1991–98*

Millions of dollars unless otherwise noted

Financial condition	1991	1998	Change (percent)
Actuarial value of plan assets	8.6	16.4	91
Actuarial accrued liability	19.6	77.7	296
Unfunded accrued liability	11.0	61.3	457
Annual plan contribution	1.7	6.8	300
Unfunded liability as percentage of payroll	5	23	372
Assets as percentage of actuarial accrued liability	44	21	–52

Source: Milwaukee Public Schools.

Retiree Medical Benefits

Of even greater financial significance is the negotiated, lifetime MPS payment of health-insurance premiums. When coupled with the early retirement pension benefits, this retiree medical insurance is a very valuable benefit. Between ages fifty-five and sixty-five, when Medicare eligibility starts, it can be difficult for some individuals to attain *any* comprehensive health insurance. But for MPS retirees, including early retirees, the coverage available while a teacher is employed simply is continued, with the district paying most or all of the cost. By comparison, many retirees "are bearing more of the burden of paying for medical care" because of cutbacks and modifications to previous plans that had relatively few limits.[42]

Regular Retirement Benefits

Full retirement benefits for MPS teachers will replace between 35 and 55 percent of preretirement income. Social security benefits will bring the total retirement benefits to between 50 percent and 80 percent of pre-retirement income.[43] Combined with retiree medical insurance, taxpayers provide a substantial share of the retirement needs for a career MPS teacher. According to the Wisconsin Department of Employee Trust

42. T. Rowe Price (1997, p. 4).
43. P. J. Beavers, member benefit specialist, Wisconsin Education Association Council, April 1997.

Funds, the "average compounded annual [retirement payment increase] has been 5.6 percent over the past ten years." Social Security benefits generally increase at a rate comparable to growth in the Consumer Price Index.

The MPS-MTEA Relationship and Its Impact on Academic Achievement

The era of collective bargaining has coincided with a worsening relationship between MPS teachers, administrators, and the school board. Bargaining has been a contributing factor. Three conclusions are clear: (1) the relationship is bad; (2) it is not conducive to improvements in academic achievement; and (3) if it is not changed to focus on improving academic achievement, there is no basis to believe academic gains will be realized.

In any union-management relationship, there will be heated, intemperate comments and calculated, stern rhetoric. However, the MPS-MTEA relationship has produced much more than isolated statements or calculated pronouncements. Instead, there is a sustained, almost relentlessly negative aura. With few exceptions, the tenor of the relationship has been adversarial for more than three decades. Our full study extensively documents the negative tenor of the relationship.

The following example is illustrative. In 1986, more than two decades into the era of collective bargaining, one of MTEA's first presidents made a presentation to the board. It was reprinted in its entirety and distributed to all members. Excerpts include the following:

—"You have great expectations of the teachers and yet you have forced them to work under conditions that make it impossible to met those expectations. . . . I tell you, you are destroying us."

—"I have occasion to meet with teachers from schools all over the city. . . . About all they are beginning to think about is—did we make a mistake going into teaching? You can't beat them over the head year after year and expect to get the kind of results you need."

—"The problem is that this school system has taken the position that teachers are to be dealt with, not worked with. . . . I'll tell you, you are beating your teachers down and we are getting discouraged. You have convinced us of one thing—we are beginning to believe you actually don't care."[44]

44. D. Feilbach, "Reprint of Don Feilbach's Presentation," March 13, 1986, distributed by MTEA.

In the end, except for brief periods, the MTEA-MPS relationship has been largely negative—perhaps, to use the union's word, at times even *destructive*. The problems that characterized the relationship were inseparable from the collective bargaining process, undermining two important conditions that must exist for learning to occur: (1) high teacher morale and job satisfaction, and (2) an atmosphere of high expectations, teamwork, and cooperation.

Teacher Job Satisfaction and Morale

A comprehensive 1984–85 study of Milwaukee-area public schools found that "perceptions and attitudes of teachers [were] consistently related to [academic] performance at all levels. This study clearly demonstrates a strong relationship between job satisfaction or teacher morale and student test scores."[45]

In MPS there is considerable evidence that teacher job satisfaction and morale have declined in the era of collective bargaining. Despite achieving most contractual objectives, teachers have received a continuously negative message from the union, which repeatedly says teachers are not respected and are "insulted" by MPS management. The union has disparaged the motives and integrity of MPS administrators. On some occasions, MPS actions appear to have justified the union's criticism.

Evidence of low teacher morale is widespread.

—A survey of Milwaukee and Milwaukee-area public school teachers was conducted in 1985. "City teachers have less job satisfaction, study says," according to a headline on the survey's results.[46] The article said that "on the matter of job dissatisfaction, teachers were asked whether they agreed . . . that the administration [in their school system] was supportive and encouraging. . . . In Milwaukee 70 percent of the teachers said they disagreed."

—Another measure of teacher discontent came in a 1987 survey by the Urban Research Center at the University of Wisconsin-Milwaukee. "Fewer than 40 percent of Milwaukee Public School teachers responding to a poll question said they would be satisfied to have their own children attend the school where they teach," according to an article on the survey.[47]

45. Walsh (1985, p. 60).
46. D. I. Bednarek, *Milwaukee Journal,* April 26, 1985.
47. "40% of Teachers Would Want Children in City Schools," *Milwaukee Sentinel,* May 12, 1987.

—A related indicator is the disproportionate percentage of teachers who send their children to nonpublic schools. According to one analysis, in 1990 one-third of Milwaukee resident teachers sent their children to private schools—more than twice the statewide rate and more than 50 percent higher than the citywide rate.[48] A separate study of 1990 census data, conducted for the *Milwaukee Journal,* concluded that an even higher percentage—49.7 percent—of public school teachers had at least one child in private school. The study said these data raise "the question of whether public school teachers, particularly those employed by [MPS], believe their children are better off attending private schools."[49]

School Climate

The 1984–85 study found "strong evidence . . . that an effective school which in the eyes of teachers has strong leadership, standards, expectations, and teamwork, performs better with both students from *low and higher income homes.*"[50] The study provided evidence that these conditions did not exist in MPS.

—Teachers also "were asked whether they agreed or disagreed with the statement that the success or failure in teaching depended on factors beyond their control. In Milwaukee, 64 percent of the teachers, the highest proportion in all the school districts surveyed, said they agreed with that statement."

—Other data indicate that negative opinions had existed for some time. In 1981 the *Milwaukee Journal* polled a representative sample of MPS teachers. The three most important concerns cited were: (1) 68 percent identified the need to involve parents in student-teacher discipline conferences; (2) 59 percent said parents should be required to take part in student-teacher academic conferences; and (3) 53 percent cited "stiffer discipline."

These and other indicators in our full study demonstrate that many teachers—perhaps most—do not see their school as "effective." We believe the collective bargaining process as practiced in Milwaukee has contributed to this, in part by lowering expectations and creating barriers to school-based reform.

48. Fuller and White (1995).
49. Richard P. Jones, "Teachers Choose Private Schools," *Milwaukee Journal,* November 14, 1993.
50. Walsh (1985, p. 60, emphasis added).

The Importance of Expectations

High expectations of students are widely recognized as an essential com-
ponent in the "climate" of effective schools. Yet for about two decades
high-level MPS administrators and the MTEA have used demographic
changes in the student body as a basis for lowering expectations. Instead of
using collective bargaining to focus on creating a more positive educational
climate, starting with high expectations, district and union officials often
have taken the opposite tack.

Former superintendent Lee McMurrin was one of the earliest MPS
officials to foster this trend. "Socioeconomic factors [present] a much
more difficult challenge" for MPS, he said, a message repeated consistently during his tenure. McMurrin frequently began presentations to
community groups by summarizing the racial and demographic makeup
of the student population and changes that had occurred. His subtext was
clear: the system was doing the best it could, considering the nature of the
student body.

Many MPS principals and other administrators followed McMurrin's
lead. In 1985 a member of this study's team interviewed a well-known
MPS principal. When asked to assess the school she administered, she said:
"We're OK . . . [pause] . . . for a city school." She explained that city and
suburban students were "different."

Her views were typical. The MPS Administrators and Supervisors
Council (ASC) said in a 1989 report that "low family income, drug abuse,
delinquency, high family mobility, poor parenting and crime are among
the barriers between students and success in school."[51] MTEA publications
also reinforced this theme.

—"The basic point which teachers have made is that many MPS students bring serious problems to school and they need a lot more personal
attention than . . . present class sizes allow."

—"Between 1970 and 1985 the percent of district students living in
poverty increased from 15 percent to over 50 percent. Today over 53 percent of district children live in families with incomes below the federal
poverty level. In 1970 about 14 percent of district children lived in a family headed by a single female . . . during the 1970–71 school year, the dis-

51. P. Ahlgren, "Report Outlines Road Blocks to Learning Success," *Milwaukee Journal,* May 21,
1989.

trict recorded 160 referrals to the school age parents' program; last year the district recorded over 700 such referrals."

Such views by administrators, principals, and union leaders foster low teacher expectations. Consider these illustrative teacher responses to a *Milwaukee Journal* survey:

—"I [have] had to lower my standards. There's no question about that. Passing used to be 70. Now it's 60. . . . When you work so hard and get so little back, it's really disheartening."[52]

—"Conditions have changed. I've aged. It's harder to cope with the changes. Kids are different—more belligerent, surly, impatient, apathetic—and less well prepared."[53]

In 1996 MPS administrators chose to begin a description of the "state of the schools" as follows:

> The students of the Milwaukee Public Schools may look somewhat different than students in Shorewood or Sheboygan, however, their expectations are no different. . . . The challenges the students of the Milwaukee Public Schools face to reach their full potential are greater than students in virtually any other school district around the state. The challenge before the community and school system is to fully understand the unique needs the students of MPS may face in order to reach their goals. . . . The percentage of students that are poor is one of the highest not only in the state of Wisconsin, but in the entire country as well. The unique challenges this provides for MPS are not an excuse for any expectation of lower student achievement or of student failure. However, the influence poverty has on the lives of students must be recognized. It is also important to note that students are in school less than 15 percent of their lives.[54]

While "not an excuse," such language legitimizes a collective sense that factors "beyond the control" of both administrators and teachers primarily explain student performance. The *Milwaukee Journal Sentinel* headline on this report was: "Jasna [the MPS superintendent] sees poverty as MPS' top issue."

52. D. I. Bednarek, "Teachers Comment on Kids Today," *Milwaukee Journal*, September 3, 1981, quoting MPS teacher Richard May.
53. Bednarek, quoting teacher and human relations coordinator David Schley, September 3, 1981.
54. MPS, "State of the Schools," 1996–97.

Demographics

Our full report describes historical changes in demographics of the MPS student body and discusses the statistical correlation established in several studies between low socioeconomic status and low student achievement.[55]

Outcomes

In 1996–97 the MPS ranked lower than almost all of the state's K–12 districts, continuing a pattern of prior years.[56] On fourth- and eighth-grade tests, only one district ranked below MPS. These dismal rankings probably *understate* the problem of low academic achievement in MPS, because a disproportionately small number of MPS students even take the exams cited. The evidence suggests those who do represent the district's better performing students.

Other measures confirm that systemwide academic achievement is too low. An independent 1997 study looked at changes in spending and achievement in four cities, including Milwaukee, from 1981 to 1992. In reviewing achievement data for Milwaukee, it found that "despite large increases in resources . . . students . . . were performing lower than national norms in the latter half of the observed period and were generally losing ground the longer they stayed in the Milwaukee Public Schools."[57] On several measures of standardized test scores, the achievement gap between low-income students and others has widened since the mid-1980s.[58] Increasingly, Milwaukee employers have said that high school graduates lack basic skills and work habits.[59]

A separate, independent study[60] of MPS achievement says that the district has "downplayed . . . realistic test results that [compare MPS students]

55. Fuller, Mitchell, and Hartmann, pp. 83–84.

56. Wisconsin Taxpayers Alliance, *SchoolFacts*, September 1997.

57. G. A. Hess Jr., "Financing Urban Schools in the Midwest: Does Money Make a Difference?" Hess is executive director of the Chicago Panel on School Policy.

58 Fuller and White (1995, pp. 25–26). Notwithstanding such data, the president and executive director of the MPS Administrators' and Supervisors' Council (ASC) wrote in the *Milwaukee Journal Sentinel* that "MPS is generally considered throughout the country as a leader and on the cutting edge of urban education." M. Sonnenberg and C. A. Gobel, letter to the editor, January 5, 1997.

59. For several years in the 1990s, Milwaukee's largest association of employers has identified this as one of the most serious problems they face. A variety of newspaper interviews with local employers produce results consistent with these business association surveys.

60. "Act on the Facts—Press for Public Schools That Work!" Paper prepared by Milwaukee Catalyst, an organization of Milwaukee parents and other community residents, assisted by foundation

against . . . rigorous statewide standards." This report showed that a disproportionately small number of MPS students score at the "advanced" or "proficient" level in reading and that the low results occur even though a disproportionately high number of MPS students did not even take the statewide test. This report also confirmed other estimates that MPS has an abysmal high school graduation rate—in 1997 the number of graduates totaled only 38 percent of the number of MPS freshmen four years earlier.

Conclusion

We found that in Milwaukee the teachers union contract and collective bargaining process historically have operated at odds with school reform. Our principal recommendations remain: that MPS and MTEA agree to bargain in public and accept responsibility for negotiating a contract that leads to improvement in academic achievement. We see these steps as minimal prerequisites to making MPS and MTEA accountable for using bargaining to improve educational outcomes.

Some reviewers suggested that if collective bargaining has been as negative as we claim, why not weaken or do away with it? We believe that in communities where teacher bargaining exists, a more realistic and constructive approach would be to strengthen it. This means using bargaining in ways that increase academic achievement. We feel this way because:

—Collective bargaining is a reality. We do not expect that teachers' rights to organize will or should be denied.

—As the major factor shaping day-to-day school operations, bargaining can be used to improve educational outcomes.

—With more public involvement and oversight, MPS and MTEA could be held more accountable for an outcome that improves education.

When we initially offered these suggestions in the fall of 1997, there was a brief period of local and national news coverage. This abated quickly. Apart from limited changes in seniority provisions in the 1999–2001 contract, no progress has occurred. It is clear that our theories about the potential of bargaining to improve educational results, and of the public's readiness to hold educators accountable for such an outcome, are wholly unproved.

grants and research by the Chicago-based Academy for Urban School Change, a program of Designs for Change.

We acknowledge the possibility that the public school establishment in cities such as Milwaukee is so entrenched, on the side of both management and labor, that the bargaining process is nearly impervious to change. Sporadic news stories and editorials do not amount to the kind of leverage that is required to produce change. Urban educators, in Milwaukee and elsewhere, know that headlines and editorial calls for change come and go quickly and rarely have real impact.

We remain convinced that collective bargaining must be strengthened and redirected to focus on academic achievement. It remains an open question as to whether this view is shared by the majority of Milwaukee's elected school board or by the staff and elected representatives of the MTEA. In the end, actions will speak louder than words.

Absent public pressure for change, why will management and labor act differently? To focus collective bargaining on improved educational outcomes involves real change. Bad teachers need to be terminated, but the current contract, and the district's approach to bargaining, largely preclude that. Individual schools and principals need more autonomy, working with their teachers to develop programs that respond to the students and parents in their schools. The current MPS-MTEA contract treats that need as the exception, not the rule. As for additional spending—something that both MPS administrators and teachers claim is needed—where will the money come from? District expenditures are both governed and driven by bargained salary and benefit levels and state spending limits. Unless voters approve a tax increase through a local referendum, the only way to acquire significant new funds is to limit future or current benefits. There is no evidence that this is likely.

We were under no illusion when we made our proposals that they alone might lead to a changed approach. We and others in Milwaukee strongly support other actions—including school choice for low-income parents and charter schools free of direct MPS regulation. Such experiments are designed to see if outside pressure will give MPS and MTEA a more direct incentive to rethink their relationship and, in the process, use bargaining to improve academic achievement.

Some signs are positive, including an increased emphasis by MPS to create or restructure schools with academic programs that are in high demand (for example, Montessori schools, language immersion programs, and other offerings for which parent waiting lists long have existed). In addition, state and federal court decisions in 1998 enabled Milwaukee's pioneering school choice program for low-income families to expand substantially. Further, a majority of new MPS board members no longer are hostile to the school choice program. The board and new superintendent also have moved to support charter schools with significant autonomy.

As for the MTEA staff and elected leadership, it worked in 1999 with state and national groups in an unprecedented, costly, and eventually unsuccessful campaign to defeat five school board candidates. All five won, creating a new majority. Following the election, the union paid a $5,000 fine after agreeing that it unlawfully failed to report at least tens of thousands of dollars in campaign expenditures. The union campaign featured a citywide mailing directly portraying incumbent John Gardner as "soft" on school violence.

It is against this backdrop that MPS schools entered the 1999–2000 academic year. Thirty-five years after bargaining began, the district and its teachers are in a tenuous relationship, one that frequently has been adversarial. When agreements have been reached, their potential to enhance academic achievement remains unclear. Provisions cited as major changes, in fact, are unproven. Perhaps they will work. Perhaps they will amount to, at best, "tinkering at the margins," to borrow the words of Charles Kerchner in describing the broader national malaise of urban education reform. For example, referring to the occasional use of contract waivers as evidence of a commitment to reform, Kerchner observes:

> Waivers are designed to loosen the constraints of the contract without losing the purpose of collective bargaining. However . . . these reforms . . . no matter how faithfully conducted and thoughtfully executed, have failed to move unions and districts much beyond the educational reform starting gate. Reduced in most cases to sporadic flirtations with flexibility, they have generally been fairly timid, focused on single issues, and hamstrung by much of the same sort of tight procedural language and bureaucratic machinery that characterizes the contracts themselves. . . . Waivers have about them a perpetual air of impermanence. Generally accorded about equal status as other pilot projects [they] tend to be seen by teachers and administrators as temporary educational aberrations. The [union and school district] bureaucracy continues to operate as if little had changed. *In the inevitable test of wills between change and the status quo, change invariably blinks first.*[61]

61. Kerchner (1997, pp. 110–11, emphasis added).

This admonition, used here by Kerchner to describe the contract waiver process, has a broader application when it comes to collective bargaining. As Shanker and Chase warned, for public schools to improve, the traditional goals of bargaining must change.

How likely is that to occur? In Milwaukee, MPS and MTEA do not act collectively as though Shanker or Chase were correct. Abetted by a historically indifferent media and a poorly informed public, many of their actions suggest they believe change poses many more risks than the status quo.

References

Backus, Julie M., and others. 1985. "District Personnel Assessment." Staff Report to the Study Commission on the Quality of Education in the Metropolitan Milwaukee Public Schools. Report 7. September 10.

Ballou, Dale, and Michael Podgursky. 1997. *Teacher Pay and Teacher Quality*. Kalamazoo, Mich.: W. E. Upjohn Institute for Employment Research.

Clear, Delbert, and William Kritek. 1993. "Teachers and Principals in the Milwaukee Public Schools. " In *Seeds of Crisis: A History of MPS from 1920–86*, edited by J. L. Rury and F. A. Cassell, 145–92. University of Wisconsin Press.

Doherty, R. E., and W. E. Oberer. 1967. *Teachers, Schools Boards, and Collective Bargaining: A Changing of the Guard*. Ithaca: New York State School of Industrial and Labor Relations, Cornell University.

Fuller, H. L., and S. B. White. 1995. "Expanded School Choice in Milwaukee: A Profile of Eligible Students and Schools." Wisconsin Policy Research Institute Report. July.

Kerchner, Charles, and others. 1997. *United Mind Workers: Unions and Teaching in the Knowledge Society.* Jossey-Bass.

Kohler, T. C. 1995. "Civic Virtue at Work: Unions as Seedbeds of the Civic Virtues." In *Seedbeds of Virtue*, edited by M. A. Glendon and D. Blankenhorn. Madison Books.

Lamers, W. M. 1974. "Our Roots Grow Deep: A History of MPS from 1836–1967." Milwaukee Public Schools.

Liebmann, George W. 1998. "The Agreement: How Federal, State and Union Regulations Are Destroying Public Education in Maryland." *Calvert Policy Brief,* Vol. II, No. 2. Calvert Institute for Policy Research Baltimore (July).

Munk, La Rae G. 1998. "Collective Bargaining: Bringing Education to the Table." Mackinac Center for Public Policy. Midland, Mich. (August).

Odden, Allen, and Carolyn Kelley. 1997. *Paying Teachers for What They Know and Do: New and Smarter Compensation Strategies to Improve Schools*. Thousand Oaks, Calif.: Corwin Press.

Poltrock, L. A., and S. M. Goss. 1993. "A Union Lawyer's View of Restructuring and Reform." *Journal of Law and Education* (Spring): 177–82.

Rury, J. L., and F. A. Cassell, eds. 1993. *Seeds of Crisis: A History of MPS from 1920–86.* University of Wisconsin Press.

Seitz, R. C. 1965–66. "Legal Aspects of Public School Teacher Negotiating and Participating in Concerted Activities." *Marquette Law Review* (49): 487–511.

T. Rowe Price. 1997. *Retiree Financial Guide.*

Urban, W. J. 1982. *Why Teachers Organized.* Wayne State University Press.

Walsh, D. J., and others. 1985. "Correlates of Educational Performance." Staff Report to the Study Commission on the Quality of Education in the Metropolitan Milwaukee Public Schools. Report 6. September 10.

5

JAMES G. CIBULKA

The NEA and School Choice

S CHOOL CHOICE HAS emerged as one of the most contentious issues in
educational reform.[1] The degree of controversy surrounding this reform
nostrum has seemed to escalate as more "radical" forms of choice, such as
publicly supported vouchers or tax credits, have gained increasing public
acceptance and come to be debated seriously. To be sure, almost all education reforms have generated some controversy. Reforms that threaten, or at
least question, vested interests cannot be expected to do otherwise. From
the viewpoint of teachers unions, what distinguishes choice from reform
proposals for education standards, reconstitution of failing schools, and
various school restructuring schemes is that they threaten the existing
structure of public education, including the stature of unions in the present
institutional arrangements. Although the school choice issue is not unique
among reform issues in generating a high degree of controversy, proposals
for school vouchers have mobilized a broad range of interests, not merely
interest groups representing teachers, administrators, school boards, and

1. In conducting this research I have relied on interviews with national and state NEA officials and
staff, knowledgeable informants concerning the NEA's positions, and review of pertinent organization
documents covering the period 1980 to the present. I wish to thank the many individuals from the
NEA who generously provided their time to share information with me, as well as the other individuals who offered me a range of perspectives on the NEA, teachers unions, and education reform.

other participants that normally dominate educational policy decisions. Moreover, as reform of the public schools has catapulted onto the national stage, so has the choice controversy, despite the fact that education is primarily a state and local function. Debates over school choice enlist the attention, resources, and prestige of the president, presidential candidates, members of the U.S. Congress, the national media, members of partisan think tanks, and others.

In addition, choice has become increasingly popular with the general public. While this is not the place to review public opinion polls in detail, a measure of the degree of support for school choice in general was offered by the Gallup Poll in which 59 percent of respondents indicated support for school choice, while 37 percent opposed it (the remaining offered no opinion).[2] Support for vouchers and tax credits, the most extreme forms of school choice in terms of their potential for changing the playing field upon which teachers unions now operate, also has been growing. Additionally, the traditional liberal labor coalition, which proved so durable on many social policy questions for decades, has come apart on this question, with many on the political left, as well as political centrists among both Democrats and Republicans, willing to support some forms of school choice.

Teachers unions, as major educational interest groups, have become important political actors in this debate. Much is at stake, both as regards traditional union issues (wages, benefits, job security, and so on) and larger issues of social policy about which union members often have decided viewpoints (such as the appropriate governance structure and funding of public education).

Critics of teachers unions charge that they are a powerful obstacle to fundamental reforms, not the least being efforts to introduce school choice. In 1994 Republican candidate Bob Dole sounded just this theme when he lambasted teachers unions in his acceptance speech after receiving his party's nomination for the presidency. While his hardball tactics were appealing to a portion of the electorate, many voters interpreted such attacks as simplistic union baiting. It certainly was true that by the mid-1990s teachers unions were trying to change their reputation for stalwart resistance to many of the educational reforms advocated since the 1980s. Under Albert Shanker, the American Federation of Teachers (AFT)

---

2. Gallup Organization (1996).

adopted a new stance that appeared to be more supportive of certain education reforms. The leadership of the largest teachers union, the National Education Association (NEA), advocated "the new unionism," which requires the union to broaden its role from one primarily concerned with improving salaries, benefits, and working conditions to an organization that also concerns itself with improving the quality of public schooling.

At the same time, the NEA has struggled to define a clear and politically defensible position on whether it supports or opposes various forms of school choice. At times, the national organization, and certain state and local affiliates, have opposed nearly all school choice proposals. These positions have varied over time, and there continues to be significant variation among states—and local jurisdictions within states—in their posture toward some forms of choice, such as charter schools. Despite union opposition to many choice proposals, the issue will not go away. Choice advocates are too well organized, with significant financial backing from business groups and conservatively oriented foundations. Public support for choice has been growing as well, perhaps reflecting the breadth of support across the political spectrum, despite efforts by Democrats who oppose choice to label it a Republican platform.

The new unionism would be one potential doctrine by which the NEA could address choice proposals in a proactive way, answering critics who charge that it is reactionary and opposed to school reform. In this chapter I address whether this is likely to occur, given what the doctrine of the new unionism has been taken to mean so far, as well as organizational constraints under which the NEA operates.

Two theoretical perspectives are presented to help interpret the NEA's behavior on school choice. The first model is *institutional*. It portrays the NEA as an interest group pursuing its strategic goals within sharply defined institutional constraints, shaped both by organizational limits and political alliances. The second model, a *leadership regime* perspective, emphasizes the role of national leadership in moving the NEA to a different set of policies concerned with educational quality. Leadership models focus on the role of ideas and strategic choice as opportunities that skillful leaders exploit to change organizations, despite the institutional constraints under which they operate. Through the juxtaposition of the two theoretical perspectives, the NEA's current and past positions on school choice can be clarified. A discussion is also included on the challenge that faces the NEA on school choice.

Choice Defined

In this discussion the concept of school choice includes any institutional arrangement in which parents are given some opportunity to choose a school for their child rather than being assigned to a particular school by the school system. There are many forms of school choice that can operate singly or in combination (for example, intradistrict open enrollment plans, interdistrict open enrollment, public specialty and magnet schools, postsecondary enrollment options, contract schools, charter schools of many sorts, voucher plans, and tax-credit plans). Some of these plans retain the school board as the sole authority, while others allow the school to remain under public authority but be operated independent of the local school board. Some plans involve private schools, whether sectarian or nonsectarian. Some are highly regulated by state or local laws and policies, while others are largely free of them, with many gradations in between. Some plans regulate the choices available to parents, while others do not. Some provide different levels of support to families or to different schools, depending on specific criteria, while others make no such distinctions. School choice, in other words, has many possible configurations and mutations, and the details of these institutional arrangements can have significant implications for cost, effectiveness, and equity, as well as other societal effects. Because of its potential complexity, any one schema for classifying choice is likely to prove inadequate or at least be disputed. For example, the NEA had tried to distinguish privatization, which it opposes, from public school choice, which it supports. However, as will be discussed below, some NEA officials now find this distinction too simplistic to offer guidance as new hybrids of local and state choice plans emerge.

Theory 1: NEA as an Interest Group in an Institutionalized Arena

Institutional theory offers a helpful theoretical perspective for understanding the role teachers unions have played in the governance of public education. While institutional theory has many manifestations, the focus here is on a few of the tenets of an institutional perspective on politics.[3] The first

3. See, for example, March and Olsen (1989).

is that institutional structures shape political outcomes. Individual actors and organizations operate within an institution, which consists of distinct cultural, structural, and normative characteristics that create a common framework for action. In institutionalized arenas, particular organizations must pursue their goals and interests within a wider institutional apparatus that constrains their options. As institutions pursue their self-interest, they not only adapt to their environments, but they also seek to actively shape their environments for their advantage. Accordingly, the distinction between the institution, with its bureaucratic apparatus, and its environment becomes blurred. Interest groups become part of the institutional apparatus, helping to legitimate it as much as to operate upon it. As arenas of action such as K–12 education become institutionalized, there is a tendency for a limited number of actors to dominate both the policy process and its outcomes. As institutional domains have become more powerful, many policy issues now are resolved within relatively closed "policy niches," where few interests are affected and the scope of conflict is narrow.[4] The traditional characterization of niche politics is a closed system controlled by an "iron triangle" of bureaucrats, legislative committees, and interest group actors.

A second tenet of institutional theory is that institutions change slowly. This is true for at least two reasons. First, institutions ignore or suppress some participants, issues viewpoints, and values.[5] Politics and administration are decoupled. Therefore, the capacity to comprehend and interpret changes in order to act in one's rational self-interest becomes problematic. Second, the tendency of institutions to expand their reach in order to control their environment limits the capacity to act coherently. The decoupling of interest and problems into discrete policies, organizations, and advocacy coalitions, while legitimating the order, also fragments it. The organizational components of institutions strive to increase capability by reducing comprehensiveness. Coordination among several components of a problem becomes decoupled.[6] Cognitive blinders and impediments to action reinforce the tendency of institutions to resist change in response to new needs and demands. Whether and how to change become central problems for institutional actors in a period of social and political upheaval such as confronts public education today.

4. Cigler and Loomis (1991, p. 392).
5. Schattschneider (1960).
6. March and Olsen (1989, p. 17).

Variants of this institutional view have been applied to elementary and secondary education.[7] Elsewhere I have argued that the institutionalized order in public education has proven to be a destabilizing factor, reducing the capacity of the educational institution to respond effectively to the demands for educational reforms coming primarily from outside the institution.[8]

What does this institutional model tell us about how organizations such as the NEA could be expected to position themselves on the issue of school choice? First, we would expect the NEA to respond as any institutional actor might when new actors seek to expand their influence, particularly when they propose reforms that would introduce new forms of governance providing parents, and possibly private firms, a greater role in delivery of school services. Such efforts will be resisted, and the resistance will take on the character of an all-out effort to exclude and overcome the adversary rather than seek accommodation and compromise. Second, apart from the political resistance that might be expected to ensue, institutional actors will have difficulty conceptualizing *how* to change. Insofar as the changes being advocated from outside require some fundamental rethinking of basic belief systems, the governing apparatus, and working relationships among stakeholders, the institutionalized arena will prove to be an impediment and perhaps even a fundamental obstacle.

A historical examination of the NEA's evolving position on issues of school choice is consistent in many respects with an institutional perspective on its activity. The organization was a tardy and reluctant player in school reform. For example, it paid little attention to the school choice issue until it appeared to be an externally imposed threat. The national organization took little interest in school choice issues until the early 1990s. The organization was not entirely silent on the issue, to be sure. A variety of voucher initiatives and referenda came before voters in various states, beginning in 1966. In 1970 the NEA first went on record in opposition to vouchers, which "could lead to racial, economic, and social isolation of children and weaken or destroy the public school system."[9] In 1974 it passed a resolution linking such plans to other "deleterious programs," such as performance contracting, planned program budgeting systems

7. Meyer and Rowan (1977); Crowson, Boyd, and Mawhinney (1996); Rowan and Miskel (1999).

8. Cibulka (1995).

9. National Education Association, Resolution A-30 (1997).

(PPBS), and evaluations by private, profit-making groups.[10] (This same position was reaffirmed and updated in 1993.) When the Reagan administration advocated tuition tax credits at the federal level, the NEA opposed such plans introduced in Congress and in state legislatures. In 1984 and again in 1989 it passed resolutions denouncing tuition tax credits.[11]

Some of the earliest forms of public school choice were introduced in the 1970s and involved choice within school districts, often for purposes of promoting desegregation. These intradistrict choice plans never attracted enough attention to warrant any resolutions adopted by the governing body of the NEA, the Representative Assembly, and, in fact, were not even treated as choice plans. The NEA's legislative program long has supported federal programs of categorical assistance, including magnet schools. The NEA's position is that such programs should not be treated as choice programs since they bear little resemblance to privatization schemes implicit in other forms of choice. According to one national official, the NEA has not done a lot on public school choice. Primarily it has concerned itself with whether students participating in such intradistrict choice programs have equitable access to information, transportation, and other services. The NEA generally supports "controlled choice" plans such as those in Cambridge, Massachusetts, which in its view protect students and families who do not have resources available to middle-class patrons utilizing choice. Such plans often have been introduced in response to a desegregation court order, and unions have sought to protect the transfer rights of teachers when efforts are made to desegregate school faculties. These matters frequently have been negotiated by unions on behalf of their members as part of the court order or in a settlement pursuant thereto. Thus while intradistrict school choice plans have not been without potential problems for teachers unions, typically they were not interpreted by local districts as posing a fundamental threat. Moreover, such matters were treated as local issues that rarely involved state affiliates.

The NEA has not supported interdistrict public school choice plans, however. In 1989 it issued its first pronouncement, in the form of a resolution, opposing federally or state-mandated choice and parental option plans:

> The National Education Association believes that federally or state-mandated parental option or choice plans compromise the Association's commitment to free, equitable, universal, and quality public

10. National Education Association, Resolution A-27 (1997).
11. National Education Association, Resolution A-29 (1997).

education for every student. Therefore, the Association opposes such federally or state-mandated choice or parental option plans.

The Association believes that local districts, in partnership with state and federal governments, must provide a quality education for every student by securing sufficient funding to maintain and to enhance excellence in each local public school district.

The Association continues to support alternative programs for specific purposes in the public schools.[12]

In other words, the NEA attempted to draw a line between the relatively narrow scope of intradistrict plans and those that involve transfers of pupils between districts. Apart from the philosophical opposition stated in the above resolution, there has been a more practical reason to view such interdistrict plans with suspicion. Revenue declines for districts that suffer a net loss of resident pupils to other districts can lead to loss of teaching jobs.

Despite the NEA's stated opposition to the above forms of choice, interest in the concept by policymakers, as well as the general public, continued to build in the 1990s. The Wisconsin state legislature had created the first voucher program in the country in 1990, and it has continued to receive widespread media coverage and attention by policymakers nationwide. That same year Oregon voters defeated a voucher initiative. Voucher legislation was defeated in Pennsylvania in 1991 and in Colorado in 1992. Choice increasingly was in the air, and the NEA found itself in a defensive posture. NEA officials throughout the country became alarmed at what they perceived as a concerted attack on public education and on the NEA by the political right. They labeled these efforts "privatization," which in some of its manifestations is a concept broader than choice.[13] Privatization obviously raised a new set of issues for teachers unions beyond those raised by interdistrict school choice plans. From the union's perspective as a protector of teachers' jobs, privatization could pose a host of threats if existing collective bargaining contracts and processes were abrogated.

Because choice proposals were being advocated for the most part by noneducators outside the relatively narrow policy niche in which unions traditionally wielded great power, these proposals also posed another threat. Direct ballot initiatives were expensive to counter and involved

12. National Education Association, Resolution A-28 (1997).

13. For example, the experiment in Baltimore to have Education Alternatives, Inc., operate nine elementary schools was a contractual arrangement between the city of Baltimore, which at that time had authority over the public school system, and a private firm.

strategies that were relatively new to educator groups in some states. (California was an exception, having experienced Proposition 13 in the 1970s and others in the 1980s.) Accordingly, state affiliates were turning to the national organization for help and guidance. Until that point all such matters were handled by the national organization's legislative affairs unit, which was not structured to provide the help requested by state affiliates facing "privatization" initiatives. (Choice is viewed as one kind of privatization by the NEA, and thus the terms are sometimes used interchangeably.) This assistance was especially critical in states whose affiliates were too small or that lacked the organizational capacity to respond to choice initiatives in their state.

The organization's board of directors decided that a coherent response was necessary. In early 1993 it brought together an interdisciplinary group to create the Center for the Preservation of Public Education, which operated out of national headquarters in Washington, D.C. The new center began to monitor activities and proposals of opponents. It prepared a training manual—"The People's Cause: Mobilizing for Public Education." The manual provided a wealth of information, political strategies, and "talking points" on various facets of the choice issue, and even provided detailed overheads for use in workshops. A lengthy section of the manual provides information about individuals and organizations advocating privatization. The center updated and augmented its manual annually and organized annual meetings for purposes of implementing the strategies contained in the manual and to provide an opportunity for representatives to network with one another.

The center represented a new strategy for NEA. It pooled information from across the country and shared successful strategies. It also developed clear statements about why the NEA opposes vouchers and privatization initiatives such as corporate takeovers, which could be used by members. For example, the manual explained that NEA believes vouchers are bad public policy because:

—Vouchers would increase the cost of education.

—Vouchers are not real choice. It is the private schools, not the parents, who have the real choice.

—Vouchers would decrease accountability in education.

—Vouchers do not enhance competition between public and private schools.[14]

14. National Education Association (1993).

The manual also instructs members on how to debunk myths perpetrated by voucher backers such as "the free market economist Milton Friedman." Among the myths cited are that public support for vouchers is large and growing, that vouchers will increase accountability in education, and that private school students outperform public school students.

The NEA's position on school choice evolved from indifference to active hostility toward choice proponents. Its efforts on this issue resembled its customary way of responding to political opponents. The NEA in the early 1990s sought to protect its role as one of the most powerful institutional players in K–12 education, with the political muscle and resources to prevail on issues it considered vital to its interests. It is useful to review how the politics of K–12 education changed to accommodate the rise of teachers unions and how they in turn exercised their power.

Teachers unions benefited from the opening of American politics in the 1960s. They came to power in the 1960s, at the same time as the civil rights movement. The collective power of teachers challenged the relatively closed system of education governance then operative. Teachers unions became an institutional player in public education with the advent of mandated collective bargaining throughout much of the United States in the 1960s and 1970s. Through this process they acquired considerable influence not only over wages, benefits, and conditions of employment but over the educational program of school districts as well.[15] Their financial and organizational resources permitted them to influence the election of sympathetic school board members[16] and members of state legislatures. In some states they gained political influence over the election of the governor or appointment/election of the state superintendent or commissioner of education. At the national level they became active and influential supporters of Democratic presidential candidates and became an influential voice on education bills being considered by Congress. So considerable has been the political influence of teachers unions in many states that they often are reputed to be one of the most powerful among education interest groups.[17]

Teachers unions rose to power in this first wave of the opening of American educational policymaking. Even if educational politics could never be

15. Cooper (1992); Kerchner and Mitchell (1988); McDonnell and Pascal (1988).

16. Zeigler, Jennings, and Peak (1974); Danzberger, Kirst, and Usdan (1992).

17. Their influence varies from state to state, depending on whether they are statutorily recognized as a bargaining agent, which is not the case in many southern states (Lieberman, 1997), and the state political culture and structure (Marshall, Mitchell, and Wirt, 1989).

described as entirely closed or autonomous from external political influence,[18] there is little dispute that in recent years the politics of education has become more open and conflictual, reducing the autonomy of the educational policy arena.[19] Federal policy helped to create a power base for many special interest groups, such as special education parents, the educationally disadvantaged, bilingual groups, and others. Such groups won representation on school boards, and in cities a return to ward or district systems legitimized an older model of constituent representation that progressive reformers had sought to eliminate in public education. Administrative bureaucracies became further fragmented and less amenable to administrative leadership.

Unions were not seeking to reform the policy process for others to participate. Initially they only asked for their rightful place at the bargaining table. Still, the broadening of educational policymaking to include many new groups did not pose a fundamental threat to union power. Through collective bargaining they enjoyed a special authority relationship, complemented by their enormous organizational resources, with a large membership and financial strength.

This institutional order, however, was sharply weakened in the 1980s by the education reform movement. Reform issues have introduced new demands for significant change in the educational system. These demands for restructuring K–12 education present a different agenda than education interest groups traditionally supported before school boards and state legislatures. In most states the political forces behind the education reform movement have come to a great extent from outside this educational "establishment," from segments of business, foundations, the Christian right, and elected officials such as governors and mayors. School choice is an example of a policy advocacy that has come largely from outside education interest groups.

18. Peterson (1974).

19. The involvement of these broader interests in K–12 education reflects a general mobilization of interest groups in American society across the spectrum of policy domains. Thus interest group politics rarely operates today as an "iron triangle" (Salisbury, 1991) controlled by bureaucrats, legislative committees, and interest groups. Cigler and Loomis (1991, p. 392) argue that the involvement of larger numbers of interests or broadened scope of conflict leads to other forms of politics, which they refer to as a policy community, symbolic and public. Within a policy community, for example, many interests contend for dominance, even though the scope of conflict remains narrow. In "public" politics, the scope of conflict broadens to include confrontation.

This institutional perspective captures the predicament in which the NEA finds itself today and helps explain how it has responded over time to demands for school choice. It has less capacity to control political outcomes within the institutional arena of public education than it had two decades ago; its ability to defeat policies that the leadership or members dislike has been weakened. Its influence in local governance through collective bargaining has come under attack.[20] Thus teachers unions have suffered from the public perception, fueled by their critics, that they are only interested in the job security of their members. Moreover, certain school choice policies have the potential to reduce the power of teachers unions. They envision scenarios in which teachers lose the right to bargain collectively, in which their membership in a bargaining unit becomes voluntary, where they are forced to become part of a separate bargaining unit, or where they lose rights of transfer by joining charter schools. Moreover, to the degree that choice policies strengthen the hands of parents, particularly vocally dissatisfied ones who demand better "qualified" teachers, choice poses a further threat to union protection of teachers' jobs. Given these fears, they have acted decisively to protect their hard-won prerogatives.

All this is consistent with the portrayal of the NEA as an institutional actor protecting its self-interest. However, this is not the full story. Although its antiprivatization drive was quite strident and uncompromising, the national NEA, in contrast to some state and local affiliates, took a more accommodating stance on a new concept called charter schools. In some ways charter schools were potentially more threatening than the interdistrict choice plans the NEA long had opposed. The NEA Representative Assembly, while continuing its hard-line opposition to any kind of voucher program, adopted a more moderate position on charter schools. Before turning to a full explanation of these developments, however, it will be useful to set them within an alternative theoretical frame that provides a very different picture of NEA's motives and actions. I described this second theoretical approach at the start as a *leadership regime* perspective.

---

20. The limitations of the traditional approach to collective bargaining are now widely acknowledged. For an excellent discussion see Kerchner and Koppich (1993), Kerchner and Koppich in this volume, and Johnson and Kardos in this volume. For a more critical assessment, see Lieberman (1997) and Fuller, Mitchell, and Hartmann in this volume.

Theory 2: A Leadership Regime Perspective on the NEA's Approach to School Choice

The analytical lens through which the NEA has been viewed as an organization so far has paid little attention to leadership as a force shaping the organization. The institutional model I have been using thus far to illustrate NEA's response to choice has portrayed the union as part of a political environment of constraints where strategic responses to uncertainty and to threats are shaped by relatively fixed imperatives, such as the search for legitimacy and survival.

Karl Weick's conception of organizations portrays them as characterized by ambiguity and a search for meaning.[21] In periods of environmental uncertainty, this tendency is exacerbated. Facts and events no longer carry clear meaning for members of an organization. What constitutes successful action is often in dispute, particularly when the organization experiences a change in leadership.[22]

Leaders help organizations deal with this uncertainty by providing new ways of viewing problems and offering new solutions. Indeed, successful leaders often must be "policy entrepreneurs"[23] who sell innovation to their peers and most especially to their followers. In this way they help organizations to move beyond "exploitative learning" in which organizations manage environmental uncertainty by seeking to pursue their self-interest.[24]

In NEA's case, the leadership posture of the national office underwent a shift. By 1993 a growing number of states had adopted or were considering adoption of charter school laws. Some state affiliates had been unqualified opponents, while others—while not enthusiastic about the concept—had worked with sponsors of charter legislation to make the bills somewhat better than they would otherwise have been if the NEA had merely tried to stonewall the bills. Those states that had used the latter strategy had sometimes ended up with particularly odious laws, from NEA's perspective. Accordingly, the national organization implicitly sided with those state affiliates who worked for compromises. The policy stated the conditions that charters should fulfill. Many of the conditions pertain to teachers' interests, and by implication those of the union that represents them:

21. Weick (1979, 1991).
22. Levitt and March (1996, pp. 522–23).
23. Roberts (1996); Mintrom (1997).
24. March (1991).

—All school employees must be directly involved in the design, implementation, and governance of these programs.

—The charter school should not impact negatively on the regular school program.

—There must be adequate safeguards covering contract and employment provisions for all employees.

—Participation should be voluntary.

—Health and safety standards must be met.

—There must be nondiscrimination and equal employment opportunity.

—Staffing must be by fully licensed professional staff.

—Programs must be adequately funded, include start-up monies and not divert funds from the regular program.

—The program must be assessed and evaluated periodically.[25]

In 1994 the Representative Assembly expanded the licensure provision to include hiring only licensed and certified counseling personnel and to provide all vital student services. Consistent with its attempt to maintain as much influence as possible in the policymaking process, the NEA also has tried to make certain that charter schools are authorized by the local school board and are part of the local school district. Unions are more likely to have some influence on local school boards than on an independently selected charter school board because unions often are active in sponsoring school board candidates and helping them get elected.

This lengthy list of provisos has been viewed by critics of NEA as a public relations gimmick that gives the appearance of supporting change while leaving ample room to oppose any charter school bill that fails to meet the NEA's litmus test. Some state affiliates have used the list that way. With the encouragement of the national office, however, many state affiliates use the list as a guide to bargain for as many provisions as they can get. They recognize from the start that compromise will be necessary but argue that being a player gives them greater influence than a strategy of steadfast resistance. The New Jersey Education Association (NJEA), for instance, worked with charter school sponsors in 1996 and was able to preserve the requirement that teachers be certified (with some qualifications), maintain some tenure provisions for teachers in charter schools, some collective bargaining provisions, rights for teachers who decide to leave charters, and

25. National Education Association, Resolution A-26 (1997). "NEA's Statement on Charter Schools," in *The People's Cause: Mobilizing for Public Education.*

preservation of pension rights and health benefits.[26] NJEA also won a time-specific limit on the number of charter schools (135 in the first four years). These and other concessions would not have been possible had the drafting of the bill been left entirely to charter school advocates, which included some key legislators and the governor.

The California Teachers Association (CTA) took a similar approach in 1992. While officially neutral on charters, they supported the "weaker" of two bills then pending in the legislature, one that would have provided collective bargaining at charter schools.[27] That bill was defeated, however, in favor of another bill. While outmaneuvered, the CTA could argue that it was not stonewalling efforts to create charter schools. Critics of the union charge that it was merely trying to forestall a voucher initiative and did not want charters at all.[28] In 1998 the CTA forestalled a charter school initiative by working with its sponsor, a wealthy thirty-six-year-old retired computer software businessman. The initiative was withdrawn when CTA agreed to changes in the charter school law, some of which it viewed as improving the existing law. Charter schools will have to have credentialed teachers and must meet state accountability standards and assessments. Stronger fiscal accountability provisions will make it more difficult for "rip-off" artists to profit from charter schools at the expense of quality. At the same time, the CTA was forced to concede on the issue of collective bargaining rights.

NEA's critics charge that these conciliatory positions on charter schools often are prompted by efforts to forestall vouchers as well as to cripple charters with onerous restrictions. This was arguably true both in New Jersey and California, depending on how one interprets the facts of each case. Other state affiliates have also negotiated in a similar manner, even when voucher proposals were not pending in their states. NEA's president Bob Chase has denied this charge. He responds that the association is only opposing loosely drawn charters, which amount to "back-door privatization." Instead, the association favors charters that strengthen public education, which is what is in the NEA's interests.[29]

26. Alternative certification is possible. The new charter school may apply the district agreement, bargain as a single unit, or not bargain at all. However, conversion schools must use district contracts.

27. Weakness, obviously, is in the eye of the beholder. Advocates of expansive or unrestricted charter school laws generally take the opposite position from the teachers unions. For example, on this issue, they claim that maintenance of existing collective bargaining agreements will hamstring charter school sponsors' efforts to be innovative and to maintain maximum control over staffing issues and conditions of employment. See Bierlein (1996).

28. Claremont Institute (1994).

29. "Which Charters Are Smarter?" *Education Week*, December 4, 1996, p. 41.

Pennsylvania provides an example. The state's Republican governor, Tom Ridge, was unsuccessful in advocating a voucher bill in the state legislature in 1995 as part of a larger "Kids One Program." Later in proposing the sequel reform package—"Kids Two"—he worked collaboratively with the Pennsylvania State Education Association (PSEA) in drafting a charter school law. Each side got some of what it wanted. For example, the governor wanted no requirement that teachers be certified, while PSEA wanted all teachers to be. The minority chair of the House Education Committee proposed an acceptable compromise that permits 25 percent of the teachers to be uncertified.

Colorado voters defeated a statewide voucher proposal in 1992 and a tax-credit proposal in 1998. The Colorado Education Association (CEA) spent $525,000 to defeat the voucher proposal. Yet the association did not oppose creation of a charter school law in 1993. It participated in the multilateral negotiations called by the governor that eventually led to a charter school law. From CEA's perspective, the law is far from perfect; teachers do not have to be certified, and private subcontracting is permitted.[30] Yet CEA also sponsors a charter school in the city of Colorado Springs. There was, in short, no correspondence between the CEA's opposition to the vouchers and its willingness to endorse a charter school law. The association also has supported interdistrict choice.

In California, Colorado, and Pennsylvania, then, a new strategy is being employed and implicitly endorsed by the national office. Rather than try to stop charter bills, which may pass anyway, they have worked to get the best law possible under the circumstances.

If the NEA has shown an increasing openness toward charter schools, it has not yet modified its stalwart opposition to contracting for services with private for-profit firms. As early as 1969 NEA went on record as opposing subcontracting of teaching and support services, a position it reiterated in 1977, 1989, and 1990.[31] The organization prepared various manuals— *Contracting Out: Strategies for Fighting Back; Contracting Out: Corporate Profiles*—for local affiliates to use in fighting the contracting out of cafeteria, transportation, custodial, and other school support services. As contractors moved from auxiliary services to educational programs and management of entire schools and districts, the array of issues surrounding the phenomenon has become more complex. Nonetheless, the NEA makes

30. A waiver is required.
31. National Education Association, Resolution D-8, F-26 (1997).

virtually no distinction among these types of arrangements. It also opposes contracting out (or subcontracting), such as the contracts provided to Sylvan Learning Systems to provide Chapter 1 remedial services. In addition, the NEA opposes "corporate takeovers" of individual schools or entire districts, such as Education Alternatives, Inc., which formerly ran in Baltimore and Hartford, Connecticut, and currently, Chris Whittle's Edison Project, which operates in approximately fifty schools in various states.

A number of state affiliates have ignored the organization's official national statement on contracting. This is because they have faced the reality, as in the case of charter schools (and sometimes as part of those deliberations) that contracting will happen whether the NEA likes it or not. As one NEA official put it, a simplistic policy of "no, no, no" has less and less credibility.[32] For example, local NEA affiliates in Michigan find it more advantageous to support contracts with the Edison Project than to have them run as charter schools. Students, jobs, and funding remain with the district. Many state regulations also remain in place, such as those on class size. Moreover, Edison must sign an exclusivity clause that says it will not open other schools in the same jurisdiction. If a charter school were to be created, the sending district would lose revenues and teaching jobs. Under California's new charter school law, there are two types of charters. If a charter is run by the local district, teachers can be part of a collective bargaining unit, in contrast to state authorized charters. In the former, contractual arrangements afford greater protection for teachers in wages and working conditions.

The choice between attempting to maintain the status quo and acceding to "conversion" schools arose in Dayton, Ohio, in 1997.[33] Initially the superintendent attempted to convert five failing schools to charter status, which would be operated by the school system. The Dayton Education Association opposed this effort. Then the superintendent proposed giving the schools "conversion" status and having the Edison project run them. The schools would have operated as a legally separate entity with a governing board but still sponsored by the city's school board. Edison officials asked the Dayton Education Association (DEA) to negotiate with them. Under the proposed provisions, the union would have continued negotiating with the city school board, which would then negotiate with the gov-

---

32. Interview, August 3, 1998.
33. In Ohio the term *contract school* is reserved for contracting for noneducational services.

erning board(s) of the conversion schools. Ohio law required the union's consent before the conversion could occur, however, and in a contract vote the DEA members overwhelmingly defeated the proposal. While the original five schools still are open, subsequently the state of Ohio authorized a charter school for the district. The result was loss of students to the school district, loss of state revenue, and potentially loss of teachers' jobs. Subsequently the union expressed some interest in working with a local community group that wished to create a conversion school. However, it was adamantly opposed to working with a for-profit organization like Edison, despite advice from the national office that this might be the preferable course. It accused members of the business community, which were active in pushing for the proposal, of intending to destroy public schools.

The Dayton incident is not isolated. NEA is confronting more and more interest on the part of school boards to contract out both core and noneducational services. According to one NEA estimate, in the 1997–98 school year at least one hundred K–12 public schools were being run by approximately twenty-five for-profit school management firms, in addition to a growing number of schools operated for at-risk students. Most of these are charter schools; the remainder are contract schools. School boards are looking at their failing schools and wanting to hand off their management to a private firm, as an alternative to reconstituting them (or having the state do so).

Thus state and local affiliates in a number of states, acting in what they regard as the prudent best interest of their organization and its members, have ignored national policy, which unequivocally prohibits private contracting. Staff at the national organization are discussing an alternative policy, but they recognize that the membership may oppose any modification. One approach under consideration would delineate criteria for acceptable contractual arrangements, much like the approach to charter schools. This approach is broached in a document released by the newly renamed Center for the Advancement of Public Education (CAPE, formerly the Center for the Preservation of Public Education), entitled "Education, Investors, and Entrepreneurs." While stopping short of developing the explicit criteria under which such contracts would become acceptable, the statement argues that the development of criteria should answer several questions:

—What kind of services do we object to school districts contracting out? (The assumption is that we do not object to contracting out purchase of goods.)

—How does the contracting out of these services harm students, employees, the public, or community interest?

—How can contracts be structured to protect the above groups?[34]

As yet, however, NEA's national leadership has not moved to alter its policy. One explanation given by some staff at the national office is the fear that the Representative Assembly would reject a more moderate approach. An attempt to broaden the policy occurred in 1994 but achieved the opposite effect when a statement was added denouncing "attempts by private corporations and individuals, such as Whittle Communications, to establish schools for profit motives."[35] Many members believe that for-profit enterprises have no place in public education. This view was advanced by the staff at CAPE for five years through its training manual and other materials and now is not easily reversed.

In a modest way NEA president Robert Chase has given support to charter schools. He endorsed a staff recommendation that the national organization, working with state affiliates, begin a small number of charter schools in Arizona, California, Colorado, Connecticut, and Hawaii. The project was intended to be a source of ideas for NEA and its affiliates, as well as for teacher educators who may wish to start a charter school. NEA staff from the Public Education Advocacy Office as well the NEA's Center for Teaching and Learning provide support to the project. One of the questions NEA hoped to answer, and which will be addressed by an outside evaluator, is whether the NEA has the organizational capacity to support this kind of work; can NEA provide the kinds of technical assistance actually needed by the schools? Of the five schools planned, four became operational. While all receive assistance from state and local affiliates, national NEA staff have been the primary impetus for the projects. State and local affiliates appear to be taking a "wait and see" attitude, which has contributed to the slow and cautious start of the charter schools initiative. At the same time, the schools reflect different approaches, which suggests that each is to some degree a home-grown effort. Two involve collaborations with local universities. One is sponsored by a state board of education and run by teachers. Most are new schools, but one is a conversion. The cur-

34. "Education, Investors, and Entrepreneurs: A Framework for Understanding Contracting-out Public Schools and Public School Services," NEA Center for the Advancement of Public Education, May 1998.

35. National Education Association, "Establishment of Schools for Profit Motive," *Proceedings of the Seventy-Third Representative Assembly* (1994): 187–89, 387–88. Two statements were passed as new business items rather than a resolution.

ricula and governance differ as well. The schools embody the principles of experimentation and deregulation at the core of the charter school concept.

According to national officials, they do not expect that the experiment will lead to dramatic changes in NEA's policy on charter schools. The schools have struggled with a variety of challenges, underscoring NEA's conviction that starting and maintaining a charter school is an arduous task.

All this suggests that while there was in 1993 a move to use the national leadership to give the charter limited endorsement, there has been no change since that time and little prospect for change. NEA officials cite other reasons for a reluctance to give the charter school concept a more qualified endorsement. First, and perhaps most important, Chase seems ambivalent. In many public statements he has emphasized that his approach to the new unionism is to improve quality for the entire educational system. Since becoming its president in 1996, Chase has been a "policy entrepreneur" selling his brand of professional unionism. His "new unionism" represents an attempt to espouse equal concern for promoting educational quality without abandoning NEA's traditional role as a protector of employee wages and benefits. This new ethic is nothing less than a struggle to redefine their organizational cultures away from industrial unionism and toward professional unionism.[36] As Chase has operationalized the concept, he emphasizes peer coaching and review, support for high student standards, and merger with the NEA's rival, the AFT. At the 1999 education summit he also endorsed a willingness to support experimentation with the controversial idea of pay for performance for teachers. At the national level, he has been instrumental in expanding organizational resources devoted to promoting educational quality. All these reform nostrums can be supported as consistent with a broad improvement in quality. Charters, he argues, can improve quality, but only for some students, and possibly at the expense of others by siphoning off students, teachers, and resources for the most needy schools. Others close to Chase make similar arguments. Charters are a "boutique" movement whose supporters

36. According to Kerchner and Koppich (1993), professional unionism involves three shifts. Old industrial style unionism emphasizes the separateness of labor and management, while the emerging union of professionals emphasizes the collective aspect of work in schools. The former emphasizes adversarial relationships, while the latter stresses the interdependency of workers and managers. Finally, industrial unionism emphasizes the protection of teachers, in contrast to the protection of teaching. Kerchner, Koppich, and Weeres (1997, p. 9) argue "that defining and measuring quality—for students, for teachers, for schools—is central to what unions need to do." They assert that teachers unions must redefine their role.

have no interest in general reform of the educational system. Some worry that they are being taken over by venture capitalists eager to make a profit.

A second explanation is that the decentralized organizational structure of NEA encourages its leader to be very selective in his or her role as a policy entrepreneur.[37] As a national organization, the NEA is a federation of state associations, which in turn have local affiliates. Furthermore, the NEA is governed by a Representative Assembly, which permits policy to be formed democratically. While the board of directors and executive committee have specific powers, it is the Representative Assembly consisting of 9,175 members who set policy and objectives. Unlike the AFT's more centralized trade union model of organization, the NEA prizes the autonomy of state and local affiliates as evidence of its commitment to professionalism.[38] This difference between the AFT and NEA was one factor making the Representative Assembly not inclined to approve a merger of the two organizations in 1998.

In these circumstances, national policy often emerges slowly and incrementally. Even when state affiliates act in ways that embarrass the national organization—as has been the case in some battles waged by state affiliates against charter school laws—national leaders have limited capacity to prevent such embarrassments. The burden of proof favors leaving discretion to fifty state affiliates and even larger numbers of local affiliates, whose circumstances, problems, and responses often differ. Problems percolate to the top when local responses prove inadequate, as judged by a sufficiently large number of the membership's delegates. It is only then that the case for responding to a problem with policy at a national level may be sufficiently compelling. In an organization such as the NEA, then, a leader may have to use considerable political resources to shape national policy. The dynamics of the organization militate toward generating policies that are reflexive in nature—reactive and coping instead of proactive and preventative.

Conclusion

In this chapter I have examined the history of NEA's position on school choice issues. NEA's position on choice, it turns out, is really a number of

37. In a sense, this is an institutional reality that surrounds any new regime, thus illustrating how the institutional, interest-group perspective in Model 1 constrains Model 2.

38. NEA's efforts to democratize included efforts to achieve equality for women in the profession and in the association and members' control of the association through the Representative Assembly. See Wesley (1957, pp. 322–33).

different positions. It has taken little interest in intradistrict choice but supports it in a qualified way and carefully distinguishes it from other kinds of choice. Vouchers are opposed. Chase denounced the Wisconsin supreme court decision upholding the constitutionality of publicly funded vouchers to send low-income Milwaukee children to religious schools. He called the decision a bad one and asserted that "these tax dollars could be better spent on smaller classes, modernizing Milwaukee schools, and helping teachers become the most qualified they can be—improvements that will help every Milwaukee child."[39] More recently he denounced Florida's statewide voucher law.

On charters, the NEA has given qualified endorsement, and individual state affiliates have acted in a variety of ways ranging from steadfast opposition to acceptance. On contracting out, the official national policy remains unequivocally opposed, despite actions in a number of states to cooperate with for-profit firms organized as contract schools or charter schools. Interdistrict choice is opposed.

Two different theoretical perspectives to interpret the NEA's position on this issue were used. While an institutional perspective does not explain all aspects of its position (the exception being qualified support for charter schools), this model is a better explanation than its rival hypothesis—that NEA's new leadership regime has shaped a new agenda that includes support for school choice. On many questions Chase has proven to be a most effective policy entrepreneur, but he has been unwilling to include choice in that reform agenda.

In his first term as NEA president, Chase successfully brought NEA into the mainstream of educational reform, so that it no longer appeared to be an all-out obstructionist of change. He has even endorsed the idea that schools should be more accountable for student outcomes.[40] How far toward the center it has moved is illustrated by the fact that the NEA and AFT, along with some other education groups, were present at the 1999 education summit with governors and major business leaders. The action statement released by the summit leaders endorsed, among other things, charter schools, but owing to differences among the participants steered clear of the voucher question. NEA's support for other themes sounded in the summit—teacher quality, higher performance by students on

39. Press release, "NEA President Says Wisconsin Voucher Decision Is Bad for Kids and Vouchers Remain Bad Policy," June 10, 1998.

40. The NEA has adopted resolutions supporting both excellence in education (A-3) and school accountability (A-10).

standards-based curricula, and greater accountability for performance—made it a credible voice in the politics of education.

There is little to suggest from its past behavior, however, that the NEA will add choice—even charters—to its core agenda for reforming schools. To be sure, like any prudent institutional actor, it will seek to preserve its role as a credible player. If support for charters gains momentum, it can be expected to move reluctantly with that consensus. Yet for the foreseeable future, the NEA's leadership on school reform will be reserved for other policies more consistent with its ideology and interests.

References

Bierlein, L. A. 1996. *Charter Schools: Initial Findings.* Denver, Colo.: Education Commission of the States.

Cibulka, J. G. 1995. "The Institutionalization of Public Schools: The Decline of Legitimating Myths and the Politics of Organizational Instability." In *Advances in Research and Theories of School Management and Educational Policy,* edited by R. T. Ogawa, 123–58. Greenwich, Conn.: JAI Press, Inc.

Cigler, A. J., and B. A. Loomis. 1991. "Organized Interests and the Search for Certainty." In *Interest Group Politics,* edited by A. J. Cigler and B. A. Loomis, 385–98. Congressional Quarterly.

Claremont Institute. 1994. *The California Teachers Association: Power Politics versus Education Reform,* #1994–36. Sacramento, Calif.: Golden State Center for Policy Studies.

Cooper, B. S. 1992. *Labor Relations in Education: An International Perspective.* Greenwood Press.

Crowson, R. L., W. L. Boyd, and H. B. Mawhinney. 1996. *The Politics of Education and the New Institutionalism.* New York: Falmer.

Danzberger, J., M. Kirst, and M. Usdan. 1992. *Governing Public Schools: New Times, New Requirements.* Washington, D.C.: Institute for Educational Improvement.

Elam, S. M., L. C. Rose, and A. M. Gallup. 1996. "The Twenty-Sixth Annual Phi Delta Kappa/Gallup Poll of the Public's Attitudes toward the Public Schools." *Phi Delta Kappan* 78, 1 (September): 41–59.

Gallup Organization. 1996. "Opinion Referendum: Ranking." *Gallup Poll Monthly* 368 (May).

Kerchner, C. T., and D. E. Mitchell. 1988. *The Changing Idea of a Teachers Union.* Bristol, Pa.: Falmer.

Kerchner, C. T., and J. E. Koppich. 1993. *A Union of Professionals: Unions and Management in Turbulent Times.* Teachers College Press.

Kerchner, C. T., J. E. Koppich, and J. G. Weeres. 1997. *United Mind Workers: Unions and Teaching in the Knowledge Society.*: Jossey-Bass.

Levinthal, D., and J. G. March. 1981. "A Model of Adaptive Organizational Search." *Journal of Economic Behavior and Organization* 2: 307–33.

Levitt, B., and J. G. March. 1996. "Organizational Learning." In *Organizational Learning*, edited by M. D. Cohen and L. S. Sproull, 516–40. Sage.

Lieberman, M. 1997. *The Teacher Unions: How the NEA and AFT Sabotage Reform and Hold Students, Parents, Teachers, and Taxpayers Hostage to the Bureaucracy*. Free Press.

March, J. G. 1991. "Exploration and Exploitation in Organizational Learning." *Organization Science* 2(1): 71–87.

March, J. G., and J. P. Olsen. 1989. *Rediscovering Institutions: The Organizational Basis of Politics*. Free Press.

Marshall, C., D. Mitchell, and F. Wirt. 1989. *Culture and Education Policy in the United States*. London: Falmer Press.

McDonnell, L. M., and A. Pascal. 1988. *Teachers Unions and Educational Reform*. Santa Monica, Calif.: Rand Corporation and Center for Policy Research in Education, Rutgers University and University of Wisconsin-Madison.

Meyer, J. W., and B. Rowan. 1977. "Institutionalized Organizations: Formal Structure as Myth and Ceremony." *American Journal of Sociology* 83, 2 (September): 340–63.

Mintrom, Michael. 1997. "Policy Entrepreneurs and the Diffusion of Innovation." *American Journal of Political Science* 41 (3): 738–70.

National Education Association. 1993. *The People's Cause: Mobilizing for Public Education*.

———. 1994. *Proceedings of the Seventy-Third Representative Assembly*.

———. 1997. *NEA Handbook, 1997–98*. Washington, D.C.

Peterson, P. E. 1974. "The Politics of American Education." In *Review of Research in Education*, Vol. 2, edited by F. Kerlinger and J. Carroll, 226–56. Itasca, Ill.: Peacock.

Roberts, N. C. 1996. *Transforming Public Policy: Dynamics of Policy Entrepreneurship and Innovation*. Jossey-Bass.

Rowan, B., and C. G. Miskel. 1999. "Institutional Theory and the Study of Educational Organizations." In *Handbook of Research on Educational Administration*, edited by J. Murphy and K. S. Louis, 359–84. Jossey-Bass.

Salisbury, R. 1991. "Putting Interests Back into Interest Groups." In *Interest Group Politics*, edited by A. J. Cigler and B. A. Loomis, 371–84. Congressional Quarterly.

Schattschneider, E. E. 1960. *The Semi-Sovereign People*. Holt, Rinehart, and Winston.

Weick, K. E. 1979. *The Social Psychology of Organizing*. 2d ed. Addison-Wesley.

———. 1991. "The Nontraditional Quality of Organizational Learning." *Organizational Science* 2(1): 72–91.

Wesley, E. B. 1957. *NEA: The First Hundred Years: The Building of the Teaching Profession*. Harper and Brothers.

Zeigler, L. H., M. K. Jennings, and G. W. Peak. 1974. *Governing American Schools: Political Interaction in Local School Districts*. North Scituate, Mass.: Duxbury.

6

WILLIAM LOWE BOYD
DAVID N. PLANK
GARY SYKES

Teachers Unions in Hard Times

How are the mighty fallen, and the weapons of war
perished!

II Samuel, 1:26–27

I N THE 1970S AND 1980S teachers unions in Michigan and Pennsylvania were among the most powerful in the United States. They won
rapid and substantial gains for their members, in large part because of their
readiness to send teachers out on strike, and they played a dominant role
in school politics and state politics more generally. With the election of
activist Republican governors in both Michigan and Pennsylvania in the
1990s, however, the power of the teachers unions began to decline precip-
itously. They now find themselves in an extremely weak position in both
states. Rather than being the protagonists of reform they are bystanders at
the reform parade. At times they are even the objects of reforms initiated
by their political adversaries.

In Michigan, Governor John Engler and his allies have devoted considerable political energy to reducing the power of teachers unions, por-

The authors' names are listed in alphabetical order.

traying the unions as obstacles to needed changes in the educational system and justifying attacks on the unions as essential steps toward educational reform. Michigan's teachers unions have played into this strategy, and arguably made their own situation worse, by responding to political attacks with transparently political counterattacks, by predictably and vehemently opposing proposals for educational change put forward by their political rivals, by insisting that educational improvement necessarily requires more money for the public school system, and by defending the claim that an attack on the teachers unions is the same as an attack on public education. This last claim has been significantly undermined, however, both by the concerted efforts of the governor to deny it and by the unions' past adherence to a strategy based on frequent strikes and "political hardball." In Pennsylvania, Governor Tom Ridge has argued that the whole public school monopoly needs to be opened up and made more efficient, effective, and accountable. Rather than attacking the teachers unions directly, he has pursued policies that implicitly damage the interests of the public school establishment, ignoring or bypassing unions and other defenders of the status quo in the process.

Neither Governor Ridge nor Governor Engler has seen any need to enlist the unions as partners in advancing their reform agendas, which include expanded opportunities for parental choice and an enhanced state role in setting and enforcing academic standards. For their part, the unions in both states have failed to advance a politically viable alternative to the reform strategies favored by their adversaries. Their energies are largely devoted to protecting their members against erosion in their economic position and to defending the public school system against the threat of vouchers. As the unions' power has diminished, however, their capacity to accomplish either of these ends has fallen into some doubt.

If the ultimate goal of educational reform is school improvement, the governors' strategy depends for its ultimate success on the recruitment of teachers to the cause of reform, independent of their unions. (If the goal is to weaken the "public school monopoly," on the other hand, there is no need to recruit teachers at all.) The question that remains to be answered is whether teachers will rally to the cause of school improvement when the reforms championed by Governors Engler and Ridge appear likely to bring them less job security, closer evaluation, and reduced salaries and benefits. This question is addressed in the concluding sections of this chapter.

Michigan: Losing Battles

The recent history of teachers unions in Michigan is a history of defeat and decline.[1] In the late 1960s and 1970s, strengthened by new legislation on collective bargaining for public sector employees, the Michigan Education Association (MEA) and the Michigan Federation of Teachers (MFT) won dramatic gains in salaries, benefits, and job security for their members. These gains were won in substantial part through the unions' exploitation of an expanded right to strike, in conjunction with pattern bargaining that sought to match gains won in one district (often after a strike) with similar gains in neighboring districts. Between 1967 and 1980 there were 454 teachers' strikes against public school districts in Michigan, an average of almost 35 a year.[2]

In the 1980s the strikes continued, at a somewhat diminished pace (18 a year, on average) and teachers' salaries continued to rise rapidly. In addition, the MEA established itself as one of the dominant forces in Michigan politics, assuming "Godzilla-like" preeminence within the state Democratic party. For example, the MEA was reported to have provided more than $1.4 million in political contributions in 1992 to candidates and causes, including more than $900,000 for Democratic candidates for the Michigan House of Representatives. The union was also identified as one of the two most powerful lobbying organizations in Michigan, along with the Chamber of Commerce.[3] The political fortunes of Michigan's teachers unions took a decisive turn for the worse in 1990, however, when John Engler upset James Blanchard to win the gubernatorial election. Engler's animosity toward the MEA was and remains one of the abiding principles of his political career. From his first election to the legislature in 1970 Engler sought two main goals: to reduce property taxes and to reduce the power of the teachers unions. According to one observer of Michigan politics:

> I think that [Engler's] anger began more as a matter of outrage and resentment against the MEA and its power. And the idea that the big

1. This section is based in part on interviews conducted with state-level leaders from the Michigan Education Association and the Michigan Federation of Teachers, and with the presidents of union locals in metropolitan Lansing. This research was conducted in the course of a larger project on "The Ecology of School Choice," which has received funding from the Spencer Foundation and the Provost's Office at Michigan State University. Brad Carl, Sharman Oliver, and Nancy Schwartz provided valuable research assistance.

2. Citizens Research Council (1994).

3. McDiarmid (1993); Farrell (1993); *Inside Michigan Politics* (1993).

unions were controlling so many legislators—and in particular the majority party—and ramming through all this legislation. And the teachers were getting more and more, higher and higher salaries, more and more benefits. And that, furthermore, they were constantly funding Democratic campaigns. . . . The guy immediately started to work up a real hate and it's never abated.

In the governor's office Engler worked systematically to reduce the power of the MEA, carrying forward the campaign that he had begun in the legislature. For its part, the MEA opposed Engler's education policy initiatives at every opportunity and mobilized to defeat him at the polls. A full year before the 1994 gubernatorial election the MEA's executive board took the unprecedented step of meeting and resolving to reject Engler as a candidate for reelection. Having chosen to play "political hardball" (in the words of Lieutenant Governor Richard Posthumus), however, the MEA suffered some major losses as Michigan's political environment changed.

Governor Engler's triumph over the teachers unions is now virtually complete. He and his allies have successfully demonized the MEA as one of the principal obstacles to educational reform in Michigan, and the union's political influence has been significantly diminished.[4] Teachers have lost their right to strike, and with it much of their leverage in negotiations with local school boards. Their salaries are effectively frozen and their benefits are under threat. Michigan's other teacher union has suffered along with the MEA, as an MFT leader acknowledges. "He killed us. He went after the MEA and ended up killing us. We were just an annoyance, not an enemy."

Shifts in State Policy

Shortly after assuming the governor's office Engler fulfilled a campaign promise and put forward a proposal to reduce property taxes and redistribute financial resources in favor of poorer school districts. The MEA organized the opposition to the governor's "Cut and Cap" plan, which was defeated in a referendum in 1992. Politically vulnerable because of his failure to deliver on his pledge to cut taxes, the governor recruited the support

4. This reflects a broader decline in the political influence of organized labor in Michigan. In the last two gubernatorial elections the candidate favored by the principal unions has lost in the Democratic primary, and the successful Democratic candidates have been easily defeated by Governor John Engler despite strong union support.

of his erstwhile opponents, including the MEA, and put forward a revised plan (the first Proposal A) the following year. Despite nearly universal support from the public school establishment (including the Chamber of Commerce) and the virtual absence of organized opposition, the governor's plan was once again rejected by the voters.[5]

The urgency of property tax reduction and school finance reform had increased substantially in Michigan when the Kalkaska school district closed its schools in March 1993.[6] The school board and the teachers union agreed to close the schools three months early rather than make program cuts, after local voters declined for the third time to approve an increase in property taxes to fund school operations. Led by the MEA, Michigan educators portrayed the closing of the Kalkaska schools as a signal that the state government needed to increase its financial support for public education. The president of the union argued that Kalkaska "could be any school district in the state. What Kalkaska has done for so many of our citizens is highlight what we said about the crisis being real."[7] Governor Engler and his allies interpreted events rather differently, however, arguing that Kalkaska illustrated the selfish and insatiable appetite of educators for additional funds and their refusal to consider measures to restrain costs or to put the interests of taxpayers or students ahead of their own.

Soon thereafter a Democratic legislator, positioning herself for a gubernatorial campaign, proposed that property taxes simply be eliminated as a funding source for public schools. Recognizing an extraordinary political opportunity, the Republican caucus supported her bill, and Governor Engler signed it. In the ensuing debate over how to replace the lost revenue, the MEA found itself politically isolated in its advocacy for the restoration of the status quo.[8] At the end of a protracted political struggle Michigan voters approved Proposal A, which shifted the main responsibility for funding schools from local school districts to the state.[9] The changes initiated

5. The first Proposal A was defeated mainly because voters in metropolitan Detroit and the urban corridor north of the city objected to the proposed redistribution of school revenues in favor of "outstate" districts.

6. Plank (1994).

7. Freeman and Hornbeck (1993).

8. Plank (1994).

9. Ballot proposals in Michigan are designated by letters. This was the second consecutive "Proposal A" to address school funding issues, following the defeat of the first Proposal A in 1993. The second Proposal A was substantially more radical than the first. Plank (1994); Courant, Gramlich, and Loeb (1994); Vergari (1995).

by Proposal A decisively altered the education policy environment in Michigan, to the disadvantage of the teachers unions.

Apart from a significant reduction in property taxes, Proposal A had two main consequences. First, it eliminated school districts' discretionary power to increase their operating revenues, by barring them from raising operational revenues from millages.[10] As a result, annual revenue increases for all of Michigan's school districts are set in the legislature, which means that the bargaining space for local teachers and school boards is narrowly constrained. Boards can no longer go to their voters to fund salary increases for teachers that exceed the rate of increase in legislative appropriations, which means that the cost of the raises awarded to teachers can be directly measured in terms of forgone expenditures in other programs.

Second, Proposal A shifted the basis of educational funding from school districts to students. Under the new funding system the only way that school districts can increase their revenues is by increasing the number of students enrolled in the district. Moreover, the per pupil subsidies provided by the state are portable, as property tax revenues were not, which opens the way to expanded opportunities for parental choice. In 1994 the Michigan legislature adopted one of the nation's strongest charter school laws, which was buttressed in 1995 by legislation allowing students to attend schools in other districts than the ones in which they reside. Michigan already has the third-largest number of charter schools in the United States, after Arizona and California, and the current Republican majority in the legislature is likely to remove the present cap on the number of charters that can be issued.[11] The legislature may also remove a provision in the interdistrict choice law that restricts transfers to schools within the same county. The strategic importance of the shift in school finance policy was signaled by Governor Engler when he signed the bill eliminating the property tax as a funding source for public schools. At the signing ceremony Engler affirmed that "the power and control the teachers unions have had over education policies in Michigan ended this morning."[12]

Emboldened by their victory on Proposal A, Republicans in the Michigan legislature shortly thereafter took advantage of their temporary majority in the House to push through a bill that directly challenged the

10. Funds for capital expenditures continue to be raised locally, through the issuance of bonds.
11. Mintrom (1998).
12. McDiarmid (1993).

power of teachers unions.[13] The bill, known as PA 112, had three main effects. First, it removed a number of significant issues from the bargaining table, making decisions about these the exclusive prerogative of school boards.

> PA 112 prohibits bargaining over the policyholder of employee group insurance benefits [a direct blow against the MEA and its subsidiary insurance operation]; the school year starting day; the makeup of site-based decision-making bodies or of school improvement committees; whether school districts should act as an authorizing body to grant a charter for public school academies [charter schools] or a leave of absence to a public school employee wishing to participate in an academy; whether to privatize non-instructional support services or to use volunteers; or the use of experimental educational or pilot programs.[14]

Second, in the event that negotiations between school boards and teachers unions reach an impasse, the Act allows the school board to unilaterally impose its "last best offer" without the agreement of the union. Finally, PA 112 imposed severe penalties on teachers who strike, including fines of one day's pay for each instructional day they are out of the classroom. Similarly, stiff fines may be imposed on the unions to which striking teachers belong.[15]

PA 112 was presented by the governor and his allies as a necessary measure to "level the playing field" in collective negotiations and to provide public school districts with the power they needed to contain costs. It was strongly supported by the Michigan Association of School Boards, as well as by business and taxpayer organizations. From the point of view of the teachers unions, however, PA 112 looked quite different. In the words of one MFT leader, "It was a stake through the heart."

13. The bill was passed by the House at midnight, with no Democratic votes. One Republican member returned from Venezuela to cast his vote. The bill passed the Senate on a party-line vote a week later, as a Republican senator returned from a two-month medical absence to cast the deciding vote, arriving on the floor from a hospital bed set up in the lieutenant governor's office.

14. Citizens Research Council (1994).

15. In September 1999 teachers in the Detroit Public Schools staged a nine-day strike at the beginning of the school year, against the advice of local and state union leaders. The school board and superintendent declined to invoke statutory sanctions against the strikers, choosing instead to continue negotiations. The Detroit school board's failure to enforce available penalties against the teachers and their union produced immediate efforts in the legislature to make the penalties mandatory.

For teachers and their unions, the damage done by Proposal A and PA 112 was compounded by the Michigan School Code revision of 1996, which increased the statutory number of instructional days for Michigan school children from 180 to 190. In the constricted fiscal environment in which school boards and teachers unions now negotiate, legislative approval of this change was widely perceived as a further attack on teachers, as there is almost no chance that teachers' salaries will be increased to compensate for their increased workload.

Political Strategy

The political strategy pursued by Governor Engler and his allies has been to draw a distinction between the unions and their members, attacking the former mercilessly while seeking to avoid the charge of teacher bashing. A Republican member of the state board of education explained how this works.[16]

> The struggle between the leadership of the Michigan Education Association and Governor Engler is clearly not a battle about education, but a battle about power. . . . We must separate the union from the union members in our thinking about educational issues. Individual teachers are concerned with educational quality. . . . The leadership of the Michigan Education Association is, and should be, concerned with promoting the political and economic power of the union. When we make this clear in our discussions it will put into proper perspective what the real issues are in the education debate in Michigan.

The strategy adopted by the MEA to respond to Governor Engler's attacks has played directly to the governor's strengths. In a dramatically changed political environment the "hardball" tactics that had been so effective in the 1980s succeeded mainly in confirming the portrait of the union that the governor and his allies were attempting to convey. The governor sought to cast the MEA as the diehard defender of a bankrupt status quo in the public school system; the MEA obliged him by defending the performance and commitment of public educators against widespread public

16. Wolfram (1994).

perceptions of crisis and decline, mobilizing opposition to virtually all of Governor Engler's policy initiatives and lobbying single-mindedly for additional revenues for schools. Fully absorbed in defending itself and its members against the governor's attacks, the union failed to identify itself with a positive commitment to change, thereby ceding the "reform" banner to the governor.[17]

As a result, Governor Engler swept from victory to victory. The power of the teachers unions in Michigan has been systematically dismantled, and the governor's other education policy goals—property tax reduction, redistribution of revenues in favor of poor rural districts, charter schools, interdistrict choice, school code revision, enhanced statewide testing— have been adopted and implemented despite the MEA's opposition. Engler plausibly presents himself as an "education governor," strongly committed to reform and the improvement of Michigan's schools. His strategy has been imitated by Republicans across the country, including Bob Dole in his 1996 presidential campaign and Governor Pete Wilson of California in his unsuccessful campaign to win approval of an omnibus package of educational reforms known as Proposal 8.

> Engler's lesson in Michigan—that it is possible to take on the teachers without committing political suicide—is resonating in other states. . . . Attacking teachers as a profession is a loser. Confronting teachers as a labor union, however, can produce political returns by portraying their opposition to such proposals as school vouchers, charter schools, and merit pay as nothing more than defense of the status quo.[18]

The MEA has recently devoted its energies to campaigns in the legislature to guarantee that per pupil funding levels will be maintained at current levels and to make the state's "model core curriculum" mandatory. The former measure would oblige the legislature to make financial provision for increases in public school enrollments and would (not coincidentally) cripple any effort to introduce vouchers in Michigan. The latter would require large increases in state funding for schools because the Michigan constitu-

---

17. In the 1998 gubernatorial campaign, the hapless Democratic candidate's education platform called for a reversal of the funding shifts enacted in Proposal A and for the repeal of PA 112 and the restoration of teachers' right to strike. It is doubtful whether anyone outside the teachers unions believed that either change would bring about improvement in Michigan's schools.

18. Mahtesian (1995).

tion prohibits unfunded mandates; if some school districts were unable to bear the cost of the "mandated" core curriculum, then the state would be obliged to provide the necessary resources. Neither of these proposals appears likely to win approval in the present political environment. Leaders from the MFT concede that it is "almost impossible" to work with the legislature and have begun to exert greater efforts to influence elections for local school boards.

Local Consequences

At the local level the unions' bargaining position has been severely undermined by Proposal A and especially by the "no-strike" provisions of PA 112. "We don't do collective bargaining any more," says one union president. "We do collective begging." The hand of school boards in negotiations has been greatly strengthened, and according to this official boards are taking advantage of the unions' weakness to "kick our butts." Most union locals consequently devote their energies to protecting past gains and resisting takebacks, with retirement and benefits the key battlegrounds. Many have also increased their involvement in local politics, trying to ensure the election of sympathetic candidates (including some Republicans) to local school boards and to the Michigan legislature.

According to an MEA leader, "in most places it is no longer an issue of economic gains for members." His members are seeking "to keep up with inflation, and keep their benefits, but the real issues they're negotiating over are quality issues, and they're frustrated." The "quality issues" identified by this official include reductions in class size, full funding for the state's model curriculum, and additional counseling and support services for students, all of which would require additional revenues and the employment of additional teachers. In the current political and fiscal environment for Michigan school districts, however, school boards have almost no bargaining room on issues that imply substantial new expenditures. Progress on these issues is simply impossible; negotiations can lead to nothing other than frustration.

Despite the affirmations of the MEA leadership, local leaders in many districts have continued to seek salary gains for their members, without much success. Teachers' consequent sense of grievance has been exacerbated by the state-mandated rise in the number of instructional days, which increases their workload without a commensurate increase in pay. The consequence has frequently been a standoff in negotiations, as the prudential obligations of school boards come into conflict with the demands of teachers for real increases in their salaries. These conflicts often focus on efforts by school boards to increase their districts' fiscal reserves by building up the "rainy day fund."[19] Such efforts are resented and resisted by teachers, who believe that for them the "rainy day" has arrived, and that financial reserves should therefore be used to improve their compensation. In September 1998 teachers in forty-one Michigan school districts were working without contracts.

Teachers are especially frustrated by their loss of the right to strike. As one local president put it, without "the ability to go on strike, there's nothing we can do." Meetings with the school board are "not really bargaining sessions," he explains, because "we have no way to express our concerns." On the other side of the bargaining table, board members and administrators are frustrated by their responsibility to hold the line on educational expenditures against the demands of teachers and parents, which has created bitter antagonisms in many districts. According to one superintendent:

I don't think bargaining at a local level fits the current system. . . . The Governor is correct that if you give us more, we'll give more away. The local pressure is so great on the board members . . . that to not give [teachers] what they want becomes a real struggle, even though we know long-term that's best. We have lots of dollars to do what we want. It just all goes to salaries.

In a few districts, however, a different pattern has begun to emerge. School boards and union locals, recognizing the common difficulties they face, have begun to work together to address issues of quality and parent satisfaction. One local union president affirms that recent negotiations in her district were marked by a "very collaborative approach," including a contract provision that ties salary increases for teachers to enrollment increases in the district. "We're very interested in the total picture. . . . We know what their budget is." At the same time, however, she makes it clear that collabo-

19. From the school boards' point of view, the "rainy day fund" has increased in importance since the approval of Proposal A, because the state aid payments that now constitute the largest share of district revenues are distributed on a schedule that does not correspond to the districts' fiscal or academic years. Those districts without a sufficient fund balance must resort to costly short-term borrowing to meet their payroll and other obligations.

ration has its limits: "If they tried to take things away, that would be draw-ing a line in the sand, [which would] posture us in a more militant mode." It remains to be seen whether this kind of cooperation can be sustained over time, or whether it will emerge in other Michigan school districts.

Summary

For Michigan's teachers unions, the future looks bleak. They are hemmed in by Proposal A and the financial constraints that it imposes on local school districts, which means that the prospect of winning real economic gains for their members at any time in the foreseeable future is vanishingly small. The unions' power to protect their members against takebacks is increasingly being challenged by local school boards. Moreover, their polit-ical power has eroded badly. The unions face the implacable hostility of Governor Engler and the decline and disarray of the Democratic party in Michigan. They have played virtually no significant role in recent educa-tion policy debates, unsuccessfully opposing each of the innovations (Proposal A, charter schools, enhanced statewide testing programs) that the Engler administration has introduced. Political action to reverse past defeats or obtain new revenues for education is consequently unlikely to bear fruit. As one union leader acknowledged, "If [the members] knew how little the union can do in return for their [annual dues] they would be leaving the union in droves."

Even if one accepts the governor's sharp distinction between teachers and their unions and concedes the proposition that teachers unions were an obstacle to reform in the past, the present powerlessness of the unions raises questions about the status of teachers and the future course of school reform in Michigan. On the one hand, teachers remain in a reasonably privileged position in most communities, with secure jobs and respectable incomes.[20] On the other hand, they are no longer politically protected, and their conditions of work are deteriorating, as the school code now requires them to work additional days with no increase in pay. Teachers in some dis-tricts have already experienced takebacks. The question that remains is whether the political destruction of the teachers unions is likely to lead to improved education for Michigan school children.

---

20. Surveys consistently rank Michigan's teachers as the best compensated in the nation when their salaries and benefits are adjusted for the cost of living in Michigan.

Pennsylvania: Institutional and Political Decline

Pennsylvania's teachers unions have not experienced losses as dramatic as Michigan's, but they find themselves in much the same circumstances.[21] Governors Tom Ridge and John Engler have much in common, philosophically and politically, and both were reelected easily in November 1998 at the head of their respective Republican tickets. Pennsylvania's teachers unions are therefore confronting a political landscape nearly as bleak as that facing their counterparts in Michigan.

To be fair, though, Governor Ridge could be called an "equal opportunity" opponent of the status quo in public education. He has consistently pushed for vouchers and charter schools and has treated all public education groups, not just the teachers unions, with suspicion and, at times, disdain. Public education groups labor under what some perceive as a "climate of official opposition to public education."[22] The state's demographics make this possible. Pennsylvania has nearly the oldest population of any state, making taxpayers and senior citizens much more important, politically, than families with children in the public schools. Moreover, it has a large Catholic parochial school constituency, to which Ridge is committed, both politically and by his background. One of his original campaign promises was to obtain vouchers to aid parochial schools, and he has tried three times without success to pass a voucher bill.

At the beginning of Ridge's administration, the Pennsylvania Department of Education (PDE) was treated like enemy territory. Ridge appointed an "alien" from outside the world of public education as its head. Within PDE, agency staff were ordered not to speak in public without first obtaining approval from PDE's press secretary, who was appointed by the governor. Ridge's assumption of "client capture" of PDE also extended to the House and Senate education committees in the Assembly. For several years he ignored or bypassed them, even when they were chaired by members of his own Republican party. For example, Ridge's KIDS I and KIDS II education reform bills bypassed the education committees as well as the key education interest groups. Ridge tried to push these reform packages through the legislature without amendments, and both failed to

---

21. This section of the chapter is based in part on interviews with Pennsylvania teacher's union representatives, legislators, legislative staff members, and education lobbyists.

22. Joe Bard, executive director of the Pennsylvania Association of Rural and Small Schools (PARSS), used this phrase in the PARSS newsletter, September 1998.

obtain the necessary votes. After these early setbacks, however, most of Ridge's education initiatives have succeeded.

Evolving Sources of Influence

As in Michigan, the 1970s and early 1980s were times of great power and success for Pennsylvania's teachers unions. Act 195 of 1970 legalized teacher strikes, and the Pennsylvania State Education Association (PSEA) and the Pennsylvania Federation of Teachers (PaFT) took full advantage of this. In the twenty-two years between 1970 and 1992—when Act 88 was passed to restrain teachers' strikes—there were 811 strikes in Pennsylvania's school districts (634 teachers' strikes and 177 classified employee strikes).[23] Since 1992 the number of strikes has declined sharply, from 36 in 1992 to only 9 in the 1997–98 school year. The political backlash against teacher strikes that produced Act 88 was augmented by anger in the early 1990s over a trend toward the use of "selective strikes." Such strikes maximized disruption by being announced unpredictably, at the last minute, and involving only selected schools within school districts.[24]

Act 88 established mandatory timelines for bargaining, new impasse procedures, a requirement of a forty-eight-hour notice before strikes, and measures allowing substitutes to be used during strikes and ensuring that no strike prevents completion of the required 180 days of instruction annually. The teachers' associations feel that Act 88—like PA 112 in Michigan—has tipped the scale heavily in favor of management, enabling school boards to force teachers to work without a new contract. Indeed, in 1998 eighty-five contracts were unsettled from 1997, eighteen unsettled from 1996, six unsettled from 1995, and one still unsettled from 1994. As a result, PSEA wants binding arbitration to replace the nonbinding version included in the Act. Not surprisingly, the Pennsylvania School Boards Association (PSBA), which sponsored the Act, is delighted with it and opposes binding arbitration.

Although PSEA's bargaining power has been greatly diminished by Act 88, and by the general political and economic climate in which it finds

---

23. From 1970 to 1980 there were 352 teachers' strikes; from 1980 to 1990 there were 227 teachers' strikes.

24. It is important to note that Act 88 was passed under the Democratic administration of Governor Bob Casey, which shows that the unions were already losing influence prior to the advent of the Ridge administration.

itself, it still exerts influence through its vast grass-roots network and its ability to make campaign contributions and mobilize campaign workers and votes. Its research and information services, which in the past used to be unequaled, are now matched by the capacities of other interest groups, organizations and think tanks, such as the conservative Commonwealth Foundation. Endorsing candidates (usually Democrats) and making campaign contributions carry risks, of course. For instance, when PSEA unsuccessfully opposed the reelection of Republican governor Richard Thornburgh in 1982 and endorsed his Democratic opponent, the union was excluded from all the administration's meetings with education interest groups during Thornburgh's second term.[25]

From Offense to Defense

In the 1970s it was remarked that PSEA had discovered that "it is easier to control one state legislature than 550 local boards."[26] Now, however, other equally powerful interests are competing with PSEA for the votes of legislators. Moreover, with the Republicans controlling both the executive and legislative branches, the issues getting voted on are different. The teachers unions, and often other education interest groups as well, are on the defensive now, not the offensive.

In the last few years PSEA began to lose on important legislative votes for the first time. So, much of what PSEA and PaFT now do is to try to protect the gains they made in the past. One area where they have been rather successful in defending their interests so far is teacher certification and continuing professional development.[27] The fact that they are having to defend, rather than advance, their interests in such matters is indicative of just how far they have fallen. As a legislative staff member remarked recently, "Five years ago, the general assembly wouldn't even have considered tenure and sabbatical changes. PSEA thought they could get the sabbatical law the way they wanted, but didn't. They also were violently opposed to charter schools. Like New Jersey, they wanted to have the law require certified teachers in charter schools [but had to give some ground on this]."

25. Karper and Boyd (1988).
26. Hess (1980, p. 66).
27. PSEA succeeded in opposing Ridge's professional development bill by taking advantage of PSBA's well-established use of the "unfunded mandate" argument. They contended that the professional development bill was going to be yet another unfunded mandate.

If Pennsylvania's teachers unions still have some influence over bread-and-butter issues concerning their work, as in Michigan, they have become mostly irrelevant to the big school reform issues of the day, such as charter schools and academic standards.[28] The latter issue illustrates how Governor Ridge was able to bypass not only the unions but also the Assembly's education committees. Rather than supporting and lobbying for an academic standards bill introduced by the Republican chair of the Senate Education Committee, Governor Ridge instead launched a successful end run around the legislature and the education interest groups, through the appointment of an Academic Standards Commission.[29] The weakness of the teachers unions was shown vividly. The commission had only one teacher on it, a young woman whose main qualification seemed to be that she was a former Miss Pennsylvania.

In contrast to the open process for developing academic standards championed by the state board of education, Ridge's Academic Standards Commission operated with great secrecy, which proved to be a tactical advantage. The task forces of professional educators involved in proposing the specifics of academic standards for the various disciplines were dismayed to see their proposals undergo radical surgery at the hands of the commission and its envoys. What ultimately emerged were not the progressive curriculum standards they envisioned but rather traditional standards that had been reviewed and revised by conservative curriculum consultants from out of state.[30]

The Battle over School Funding

The continuing battle over state funding for public schools is another major issue illustrating Governor Ridge's power and the weakness of the unions and other mainline education interest groups. This battle set the stage for the "Kalkaska-like" crisis being played out in Philadelphia. From Philadelphia's point of view, it is a story of rural and suburban interests versus urban interests, and of poor and advantaged whites versus poor, urban blacks. It also reveals the profound political shifts that are occurring in urban school systems.

28. The unions were also irrelevant to the biggest education policy controversy during Governor Casey's administration, the donnybrook over outcome-based education. Boyd, Lugg, and Zahorchak (1996).
29. Makosy (1998).
30. Makosy (1998).

In July 1999 the long-running court case brought by the Pennsylvania Association of Rural and Small Schools (PARSS) challenging the constitutionality of Pennsylvania's system of school finance—its equity and adequacy in regard to the constitutional promise of a "thorough and efficient system"—was dismissed by the Commonwealth Court. Later, this case, plus a similar one brought against the state by the Philadelphia school district, was dismissed by Pennsylvania's Supreme Court.

If PARSS has failed judicially so far, Michael DiRaimo, a lobbyist for the Pittsburgh school district, contends that its case has been successful politically.[31] Soon after PARSS brought its lawsuit in 1991, Pennsylvania's Equalized Subsidy for Basic Education (ESBE) formula system was frozen and replaced by an ad hoc system in which new dollars are added to it each year. Rather than being allocated by the formula, these new dollars are fought over each year, and in the first several years rural and suburban interests prevailed over urban interests. The ESBE formula gave priority to districts where there were high concentrations of poverty. By contrast, the new ad hoc approach has favored low wealth and low expenditure districts—that is, poor, white, rural school districts. Put another way, the limited additional state money has been allocated more to reduce expenditure disparities than to address the "difficulty of the educational task."[32] The result, according to an analysis by the Council of Great City Schools, is that poor, black, urban districts get less of the new money than poor, white, rural districts. So, the Philadelphia school district is contending, in a new federal civil rights lawsuit, that Pennsylvania's education funding is now racially discriminatory. According to its complaint, "the result of the changes in the formula has been a shift of Commonwealth treasury revenues away from Philadelphia schools . . . which the Commonwealth Defendants knew or should have known represents a disproportionate allocation of funds away from the largest concentration of minority students in the Commonwealth."[33]

This alteration of the ESBE system has added to the funding woes of the big cities and contributed to the mounting fiscal crisis faced by the Philadelphia school district. Believing that his district could afford no further cuts in spending, in February 1998 Philadelphia's superintendent, David Hornbeck, asked the legislature to make up a projected $55.2 mil-

31. Interview with Michael DiRaimo on August 26, 1998.
32. Reis and Hartman (1997).
33. Council of Great City Schools (1998).

lion budget shortfall for the 1998–99 school year. To get their attention, he warned that if this money was not forthcoming he would have to close Philadelphia's public schools as early as March 1999.

Governor Ridge and the Republican leadership of the legislature viewed Hornbeck's proposal as blackmail, and as both a threat and an opportunity. With relish and alacrity, they drafted a draconian bill that would allow the state to take over the Philadelphia school district if Hornbeck were to pursue his threat. All the unions opposed this bill, but it passed easily, despite its numerous incendiary features, such as provisions for replacing the school board and superintendent, suspending the teachers' contract, laying off teachers, and, in the words of the PaFT, "unilateral school closings and privatization by converting public schools to charter schools without approval by teachers and parents."[34] It was then Philadelphia's turn to be "motivated" to find a way to avoid school closure and state takeover. Rather than cutting the proposed school budget, an eleventh-hour solution was found when two local banks issued the district letters of credit enabling it to borrow $250 million to keep operating through June 1999.[35]

Underlying Philadelphia's crisis and the legislature's takeover bill are momentous political shifts that are redefining not only the politics of urban education but, more broadly, the character of state and national politics. A new coalition is emerging between traditionally Democratic African Americans and the Republican party. Both share a conviction that the unions will never make the changes necessary to rescue urban education. Remarking about this, a legislative staff member noted that,

> Louis Farrakhan's representative in Philadelphia, Rodney Mohammed, made an impassioned appeal for vouchers as part of the Legislative Commission on Urban Restructuring's recommendations for urban education. We know, he said, that the Democrats aren't going to take on the unions and really change things. [Thus, House Majority Leader] John Perzel [a Philadelphia Republican] and Rep. Dwight Evans [an African American Democrat from Philadelphia] have become very unlikely allies.

34. "Breaking the Ranks," *Wall Street Journal*, May 15, 1998, p. A14. The strong support for this bill reflected the legislature's negative view of Philadelphia as an insatiable and "bottomless pit," as well as their antipathy toward the unions and Philadelphia's school superintendent.

35. White (1998).

Indeed, Dwight Evans was among the legislators pushing for the passage of the Philadelphia takeover bill, for which he earned the ire of Philadelphia's unions. They previously had supported him, but spent heavily in an unsuccessful effort to defeat him in the Democratic primary in May 1998. Evans was a leading contender to succeed Mayor Rendell in 1999, and had come out in favor of vouchers and of transferring responsibility for education to the mayor's office.[36]

In sum, Pennsylvania's teachers unions face an uncertain and challenging future. Although Governor Ridge has stopped pushing for a voucher bill, following a third unsuccessful effort in 1999, he is trying to maximize the expansion of Pennsylvania's growing charter school sector. Over the long haul, Ridge's chances of success in school choice seem to be increasing. The charter school bill has no limit on the number of such schools that can be created. Polling data suggest that support for school choice is growing among union members as well as among African Americans, in part because of an increasing divide between public and private sector union members. In this regard, the *Wall Street Journal* notes that "the wage gap between public sector and private sector salaries is larger in Pennsylvania than in any other state.[37] In 1995 the average teacher in the state earned $46,000 for nine months' work, while the average salary for all workers was $27,900." This kind of disparity makes it harder for the teachers unions to avoid being perceived (at least by a growing segment of the population) as advantaged special interest groups, rather than being seen, as they wish, as the champions and defenders of public education. This leaves their leaders and strategists facing a difficult political and public relations problem.

The Politics of the "New Unionism"

The changes that have been described in the position of the teachers unions in Michigan and Pennsylvania appear irreversible, part of a secular trend defined both by the general loss of confidence in many of our society's institutions and by the decline of industrial unionism and its preferred strategies for advancement. Some analysts see the present moment as transitional.[38] Positing a generational theory of development, they predict that

---

36. "Breaking the Ranks," *Wall Street Journal*, May 15, 1998, p. A14.
37. "Breaking the Ranks," *Wall Street Journal*, May 15, 1998, p. A14.
38. For example, Mitchell and Kerchner (1983); Kerchner and Mitchell (1988).

teachers unions will evolve into hybrid organizations typically characterized as "professional unions." They recognize that traditional unionism
continues in the mainstream and is institutionalized in labor law, organizational culture, and in the interests and cognitions of many union leaders,
but they characterize such forms as ultimately vestigial. As evidence of evolution they point to such vanguard developments as joint union-
management committees, educational policy trust agreements, and contract waivers that promote innovation at the school level. Instances of these
emerging practices in such locales as Pittsburgh, Pennsylvania; Louisville,
Kentucky; Cincinnati, Toledo, and Columbus, Ohio; Rochester, New
York; and Glenview, Illinois, are said to constitute the leading edge.

Other developments abet these tendencies. Most notably, the National
Board for Professional Teaching Standards (NBPTS), launched in 1986,
enters its second decade in reasonably good health. With two-thirds of its
membership made up of teachers (equally divided among the NEA, the AFT,
and "other" teacher associations, such as the National Council of Teachers of
Mathematics), the NBPTS has emerged as a powerful champion of the professional theme in teaching. Its standards and assessments constitute not only
a representation of knowledge and skill in teaching, but also a practical
means to institute performance-based compensation; to organize teacher
professional development; to identify teacher leaders; to rationalize the curriculum of teacher education; and to introduce greater rigor and relevance
into initial teacher licensure (see the work of the Interstate New Teacher
Assessment and Support Consortium, supported by the Council of Chief
State School Officers).[39] Likewise, although the merger of the NEA and the
AFT suffered a setback with the NEA vote in the summer of 1998, the
prospect remains alive, substantially driven by the common interest of the
two unions (at least at the national level) in increased professionalism.

These developments may indeed be harbingers or portents, but the
state-level political developments described in our case states give pause.
Writing some years ago, McDonnell identified a fundamental obstacle to
the development of successful state teacher policies. Such policies, she
argued, must accommodate two different, yet legitimate values—popular
control and professionalism:

Popular or democratic control requires that schools, as public institutions, be held accountable to the citizenry and its elected representatives.

39. See Odden and Kelly (1996); Ingvarson (1998).

This form of accountability assumes that public officials have the right to impose on schools and those who work there a set of performance standards consistent with the norms and expectations of the larger community. Professionalism assumes that because the members of a particular profession possess a specialized body of knowledge and have been judged competent to practice that profession, they should be free to decide how best to serve their individual clients. In other words, accountability should be based on norms and standards collectively defined and enforced by peers. In their pure forms, these values each suggest different modes of governance and accountability for education.[40]

Teacher policy in Michigan and Pennsylvania lately has shifted decisively in favor of popular control, in significant part because the states' teachers unions were widely perceived to have deployed the banner of professionalism in order to advance the material and political interests of their members rather than to improve the performance of schools. Teachers and their unions have consequently been sidelined in current debates about educational reform; strengthening public control and accountability through mechanisms including expanded parental choice and state or mayoral takeovers of public school districts has been put forward as the solution to a host of educational problems.

The dilemma identified by McDonnell has hardly vanished, however. The "new unionism" described by Kerchner and others represents a possible resolution, one in which the competing values of popular control and professional autonomy are reconciled in a common commitment to improved service for the clients of the school system.[41] Progress toward such a reconciliation has been achieved in a few school districts, and both unionists and politicians have acknowledged that moves toward enhanced professionalism among teachers and increased cooperation between professionals and the broader public are essential to the tasks of improving schools and school outcomes. We share this view and salute the promise of the "new unionism," but we are nevertheless pessimistic about the likelihood of a widespread move in this direction. The politics needed to reconcile the values of public and professional control plainly have not

40. McDonnell (1989, p. v).
41. See Kerchner and Koppich (1993); Kerchner, Koppich, and Weeres (1997).

emerged in Michigan or Pennsylvania, nor is there much prospect that they will any time soon.

To see why, we need to explore in greater depth the competing interests represented in the contest, along with the incentives and risks facing the respective players. On one side of the table, powerful interests within the teacher union movement seek to preserve and advance the traditional strategies and postures that have secured gains in the past. This is understandable, first from a historical perspective. An entire generation of union leaders and staff, especially at state and local levels, has made careers out of mastering the processes of local collective bargaining and state-level lobbying for teacher interests. In most states, but particularly in those with strong collective bargaining statutes, teachers unions acquired considerable political influence by operating in a largely adversarial and partisan manner. Contract negotiations at the local level and budgetary politics at the state level were treated as zero sum games, and the unions' readiness to resort to strikes, job actions, and hard-edged electoral politics around wages, benefits, job protections, and working conditions produced large gains for teachers. As indicated, states such as Michigan and Pennsylvania represent this tradition, but many national staff also have made careers in the spheres of collective bargaining and lobbying. The teachers unions, then, have a strong vested interest in these strategies around which staff have developed expertise and to which they are committed through a lifetime of work.

The decisive decline of the unions in these case states suggests that these traditions are no longer serviceable. The circumstances leading to this outcome have already been explored, but its import can be amplified. "What's good for teachers is what's good for education" is the claim that always has undergirded teacher demands. Other interests rely on similar claims (what's good for General Motors . . . "; "the business of America is business"). When this equivalence between public and private interest was firmly established in the public mind, the unions were relatively free to pursue an agenda focused on wages and protections for their members. The rhetoric of professionalism was extremely useful to the task of public persuasion and has been employed successfully over the years. While it would be wrong to assert that the teachers unions have paid mere lip service to the professional ideal, it is surely accurate to claim that the unions' muscle has resided in their negotiators and lobbyists, rather than in their professional development staff. So, while the unions could point to steady investment in "professional" activities, these were secondary to the primary pursuits of bargaining and lobbying.

In recent years new voices have emerged within the teachers unions that seek to modify if not transform teachers' collective advancement strategy by drawing explicitly on the professional theme. The vanguard developments already indicated exemplify this strand within the union movement. Union progressives reckon that in order to restore public confidence in organized teachers, the unions must engage proactively in school improvement and must alter certain traditional features of unionism. These include the shift from distributive bargaining (for example, dividing the "spoils" of money, power, rights) to integrative bargaining (for example, seeking mutual benefits and a common agenda), a distinction Koppich and Kerchner derive from Walton and McKersie; the introduction of peer review into the evaluation of teaching competence; the championing of rigorous professional standards for teachers; and the genuine participation of teachers in school and policy decisionmaking.[42]

In pursuing these matters, however, union progressives do not seek to overthrow the institutional framework of industrial unionism but to bend it to more professional purposes. They recognize the necessity for some form of collective negotiation and of dispute resolution. They hope, however, to supplement the traditional concerns for teacher rights, wages, and benefits with broader concerns for educational improvement. By creating both the appearance and the reality of direct teacher engagement in professional accountability and educational improvement, they hope to enhance teachers' cultural authority as well as their economic status.

Union progressives face two main problems. First, in challenging certain cherished tenets of industrial unionism, they incur internal opposition from traditionalists. Peer review is the most obvious instance. Unions protect their members, but peer review requires some teachers to sit in judgment over others, potentially affecting their employment. This is a matter of great symbolic import that is deeply divisive.[43] If teachers do not police their own ranks, they abandon one pillar of professionalism. If they do, they come into direct conflict with worker solidarity promoted by industrial unionism. Second, and equally troublesome, is the political weakness of professionalism as an advancement strategy. Teachers may choose to become involved in school reform, but democratically elected bodies may

---

42. Koppich and Kerchner (1999); Walton and McKersie (1965).
43. See Kelly (1998).

still choose not to provide sufficient funds to support instructional improvement, yielding large classes, run-down schools, inadequate instructional materials, and meager salaries. They may also enact deprofessionalizing policies that, for example, open the occupation to the unqualified or create rigid bureaucratic structures and processes constraining the exercise of professional judgment.

In such cases, organized teachers require more than persuasion and advocacy to counter the excesses of public control. They must possess some form of political muscle that they can flex, not simply on their own behalf but ultimately on behalf of their students. Labor law and the institution of collective bargaining, together with political action at the state level, have supplied organized teachers with the principal forms for the exercise of power. While doctors and lawyers were able to convert the professional theme into cultural authority, political power, and highly favored economic position, that path is not open to teachers. Consequently, classic professionalism by itself cannot protect the interests of teachers nor counterbalance the potential disadvantages of democratic control.

The strategic problem for teachers unions may therefore be framed in the following terms. In the contest over scarce public resources and the control of work, teacher organizations require some basis upon which to mobilize power and influence. Elusive yet vital cultural support for teacher militance in states such as Michigan and Pennsylvania has eroded to the vanishing point. Frontal assaults on teachers unions now make good electoral politics in these states, leading to new statutes that further weaken the unions. Continuing the strategies of industrial unionism no longer appears to be a viable option. Yet the cultural and political bases upon which to reassert influence have not yet emerged. So, while union leaders, in our view, are correct in asserting the necessity of wielding power in defense of teacher interests, the means that would make this effective are no longer readily available.

On the other side of the table, politicians such as Michigan's Engler or Pennsylvania's Ridge at first glance face no downside in either attacking or bypassing the teachers unions. The erosion of public support for the unions, the ascendance of the Republican party, and the perceived affluence of teachers conduce to a political climate that favors antiunion political appeals. Recent state legislation in both states has further weakened the unions' power, so they are no longer as potent an adversary as in years past. Electoral politics, of course, can change as suddenly as the weather, but for the moment there is no cloud on the horizon.

Consider the prospect of serving as an "education" governor who is opposed to the organizations representing teachers. That posture contains its own difficulties. At some point in the chain of logic linking reform ideas to instructional improvement to student learning, teachers are necessarily implicated. As Cohen among others has pointed out, one of the troubling ironies of educational reform is that teachers are regarded simultaneously as the source of the problem and of the solution.[44] If student learning standards are vague, weak, and unenforced, then new standards can only achieve effects if teachers use them. If "break the mold" schools established by charter or by private firms such as the Edison Project are to revitalize urban education, those school designs require committed, expert teachers for their realization. If class size reduction appears as a potent state policy, it can achieve effects on learning only so far as the state is capable of recruiting enough qualified teachers.

The strategic problem faced by public officials is therefore that what makes for good electoral politics may not produce good educational policy, when "policy" is construed not as the output of legislators but as the actions of educators—street-level bureaucrats in Lipsky's phrase.[45] Politicians cannot do without the energetic collaboration of teachers if the long-term goal of improving public school systems is to be achieved; but their short-term interest in restraining public expenditures, strengthening the institutions of public control, and winning elections may preclude the kinds of concessions that would win the trust and cooperation of organized teachers. Permanently alienating teachers may be destructive of their long-term ends, but premature conciliation may surrender the leverage politicians need to encourage educational improvement.

The problem facing teachers unions and public officials can be framed as an instance of the "prisoners' dilemma" game, in which the players must decide whether to act selfishly to advance their private interests or altruistically to achieve shared gains (see box 6–1). The mutual dependence between teachers and public officials may argue for partnership between public and professional interests along the lines defined by advocates of the "new unionism," but the mutually beneficial outcome is not available, since for each side the real short-term advantage of opposing the other outweighs the notional benefits of cooperation. Under these circumstances,

44. Cohen (1988).
45. Lipsky (1980).

the predicted outcome is continued standoff, which is unlikely to produce much in the way of school improvement.

In the longer term, more desirable outcomes may become available.[46] Cooperation in the interest of shared gains may come about through the establishment of trust between the players, or through expanded opportunities to communicate with one another about their respective strategies.[47] In Michigan and Pennsylvania, however, such cooperation will only be achieved in a substantially changed political environment, which is not an immediate prospect. When it comes, it most likely will emerge around two broad policy themes, which are discussed in our conclusion.

Reform without Teachers?

In Michigan and Pennsylvania, as in many other states, two streams of policy are unfolding simultaneously with unpredictable futures. One stream involves the creation of strong standards for student learning and curriculum, together with development of state assessment systems. The other stream introduces new forms of school choice on both the supply and demand side, often in conjunction with the privatization of educational services. Each of these policy streams poses opportunities and impediments for public-professional forms of cooperation. Each might enhance professionalism in teaching or serve to deprofessionalize the occupation.

Higher Standards for Teachers and Students

Consider first the movement to introduce high standards into education. Policy efforts along these lines have emerged at national, state, and local levels around the core academic subjects. Standards constitute a natural point of convergence between public officials interested in raising academic achievement and organized teachers interested in promoting professionalism. Consequently, standard setting is an inviting activity around which to build common ground. Standards-related policy incorporates attention to curriculum reform, to student learning, to assessment of student learning,

---

46. Relations between governors and teachers unions are far less acrimonious and potentially more constructive in other states, including New York.

47. Axelrod (1978).

Box 6-1. *Playing "Political Hardball"*

The problem facing the governors and the teachers unions can be presented in the form of a game known as the "prisoners' dilemma," in which the principals must choose whether to fight to advance their particular interests or cooperate with their adversaries to achieve shared gains. In the original prisoners' dilemma game, two prisoners have been arrested for the same crime. They are placed in separate cells to prevent them from communicating with one another and separately offered a similar bargain by their jailers. If one betrays the other he will be set free, while his confederate serves the maximum time, provided that his partner does not betray him. If he refuses to "defect" and betray his partner he will serve an intermediate sentence. If neither of the two prisoners defects, both will go free; if each betrays the other, both will serve maximum time. The socially optimal outcome is for both prisoners to refuse to defect, but the equilibrium solution is for both to defect and serve maximum sentences.[1]

The conflict between the teachers' unions and the governors is presented graphically in the accompanying figure. The absolute magnitude of the gains (or losses) associated with the choices available to the two players is not important to the analysis. The critical condition is that the payoff for fighting exceeds the payoff for cooperating for each party, regardless of the other party's choice. In the figure, for example, if the governors choose to fight and the unions choose to cooperate, then the governors' payoff is 4, which is greater than the payoff of 2 that the governors would receive if they chose to cooperate. Similarly, if the unions choose to fight, the governors' payoff is 0 for fighting and −2 for cooperating. The same conditions hold for the unions. Under these circumstances, both players will choose to fight and the outcome of the game will be (0,0), as shown in the lower right-hand cell. Collectively, the best available outcome is that in the upper left-hand cell (2,2), but this socially preferred outcome is not readily attainable.

From the governors' point of view, there is little to gain from cooperating with the teachers unions. Public support for restraining or reducing taxes remains widespread, and in Michigan and Pennsylvania there appears to be further political mileage in attacks on the education establishment. The governors' policy priorities in both states include expanded opportunities for parental choice and stricter accountability for schools, teachers, and students, both of which are strongly resisted by the teachers unions. Under

Conflict between the Teachers Unions and the Governors

		Unions	
		Cooperate	Fight
Governors	Cooperate	2,2	−2,4
	Fight	4,−2	0,0

these circumstances, the governors' best strategy is to move forward with their reform agendas, confronting the unions when necessary and ignoring them otherwise.

From the unions' point of view, cooperation with the governors opens up a dismal prospect for their members, including more work for less pay, peer evaluation, stricter external accountability (including tests for practicing teachers and "merit pay"), and reduced job security. In the present political environment it is unlikely that unilateral concessions on any of these issues would produce reciprocal concessions from the governors; rather, they would almost certainly result in unpredictable but potentially large losses for union members and a further deterioration in the power of the unions. The "new unionism" seems to offer unions little or no political leverage; their best strategy is to fight to protect their members' past gains, while mobilizing politically to shift the electoral balance in their own favor.

At present it is clear that the governors hold the winning hand, but this does not mean that it is in their interest to be magnanimous, or that it is in the unions' interest to be conciliatory. The governors maximize their gains by confronting the unions, while the unions minimize their losses by confronting the governors. If both were to adopt cooperative strategies like those admired by the proponents of the "new unionism," this might lead to quicker or deeper improvements in educational performance than can be achieved by continued confrontation, but for the moment it serves each individual interest to fight on.

1. Fudenberg and Tirole (1991); Axelrod (1978).

to teachers' professional development, to rewards and incentives for performance, and to the articulation of standards for teaching and those for learning. On these matters and on their coordination into systematic approaches to instruction, there is considerable room for teacher involvement at all levels of governance. At the same time, these are public policy issues that also engage the authority of government and the responsibilities of state and local policymakers.

Although these are not the traditional "bread-and-butter" issues of unionism, the teachers unions might opt for more aggressive involvement in such issues as part of a campaign to enlarge public confidence and to influence instructional conditions for teachers. Such activity cannot substitute for negotiation around wages, benefits, and job protections, but it can supplement and complement bargaining, and it can assume greater importance in the public posture of unions, particularly as systemic reform includes attention to accountability. This is really the crux of the matter. The traditional union stance allocates teacher evaluation to management and protection of workers to the union. This equation, however, leaves organized teachers in a weak position to advocate for professional standards of practice, if they are unwilling to play a major role in defining and implementing those standards. Peer evaluation is a critical element of professional accountability and may constitute a vital quid pro quo in the larger effort to introduce professional standards into schools.

Other policies, however, also serve as starting points for public-professional partnerships around standards. States and districts can begin to make use of national board certification and of NBPTS standards and assessments as a basis for teacher evaluation and professional development, teacher compensation, teacher advancement, and other personnel decisions. The scope of bargaining at the local level can expand, as it has in such vanguard districts as Cincinnati, to incorporate issues of educational reform that may be proposed by either labor or management. Structural reforms such as site-based management can create conditions under which teachers can exercise greater authority in forming academically oriented school communities.

Public policy can also contribute to the deprofessionalization of teachers, however. Curricular and assessment mandates developed without teacher input often violate professional standards and judgments. State and district testing systems in particular often create constraining conditions for teachers and students alike, in the name of public accountability. Some state legislatures are even beginning to mandate instructional methods, around literacy instruction for example, where phonics-based approaches have gained favor over so-called whole language methods. In such instances, policymakers clearly reject teachers as partners, viewing them instead as bureaucratic functionaries expected to dispose what others propose. Under these circumstances, both union power and professional suasion appear incapable of exerting influence over curriculum and instruction. Pennsylvania's recent experience with their standards commission is a clear instance of standard setting as the triumph of public over professional values.

Under present political circumstances, state policymakers in Michigan and Pennsylvania have little incentive to engage directly with organized teachers around standard setting. This remains a potential area for resumed dialogue and collaborative activity in the future, to the extent that state policymakers come to believe that reform itself cannot bear fruit without the constructive involvement of teachers. How to engage rank-and-file teachers in state standard setting becomes the task, and for that, the professional model may be the best entrée.

Choice and Privatization in the Educational System

The second major stream of policy further complicates efforts to find common ground around standard setting. Many states today, including Michigan and Pennsylvania, are experimenting with a variety of school choice and privatization policies. There are many varieties of choice policy, but Michigan, as we have indicated, has a "strong" charter school statute together with an interdistrict transfer policy.[48] Pennsylvania's charter schools law, passed more recently (in July 1997), is not as strong. Its first year of implementation produced only a few charter schools, since only local school boards could grant charters and no appeals of rejected proposals were allowed until the second year.[49] The fact that charter schools are now possible has already changed some of the dynamics of educational politics in Pennsylvania, but not much is yet known about the impacts and consequences associated with Pennsylvania's charter schools.[50]

48. See Cookson (1994, pp. 14–16) for one account.

49. As reported in the *Harrisburg Patriot* on August 30, 1998, thirty-one charter schools were approved for operation in Pennsylvania during the 1998–99 school year.

50. Daniels (1997).

Having won control of both houses of the Michigan legislature in the November 1998 elections—and with the U.S. Supreme Court declining to review the Wisconsin state supreme court decision that allowed public vouchers for private and parochial schools—a conservative coalition has proposed an amendment to the Michigan constitution that would clear the way for the introduction of a state voucher plan for Detroit and other urban districts. Although Governor Ridge has not succeeded in three voucher efforts, as in Michigan and other states it would be much easier to pass a voucher plan limited to a few big cities in Pennsylvania than one that would embrace the whole state, which would require massive funding and widespread political support. In Michigan, private firms such as the Edison Project and others now operate a number of schools, including both charter schools and district schools. The main "privatization" venture in Pennsylvania to date involved a controversial effort by the Wilkinsburg school board to contract out the management of one of their elementary schools. This effort received moral and legal support from the secretary of education, but after some protracted legal disputes was ultimately declared illegal, because the outside management firm replaced the existing teaching staff in violation of the teachers' contract.[51]

To date teachers unions have opposed choice and contracting policies. They particularly fear the potentially weakening effects of vouchers on the public school system, redirecting resources away from struggling public schools to private schools. Choice and privatization policies also threaten teachers' organized interests insofar as they encourage the employment of nonunionized and noncertified teachers. For many choice advocates, however, this is the point. They argue in part that choice policy frees schools from many of the constraints that hinder more effective education. Chief among such constraints are the bureaucratic organization of school districts embedded in state regulatory policy and collective bargaining agreements.

Traditional and progressive unionists are of one mind on this issue. If choice and privatization policies weaken standards for entry and for employment of teachers, then they are hostile not only to the interests of unions but also to the advancement of professionalism. On this point, studies in progress of charter schools and choice in Michigan by Plank and Sykes contain some anecdotal evidence. By law, charter schools must hire certified teachers, but it appears that many such schools are having difficulty attracting experienced, highly qualified candidates. While such

---

51. Thomas, Moran, and Resnick (1996); Ponessa, (1996); Walsh (1996); Wills (1998).

schools may offer greater autonomy and the appeal of a focused, distinctive mission, they also offer fewer job protections, less attractive benefits, and more demanding work schedules to their nonunionized workers. In a number of cases, Michigan charter schools have had to bring in outside management companies to cover cash flow problems and to provide administrative services. Such companies often become the employers of record; they determine such matters as teacher salary increases, work schedules, and employment itself, because charter teachers lack tenure and typically work on annual or "at-will" contracts that need not be renewed. The freedom teachers may have in charter schools is offset by their vulnerability in many cases, and this trade-off lacks appeal for many teachers.

The involvement of for-profit firms in education raises another issue as well. Firms such as the Edison Project or the National Heritage Academies seek not only to provide better education for students and families, but to do so at lower cost in order to produce profits for their investors. If firms are accountable to stockholders for profits and schools are accountable to parents for educational quality, these two forms of accountability may not mesh. While competition among producers may force automakers, for example, to produce a reasonably good car at a competitive price, the complexity of evaluating educational services makes it more difficult for consumers to judge the quality of what they are receiving. Thus accountability for profits might take precedence over accountability for educational quality, constituting a wholly new development in American education. How have for-profit firms sought to reduce costs while maintaining educational quality? Again, the evidence from Michigan is anecdotal, but a tendency can be seen. Firms can most easily economize by (1) achieving economies of scale via "franchising" their school model; and (2) hiring nonunionized employees, including teachers' aides, bus drivers, janitors, secretaries, and food service workers, and offering them lower wages and fewer benefits. To the extent that profits are generated at the expense of other school workers or ultimately teachers themselves, however, organized teachers might be expected to resist.

Choice and privatization policies, then, can be inimical to both union and professional interests, weakening teachers' influence in school decision-making and undercutting worker solidarity. Yet at least some advocates for choice argue its merits on the basis of supporting teacher professionalism.[52] The typical conditions of teachers' work in many large, urban districts are

---

52. For example, Raywid (1990); Chubb and Moe (1990).

deprofessionalizing, if not downright demoralizing. Charter laws create opportunities for entrepreneurial teachers to open their own schools free, at least, of some of the alienating constraints. Chubb and Moe, for example, argue that schools of choice under voucher or charter school plans will feature less bureaucratic oversight from the district level and fewer entanglements from district-bargained contracts.[53] Consequently, there will be greater scope for professional community to form in schools of choice than in schools operating within the traditional public system. In addition to greater freedom from bureaucratic constraints, schools of choice also offer teachers the benefits of a small-scale, focused mission and a values match between school faculty, parents, and community. Anecdotal evidence from our studies and others suggests that some teachers have taken advantage of these opportunities. The philosophy and practice of charter schools, then, are not inhospitable to the professional aspirations of teachers. But charter school teachers may wish to retain their membership in teachers unions, as has occurred in charter schools in other states. Indeed, teachers unions themselves have begun sponsoring charter schools as part of their own effort to participate in school reform.

At issue is the role of teachers in charter schools, together with their organized involvement in them. Will charter schools genuinely create conditions where teacher professionalism may flourish, or will charter schools more often be thin masquerades for domination by for-profit firms and community interests that seek to control schools for a range of ideological purposes? Will charter schools and contract schools accommodate organized teachers and work within the framework of collectively negotiated agreements that promise parity in labor-management disputes? Or, will they become maverick organizations that continue to hire teachers on annual contracts without the protections of tenure and formal teacher involvement in decisions regarding conditions of employment and work? Both potentialities can be seen unfolding in Michigan's charter schools (with Pennsylvania's charter schools just getting underway), so the issue remains open at this writing.

In her analysis of the requirements for democratic education, Gutmann has written,

> When democratic control over schools is so absolute as to render teachers unable to exercise intellectual discretion in their work, (1) few independent-minded people are attracted to teaching, (2) those who

53. Chubb and Moe (1990, pp. 86–91).

are attracted are frustrated in their attempts to think creatively and independently, and (3) those who either willingly or reluctantly conform to the demands of democratic authority teach an undemocratic lesson to their students—of intellectual deference to democratic authority. A democratic conception of professionalism supports those union claims to educational authority necessary to cultivate a democratically tempered sense of professional mission among teachers.[54]

Gutmann argues that organized teachers are an institutionalized counterbalance to the excesses of democratic authority, but she also acknowledges that teachers unions can secure too much power, using it to their benefit rather than to the benefit of the students they serve. In our case states, the pendulum has swung mightily from strong union influence to near negligible union influence; if Gutmann's arguments are to be credited, neither extreme is healthy for democratic education. From our perspective, if organized teachers could come together with public officials around a professional agenda that accords weight to both the legitimate desires of the public and the necessary discretion allocated to teachers, this would be the best course. The twin policy themes of standards and choice have emerged as the likely foci for such partnership, but each theme contains the seeds of both collaboration and conflict around professionalized conceptions of the teacher's role and of participation in reform by organized teachers.

Along with Pennsylvania, Michigan is an important state to watch, for it represents one kind of future. Unlike in California where districts form charter schools under existing regulations, including collectively bargained contracts, Michigan has opted for choice policies coupled with other legislation that dramatically weakens teachers and their organizations from the school to the statehouse. If present trends continue unchallenged, increasing numbers of teachers will work in charter, contract, and private schools at the discretion of administrators, corporate directors, and private boards who have little incentive to negotiate with them.

Conclusion

Both standards and choice as policy themes contain possibilities for enhancing teacher professionalism and supporting the growth of "new

---

54. Gutmann (1987, p. 80).

unionism" among teachers, but we are pessimistic about this potential in the short run. Politicians in Michigan and Pennsylvania have discovered real advantages in politics and policies that attack or bypass unions. They do not need to bargain; they do not need to form public-professional partnerships. They have won the war, and they are in charge. In response, the unions may feel their best option is to continue fighting a rearguard action and to wait for a more propitious political environment, rather than searching for détente and common ground with their present adversaries. In this political context, appeals to professionalism carry little weight on either side.

Michigan and Pennsylvania thus represent cases of educational reform in which the purported excesses of organized teachers who acquired too much power and used it to their own benefit have been successfully challenged. Replacing teacher power is a combination of public and market power that has substantially reduced the potency of the teacher's voice. Whether this new regime will lead to improvements in educational quality or equity remains to be seen, but we have our doubts. Meaningful school reform without the wholehearted participation of teachers appears an unlikely prospect. How individual teachers respond to the decline of their unions and to their own loss of influence in educational policy debates is therefore likely to emerge as the critical issue for reformers in the coming years.

References

Axelrod, R. 1978. *The Evolution of Cooperation.* Basic Books.

Boyd, W. L., C. Lugg, and G. Zahorchak. 1996. "Social Traditionalists, Religious Conservatives, and the Politics of Outcome-Based Education." *Education and Urban Society* 28, 3 (May): 347–65.

Chubb, J., and T. Moe. 1990. *Politics, Markets, and America's Schools.* Brookings.

Citizens Research Council. 1994. "Public Sector Strikes in Michigan: An Update." *Council Comments* (no. 1026).

Cohen, D. 1988. "Teaching Practice: Plus Que Ça Change." In *Contributing to Educational Change: Perspectives on Research and Practice,* edited by P. Jackson, 27–84. Berkeley, Calif.: McCutchan.

Cookson, P. 1994. *School Choice: The Struggle for the Soul of American Education.* Yale University Press.

Council of the Great City Schools. 1998. "Adequate State Financing of Urban Schools. Part I: An Analysis of Funding to the Philadelphia Public Schools" (May). Washington, D.C.

Courant, P. N., E. Gramlich, and S. Loeb. 1994. "A Report on School Finance and Educational Reform in Michigan." In *Midwest Approaches to School Reform*, edited by Thomas A. Downes and William A. Testa. Federal Reserve Bank of Chicago.

Daniels, T. H. 1997. "The Development of Charter Public Schools in Pennsylvania." *Pennsylvania Educational Leadership* 17, 1 (Fall): 4–10.

Farrell, D. 1993. "Political Hardball Is the MEA's Game." *Detroit News,* December 12, 1A.

Freedman, E., and M. Hornbeck. 1993. "Kalkaska Parents Are Angry at State." *Detroit News,* March 26, B1.

Fudenberg, D., and J. Tirole. 1991. *Game Theory.* MIT Press.

Gutmann, A. 1987. *Democratic Education.* Princeton University Press.

Hess, P. K. 1980. "An Analysis of the Influence of the Pennsylvania State Education Association within the State Legislative Policy Process." Ph.D. dissertation, Pennsylvania State University.

Ingvarson, L. 1998. Professional Development as the Pursuit of Professional Standards: The Standards-Based Professional Development System." *Teaching and Teacher Education* 14: 127–40.

Inside Michigan Politics. 1993. "Multi-Client Firms (and Much More) Top Lobbyist Survey," September 4.

Karper, J. H., and W. L. Boyd. 1988. "Interest Groups and the Changing Environment of State Educational Policymaking: Developments in Pennsylvania." *Educational Administration Quarterly* 24, 1 (February): 21–54.

Kelly, P. 1998. "Teacher Unionism and Professionalism: An Institutional Analysis of Peer Review Programs and the Competing Criteria for Legitimacy." Ph.D. dissertation, Michigan State University.

Kerchner, C., and J. Koppich, eds. 1993. *A Union of Professionals: Labor Relations and Educational Reform.* Teachers College Press.

Kerchner, C., J. Koppich, and J. Weeres. 1997. *United Mind Workers: Unions and Teaching in the Knowledge Society.* Jossey-Bass.

Kerchner, C., and D. Mitchell. 1988. *The Changing Idea of a Teachers' Union.* New York: Falmer Press.

Koppich, J., and C. Kerchner. 1999. "Organizing the Other Half of Teaching." In *Teaching as the Learning Profession: Handbook of Policy and Practice,* edited by L. Darling-Hammond and G. Sykes. Jossey Bass.

Lipsky, M. 1980. *Street-Level Bureaucracy: Dilemmas of the Individual in Public Services.* Russell Sage Foundation.

Mahtesian, C. 1995. "The Chastening of the Teachers." *Governing* (December 9).

Makosy, S. 1998. "Academic Standards-Setting in Pennsylvania: The Confluence of Problems, Policies, and Politics." Ph.D. dissertation, Pennsylvania State University.

McDiarmid, H. 1993. "School Yard Bullies Put the Kids at Risk." *Detroit Free Press,* November 16, 1B.

McDonnell, L. 1989. *The Dilemma of Teacher Policy* (JRE–03). Santa Monica, Calif.: RAND.

Mintrom, M. 1998. "Michigan's Charter School Movement." Working Paper 98–14, Political Institutions and Public Choice Program, Michigan State University.

Mitchell, D., and C. Kerchner. 1983. "Labor Relations and Teacher Policy." In *Handbook of Teaching and Policy,* edited by L. Shulman and G. Sykes, 214–38. New York: Longman.

Odden, A., and C. Kelly. 1996. *Paying Teachers for What They Know and Do: New And Smarter Compensation Strategies to Improve Schools.* Thousand Oaks, Calif.: Corwin Press.

Plank, D. N. 1994. "Michigan: Slouching towards Kalkaska." *Politics of Education Bulletin* 20 (Winter).

Ponessa, J. 1996. "Wilkinsburg Should Rehire Teachers, Arbitrator Says." *Education Week on the Web* (http://www.edweek.org/ew/vol-15/18wilk.h15 [January 24]).

Raywid, M. 1990. "Rethinking School Governance." In *Restructuring Schools: The Next Generation of Educational Reform,* edited by R. Elmore and associates, 152–206. Jossey-Bass.

Reis, S. C., and W. T. Hartman. 1997. "Education Funding in Pennsylvania: A Legal Challenge and a Fiscal Response." *Pennsylvania Educational Leadership* 17, 1 (Fall): 11–21.

Thomas, W. B., K. J. Moran, and J. Resnick. 1996. "Intentional Transformation in a Small School District: The Turner School Initiative." In *The Politics of Education and the New Institutionalism: Reinventing the American School,* edited by R. L. Crowson, W. L. Boyd, and H. Mawhinney, 115–26. Washington, D.C.: Falmer Press.

Vergari, S. 1995. "School Finance Reform in the State of Michigan." *Journal of Education Finance* 21 (Fall).

Walsh, M. 1996. "Proponents of Private Management Weigh Options." *Education Week on the Web* (http://www.edweek.org/ew/vol-15/41priv.h15 [August 7]).

Walton, R., and R. McKersie. 1965. *A Behavioral Theory of Labor Negotiations.* McGraw-Hill.

White, K. A. 1998. "Philadelphia Budget Passes, Easing Takeover Threat." *Education Week* 17, 39 (June 10): 6.

Wills, D. J. 1998. "Can School Districts in Pennsylvania Legally Privatize Management and Instructional Services?" Ph.D. dissertation, Pennsylvania State University.

Wolfram, G. 1994. "Education, Power, and the Teachers' Union in Michigan." *Michigan Forward* (October).

7

MARIS A. VINOVSKIS

Teachers Unions and Educational Research and Development

T HE OVERALL ROLE OF teachers unions and their effect on education
has not been thoroughly investigated—although there have been
some recent studies that are helpful.[1] Even fewer analyses exist of the contributions of teachers unions to educational research and development
(R&D), even though this topic is potentially of great interest to many educators and policymakers. The one notable exception is the fine study of the
creation and evolution of the research division of the National Education
Association by noted educational historian Wayne Urban.[2]

In order to provide a broad overview of the changing role of teachers
unions in sponsoring and synthesizing educational research and development, this chapter briefly sketches some of the past contributions of the
American Federation of Teachers (AFT) and the National Education
Association (NEA). Some of the more recent developments in the AFT and
NEA with regard to research (and pay) are examined, with particular attention given to how those organizations have interacted with the Office of

---

1. Among some of the recent books about teacher unions and education are Kerchner, Koppich,
and Weeres (1997); Lieberman (1997); Murphy (1990). Some of these analyses are quite controversial,
as they tend to be strongly opinionated about the value of teacher unions in promoting educational
improvements.

2. Urban (1998).

Educational Research and Improvement (OERI) in the U.S. Department of Education.

The chapter also explores some of the conceptual, methodological, and political issues involved in the provision and use of research by teachers unions and concludes with some suggestions for future improvements. For example, should teachers unions leave educational R&D to the federal government or private foundations in order to use their own scarce resources for other purposes? If teachers unions continue to support research, what types of projects should they fund? Original educational research? Synthesizing existing studies? Disseminating findings from other research and evaluation projects? And given the political activism of both the NEA and AFT in recent years, how can they ensure that their R&D activities are as scientifically rigorous and objective as those produced by other organizations?

Naturally, given the limited secondary analyses on this important topic as well as the large number of issues that might have been addressed, this analysis should be seen as a modest contribution that hopefully will stimulate other scholars and policymakers to examine more thoroughly the efforts of teachers unions in providing and using educational research and development.

The NEA and AFT and Educational Research before 1970

Before the mid-nineteenth century national teacher organizations did not exist—although educators in several states had established their own statewide associations. In 1857 the presidents of the Massachusetts and New York teacher associations drafted a letter calling for a convention to create a national organization. At that convention in Philadelphia, an address by William Russell was read that listed some of the benefits of a national association of teachers, such as sharing educational innovations and effective teaching practices among themselves.[3] Russell acknowledged the special importance of expert knowledge and teacher training in promoting professionalization.[4]

---

3. William Russell was scheduled to deliver a keynote address on the "National Organization of Teachers," but illness prevented his attendance. Therefore T. W. Valentine read Russell's speech before the convention. See Wesley (1957, pp. 22–23).

4. William Russell, quoted in Cohen (1974, p. 1403).

The delegates voted to create the National Teachers' Association (NTA), which was renamed and reorganized in 1870 as the National Educational Association. During the second half of the nineteenth century, the membership of the NEA remained small and fluctuated considerably from year to year. Before 1883 the organization never reached 400 members; in 1887 it jumped to 9,115 but then fell to 1,984 two years later. At the beginning of the twentieth century membership hovered around just over 2,000.[5] In the nineteenth century the NEA was basically a small educational organization with an elected rotating presidency but no permanent full-time staff. Its activities were focused on the annual conventions where teachers, administrators, policymakers, and others presented about 100–200 papers or speeches and passed resolutions on behalf of improving education.[6]

The decentralized organizational structure of the NEA consisted of numerous and often overlapping departments that brought together like-minded individuals. The NEA also appointed committees and commissions to deal with more particular problems and issues. While the work of most of these departments and committees only had a limited impact, a few like the famous Committee of Ten on Secondary School Studies in 1893 had a major influence on education by trying to standardize American high school curriculum.[7]

The NTA and the NEA called for increased federal educational assistance. The NTA strongly endorsed the idea of creating a federal Department of Education and helped to secure its passage in 1867.[8] The NTA and its successor, the NEA, worked closely with the soon renamed federal Bureau of Education throughout the second half of the nineteenth century. Commissioner John Eaton, for example, used the bureau's franking privileges to distribute NEA publications. And on several occasions the NEA worked hard, but unsuccessfully, to persuade Republican or Democratic administrations to appoint Emerson White as the next commissioner of education.[9]

In the early twentieth century the NEA membership grew rapidly and the organization was restructured. Membership by 1910 had grown to 6,909; in 1920 it reached 52,850 and it rose to 216,188 in 1930.[10] Initially

---

5. On the annual changes in the NEA membership from 1857 to 1956, see Wesley (1957, p. 397).
6. Wesley (1957, pp. 20–55).
7. Cremin (1988, pp. 233, 386, 546–47).
8. The best discussion of the creation of the Department of Education in 1867 is Warren (1974).
9. Warren (1974).
10. Wesley (1957, p. 397).

decisions about the organization were decided at the open annual meetings where anyone who attended could vote; after 1921 the conventions became representative assemblies with delegates sent from state associations and other local groups officially affiliated with the NEA.[11] The NEA transferred its headquarters to Washington, D.C., in 1917 and hired a full-time, permanent staff to minister to the needs of its members.[12]

During the nineteenth century the NEA did not specifically focus on the more basic needs of its individual members (such as increasing salaries or improving working conditions). Instead, the organization sought to improve the profession of teaching as a whole and tried to reform American education. By the early twentieth century, however, teachers and administrators had become more concerned about their own immediate needs and urged the NEA to become more attentive to their welfare.[13] The creation of the AFT in 1916 also increased the pressures on the NEA to improve teacher working conditions.[14]

As the NEA reorganized its operations and focused on the more personal, economic concerns of its members, the organization created the Research Division in 1922. In the post–World War I period, teacher salaries had suffered greatly due to high wartime inflation and the inability of local communities to provide adequate funding. The Research Division was established in large part to gather school financial data that school superintendents and teachers needed as well as to discover more scientific ways of running the schools. An additional reason given for creating the unit was the failure of the federal Bureau of Education to provide adequate educational statistics and information that the NEA members now needed.[15]

The Research Division grew rapidly during the 1920s and 1930s under the able leadership of John K. Norton, William G. Carr, and Frank W. Hubbard. Research focused mainly on issues of school finance, instructional salaries, and teacher working conditions—but only rarely on pedagogical or curriculum-related matters. Reflecting a long-standing tension

11. Wesley (1957, pp. 322–33).

12. Wesley (1957, pp. 374–80).

13. Wesley (1957, pp. 334–41).

14. Eaton (1975); Murphy (1990).

15. For an excellent discussion of the creation of the Research Division as well as its subsequent developments over the years, see Urban (1998). Much of my discussion of the history of the Research Division throughout this chapter draws upon the work of Urban. On the federal Bureau of Education in the early twentieth century, see Smith (1923).

within the NEA, teachers and school superintendents were sometimes at odds with each other. The Research Division catered more to the needs and interests of the superintendents than to the teachers, but both groups benefited considerably from the more service-oriented research that was being published in its *Research Bulletin*. And with the onset of the Depression, the Research Division shifted more of its attention to working with state education departments.[16]

Not everyone in education was pleased with the work of the Research Division. An editorial in 1928 in *School Review* questioned the objectivity of the NEA researchers:

> If any organization has ever used the methods of propaganda to promote the interests of its members, it is the National Education Association. A paid bureau—the Research Division—has issued statistical compilation after statistical compilation to coerce boards of education to increase teacher salaries.
>
> Members of Congressional committees have repeatedly complained at public hearings that they are bombarded by letters favoring a Federal Department of Education on the ground that it would be able to increase salaries for teachers.[17]

But the NEA leaders and members appreciated the practical orientation of the Research Division and provided additional resources for its studies and publications.

The nature and quality of the work of the Research Division before World War II have been aptly characterized as "social bookkeeping."[18] The unit compiled statistical information on topics such as teacher salaries, school finance, and enrollment trends, but did not use sophisticated statistical techniques to analyze those data. Nor was the research scope of the Research Division very broad.

The American Educational Research Association (AERA) was created as an NEA department in 1931 and attracted the more academically oriented researchers within the union. The AERA pursued a broader and more encompassing research strategy than the Research Division—but one that

16. Urban (1998, pp. 1–40).
17. Quoted in Urban (1998, p. 18).
18. Urban (1998, p. 17).

had less direct relevance for most NEA members.[19] As Urban put it, "What seemed characteristic of AERA in the 1930s, then, was a movement toward entertaining a wider range of methods in the pursuit of educational research. All of these methods were encompassed under the term 'scientific,' which guided the efforts of AERA, though the meaning of scientific certainly was broadened by the embrace of more, and more diverse, approaches. The Research Division, on the other hand, scientifically suspect for the AERA from the beginning, in the late 1930s continued its efforts from earlier in the decade, and from the previous decade, largely unchanged."[20]

World War II had a major impact on research and development in the United States. The federal government greatly expanded its support of the sciences and they flourished as the public and policymakers became aware of their major contributions to the war effort.[21] Federal spending on R&D rose from about $100 million in 1940 to approximately $1.5 billion in 1945.[22] The behavioral and social sciences did not fare as well, but some economists did play a prominent role in the Office of Price Administration and the War Production Board and many historians worked for the new Office of Strategic Services.[23]

Educational research was not seen as particularly vital to the war effort and the U.S. Office of Education actually reduced its research staff by two-thirds during the war.[24] But the NEA Research Division prospered during World War II and even experienced an increase in its budget (but not in the number of its staff). As a response to the worsening economic conditions for teachers during the war, the Research Division focused on assembling statistics and arguments on behalf of increasing teacher salaries in its *Research Bulletin*.[25]

19. In 1915 the National Association of Directors of Educational Research (NADER) had been created in the NEA and the group worked closely with the Department of Superintendence. It was renamed in the 1920s as the Educational Research Association and became more academically research oriented with a focus on educational psychology. That group then was designated an NEA department in 1931—the American Educational Research Association and published its own journal, *Review of Educational Research*.

20. Urban (1998, pp. 37–38).

21. Featherman and Vinovskis (forthcoming).

22. Reagan (1969, p. 320).

23. Hauser (1945); Novick (1947); Smith (1973); Vinovskis (1999a).

24. Vinovskis (1998a). This was a background paper prepared for the National Education Research Policy and Priorities Board, U.S. Department of Education.

25. Urban (1998, pp. 41–65).

In the postwar period, the Research Division continued to emphasize providing timely and useful information to the growing number of NEA members (the membership more than doubled from 1940 to 1950).[26] Sam Lambert became the director of the Research Division in 1957 and increased its budget from $250,000 to just over $1 million by 1972. While the agency continued with its focus on teacher salaries and school finances, it also expanded into new areas (such as polling teachers, providing information for Congress, and computerizing its operations).[27] During these years, the unit received considerable outside recognition of its work. For example, Lawrence G. Derthick, commissioner of the U.S. Office of Education, in 1960 stated that "the NEA Research Division is acknowledged to be the best and largest agency of its kind maintained by any professional association in the world."[28]

But there were also some troubling signs for the future of research at NEA in the 1960s and early 1970s. A few delegates at NEA meetings now questioned the usefulness of the work of the Research Division and challenged its close alliance with school administrators. As the NEA became more concerned about teacher negotiations and battling the AFT, the more academically oriented researchers in the organization felt less appreciated. Reacting to the NEA efforts to increase departmental financial contributions, the AERA left the NEA and created its own, independent association—thereby further weakening the already small, but more theoretically oriented research community within the organization.[29]

While producing and disseminating research had been a major part of NEA activities before 1970, the AFT did not show much interest in that area. When the AFT was created in 1916, its limited financial resources and precarious situation did not allow for much opportunity to sponsor research. The continued problems of the AFT during the Depression as well as its internal struggles over what to do about its communist members in the late 1930s and 1940s hampered the organization.[30]

Occasionally the AFT published in its *American Teacher* short research-based essays. For example, in 1945 the journal presented the results of a small study that found that a higher proportion of draftees who failed the

---

26. Wesley (1957, p. 397).
27. Urban (1998, pp. 67–86).
28. Urban (1998, p. 72).
29. Urban (1998, pp. 81–86).
30. Eaton (1975); Iverson (1959); Murphy (1990).

army's literacy tests came from states that paid their public school teachers the least.[31] Yet the AFT waited until 1948 to appoint a nominal research director, Florence R. Greve, and even then that operation remained very small.[32] Moreover, many members of the AFT questioned the need to expend scarce resources on research when those monies might be better spent on organizing teachers. For example, when the AFT created a Commission on Educational Reconstruction in 1944 to set goals for American education in the post–World War II period, AFT secretary Irvin Kuenzli remarked that many members questioned the value of the entire enterprise.[33]

Rather than spend money it did not have on collecting and disseminating research, the AFT realized that often it could obtain that same information from the NEA Research Division. For instance, when the NEA established the *Negotiations Research Digest* in 1967 to help its own affiliates in the increasingly bitter union battles with the AFT, the AFT locals simply paid $15 to subscribe to that publication and thereby benefited from the expensive and time-consuming research work done by their rival.[34]

Changes in Teachers Unions and Research in the 1970s and 1980s

The 1970s and 1980s were a period of considerable turmoil and organizational change for both the AFT and NEA as they became even more involved in promoting collective bargaining and competing against each other for new members. The NEA Research Division was reorganized as NEA Research Services and lost much of its autonomy; and its role and importance within the NEA diminished. On the other hand, the previously limited R&D activities of the AFT increased as that organization tried to match NEA's even diminished professional services. The AFT's new president, Albert Shanker, promoted broader educational reforms and worked more closely with federal research agencies such as the National Center for Education Statistics (NCES).

31. American Federation of Teachers (1945, p. 20).
32. American Federation of Teachers (1948, p. 7).
33. Quoted in Eaton (1975, p. 136).
34. Urban (1998, pp. 76–81). See also Murphy (1990, pp. 222–23).

Before World War II few teachers went on strike for higher wages or better working conditions, and in principle both the AFT and NEA opposed teacher strikes. During the late 1950s the AFT became more sympathetic to teacher strikes and collective bargaining. The AFT-affiliated United Federation of Teachers (UFT) went on a one-day strike in New York City in November 1960; the AFT won the right to a collective bargaining election for the following year, at which time the teachers chose to stay within the AFT.[35]

Successful teacher strikes in the 1960s resulted in more collective bargaining and encouraged the AFT and the NEA to compete aggressively against each other for new members. The NEA initially relied only upon sanctions against communities or states that refused to negotiate with teachers rather than encourage local strikes, but it quickly became apparent that many teachers insisted on the right to bargain collectively and go on strike if necessary. Although the NEA was more successful in organizing workers in rural areas and smaller communities, the AFT did much better in the largest cities.[36]

NEA teachers, especially those from the urban areas, increasingly demanded that their union focus more on winning the right to collective bargaining; these teachers also challenged the dominance of the school administrators in NEA and complained that the work of the Research Division often was either irrelevant or designed mainly to help the school superintendents.[37] As part of a larger NEA reorganization in the early 1970s, the Research Division was renamed and reduced to a service unit and its work was assessed by the newly established Program, Planning, Budgeting, and Evaluation System (PPBES). The new Research Services unit no longer was allowed to initiate independent projects; instead it had to await service requests from the other NEA units.[38]

Along with the new emphasis on service, the need for publishing research findings was downplayed. The NEA abandoned publishing the *Research Bulletin* in 1972 and the *Research Reports* series in 1973. At a conference on the role of NEA research in 1974, the Director of Field Services criticized the practice of publishing NEA's research because this provided

---

35. Lieberman and Moskow (1966); Selden (1985); West (1982).

36. Murphy (1990).

37. One of the more militant groups within the NEA was the National Conference of Urban Education Associations, which questioned the usefulness of the work of the Research Division.

38. Urban (1998, pp. 87–104).

those findings readily to hostile public school administrators as well as to opposing AFT members.[39]

Most of the NEA Library and Archives were disbanded and the remaining services were closed to the public and outside scholars. Glen Robinson, director of the old Research Division who had stressed the need for objective analysis, retired in 1973. Two of the next three directors of Research Services did not have the equivalent of a doctorate; the third one, Frank Masters, had little research experience since he came from a long career in field services. Reflecting the growing NEA interest in politics, Research Services tracked federal and state educational legislation and tried to develop a computer network capable of providing information quickly to NEA members. Staff morale in Research Services remained low, but there were some improvements in the late 1980s when Margaret Jones became the new director and Ron Henderson the associate director.[40]

The AFT had not devoted much attention to providing research for its members. But as that union grew in size and became more secure financially in the 1980s, it also began to collect teacher salary information in order to provide comparable data to those still being distributed by the NEA to its members—especially since the NEA was no longer sharing all its research materials with outsiders and competitors. In 1981 the AFT created the Educational Research and Dissemination (ER&D) Program "to translate, codify, and disseminate quality educational research findings about teaching and learning to classroom teachers and paraprofessionals."[41] In the late 1980s the AFT cosponsored the Education for Democracy Project, which published a popular book, *Democracy's Half Told Story*.[42] Yet even compared to the reduced NEA research efforts, the overall work of the AFT in research and development was still smaller in scale and operation than at the NEA.

The 1970s were an important but troubled period for federal support of educational research and development. Dissatisfaction with the quality and usefulness of educational research in the 1960s led to the creation of the National Institute of Education (NIE) in 1972—just as the NEA was dismantling and reorganizing its Research Division. Neither the NEA nor the AFT showed much interest in the creation or support of NIE during the

39. Quoted in Urban (1998, pp. 88–89).
40. Urban (1998, pp. 87–123).
41. American Federation of Teachers (n.d.).
42. Gagnon (1989).

1970s (nor did most other major educational groups express much interest in research and development).[43]

Even during the 1980s, when the NEA and the AFT angrily denounced the Reagan administration's severe cutbacks in educational funding, there was little effort by the teachers unions or other supporters of education to make special pleas for preserving federal R&D funding. Even the few members of Congress who had been strong supporters of the NIE during the 1970s were not willing to fight for more research monies at the expense of funding for service programs such as Title I of the Elementary and Secondary Education Act of 1965.[44] While overall the Department of Education was reduced in real dollars by 11 percent between FY81 and FY88, NIE/OERI lost 70 percent during those years.[45]

The AFT and the NEA were not particularly active in supporting federal R&D activities during the 1970s and 1980s, but they did become more involved in a few situations. For example, the teachers unions in the early 1970s opposed the Education Voucher Experiment put forth by the Office of Economic Opportunity (OEO) that analyzed giving parents an opportunity to choose public schools in the Alum Rock District in San Jose, California.[46] And the AFT opposed the OEO experiments to study contracting out public school services in New York City.[47]

One of the more interesting and controversial issues was NEA's support for many of the recommendations of the Council on Educational Development and Research (CEDaR) about the federally funded regional educational laboratories and the R&D centers. In 1965 the Johnson administration created a system of regional educational laboratories that initially were envisioned as providing large-scale, systematic development (the R&D centers had been created the previous year). In the late 1960s the anticipated funding increase for these institutions did not materialize, and many educators and policymakers became disillusioned with the quality of the R&D work being produced. Efforts were made to reduce or discontinue the guaranteed funding of these institutions in the early 1970s. The laboratories and centers, through CEDaR, persuaded Congress to earmark NIE/OERI research monies for themselves—despite protests from

43. Sproull, Weiner, and Wolf (1978, p. 69).
44. Vinovskis (1998a).
45. Verstegen and Clark (1988).
46. Ascher, Fruchter, and Berne (1996, pp. 38–42); Sproull, Weiner, and Wolf (1978, pp. 96, 101, 134, 170–71).
47. Gramlich and Koshel (1975); Lieberman (1997, pp. 115–16).

the agency as well as many educators. At several crucial moments in these congressional battles in the 1970s and 1980s, the NEA (but not the AFT) intervened and lent its support to CEDaR for the preservation of the laboratories and centers.[48]

The other major development in the 1970s and 1980s was the highly publicized effort of AFT president Shanker to promote educational improvements through standards-based reforms. Shanker was elected AFT president in 1974 and increased the union's membership from 125,000 in 1974 to 750,000 in 1990.[49] He was a visible and successful labor leader who spoke out forcefully for the need for teachers to become involved in the broader educational reform efforts. Through his paid advertising columns in the media, Shanker urged Americans to set high standards for all students and to hold everyone accountable for achieving those goals. While Shanker was not a researcher himself, he frequently reported research findings in his newspaper and magazine columns to support his analyses and arguments.[50]

Teachers Unions and Educational Research in the 1990s

Both the NEA and the AFT expanded their research and development during the 1990s. The NEA in particular reversed the serious cutbacks in research it had instituted in the 1970s and 1980s. Urban's 1998 analysis of NEA's reconstituted Research Division found that the agency had made substantial progress:

> When Ronald Henderson became the Director of the Research Division in 1990, the enterprise seemed more secure than it had been for almost two decades. Events in the ensuing years of the decade confirmed that research and the Research Division indeed had again become an important part of the operation of the headquarters of the National Education Association. In a sense, the Research Division and the rest of the National Education Association came full circle in

48. On the regional educational laboratories and the R&D centers, see Dershimer (1976); Sproull, Wiener, and Wolf (1978); Vinovskis (1993).

49. Mungazi (1995, p. 91).

50. For a highly flattering portrait of Shanker in the 1970s and 1980s, see Mungazi (1995). For a much more critical evaluation of his contributions to educational reform, see Lieberman (1997, pp. 191–206).

the 1990s, arriving at a place they had been many years earlier, expressing values such as professionalism that had earlier been stressed, without abandoning completely the trade union orientation of the 1970s and 1980s.[51]

NEA's renewed interest in research and development received a boost in the mid-1990s with the election of Robert Chase as the president of the organization. Chase spoke of a "new teacher unionism" that called for more teacher professionalism and more cooperation with school administrators. He also called upon teachers to join in the broader public school reform efforts. Whether or not Chase's reform initiatives succeed remains to be seen, but they clearly have reinforced the Research Division's activities to improve the quality and scope of its research and professional endeavors.[52]

The Research Division expanded and improved its earlier work and publications.[53] The agency continued to produce its *Rankings of the States,* which provided rank-ordered educational statistics for the fifty states and the District of Columbia.[54] The survey of the working conditions of teachers every five years was maintained and provided up-to-date information on educational background, teaching experience, teaching assignments, instructional resources, professional development, economic status, personal life, and community involvement.[55] New compilations of data and essays on topics such as higher education were added.[56]

Much of NEA's research continues to focus on school finance and other economic aspects of schooling. Studies of state school finance and tax options have been made.[57] One investigation considered the long-term effects of linking school funding to different types of state taxes. For example, school funding based upon an income or general sales tax ordinarily grows more rapidly than funding based upon a cigarette or gasoline tax (which are usually dependent upon the quantity of the product sold rather

---

51. Urban (1998, p. 125).

52. Urban (1998, pp. 140–42); "NEA Shifts Focus to Education Reform," *Teacher Magazine* (September 1995) (http://www.edweek.org/htb).

53. Some of these studies were done under contract with outside groups like the Corporation for Enterprise Development or individual scholars from organizations like the Urban Institute. The analyses done by those outside the Research Division usually were quite sophisticated analytically and well done.

54. National Education Association (1998b).

55. National Education Association (1997b).

56. National Education Association (1998a).

57. National Education Association (1998c); National Education Association (1994b).

than its value).[58] Studies have explored the linking of education finance and student performance.[59] Considerable effort has been made to analyze the health and pension needs of retired teachers.[60] A new initiative is under way to investigate the characteristics and working conditions of educational support personnel.[61]

Rather than presenting one-sided efforts espousing a particular point of view, the analyses reviewed usually have tried to present a more complex and balanced interpretation. For example, on the highly controversial issue of whether additional school expenditures improve educational outcomes, the NEA research publication summarized its findings:

> The relationship between education spending and economic development is not a simple one, but rather one which involves a series of complex interrelationships. In exploring the connection between the two, we have come to the conclusion that there are no easy answers to the question of the impact of education spending on economic development.
>
> On the one hand, it is clear that investments in education can have a significant impact on long-term economic health. . . .
>
> On the other hand, the on-going debate about the link between education spending and student achievement raises the issue of how efficiently education dollars are spent currently and whether education spending really "matters." While recent research cautions against a simplistic conclusion that "money doesn't matter," this research is equally clear in noting that simply investing more in education—without changes in the way education dollars are spent—will not alone lead to greater student outcomes.[62]

Working more closely with teachers and providing them with research-based curriculum information and mentoring are among the more ambitious efforts within NEA in recent years to provide more professional assistance. The Learning Laboratory Initiative was begun in 1989 as a partnership

58. National Education Association (1996c).

59. National Education Association (1996a).

60. National Education Association (1997a); National Education Association (1995b).

61. National Education Association (1994a); National Education Association (1996b).

62. National Education Association (1995a, p. 34). For a good review of the entire debate on the importance of money in education, see Burtless (1996); Mayer and Peterson (1999).

between NEA's Center for Innovation and local school districts (approximately thirty districts are now participating in this effort). The program brought together teachers, school administrators, and local school boards to promote educational reforms.[63]

The NEA also sponsored the Teacher Education Initiative, which created a seven-site network to develop partnerships between schools, universities, and local associations.[64] And the NEA's project on Keys to Excellence for Your Schools (KEYS) is a five-year R&D project that has identified thirty-five factors that are particularly important for improving education. School staff fill out questionnaires about their institution and the NEA team analyzes those instruments and provides summaries of that information to the schools. Suggestions are made on how to improve the individual schools based upon existing research available through the KEYS project as well as the insights provided by the diagnostic staff questionnaires.[65]

The AFT continued to expand its R&D activities in the 1990s. Unlike the NEA, however, the AFT devoted much less attention and resources to studying teacher salary patterns and trends.[66] Instead, the AFT focused more on analyzing and promoting domestic and international education standards. Building upon Shanker's lengthy involvement with the work of the National Education Goals Panel and the National Assessment Governing Board (NAGB), the AFT published criteria for judging the quality of state educational standards.[67] The organization also annually critiqued the state standards-setting process.[68] The AFT was a leader in defining world-class

---

63. A recent outside evaluation of the Learning Laboratory Initiative concluded: "The Learning Lab initiative has been a valuable forum for testing theories and strategies about the role of a national union in the local education reform arena. The successes and challenges of the eight years of Learning Labs show clearly that by focusing on issues such as building capacity in teachers' associations and encouraging an emphasis on substantive change, NEA is making a significant contribution to the development of unionism more generally. By building on the lessons that have emerged from the experience of both NCI staff and participants in the thirty Learning Lab sites, NEA will [be] likely to have an even more influential role in successful education reform in the future." Bascia and others (1997, p. 6).

64. National Education Association (1998d).

65. For a description of KEYS see Schneider (1995); for some analysis related to the KEYS effort, see Henderson and others (1996, pp. 162–84); Schneider and others (1993); Verdugo and others (1997, 1996).

66. The AFT produced several publications on salary-related matters such as Nelson and Schneider (1998); Nelson and O'Brien (1993).

67. Gandal (n.d.).

68. Gandal (1995, 1960, 1997a).

standards for different subjects and making that information readily available to teachers and policymakers throughout the United States.[69]

The AFT provided teachers with brief descriptions about a handful of promising instructional programs as well as six schoolwide reform efforts.[70] It also supplied guidance about effective reading and mathematics programs.[71] Research on the widespread practice of social promotion was reviewed and then followed by an analysis of actual promotion policies in eighty-five school districts:

> Social promotion is an insidious practice that hides school failure and creates problems for everybody—for kids, who are deluded into thinking they have learned the skills to be successful or get the message that achievement doesn't count; for teachers who must face students who know that teachers wield no credible authority to demand hard work; for the business community and colleges that must spend millions of dollars on remediation, and for society that must deal with a growing proportion of uneducated citizens, unprepared to contribute productively to the economic and civic life of the nation.[72]

Much of the research effort of the AFT was focused on refuting private school and voucher proponents. One study tried to dispel the impression that public school teachers were more likely than the general public to send their children to private schools.[73] Another investigation analyzed the impact of the charter school laws.[74] A series of studies challenged the effectiveness of the recent contract to Education Alternatives, Inc. (EAI), a private, profit-making company, to operate some of the Baltimore public schools.[75] Based upon their research, the AFT has questioned the effectiveness and usefulness of the some of the major school voucher programs.[76]

69. Gandal (1994, 1996, 1997b); Krusemark (1995).

70. American Federation of Teachers (1998a, 1998b).

71. The AFT was one of the members of the Learning First Alliance, which put out a document on how to improve children's reading. See Learning First Alliance (1998). The AFT has also been involved for many years in improving mathematics learning through its program, Thinking Mathematics.

72. American Federation of Teachers (1997, p. 5).

73. Nelson (1996).

74. American Federation of Teachers (1996a).

75. American Federation of Teachers (1994, 1995, 1996b).

76. Murphy, Nelson, and Rosenberg (1997); Shanker and Rosenberg (1991, 1994); Rosenberg (1989, pp. 8–14, 40–45).

On some specific issues the AFT seems to present a selective review of the existing research literature in order to support a particular policy position. For example, on January 27, 1998, President Bill Clinton in his State of the Union address proposed to reduce class size for the first three grades of school, citing highly favorable recent research results on small class size. While some scholars and policymakers have endorsed Clinton's proposals, others have challenged his overall interpretation of the research evidence and questioned the cost-effectiveness of reducing class size for improving student achievement.[77]

Rather than acknowledging and documenting the contested nature of the research debate on class size and student achievement, the AFT's publication, "What Works: Recent Research Demonstrates Major Benefits of Small Class Size," presents a more one-sided, enthusiastic endorsement of the benefits of reducing class size:

> Taken together, these studies strongly support President Clinton's class size initiative. They provide compelling evidence that reducing class size, particularly for younger children, will have a positive effect on student achievement overall and an especially significant impact on the education of poor children. Moreover, lower class size trumps even the most generous results from the highly contested research on vouchers.
>
> Of course, small class size is not a panacea. Reducing class size is a significant means of improving student achievement, but it is not the only piece. High academic standards and a challenging curriculum, safe and orderly classrooms, and qualified teachers are no less significant in the arsenal of solid research-proven reforms. And, in fact, when smaller class size is pursued in conjunction with these standards-based reforms, the combined impact on student achievement is far greater than either strategy alone.[78]

While one can certainly make an argument for the value of reducing class size, perhaps one should also acknowledge that the scholarly evidence in this area is also still quite contested—especially in regard to the cost-effectiveness of this approach compared to other educational reforms.[79]

---

77. There are many discussions of the importance of reducing class size. For a useful summary of some of the latest work, see Bohrnstedt and Parrish (1998).

78. American Federation of Teachers (1996c, 1998c).

79. The NEA has also passed resolutions endorsing smaller class sizes. Lieberman (1997, p. 30).

The AFT's research and dissemination efforts in the 1990s have improved considerably, but overall they are still more modest in size and scope than comparable work at the NEA. One major advantage for the AFT had been the extraordinary intellectual and political leadership of Albert Shanker, whose frequent and well-publicized use of research was widely acknowledged and greatly appreciated.[80] Upon his death in February 1997, memorials from a broad spectrum of policymakers testified to his unique role in American education.[81] Maintaining the same high profile and stressing the relative impact of AFT's research-oriented operations without Shanker's unique internal and external leadership, however, will be a major challenge for the future.

Conclusion

As I conclude this brief overview of the role of teachers unions in fostering educational research and development, perhaps it is time to ask why these organizations should expend any of their scarce dollars on research or development. The teachers unions might be better advised to focus more attention on increasing the federal, state, and local resources available for education or providing for the professional needs of their members. Should teachers unions just leave research and development to academic researchers or the Department of Education while they focus their attention more directly on educating students and providing for the economic and professional improvement of their members?

If the quality of educational research and development in the United States were sufficiently high and we already knew how to help all students thrive in our schools, perhaps teachers unions might leave most of those tasks to others. Unfortunately, our knowledge of what needs to be done to help at-risk children as well as other students is inadequate and our current R&D efforts too limited. During the past three decades, the federal government by itself has spent more than $150 billion on compensatory education programs, yet we have made insufficient progress in improving the academic achievement of these at-risk students. Despite the expenditures

80. Lieberman agrees that Shanker was widely admired, even by neoconservatives. But he argues that Shanker and the AFT in practice are as opposed to fundamental educational reforms as the NEA. Lieberman (1997, pp. 191–206).

81. Resolution of the National Assessment Governing Board (NAGB), adopted May 10, 1997, Washington, D.C. Available in "NAGB Briefing Book" (July 1997).

of considerable federal research monies, it is still not known which programs or policies are the most effective in helping particular children going to school in different neighborhoods.[82]

Many policymakers and educators often believe that there is a "treasure chest" of promising and proven practices simply awaiting better dissemination to school principals or classroom teachers. While there certainly is an abundance of innovative ideas and practices in the field of education, there are no in-depth, rigorous evaluations of them in order to know which ones might be particularly effective in different environments.

Much of the responsibility for the collection of educational statistics and the evaluation of promising practices has rested with the federal government since the mid-nineteenth century. The U.S. Department of Education was created in 1867 and many educators, including NEA members, looked to that agency for leadership and assistance. When sufficient help was not forthcoming, the NEA felt compelled in the early twentieth century to create its own Research Division in order to help its members with the information that the federal government was not providing.

Educators and policymakers recognized the need for large-scale systematic research and development in the mid-1960s when the R&D centers and the regional educational laboratories were created. These institutions initially were envisioned as producing the in-depth and rigorous research and development necessary to provide better educational materials and models for improving American schooling. Yet having spent more than $1.5 billion on the laboratories and $1.1 billion on the centers (in constant 1996 dollars) from fiscal year (FY) 1964 through FY 1997, there still are no large-scale, scientific studies that outline which programs work the best in different circumstances. Some of the laboratories and centers have sponsored useful analyses or provided other types of services such as technical assistance to local schools, but many outside observers have been disappointed with the overall nature and quality of the research and development from these institutions (although the reasons for the frequent changes in their direction and orientation during the past three decades are complex and the subject of considerable disagreement among analysts and policymakers).[83]

Nor should too much attention to the lack of large-scale, scientific research and development be focused on just the regional educational

---

82. Vinovskis (1999a).
83. On the history and quality of the work of the laboratories and centers, see Vinovskis (1993); on the general problems of research and development at OERI today, see Vinovskis (forthcoming).

laboratories and the R&D centers. Congress often calls for ambitious, in-depth studies but then only provides funding for small-scale investigations. And neither the OERI nor the Planning and Evaluation Service (PES) in the Department of Education has made systematic program development and evaluation a major priority in the 1980s and 1990s.[84] As Robert Slavin has observed:

> For decades, policymakers have complained that the federal education research and development enterprise has had too little impact on the practice of education. With a few notable exceptions, this perception is, I believe, largely correct. Federally funded educational R&D has done a good job of producing information to inform educational practice, but has created few well-validated programs or practices that have entered widespread use. The limited direct influence of federal educational R&D, compared to that of, say, research in medicine, physics, and chemistry can certainly be ascribed in part to the far more limited federal investment in educational R&D, coupled with federal policies opposing investment in curriculum development dating back to the Nixon administration and a conservative backlash against such values-laden curricula as "Man: A Course of Study" in the 1970s.[85]

Given the continued lack of large-scale, systematic research and development, the teachers unions should join other concerned groups and individuals in correcting this long-standing deficit. Federal programs like Title I of America's Improving Education Act of 1994 and OERI will be reauthorized in 2000 and will provide an opportunity for those interested in better research and development to make their voices heard in Congress. The AFT and the NEA, which have been influential participants in previous reauthorizations of Title I, should consult with their own research units and then strive to improve the legislation governing current federal research and development. The AFT and NEA should also work more closely with OERI and PES to encourage the Department of Education to enhance the type and quality of research and development being done under the current legislation.

---

84. On the generally perceived idea that the quality of educational research and development is inadequate, see Kaestle (1993). For a discussion of the problems of fostering high-quality research and development by the federal government, see Vinovskis (1999b).

85. Slavin (1997, p. 22).

Teachers unions also can make an important contribution by undertaking their own large-scale R&D activities. Yet their work in this area will be constrained by the high cost of such endeavors—unless the organizations are able to solicit significant outside funding. A few projects like the NEA's KEYS could evolve into a more systematic, large-scale effort to develop more effective ways of improving education, but this may require some redesign of the current project as well as additional testing and analysis. One of the major advantages of having teachers unions involved in this process is that it encourages a larger role for teachers in the development of any new educational models and approaches. When the effectiveness of any program development efforts is being assessed, however, it will be useful to have credible outside evaluators doing that work.[86]

Much of the research work of the teachers unions has focused on instructional salaries and working conditions. While the NCES now also collects statistics on teachers, the salary data have not been released quickly enough to provide teachers union and local school board negotiators with the information they need.[87] Given the importance of timely teacher salary information to the teachers unions as well as the school boards, perhaps NCES could be persuaded to collect these data (assuming that Congress provides the additional necessary funds). In the past NCES sometimes has not been able or willing to collect and report data quickly, but there now appears to be more of a willingness within that agency to work more closely with its customers in order to make such information more readily available. The involvement of NCES in the collection of teacher salary data would benefit everyone and assure that the results would be as accurate and objective as possible. It would also allow the teachers unions and others to focus their research efforts on analyzing those data rather than on the expensive and time-consuming process of assembling them.[88]

The AFT has been one of the leaders in championing the national- and state-level National Assessment of Educational Progress (NAEP) tests. It has also played a key role in supporting the development of NAEP performance standards that provide parents and educators with an indication of

---

86. Few education programs are thoroughly evaluated and some of those that are assessed are evaluated by their developers—an unfortunate situation as one would prefer an evaluation by someone other than the creator of the program. For example, see Vinovskis (1999d).

87. National Center for Education Statistics (1996); Choy and Chen (1998).

88. Since the aggregate teacher salary information is not confidential information, NCES may be able to release the raw data immediately to everyone, thereby making that information available much more quickly.

the expected levels of student achievement. The federal government has spent nearly $500 million (in constant 1996 dollars) since 1969 on NAEP and everyone has gained much from that investment. Yet the AFT has called for using the NAEP data for more than just an index of national and state educational achievement. These data might also be used analytically to provide additional hypotheses and insights about the functioning of the American educational system. While there are serious limits to the use of existing aggregate, cross-sectional NAEP data, the teachers unions could work with NAGB and NCES to develop more effective ways of using NAEP data analytically—perhaps along some of the general lines suggested in the original Lamar Alexander–H. Thomas James report on how to improve NAEP and the National Academy of Education's response to it in 1987.[89]

One of the more useful services of the AFT and the NEA is the synthesis of educational research for its members. Not only is it hard for anyone to keep up with the large volume of research produced annually, but it is difficult for the nonexpert to assess the strengths and weaknesses of that work. Moreover, the average teacher or educator benefits from having that research summarized and presented in a more comprehensible manner— without much of the academic jargon and the technical details present in most research publications.

It is expensive and time-consuming to do in-depth, thoughtful research syntheses. Therefore, whenever possible, the teachers unions should try to rely upon existing well-done, objective research synthesis produced by other individuals or groups such as the R&D centers, the regional educational laboratories, NCES, or OERI. On important topics such the effects of reducing class size, the value of early childhood education, or the best ways of teaching reading skills, we often already have useful syntheses. At the same time, however, some of these research syntheses differ among themselves on how they assess the quality of the existing research or how they interpret the findings. Therefore, it is essential that the researchers within the teachers unions be able to read and assess critically the validity of these other syntheses in order to determine which ones, if any, they feel are technically competent and useful enough for wider distribution.

Another valuable role for the teachers unions is to help their members in obtaining appropriate research-related information, either by providing it

---

89. On the changes in NAEP and the operation of NAGB in the 1990s, see Vinovskis (1998b). This was a background paper prepared for the NAGB.

directly themselves or directing teachers to other sources of assistance. With the development of numerous Internet websites devoted to the dissemination of research-related information about education, consumers often have difficulty in deciding which ones are the most appropriate for them or how to access them efficiently. As the AFT and NEA move toward the so-called new unionism, providing teachers with a central location to which they can go for assistance in navigating the increasingly rich and complex information systems available to educators will be helpful.[90] While teachers now can go directly to institutions such as the regional educational laboratories, the federal comprehensive service centers, the R&D centers, or the ERIC system for assistance, in practice many teachers would benefit by having a knowledgeable person listen to their particular needs and then explain the various options for obtaining the necessary information.

Research played an important role in the NEA before 1970, but it suffered severe cutbacks during the next two decades. Now research has regained some of its former role within NEA, and this is a welcome development for helping to improve American education in the future. Yet the day-to-day ties between the rest of the NEA and the Research Division still could be improved—especially if more efforts are made to work with the executive and legislative branches in order to improve federal research and development.

Thanks to the vigorous and research-oriented leadership of Albert Shanker, the division between union governance and research within the AFT has not been large during the past twenty-five years. But what will happen to the AFT in the future now that the unique contributions of Shanker have ended? Will his successors be able to play the same demanding role both within the union and the larger educational reform community? Will the research staff and activities within the AFT be expanded in order to be more comparable to that of the NEA? And what will happen to the nature and type of research being done by the two unions if the AFT and NEA finally merge?[91]

As research plays a larger and more important role within the AFT and NEA, it is essential that both organizations have adequate staffs who are trained and experienced in dealing with highly sophisticated research

---

90. On the "new unionism," see Kerchner, Koppich, and Weeres (1997).

91. Both the AFT and the NEA now are in the process of revising their research and development priorities—moving closer to each other on many of the issues that they have been pursuing. Bradley (1998, pp. 1, 14–15).

designs and rigorous statistical analyses. While the relatively straightforward collection of data and simple descriptive reporting of them may have been sufficient earlier, today it is important that the research staff be able to design, interpret, and disseminate the increasingly complex data and technically sophisticated studies now prevalent in the social sciences. Even when specific topics are researched by outside experts under contract, the AFT or NEA research staff need to be able to understand the issues involved in order to make wise decisions about whom to hire as well as to know how to evaluate the quality of the work that has been produced.

Teachers unions, like many other educational associations, often function as advocates—interested both in improving American education in general and providing for the more immediate needs of their members. They are to be commended for increasingly seeing the value of research and development in carrying out their missions. At the same time, sometimes there is an inevitable tension between conducting or reporting research objectively and using the results to argue for a particular policy position. While the research units within the AFT and NEA have been sensitive to this dilemma and seem to have handled it well in many situations, this is certainly an area that might benefit from further discussion and improvement. Should there be a more explicit and visible separation in the publications of the research units and the offices of public affairs? What might be learned from the experiences of other groups, such as the division of labor between the Planned Parenthood Federation of America and its sympathetic but technically independent research agency, the Alan Guttmacher Institute?[92] Would convening more outside groups of experts to help oversee specific or more general research activities within the AFT or NEA be helpful?

Finally, everyone might benefit from additional professional interactions between researchers within and outside teachers unions. Despite some notable exceptions, many academics or those who have worked in the Department of Education have not always been familiar with the research and development produced by the AFT and NEA. At the same time, the

---

92. On the problems faced by the Alan Guttmacher Institute in balancing its interests in advocacy with its commitment to objective research on the issue of parental notification when unemancipated teenagers go to family planning clinics, see Vinovskis (1988, pp. 87–130). Outside groups are not the only ones plagued with problems of balancing their advocacy activities with their research functions. For example, the Planning and Evaluation Service in the Department of Education may have manipulated how it released findings from its Longitudinal Evaluation of School Change and Performance in order to affect ongoing education policy discussions about the effectiveness of systemic reform. See Vinovskis (1999c) and the reply by the Planning and Evaluation Service (1999).

staff of the teachers unions have not always been aware of or involved with nonunion research projects that might have been of interest to themselves or to the teachers who are members of their organizations.

References

American Federation of Teachers. No date. "Educational Research and Dissemination (ER&D) Program." Washington, D.C.

———. 1945. "Bayonne Teacher Makes Study of Economic Status of Bayonne Teachers." *American Teacher* (February): 20.

———. 1948. No title. *American Teacher* (February): 7.

———. 1994. *The Private Management of Public Schools: An Analysis of the EAI Experience in Baltimore.* Washington, D.C.

———. 1995. *How Private Managers Make Money in Public Schools: Update on the EAI Experiment in Baltimore.* Washington, D.C.

———. 1996a. *Charter School Laws: Do They Measure Up?* Washington, D.C.

———. 1996b. *Setting the Record Straight: Update on Student Achievement in the EAI-Run Schools in Baltimore.* Washington, D.C.

———. 1996c. *Vouchers versus Small Class Size: Comparing Effects, Costs, and Public Support.* Washington, D.C.

———. 1997. *Passing on Failure: District Promotion Policies and Practices.* Washington, D.C.

———. 1998a. *Building on the Best, Learning from What Works: Seven Promising Reading and English Language Arts Programs.* Washington, D.C.

———. 1998b. *Building on the Best, Learning from What Works: Six Promising Schoolwide Reform Programs.* Washington, D.C.

———. 1998c. "What Works: Recent Research Demonstrates Major Benefits of Small Class Size." Washington, D.C. (February).

Ascher, Carol, Norm Fruchter, and Robert Berne. 1996. *Hard Lessons: Public Schools and Privatization.* New York: Twentieth Century Fund.

Bascia, Nina, and others. 1997. "Teacher Associations and School Reform: Building Stronger Connections." External review prepared for the National Education Association by the Ontario Institute of Studies in Education, University of Toronto (November).

Bohrnstedt, George W., and Thomas B. Parrish. 1998. "California's Class Size Reduction Initiative: Is It Likely to Reduce or Create Further Inequities in California Districts?" Paper presented at the meetings of the American Sociological Association, San Francisco, August.

Bradley, Ann. 1998. "NEA, AFT Strategies for Upgrading Quality of Teachers Drawing Nearer." *Education Week* 18 (September 23): 1, 14–15.

Burtless, Gary, ed. 1996. *Does Money Matter? The Effect of School Resources on Student Achievement and Adult Success.* Brookings.

Choy, Susan P, and Xianglei Chen. 1998. *Toward Better Teaching: Professional Development in 1993–94,* NCES 98–230. National Center for Education Statistics. Government Printing Office.

Cohen, Sol, ed. 1974. *Education in the United States: A Documentary History,* vol. 3. Random House.

Cremin, Lawrence A. 1988. *American Education: The Metropolitan Experience, 1876–1980.* Harper and Row.

Dershimer, Richard. 1976. *The Federal Government and Educational R&D.* Lexington Books.

Eaton, William Edward. 1975. *The American Federation of Teachers, 1916–1961: A History of the Movement.* Southern Illinois University Press.

Featherman, David L., and Maris A. Vinovskis. Forthcoming. "Growth and Use of Social and Behavioral Science in the Federal Government since World War II." In *The Social Sciences and Policymaking,* edited by David L. Featherman and Maris A. Vinovskis. University of Michigan Press.

Gagnon, Paul. 1989. *Democracy's Half Told Story: What American History Textbooks Should Add.* Washington, D.C.: American Federation of Teachers.

Gandal, Matthew. No date. *Setting Strong Standards: AFT's Criteria for Judging the Quality and Usefulness of Student Achievement Standards.* Washington, D.C.: American Federation of Teachers.

———. 1960. *Making Standards Matter: An Annual Fifty-State Report on Efforts to Raise Academic Standards.* Washington, D.C.: American Federation of Teachers.

———. 1994. *What College-Bound Students Abroad Are Expected to Know about Biology: Exams from England and Wales, France, Germany and Japan.* Washington, D.C.: American Federation of Teachers.

———. 1995. *Making Standards Matter: A Fifty-State Progress Report on Efforts to Raise Academic Standards.* Washington, D.C.: American Federation of Teachers.

———. 1996. *What College-Bound Students Abroad Are Expected to Know about Chemistry and Physics: Exams from England and Wales, France, Germany and Japan.* Washington, D.C.: American Federation of Teachers.

———. 1997a. *Making Standards Matter, 1997: An Annual Fifty-State Report on Efforts to Raise Academic Standards.* Washington, D.C.: American Federation of Teachers.

———. 1997b. *What Students Abroad Are Expected to Know about Mathematics: Exams from France, Germany and Japan.* Washington, D.C.: American Federation of Teachers.

Gramlich, Edward M., and Patricia P. Koshel. 1975. *Educational Performance Contracting.* Brookings.

Hauser, Philip M. 1945. "Wartime Developments in Census Statistics." *American Sociological Review* 10 (April): 160–69.

Henderson, Ronald D., and others. 1996. "High-Quality Schooling for African American Students." In *Beyond Desegregation: The Politics of Quality in an African School,* edited by Mwalimu J. Shujaa, 162–84. Corwin Press.

Iverson, Robert W. 1959. *The Communists and the Schools.* Harcourt, Brace, and Co.

Kaestle, Carl F. 1993. "The Awful Reputation of Educational Research." *Educational Researcher* 22 (January–February): 23–31.

Kerchner, Charles Taylor, Julia E. Koppich, and Joseph G. Weeres. 1997. *United Mind Workers: Unions and Teaching in the Knowledge Society.* Jossey-Bass.

Krusemark, Dawn. 1995. *What Secondary Students Abroad Are Expected to Know: Gateway Exams Taken by Average-Achieving Students in France, Germany, and Scotland.* Washington, D.C.: American Federation of Teachers.

Learning First Alliance. 1998. *Every Child Reading: An Action Plan of the Learning First Alliance.* Washington, D.C.

Lieberman, Myron. 1997. *The Teacher Unions: How the NEA and AFT Sabotage Reform and Hold Students, Parents, Teachers, and Taxpayers Hostage to Bureaucracy.* Free Press.

Lieberman, Myron, and Michael H. Moskow. 1966. *Collective Negotiations for Teachers.* Rand McNally.

Mayer, Susan E., and Paul E. Peterson, eds. 1999. *Earning and Learning: How School Matters.* Brookings.

Mungazi, Dickson A. 1995. *Where He Stands: Albert Shanker of the American Federation of Teachers.* Praeger.

Murphy, Dan, F. Howard Nelson, and Bella Rosenberg. 1997. *The Cleveland Voucher Program: Who Chooses? Who Gets Chosen? Who Pays?* Washington, D.C.: American Federation of Teachers.

Murphy, Marjorie. 1990. *Blackboard Unions: The AFT and the NEA, 1900–1980.* Cornell University Press.

National Center for Education Statistics. 1996. *The Patterns of Teacher Compensation, NCES 95–829, by Jay Chambers.* Government Printing Office.

National Education Association. 1994a. *Educational Support Personnel Membership Study by State, 1993.* Washington, D.C.

———. 1994b. *Tax Options for States Needing More School Revenue.* Washington, D.C.

———. 1995a. *How Education Spending Matters to Economic Development.* Washington, D.C.

———. 1995b. *Retirement and Health Care in the 21st Century: Ready or Not? Selected Proceedings of the NEA Retirement and Benefits Forum.* Maui, Hawaii, October 13–16, 1994. Washington, D.C.

———. 1996a. *Linking Education Finance and Performance: Selected Proceedings State Education Finance Workshop.* Denver, Colo., May 18–19, 1995. Washington, D.C.

———. 1996b. *National Educational Support Personnel Membership Study.* Washington, D.C.

———.1996c. *Separating the Wheat from the Chaff: How Much Do Schools Really Benefit When States Raise Taxes on Their Behalf?*

———. 1997a. *NEA-Retired National and State-Level Membership Studies, 1994.* Washington, D.C.

———. 1997b. *Status of the American Public School Teacher, 1995–96.* Washington, D.C.

———. 1998a. *NEA 1998 Almanac of Higher Education.* Washington, D.C.

———. 1998b. *Rankings of the States, 1997: A Data Resource for Examining State Public Education Programs.* Washington, D.C.

———. 1998c. *Survey of 1996 State School Finance Legislation: Overview and Abstracts of Legislation from the Fifty States.* Washington, D.C.

———. 1998d. *Teacher Education Initiative: Second Year Report, May 1998.* Washington, D.C.

Nelson, F. Howard. 1996. *Public School Teachers and Their Private School Choices: Getting the Facts Straight.* Washington, D.C.: American Federation of Teachers.

Nelson, F. Howard, and Timothy O'Brien. 1993. *How U.S. Teachers Measure Up Internationally: A Comparative Study of Teacher Pay, Training, and Conditions of Service.* Washington, D.C.: American Federation of Teachers.

Nelson, F. Howard, and Krista Schneider. 1998. *Survey and Analysis of Salary Trends, 1997–1998.* Washington, D.C.: American Federation of Teachers.

Novick, David. 1947. "Research Opportunities in the War Production Board Records." *American Economic Review* 37 (May): 690–93.

Planning and Evaluation Service. 1999. "Response to Maris Vinovskis' Paper Critiquing the Longitudinal Evaluation of School Change and Performance" (August).

Ravitch, Diane, ed. Forthcoming. *Brookings Papers on Education Policy, 2000*. Brookings.

Reagan, Michael D. 1969. *Science and the Federal Patron*. Oxford University Press.

Rosenberg, Bella. 1989. "Public School Choice: Can We Find the Right Balance?" *American Educator* 13 (Summer): 8–14, 40–45.

Schneider, Jeff. 1995. "KEYS to Excellence for Your Schools." National Education Association (May).

Schneider, Jeffrey M., and others. 1993."Statistical Quality Control and School Quality." *Contemporary Education* 64 (Winter): 84–87.

Selden, David. 1985. *The Teacher Rebellion*. Howard University Press.

Shanker, Albert, and Bella Rosenberg. 1991. *Politics, Markets and America's Schools: The Fallacies of Private School Choice*. Washington, D.C.: American Federation of Teachers.

———. 1994. "Private School Choice: An Ineffective Path to Educational Reform." In *Privatizing Education and Educational Choice*, edited by Simon Hakim, Paul Seidenstat, and Gary Bowman, 60–71. Praeger.

Slavin, Robert E. 1997. "Design Competitions: A Proposal for a New Federal Role in Educational Research and Development." *Educational Researcher* 26 (January–February): 22–28.

Smith, Darrell Hevenor. 1923. *The Bureau of Education: Its History, Activities, and Organization*. Johns Hopkins University Press.

Smith, R. Harris. 1973. *OSS: The Secret History of America's First Central Intelligence Agency*. New York: Delta.

Sproull, Lee, Stephen Weiner, and David Wolf. 1978. *Organizing an Anarchy: Belief, Bureaucracy, and Politics in the National Institute of Education*. University of Chicago Press.

Urban, Wayne J. 1998. *More Than the Facts: The Research Division of the National Education Association, 1922–1997*. Lanham, Md.: University Press of America.

Verdugo, Richard R., and others. 1996. "Statistical Quality: Control, Quality Schools, and the NEA—Advocating for Quality." *Contemporary Education* 67 (Winter 1996): 88–93.

———. 1997. "School Governance Regimes and Teachers' Job Satisfaction: Bureaucracy, Legitimacy, and Community." *Educational Administration Quarterly* 33 (February 1997): 38–66.

Verstegen, Deborah A., and David L. Clark. 1988. "The Diminution in Federal Expenditures for Education during the Reagan Administration." *Phi Delta Kappan* (October): 134–38.

Vinovskis, Maris A. 1988. *An "Epidemic" of Adolescent Pregnancy? Some Historical and Policy Considerations*. Oxford University Press.

———. 1993. "Analysis of the Quality of Research and Development at the OERI Research and Development Centers and the OERI Regional Educational Laboratories." Final Report, Office of Educational Research and Improvement (June).

———. 1998a. *Changing Federal Strategies for Supporting Educational Research, Development, and Statistics*. Government Printing Office (September).

————. 1998b. *Overseeing the Nation's Report Card: The Creation and Evolution of the National Assessment Governing Board.* Government Printing Office (November).

———— 1999a. "Do Federal Compensatory Education Programs Really Work? A Brief Historical Analysis of Title I and Head Start." *American Journal of Education* 107 (May): 187–209.

————. 1999b. *History and Educational Policymaking.* Yale University Press.

————. 1999c. "Improving the Analysis and Reporting of Policy-Related Evaluations at the U.S. Department of Education: Some Preliminary Observations about the Longitudinal Evaluation of School Change and Performance." Unpublished paper (August).

————. 1999d. "Missing in Practice? Systematic Development and Rigorous Program Evaluation at the U.S. Department of Education." Paper presented at the Conference on Evaluation and Educational Politics, American Academy of Arts and Sciences, Cambridge, Mass. (May).

————. Forthcoming. "Restructuring the Office of Educational Research and Improvement and Enhancing the Federal Role in Educational Research and Development." In *Brookings Papers on Education Policy, 2000,* edited by Diane Ravitch. Brookings.

Warren, Donald R. 1974. *To Enforce Education: A History of the Founding Years of the United States Office of Education.* Wayne State University Press.

Wesley, Edgar B. 1957. *NEA: The First Hundred Years, The Building of the Teaching Profession.* Harper and Brothers.

West, Allan M. 1982. *The National Education Association: Power Base for Education.* Free Press.

8

BRUCE S. COOPER

An International Perspective on Teachers Unions

TEACHERS WORLDWIDE HAVE shown amazing resiliency and adaptability, embracing the labor movement and greatly improving their
status and income. In less than a half century teachers have risen from
underpaid, undervalued "semiprofessionals" to powerful voices in education, becoming key leaders within the larger labor movement and prime
movers in regional and national politics. To a large degree, this emergence
from obscurity to prominence and transition from exploited, sympathy-
invoking martyrs to respected agents at the bargaining table and in the
halls of government are the result of the unionization of teachers—a phenomenon common in virtually every developed nation on earth.[1]

As we enter the new millennium, teachers and their unions face new
problems across the world. First, students are gaining access to interactive
learning electronically and "home schooling," which could lead to a weakening of the hegemony of formal, publicly controlled education. Second,
governments are experimenting with radical decentralization, whereby the

A special thank you to Stephen B. Lawton, professor at the Ontario Institute for Studies in
Education, University of Toronto, for his help in revising this chapter. Also, thanks to Anne Gargan for
her assistance in editing this chapter.
1. Etzioni (1969); Lortie (1969, 1975); Conley and Cooper (1991); Rosenholz (1985); Urban
(1982); Berube (1988).

management of schools is handed over to the parents, teachers, and administrators. How can a teachers union organize thousands of tiny "locals" and bargain thousands of contracts, when school decisionmaking is at each school site, no longer controlled by the district, state, or nation? Perhaps the greatest threat to the long-term survival of teachers unions is what the movement ungracefully has called "privatization," the conversion of education from a public, government service to a private, entrepreneurial effort, using vouchers and other market-centered devices.

This chapter discusses how, in the postindustrial "Information Age," "education" is now available in myriad places other than formal schools. And already, a number of jurisdictions, including the United States, Canada, England and Wales, and New Zealand, have experimented with the "privatization" of education (for example, vouchers, aid to nonpublic and even religious schools), radical decentralization, outsourcing education to private providers and managers, and opting out (for example, charter schools; city technology colleges; and schools run by private, for-profit corporations). These and other reforms threaten the traditional role of teachers unions—much as postindustrialism has changed the shape of business and reduced the size and effectiveness of private-sector unions in many nations.

Understanding teachers unions and how they adapt to their environment—particularly across nations and societies—starts with a common set of definitions and process, within highly diverse and differentiated structural, financial, and political environments. The core mission and processes of unions are all essentially the same: united transactions to help teachers improve their work lives by balancing the asymmetrical relationship between the more powerful employers in the enterprise (usually the government in K–12 education) and the less powerful employees. Teachers typically become part of a labor-management relationship, as equals at the "bargaining table," where employees and employers seek to co-determine the levels of pay, benefits, conditions of employment, and any other job-related issues that trouble either "side." Thus nations with free, democratic labor movements have these characteristics in common.[2]

Figure 8-1 places this common core activity (called "Union Rights and Transactions") at the epicenter of the labor-management system, with five related processes shaping and affecting the central activities of representing,

2. Maeroff (1988); Wattenberg (1990); World Confederation of Organizations of the Teaching Profession (1986, p. 43).

Figure 8-1. *Teacher Unionization Model: Five Foci for Making International Comparisons*

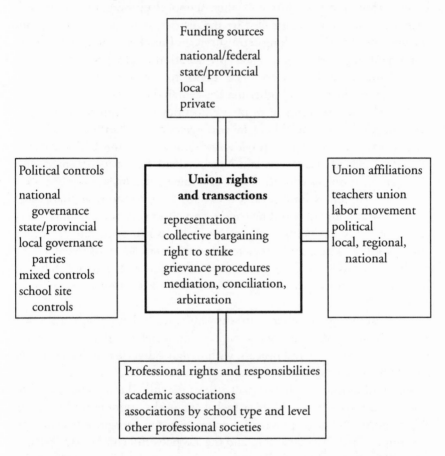

bargaining, striking, grieving, and mediating. But here the similarities stop. Each nation and, in some cases, each state or province within a country, has the following four contextual differences that affect the basic union functions.

FUNDING SOURCES. Unions are concerned about the economic well-being of their members; hence the centerpiece of collective negotiations and the most often cited cause of strikes are unmet demands for higher pay and better benefits. Nation by nation, the source of funding is a good predictor of the nature and focus of bargaining. In those nations with federal (national) funding of education, one expects to see national bargaining and contracts. In other countries funding is primarily provided by regional jurisdictions (states in the United States, provinces in Canada, and länder in Germany). In nations with local taxation for schools and local control (United States, Canada, and Germany) and where private sources of funding for schools are common, unionization is weaker and more diffuse, as is illustrated by the rise of charter schools and private schools (many of which hire nonunionized teachers).

POLITICAL CONTROLS.   Closely related to funding, as shown in figure 8-1, is the locus of political control over schools. Again, those nations with federal or national school systems, controlled legislatively and judicially from the nation's capital, find teachers unions bargaining, lobbying, striking, and grieving within a national political context. Where control is "mixed," as in Canada, the United States, England and Wales, Germany, and Australia, the behavior of teachers' organizations is more diffuse and confusing. Often reflecting the political structure, the unions form local, state, and national offices—each with special staff to deal with that level of jurisdiction. Functionally, too, each level of government may take on slightly different roles, meaning that the union may do different things at different levels. For example, the union may set up lobbying offices at provincial or national levels, while engaging in collective bargaining at the local level, as in most states of the United States and several provinces of Canada.

UNION AFFILIATIONS.   As indicated in figure 8-1, unions perform more functions than bargaining and striking. They have a major role in uniting employees, affiliating teachers with other teachers in one or more teachers unions and joining teachers to the general labor union movement, or branches of it, in their country. The national labor union(s) in some countries, in turn, affiliate with key political parties, forming either a Labor party or Workers' party. In other countries, teachers unions and the national labor federations may refrain from joining one political party; instead, they "support" (or become identified as supporting) a particular party that seems best to promote compatible, supportive ideologies and policies.[3]

---

3. Rosow and Zager (1989).

This tendency of unions to affiliate, merge, and unite with other associations creates ever-larger union groups—increasing political power but sometimes diminishing local autonomy. In cases such as Mexico, as discussed later in this analysis, teachers unions sometimes made tough choices not to support laws that directly helped teachers in their classrooms (through radical decentralization) but instead backed the status quo, so teachers union leadership could retain control over education by keeping the system nationalized and centralized.

PROFESSIONAL RIGHTS AND RESPONSIBILITIES. Teachers are not carpenters, steelworkers, or shipbuilders. They are trained professionals with major responsibilities for transmitting and improving the culture of nations (see figure 8-1). This idealistic role of schooling interacts with the teachers union's functions in some cases, influencing what educators favor, what they are willing to fight for, and how they define their mission. In many cases, the teachers union will adopt the essence of the school's mission and will claim to be bargaining, grieving, and even striking to benefit teachers and students. But professionalism and unionism are not always compatible and appear to distort the union-management process in some nations.[4]

This chapter analyzes data on teachers unions in fifteen nations across the globe, from Greece to Sweden, Israel to Australia, to determine how the core behaviors that define unionization relate to the patterns of funding, political control, affiliation, and professionalism in K–12 education.

Core Activities

The basic or core processes in the fifteen countries are explored, including the legitimacy and means by which unions: (a) seek official public representation for teachers as their recognized bargaining agent; (b) bargain collectively with management for better economic benefits and improved conditions of work; (c) withdraw services (that is, to strike) if management refuses to recognize the union's rights, ceases to bargain in good faith, and/or fails to carry out the contract in a mutually satisfactory way; (d) seek third-party intervention (mediation, reconciliation, and

4. Ravitch (1974).

arbitration—voluntary or binding) to help settle impasse and disputes; and (e) gain access to management decisionmaking through a united, collective voice in key deliberative groups. While these processes may vary in their level (federal/national, state/provincial, local), timing, and participation, the net effect of these core union-management interactions remains similar in most nations.

Founding of Teacher Organizations

Teachers' associations, clubs, and societies were formed most often in the late nineteenth century—many years before the advent of collective bargaining and the labor movements in the public sector (see table 8-1). However, teachers early on perceived the need for some kind of formal association, even though real unionization was to come later. For example, the following countries formed educator associations on these dates: Australia, 1889; Great Britain, 1870; Greece, 1872; New Zealand, 1883; Sweden, 1880 for primary school teachers, 1885 for secondary staff. The National Education Association (NEA) was formed in the United States in 1857.

These dates correspond roughly to the formation of the official public education systems in those countries, whereby governments established universal, often compulsory, primary schools, with significant public resources devoted to education. In Australia, for example, education is the responsibility of the states. Hence the oldest teachers' association, the Queensland Teachers' Union, was started in 1889, at the point where the state of Queensland passed laws establishing a public school service.

Similar histories can be told in Great Britain. The passage of the Elementary Education Act of 1870—"the most workable piece of compromise legislation in English 19th-century history," according to John Lawson and Harold Silver—was also the year of the founding of Britain's preeminent teachers' association, the National Union of Teachers (NUT).[5] As Britain established a government-sponsored primary school system, teachers perceived the need to form and join an association to enhance their voice and to build stronger collegiality.

Sweden's Sveriges Allmanna Folkskollararefonig, the country's first primary school teachers' group, was formed in 1880, followed by the secondary teachers union in 1884. Both were in part reactions to the effort of

5. Lawson and Silver (1978, p. 314).

Table 8-1. *Dates of Founding and Initiating Collective Bargaining for School Teachers, in Sample Nations*

Nation	Date of first teacher organization	Date of unionization	Number of teachers[a]	Level of bargaining
Australia	1889	1916	210,000	State
Canada	1890	1965	460,000	Provincial/local
China	1949	1950	9,000,000	Local/national
France	1906	1919	817,368	National
Germany	1900	1967	434,300	National
Great Britain	1870	1907	498,000	National
Greece	1872	1964	102,000	National
Hungary	1975	1988	230,000	National
Israel	1903	1948	102,000	National
India	1890	1909	6,400,000	National/regional
Italy	1901	1947	953,000	National
Mexico	1932	1960	1,090,000	National
New Zealand	1883	1962	31,694	National
Sweden	1880	1963	223,300	National
United States	1857	1968[b]	4,500,000	Local

a. In 1989.

b. Each state regulates teacher collective bargaining as it sees fit; hence, no single date is possible. The year 1968 was the beginning of official bargaining in New York.

the Swedish government to expand the provision of free education to all in the late nineteenth century.

In the United States, the founding of the first national teachers group in 1857—the National Teachers' Association (later renamed the National Education Association)—was the result of the joint effort of ten state teachers' organizations. This merger, indicating a fair amount of earlier organizational activity at the state level, was a partial result of state and local actions: the creation of the universal, publicly funded public or "common" school, beginning in the 1830s in Massachusetts and spreading south and westward as the nation grew.[6]

The leadership in the United States education association came not only from among the teachers but also from a whole set of new educational

6. See Tyack (1974).

managers, including the principal teachers (the heads of schools) and assistants, and the school superintendents—the emerging "captains of education efficiency."[7] Administrators, too, saw the need to form an education association to give voice to their new enterprise—and, ironically, to combat early attempts of teachers to unionize. Later the school superintendents were expelled from the NEA when teachers started to organize for collective negotiations with the passage of state-level bargaining laws.

All these examples, and more, show the emerging relationship between government action and teacher unionism: the more active the government was in establishing a large, standard public system, the greater the response of the teachers to organize.[8] The growth of school structure and school employees' associations went hand in hand. Job descriptions and qualifications, standards for licensing and certification, contractual employment, standard salary schedules, and job review, for example, as promulgated in government regulations, seemed to stimulate a collective response from teachers in the education system.

Further, these early associations were mainly composed of primary (or elementary) school teachers, since nations concentrated first on creating universal elementary school education, for children from about ages six to fourteen. Later, as secondary schools became more common, so did the rise of high school teacher associations. In Sweden, for example, the primary teachers' group was begun in 1880, followed a few years later by the secondary school teachers' group. In Australia, a number of states (for example, Victoria) had primary schools groups, then secondary, and later a merger of the two associations to form one, more powerful teacher group.

Collective Bargaining

The right to bargain collectively is necessarily a matter of law and policy. Without legal protection, unions cannot easily pursue their goals of co-determination through negotiations. This right to bargain, as spelled out in government policy, may come from three levels: a national system of laws and practices (as in China, France, Great Britain, Greece, Hungary, Israel, Italy, Mexico, and New Zealand); state or provincial legislation (as in Australia, Canada, Germany, and the state of Hawaii in the United States); or the local level, where teachers' groups are recognized for negotiations

7. Callahan (1962).
8. Cooper and Bussey (1982).

through local committees (as in the United States, some states in Australia, and Canada).

As shown in the second column of table 8-1, the dates of the beginning of collective bargaining between the teachers union(s) and the governmental jurisdictions came over a wide span of years, with Australia, France, and Great Britain seeing teachers (and other public sector employees) joining in collective negotiations at about the same time as did industrial employees. Typically, however, teachers were granted official rights to bargain later than blue collar employees in the private sector, mostly in the second half of the twentieth century: 1965 in Canada, 1968 in the state of New York (United States), and 1962 in New Zealand.

Most nations in this limited sample have established (1) national laws regulating bargaining, (2) national mechanisms for bringing school employees and government employers to the bargaining table, (3) national pay and benefit scales, and (4) national strikes and lobbying, since authority over teachers is national in scope. The case of Italy illustrates the process of recognition.

Long-suffering teachers in Italy watched their pay levels decline, putting them near the bottom in salary among all public employees. Divided, disorganized, and unable to bring political force to bear, the mainstream teachers unions were unwilling to risk direct action. Instead, breakaway "autonomous" organizations, also called "grass roots committees," led a long but successful strike, which ended in 1988 with the Italian government's increasing teachers' pay significantly above the rate of increase extended to other public employees.

Australia, the United States, and Canada—all nations with decentralized labor relations—are by far the most complex. Australia has full bargaining structures in each state and territory, which in turn negotiate and deal with the state teachers unions. Canada has different bargaining arrangements in the eleven provinces and two territories, with an enormous variety of unions, each bargaining at provincial or local jurisdictions, and some at both levels.

The United States has 14,800 local education authorities (called school districts) and thus 14,800 different labor relations environments (that is, "contracts," pay scales, and conditions of employment). Only in school districts located in the thirty-two states that legally protect teachers' prerogative to bargain can teachers be assured of collective rights, for the United States has no national public employment relations law and no national teacher negotiations. Unionization tends to occur in the larger, more industrialized states (for example, California, New York, Michigan, Pennsylvania, and New Jersey). Thus while thirty-two states protect union recognition for teachers, some 82 percent of American teachers engage in collective bargaining with school boards.

Nations extend these rights to teachers in different ways. Australia, for example, has established special tribunals to which teachers unions can appeal and which have had the authority since 1916 to determine at least the teachers' salaries. Various states and territories have slightly different arrangements, with Queensland, New South Wales, the Australian Capital Territory, and the Northern Territory using an industrial commission to settle disputes between the union and the state or territorial bargaining agency.

Other states, such as Western Australia, Victoria, and Southern Australia, extended the existing industrial (private sector) machinery to include teacher unionism; still others created a special commission, the so-called Teachers' Tribunal or the Victorian Teaching Service Conciliation and Arbitration Commission, to encourage bargaining and provide voluntary arbitration, should union and management reach an impasse. Hence Australia has created elaborate mechanisms in each state to assist teachers in reaching wage agreements with their state governments.

New Zealand followed suit, although much later. In 1948 the government established the arbitration system and the arbitration court to adjudicate differences between public sector unions and the government. When this mediation process failed in 1986, the teachers appealed to another body, the Higher Salaries Commission, an independent group in charge of setting salaries for members of parliament and judges, which restored teachers' salaries after a national freeze.

In the fall of 1989 the government in New Zealand attempted unsuccessfully to abolish all collective bargaining with national unions, shifting this activity to individual schools and individual teachers. While it may have been the intent of the government to make these dramatic changes— including shutting down school boards at the elementary school level and issuing charters to each school as a freestanding agency—nationwide collective bargaining between the government and the New Zealand teachers unions was maintained.

After granting "bulk funding" directly to about fifty schools under their charters, individual contracts were issued to teachers in those schools. When the government tried to expand bulk funding to other schools, the teachers unions strongly opposed this effort. On September 3, 1998, the New Zealand Post-Primary Teachers' Association "lodged a counter-claim, in response to the government's opening offer for a settlement of the Collective Employment Contract." Obviously, national unions are alive and fighting in New Zealand, seeking increased national salaries and a stronger voice for teachers. A leader stated in an interview with the author, "We have also rejected strongly all other antiunion aspects of the government's offer, including abolition of paid union meetings and paid Presidential leave."[9]

In Great Britain in the 1980s Prime Minister Margaret Thatcher ended a three-year teachers' strike (1984–87) by granting teachers a wage increase of more than 16 percent, while at the same time abolishing collective bargaining for teachers in England and Wales (Scotland has its own system). Between 1988 and 1991 Britain had tried unilateral decisionmaking, as well as discussions of returning to the representational style of bargaining, known as the Burnham Commission, a representative body or syndicate that acted for decades as a bargaining group for all parties and unions, or some other device. A commission to "set" wages was established, a similar system now being used among professional employees (doctors and nurses in the National Health Service). A national commission reviews the salary situation, hears testimony from teachers and employers, and sets wages and conditions of employment—a retreat from the basic tenets of co-determination in union-management relations: that is, union recognition, collective bargaining, and shared decisionmaking.

In all, then, nations have turned to national and state or provincial legislatures to legitimize the rights of teachers to form unions and to seek co-determination with their employers, the government. While a definite movement toward universal rights of teachers to form unions can be seen, we also note interesting means for extending this right—and the restriction of these rights under government policies in Great Britain, New Zealand, eighteen of the fifty states in the United States, and even Japan, where bargaining rights are not enjoyed.[10]

Structure of Teacher Unionism

The structure of teacher labor relations reflects the complexity of societies and the legal systems in which they exist. Nations with diverse ethnic, confessional, linguistic, and social groups; with complex federal republican

---

9. See www.ppta.org.nz.
10. Ota (1985); Lawn (1985); LeClearcq (1984).

governments; and with traditions of local, democratic control of education are more likely to have elaborate teachers unions and complex bargaining arrangements. In contrast, countries with less socioethnic and political diversity and more highly centralized school control systems will have fewer teachers unions (even just one) and a more nationalized, monolithic view of union-management relations.[11]

Several countries cluster at either end of a continuum that runs from monolithic-centralized to diverse-decentralized, illustrating the qualities of teacher unionism across the globe. At the centralized, nondemocratic, unified end of the spectrum are those nations with strong, national political systems. China, Hungary, and Mexico are good examples. Each country has basically a one-party political system, with a strong, singular political ideology that is reflected in government-union relationships. At the decentralized-particularized end of the spectrum are those nations with multiple political parties, unions, and bargaining units, creating particularistic units of representation instead of large, national structures and controls.

The level of union-bargaining complexity is defined by four variables.

Legislative/Regulatory Level for Teacher Labor Relations

The governance and control of collective bargaining may be vested in a variety of national, state, and even local agencies. In countries in this study, the variation includes (1) national legislation or even national constitutions that guarantee the right to form unions, implemented nationally; (2) regional—state or provincial—laws that govern teacher labor relations within their own jurisdictions; or (3) no laws at any level protecting the rights of teachers to engage in collective negotiations. Where states or provinces, rather than the national government, determine labor relations policies, one might expect greater diversity since a number of jurisdictions are making policy. Where national law prevails, one might assume somewhat greater similarities of qualities and unity of control.[12]

Levels of Bargaining and Contracts

Nations vary by the level at which collective bargaining occurs between the national, state or provincial, local, and even bilevels of government and

11. Lipset (1956, 1962).
12. Michels (1959).

the union(s) of teachers. Similarly, the jurisdictions of teachers' contracts will correspond to that unit of government.

NATIONAL. Most countries in this research have national teacher collective bargaining and contracts, as well as national salary scales. These countries have a nationalized education system, with national tests, certification, salaries, and policies. These include China, Italy, France, Mexico, Hungary, Israel, Great Britain, Greece, Sweden, and New Zealand.

STATE OR PROVINCIAL. Countries with state or provincial school governance usually have state-level bargaining and contracts, making the state teachers' associations of prime importance. Examples of state jurisdictions include the länder in Germany, the Canadian provinces of New Brunswick, Prince Edward Island, and Nova Scotia; the state of Hawaii (alone among the fifty states of the United States), and the nine states in Australia.

LOCAL. The remaining countries engaged in teacher collective bargaining activities involving local education authorities or school districts, with local unions and school boards doing the negotiating and implementing the contract. These include thirty-one of the states in the United States, four Canadian provinces (Ontario, Manitoba, Alberta, and British Columbia), two territories (Yukon and Northwest Territory), and the redesigned New Zealand system since 1990. Several provinces in Canada (Saskatchewan, Quebec, and Nova Scotia) also use bilevel (provincial and local) bargaining. Furthermore, eighteen states of the United States have no bargaining law at all or forbid local school boards from recognizing teachers unions for bargaining.

Hence nations can be categorized by how they organize and govern their public schools: most run the schools from the nation's capital, and have a single bargaining unit and contract; others (mainly the United States, Canada, and Australia) delegate authority for education to the several states or provinces; still others govern schools locally, with contracts, conditions of work, and pay levels determined by each local education authority (the United States, except Hawaii, and about half of Canada).

Number and Type of Unions

Nations also differ in how many bargaining units or unions are recognized in any jurisdiction. These units (also called branches, locals, or union organizations) may reflect the heterogeneity of the nation, state, or locality, as various types of unions (representing teachers from primary schools, secondary schools, or holding left-wing/right-wing political positions, various religious groups, or language groups) that bargain for these different teacher constituencies. Thus even nations with a single national bargaining process may recognize the interests of a range of teachers' organizations and permit them to join the government at the bargaining table. Nations with state-level and local bargaining may involve a number of union types or require—as in the United States—a single, majority-elected association to represent all of a system's teachers.

Number and Type of Management Units

The level, type, and number of government or employer units are also important in defining the complexity of teacher labor relations. In some nations, multilevel bargaining occurs; in others, the same school board, treasury board, or Ministry of Education bargains with a range of unions. Often, too, certain issues (pay and benefits) are bargained by one group, such as the state or provincial level, while the lower level (local education authority) conducts contract negotiations about the nonfinancial matters (hiring, working conditions, sabbatical leaves, and other employee policies).

When these four variables are combined, an amazing range or "mix" of teachers union activities can occur. A nation may have regional laws, may devolve bargaining to a number of local boards, and may bargain with a diverse panoply of local unions over a wide array of issues. One can also imagine a national government, passing a single national law, creating one labor relations system, in which a single national teachers union bargains with a single government agency, under one set of labor policies. In between, one finds a diverse set of combinations.

Table 8-2 presents the cases in this study, across the four variables, arranged from the simplest structurally (monolithic/centralized) to the most complex (multiple/decentralized). At the extremes, quite clearly Mexico, China, and Hungary present the most centralized labor relations system, with a national government setting the conditions of employment, and a single teachers union negotiating for all.

Case Studies

Mexico has one national teachers union (the Sindicato Nacional de Trabajadores de la Educación, SNTE), which is closely tied with one

Table 8-2. *Structure of Teacher Collective Bargaining, by Nation*

Nation	Level of government labor legislation	Level of union bargaining	Number of bargaining units	Number of management units/contracts
Monolithic/centralized				
Mexico	National	National	1	1
China	National	National	1	1
Hungary	National	National	2	1
Moderate				
New Zealand	National	National	2	1
Sweden	National	National	2	1
Israel	National	National	3	3
Greece	National	National	2	4
France	National	National	3	1
Great Britain	National	National	7	1
Italy	National	National	3	3
Multiple/decentralized				
Germany	Länder (state)	Länder	3	1
Australia	State	State	10	10
United States	State	Local (state in Hawaii)	11,400	1
Canada	Provincial	Provincial/local	33	33
Total	10 national/ 4 state	10 national/ 4 state	11,473	17,458

national political party, the Partido Revolucionario Institucional (PRI). In fact, Cortina describes how the then president of Mexico, Avila Camacho, actually outmaneuvered the three competing teachers unions, supporting the two weaker unions against the strongest of the three, which was opposed to his regime.[13] The national party then convinced the three competing unions to sign a unification pact, which strengthened the hand of the president of Mexico and his party, the PRI.

These developments wedded the interests of the teachers union to those of the national party and weakened the left-wing and communist factions within the teachers union movement. In merging the future of the SNTE with that of the PRI, the teachers union became the dominant partner in

13. Cortina (1992, 1998).

the national public sector union, the Sindicato de Trabajadores al Servicio del Estado, Mexico's largest workers' organization. This merger of teachers with public employees and with the national party gave teachers a powerful voice in the affairs of Mexico, but also limited the chances of the teachers expressing real opposition to the ruling PRI.

Hungary and China, too, are basically one-party nations, and the role of the union is to support the beliefs and values of the political regime. This joining of union and state does not completely wed them and suppress dissent.

In Hungary, for example, the Union of Pedagogues (UP) has been the official organ of the government in dealing with teachers, although it has some power by virtue of its most favored status. It has tried at certain times to focus attention away from political "training" and control, and toward pedagogical and educational concerns.[14]

During periods of liberalization and democratization (briefly after the death of Stalin in 1953 and more recently during Gorbachev's effort toward economic and social openness), the teachers union in Hungary worked to improve the pay and working conditions for teachers and to bring public attention to the quality of schooling itself. Hungarian teachers recently have moved to raise their pay, to gain bonuses for improved training, and to better working conditions.

In 1988 the nation actually saw the emergence in Dombovar, a town in southern Hungary, of a grass-roots movement demanding wage increases to keep pace with rising inflation and a year-end bonus. Strikes were threatened against the government for the first time since before World War II. Teachers from more than half the nation's schools signed petitions demanding better pay.

In Budapest, the Democratic Union of Pedagogues (DUP) was founded, threatening the monopoly of the Union of Pedagogues. The official organ of the DUP argued that teaching was a "profession" and needed additional funds and autonomy to improve Hungarian education by deregulating schools and decentralizing authority. Such changes would give schools greater control over program, students, staff, and funds. While such public discourse was unheard of even eight years ago, the outcome of this movement in Hungary and other Eastern European nations must be watched over time.

China, too, has one workers' union, the China Trade Union, and since 1950 one teachers union, the China Education Trade Union (CETU). As

14. Darvas (1992).

one of China's largest unions, and certainly the world's biggest teachers union, CETU plays a prominent role in party and national developments. Under the Chinese version of "democratic" management of local affairs, the local Teaching Faculty Congress and Teachers' Congress play a key role in carrying out the national purpose and controlling workers in the schools. However, many would argue that unions in China are neither free nor democratic, given the lack of civil liberties in the nation as a whole.

China, Hungary, and Mexico, then, are examples of a relatively simple union structure, mirroring the single-party and single-union political system. In contrast, there are several nations with highly localized control and highly diverse unions serving widely different interests and political groups.

Canada has by far the most complex labor relations system for teachers unions covered in this fifteen-nation analysis, and perhaps in the world, although there are some signs recently of attempts to simplify and consolidate the effort. For example, in the province of Quebec, the basis of teacher affiliation and, thus, bargaining for teachers shifted from religious (Protestant-Catholic) to "linguistic" (French-English) on January 1, 1998. Previously teachers formed unions around both their religious and linguistic affiliations, leading to French-Catholic, English-Catholic, Protestant-English school systems and unions. However, all the French-speaking schools have a single union, as do the English-speaking ones, although schools are demarked as "public" versus "Catholic" in some provinces— and even "joint" or "mixed" public-Catholic. Furthermore, under court order in 1998, the men and women teachers associations in the province of Ontario merged.[15]

Canada has no single teachers union, but rather an incredibly complex array of associations, based on the following: (1) linguistic differences (Anglophone or Francophone); (2) grade levels (elementary and secondary teacher groups); (3) the gender of teachers (a women's and men's union existed until a 1998 court order merged them in Ontario); and (4) government jurisdictions, with bargaining mostly done by province, occasionally by local education authority, and even at both local and provincial levels, with the Newfoundland and Labrador Teachers' Association bargaining under a single, interprovincial structure.

Nova Scotia has a two-tier system of collective negotiations, where the Nova Scotia Teachers' Federation and the provincial education authority

15. Lawton (1997, p. 3).

bargain at the "central table" over key issues of pay and allowances. With impasse, teachers in Nova Scotia have the right to strike but only at the provincial level. Seven local school boards (6 Anglophone and 1 Francophone public school board) handle lesser issues such as sick, sabbatical, and educational leave policies; staff development; and other programs. But Nova Scotia school teachers do not enjoy the right to strike their local school boards, only province-wide.[16] Saskatchewan, likewise, has only one bargaining agency, the School Trustees' Association, which negotiates bilevel agreements with its Saskatchewan Teachers' Federation (STF). Under the Public Schools Act, provincial-level bargaining occurs with the provincial staff of the STF union around major issues of pay and benefits.[17] With 124 local school boards (89 public, 21 Catholic, 8 Francophone, and 6 joint boards), local bargaining is done again by the STF's local branches over issues of local concern to teachers and school management. Teachers are permitted to seek arbitration or to strike at both the local and provincial levels, although th   on must declare in advance whether they wish to arbitrate the settlem.   or use the strike.

Teachers in British Columbia can also bargain two-tier contracts under the Labour Relations Code.[18] All key economic concerns must be negotiated at the provincial level with the British Columbia Teachers' Federation, leaving the 59 local school boards (58 public and 1 Francophone education authorities) to settle issues of working conditions and leave policies. Like Nova Scotia, British Columbia teachers may strike only province-wide, not at the local level and not during collective bargaining. Quebec has provincial bargaining using employer management committees representing Francophone and Anglophone school boards. Teachers have a joint bargaining committee, composed of members from three different unions, including the French- and English-speaking, Catholic and Protestant teachers unions: (1) the largest is the French-Catholic union, the Centrale de l'enseignement du Quebec, the Quebec Teachers Federation, which includes some 52,400 teachers; (2) English-speaking teachers are members of the Provincial Association of Protestant Teachers, with 4,978 teacher members; and (3) the Provincial Catholic Teachers Association, which is for teachers who are English and Catholic, with some 2,500 teacher members.

16. Teachers' Collective Bargaining Act, 1974, p. 23.
17. See the Manitoba Schools Act, RSM, 1987, p. 250, Bill 72.
18. Labour Relations Code, 1994, c.82, Bill 84.

In Quebec teachers are allowed to strike (and lockouts are permitted) at the provincial level but only (1) over provincial matters, (2) after a compulsory mediation through the Ministry of Labour, and (3) following a twenty-day cooling-off period.

New Brunswick has Canada's most centralized form of teacher bargaining, with provincial bargaining, no local school boards at all (rather, parent councils at schools), and 100 percent provincial funding of schools from general revenues and a provincial property tax. Under the Public Service Labor Relations Act of 1973, teachers may bargain only over pay, work hours, and discipline standards but not concerning preparation periods, class size, and leave policies. While the teachers have French and English teachers' associations, for purposes of bargaining they combine to form the New Brunswick Teachers' Association.

Newfoundland and Labrador are unique in Canada, having an interprovincial system of labor relations in education. The Newfoundland and Labrador Teachers' Association bargains for the employees, while management is represented for provincial purposes by a team selected by the minister of the Treasury Board, with members representing the ten interdenominational school boards (trustees) and chief administrators. Strikes are legal seven days after a report of impasse is made by the Conciliation Board, appointed from the Department of Manpower and Industrial Relations.[19]

Prince Edward Island also has provincial teacher bargaining, with representatives from the two Anglophone and one Francophone school boards and members of the Prince Edward Island Teachers' Federation. The scope of bargaining is unspecified and teacher strikes are not allowed under the 1993 Schools Act.[20] Should impasse occur, the minister of labor may appoint a conciliation officer and an arbitration board, with binding arbitration as the final step in bargaining.

Ontario is the most elaborate of any jurisdiction described thus far, perhaps most resembling teacher unionism in the United States. It has no fewer than five separate teachers unions and one provincial association, the Ontario Teachers' Federation (OTF). All bargaining is done locally for the 116 different school boards (31 public Anglophone and 4 Francophone; 30 Catholic Anglophone; and 7 Francophone, plus 44 isolates) with the OTF across the province. The OTF has little real power other than through supporting local negotiations.

19. See the Newfoundland Teacher Collective Bargaining Act, 1973.
20. Schools Act, 1993, c.35, Bill 31.

Bargaining thus occurs between the branches of these organizations and the relevant school board or group. The number of local branches (local unions) is more than 480 since bargaining often occurs separately at the elementary and secondary levels for each unit. Strikes are permitted locally, but only after a sixteen-day conciliation and after impasse has been declared by the Ministry of Labour. Hence in Ontario alone, there is an incredible diversity of Canada labor relations, with different unions based on confessional, language group, and type of school (secondary and elementary), each bargaining locally for its membership.

Manitoba is quite similar, with a single teachers union, the Manitoba Teachers' Society (MTS), but with only local (no provincial level) collective bargaining between local teacher affiliates of MTS and the 57 local boards of education (56 Anglophone and 1 Francophone). The scope of bargaining is not proscribed. If an impasse is reached, strikes are not permitted; rather, teachers can apply for final and binding arbitration.[21]

Alberta has a single union, the Alberta Teachers' Association (ATA) responsible for local bargaining with the 66 local school boards: 42 public, 21 Catholic, and 3 Francophone.[22] The provincial union provides leadership to help in local teachers' group bargaining and reserves the power to approve the contact. In fact, the provincial teacher leadership actually sits at the local bargaining table to help its local affiliate. The scope of bargaining is not proscribed. Teachers reserve the local right to strike, although compulsory mediation occurs prior to a strike vote, as supervised by the Labour Relations Board, and a fourteen-day cooling-off period has to have elapsed.

Finally, in the Yukon and the Northwest Territory, local bargaining occurs under federal ordinances or laws. At the national level, the Canadian Teachers Federation is fairly weak, handling mainly crossborder relations among unions and looking out for federal school programs in the nation's capital. In all, there is an incredible mix of teacher union/government relations, with bilevel bargaining in three provinces (Nova Scotia, Saskatchewan, and British Columbia), provincial bargaining only in New Brunswick, Quebec, Prince Edward Island, and Newfoundland-Labrador, and only local bargaining in the remaining provinces (Ontario, Manitoba, and Alberta, plus the Yukon and the Northwest Territory). The remaining nations fall in between, in the moderate category. The United States, like

21. Manitoba Schools Act, 1987.
22. Labour Relations Code, 1988, c.L-1.2, Bill 22.

Canada, leaves education governance primarily to the fifty states.[23] In the absence of a national collective bargaining law in the public sector, all state, country, and local employees in the United States depend on their state legislatures either to vote these workers the right to unionize, to deny such rights, or to remain silent (thus not guaranteeing recognition of teachers' groups by local school boards). Only thirty-two states have passed public employment relations laws (twelve states are silent on the rights of teachers and an additional six states do not allow school boards to engage in collective bargaining with teachers). In thirty-one of these states, the laws hand bargaining over to the local school districts, meaning that each district's union contract is different, depending on the results of collective negotiations.[24]

Only the state of Hawaii has one statewide school district, one recognized teachers union for purposes of negotiations, one teachers' contract, and one teachers' pay scale. The remaining thirty-one states, including some 11,000 of the nation's 15,400 local education authorities, bargain directly with teachers, who may vote to affiliate with either the American Federation of Teachers (AFT) or the National Education Association (NEA) through their state affiliates or to remain independent and have no state or national representation.

While Canada has by far the greatest variety of unions and relations, the United States has the widest breadth of labor relations policies, ranging from an absolute prohibition against local boards' bargaining with their teachers' association (for example, in Virginia, North Carolina, Georgia, and Arkansas), to state mandates that employers must recognize their teachers. Two states even allow teachers the legal right to strike, although many teachers unions in the United States engage in illegal strikes where necessary to gain a power advantage. In 1991 in the state of Washington, for example, teachers actually walked off the job all across the state when the legislature cut resources for education; typically, however, strikes are local, with the teachers union striking against their local board of education.

Nationally, the two major U.S. teacher groups—the 980,000-member AFT and the 2.1-million-member NEA—sought the nation's biggest merger, attempting to form the largest single union in the United States. On July 4, 1998, the NEA's 10,000-member Representative Assembly convened in New Orleans and voted by 55 percent *not* to amalgamate with the

23. McDonnell and Pascal (1988); Mills (1978).
24. Eberts and Pierce (1980).

AFT, while in contrast the AFT two weeks later voted by 97 percent in favor of a merger with the NEA. Work is under way to join together some state and local AFT and NEA unions, but the effort to give the United States one "voice for school teachers," to quote the late AFT president, Albert Shanker, was not yet acceptable to the larger of the two national U.S. unions, the NEA.[25]

In Sweden the four teachers unions correspond to the four levels of their educational program: the primary school teachers, the vocational teachers, the secondary teachers, and finally the university teachers. The constituent teachers of each of these unions are employed either by the local government (for example, vocational teachers) or the national government (for example, secondary, primary, and university teachers). The unions of both the vocational teachers and the primary school teachers are affiliated with the Central Organization of White Collar Employees—the national union of professionals. Additionally, the unions for the secondary teachers and the university teachers are allied with the Swedish Confederation of Professional Associations. As far as politics is concerned, the unions are largely independent of all political parties.

In contrast to these decentralized, diverse union structures in Canada and the United States, the educational system and its unions in New Zealand are highly centralized. All educational policies and legislation are determined at the national level. The two unions of New Zealand are the New Zealand Education Institute (NZEI), which represents the primary school teachers, and the Post-Primary Teachers' Association (PPTA) for secondary school staff. Although both unions are national, they are composed of local branches that are subdivided among the twenty-four regions of the country. The NZEI is not politically aligned, but it recently joined the newly formed New Zealand Council of Trade Unions. In contrast to the NZEI, the PPTA has tremendous political clout.

France has different unions for the different levels of education—each allied with a national trade union. The Federation de l'Education Nationale (FEN) is independent of all other national trade unions and acts as an umbrella union for the forty-eight other national subunions, the largest representing primary school teachers. Many of these subunions are again divided into "departments," which may signify a district or may be a designation of a particular category within an area of education. Each union within the FEN is autonomous but the FEN serves as a kind of

25. Cooper (1988, 1992, 1998).

labor syndicate, negotiating between teachers and the governmental agencies (their own syndicate). The FEN is politically composed of several factions, such as the communists, ex-communists, socialists, anarchists, and Trotsky-ites. Clearly, the FEN can be characterized as supporting the radical left.

Another French union is the Sindicat General de l'Education Nationale (SGEN). This union does not separate out the different sub-unions, although it is also an umbrella union. The SGEN is affiliated with the Confederation of Federal Democratic Workers, which is politi-cally aligned with the democratic-socialists. France also has two other smaller national unions, the Force Ouvriere and the Confederation Generale du Travaill.

The Right to Strike

Besides recognizing the rights of teachers to form unions and to bargain contracts collectively, the next most important core activity of unions has been exercising the right to strike. Without the ability of employees to "withdraw their services," as the euphemism goes, workers are virtually powerless against management—in this case, the government. As shown in table 8-3, most nations have granted teachers and other public employees the right to strike, as part of the policies that recognize the legitimate rights of workers to form unions and bargain collectively.

However, strikes are not always over money. Several interesting cases illustrate the use of strikes for professional and more strategic purposes, showing the interaction of politics, professionalism, and union structure.

Canada in October 1997 suffered a unified, pervasive strike of all teach-ers in Ontario, including support staff, bus drivers, and school secretaries. The issue concerned attempts by the new government to cut taxes and thus resources for schools and teachers. It was the largest strike in North American history, with Ontario teachers losing more workdays than New York City teachers had in their mammoth 1975 walkout.

As George Bedard and Stephen Lawton explain,

Public opinion during the strike began to swing more favorably towards the educators when a leaked performance contract of the deputy minister indicated that the government indeed had some hard numbers to suggest that a further cost-cutting of around $670 mil-lion was anticipated in the next round of cuts—a revelation that enforced the claim of the government's critics who contended all

Table 8-3. *Teachers' Legal Right to Strike: An International Perspective*

Nation	Right to strike	Granted by what institution?	Restrictions on teachers' strikes
Australia	Yes	States grant right to teachers	Few restrictions
Canada	Yes	Conditions depend on local and provincial policies	
China	No	n.a.	
France	Yes	Nat. law: Sec. I Article 10	Five days' notice, no pay loss
Germany	Yes	Under national law; enforced by each state	
Great Britain	No		Right to strike lost when collective bargaining discontinued
Greece	Yes	National law: must give 4 days' notice	
Hungary	No	n.a.	
Israel	Yes	National law	Few effective strikes occurred
Italy	Yes	National law	After other processes fail
Mexico	Yes	Guaranteed by national government	
New Zealand	No	National law	Local bargaining, no strikes
Sweden	Yes	National law	Same as private sector (first strike in 1966)
United States	No		Most states ban strikes; 3 states allow strikes after third-party mediation

n.a. Not available.

along that beneath the smoke and mirrors, Bill 160 was about "gutting public education" to finance an over ambitious tax cut.[26]

Sweden's law specifies that, during the period of their contract, teachers are bound by the agreement; when it expires, however, and impasse occurs, unions may strike and management may "lock out" union workers to ensure the safety of the premises and equipment and then force management and unions to reach mutual agreement.

26. Bedard and Lawton (1998, p. 13).

Israel is admittedly not a typical country. Its great "association of teachers," the Histadrut Hamorim, reflects that special role and evolution of the Zionist state.[27] Started by an Odessa Jew, Menahem Ussishkin, in 1907—forty-one years before the founding of the nation of Israel itself—the teachers union helped to open and manage twenty-seven Hebrew-speaking schools in Palestine. In 1914 the Histadrut Hamorim called its first strike, not for higher salaries but fortuitously to support Hebrew instead of German as the language of instruction at Tel Aviv's Technion (a college of engineering).

After World War I and the British Mandate by which Britain held control over Palestine, the teachers' group joined the left-wing, labor Zionist Federation, mainly to obtain resources. With independent statehood in 1948, the 86,000-member teachers' association and Israel's other major teachers' groups—the Irgun Hamorim for secondary teachers and the Agudith Israel Organization for Orthodox Jewish teachers—affiliated with the General Workers' Federation (Histadrut Haovdim), with provisions for autonomy and the right to strike without the federation's approval.

A few nations, including the United States (excluding two states), still treat teacher strikes as a misdemeanor, and judges can and occasionally do send union leaders to jail, deduct amounts per strike-day from teachers' pay, and even take away bargaining rights when and if teachers go out on strike. However, in most jurisdictions, teachers strike regardless of the law; judges often become involved in helping to mediate the impasse and end the walkout. But, in general, in the nations treated in this study strikes are commonplace and most are done legally under the process of bilateral decisionmaking at the heart of collective bargaining and union-management co-determination.

Affiliation and Teacher Unity

As part of the "labor movement," the teachers unions affiliate with other teacher groups, with unions in the public or "state" sector, with the industrial unions, and even with national political parties. This web of political relationships is important for several reasons. It gives the teachers' organizations an identity, being part of a labor or trade union association, a partisan group (Socialist or Labor party, Communist party, Centrist-Democratic party), and the power to force government to support education more completely.

27. Elboim-Dror (1982, 1986); Gaziel (1992).

Affiliation also gives rise to the organization of teachers unions: with larger membership come the resources to hire more full-time union staff, establish national and regional (state/provincial) offices, and offer teachers direct union services (expertise in collective bargaining, financial planning, political strategy, lobbying, benefits planning, and union organization). In all nations included in this study, the rise of unions was accompanied by the growth of a professional union staff.[28]

As shown in box 8-1, most nations have more than one union of teachers. They are often organized around (1) location—the province or state in which the teacher works (Australia, Canada, and the United States), (2) grade level taught or education specialty (Israel, New Zealand, Sweden, Germany), or (3) political opposition as in Hungary, France, and Italy. These unions are, in turn, affiliated with a national public sector union or division (for example, France's National Federation of State Employees Unions, the Federation Nationale des Associations Professionnelles de Employes de l'Etat, the German Association of Civil Servants, and Greece's Confederation of Civil Service Unions).

In turn, most teachers unions are members of some national trade union council. In the United States, for example, one of the two national teachers unions, the American Federation of Teachers, is a member of the Public Employees Council of the American Federation of Labor-Congress of Industrial Organizations (AFL-CIO), the nation's largest and most powerful labor union. Similarly, in Great Britain, the National Union of Teachers is affiliated with the Trade Union Congress, Britain's main national union federation. The major Swedish teachers groups are members of the Central Organization of White Collar Employees.

Finally, some teachers unions are members of national political parties. Mexico's SNTE is integral to the PRI, Mexico's one political party. Hungary's Union of Pedagogues and China's Education Trade Union are directly linked with the regime and its national party.

Participation in the labor movement puts teachers in the center of government policymaking, since in nations with strong national affiliations teachers become part of the government's deliberations. The trade-off, however, is the difficulty that closely affiliated teachers unions experience when called upon to take drastic action against the regime.

Italy's major teachers unions, for example, were part of the Trade Union Confederation and were unwilling to call a strike against the government.

28. Jessup (1985); Grimshaw (1979).

Box 8-1. *Teachers Union Affiliation, by Nation and Level*

Australia

Nine state/provincial unions; one national union

Labor affiliation: Australian Council of Trade Unions

National teachers union: Australian Teachers' Federation

Canada

Twenty-one provincial and territorial unions that are not related to trade unions or political parties; all part of Canadian Teachers' Federation.

China

China Education Trade Union: part of the China Trade Union (not a free, democratic union)

France

National Federation of Education Employees: affiliated with the National Federation of State Employees Unions; and with the Socialist party

General Syndicate of National Education: affiliated with the Confederation of Workers and the Democratic Socialist Party

Germany

German Teachers Union: affiliated with the German Association of Civil Servants and the German Federation of Trade Unions; no party affiliations

Association of Culture and Education: affiliated with the German Association of Civil Servants and the German Federation of Trade Unions; no party affiliations

Union of Education and Culture: affiliated with the German Trade Union Congress

East German Union of Instruction and Education: nonaffiliated, "independent"

Great Britain

National Union of Teachers: part of the Trade Union Council, strong ties to Labour party

National Association of School Masters/Union of Woman Teachers: part of Trade Union Council; no party ties

Assistant Masters and Mistresses Association: no ties to national union or party

National Association of Head Teachers: no ties to national union or party

Secondary Heads Association: no ties to national union or party

Professional Association of Teachers: no ties to national union or party

National Association of Teachers in Further and Higher Education: no ties to national union or party

Greece

Teachers Federation of Greece

Federation of Secondary Education   } all affiliated with the Confederation of

Federation of Private Instructors   Civil Service Unions; no party affiliations

Hungary

Union of Pedagogues: affiliated with the National Council of Hungarian Social
   Workers Trade Unions Party

Democratic Union of Pedagogues: independent

Israel

Histadrut Hamorim (Union of Teachers): affiliated with the General Workers
   Federation and the Labour party

Irgun Hamorim (Federation of Secondary Teachers)

Organization of Agudith Israel Teachers (Orthodox Jewish schools)

Italy

CGIL: affiliated with the National Federation of Unions

SNALS: connected to Christian Democratic Party

UIL: part of autonomous trade unions

CISL: no affiliation

DITSTAT: Administrative employees; no affiliation

Mexico

Sindicato National de Tradajadores de la Educación: affiliated with the National
   Union and the Partido Revolucionario Institucional

New Zealand

New Zealand Education Institute (primary education): affiliated with the New
   Zealand Council of Trade Unions and aligned with the Labour party

Post-Primary Teachers' Association: not affiliated

Sweden

SL (primary) and SFL (vocational): both affiliated with Swedish Confederation of
   Professional Employees and Central Organization of White Collar Employees;
   center-left politically but party neutral

LR (secondary) and SULF (higher education): both affiliated with the Swedish
   Confederation of Professional Associations and the Central Organization of White
   Collar Employees and neutral

United States

National Education Association (NEA): not affiliated with national labor movement
   (AFL-CIO); often supports Democratic party

American Federation of Teachers: affiliated with the AFL-CIO, Public Employees
   Dept., no party affiliation; sympathetic to Democratic party

In the winter of 1987–88 a grass-roots teachers "union" called Comitati de Base (COBAS) emerged to represent the dissidents. Its strategy was bolder, more critical of the government, and even disruptive, staging strikes and "work to the rule" protests carried out over a twelve-month campaign. These actions embarrassed the government into raising salaries well above the norm for other public employees.

In summary, the range of union relationships is wide, with various teachers' groups relating to professional and trade union groups or to the union that represents their own level (primary versus secondary, French Catholic or English Catholic). In some cases teachers unions work closely with various political and trade union groups without actually joining or affiliating with them. This relationship, with its affiliation and political alignments, shows the importance to teachers and other government employees of forming ties not only with other similar employees (teachers with teachers) but also with broader groups (white-collar employees, public employees) and, finally, with workers of all kinds.

The Future of Teacher Unionism—International

The new millennium poses problems and issues for school teachers worldwide. As with other employee groups, teachers always run the risk of losing their hard-won recognition, access to power, and rights to bargain. In the late 1980s, for example, after a prolonged teachers' strike, the Tory government in Great Britain changed the education decisionmaking structure, excluding the teachers unions from a "place at the table," purposely marginalizing the unions, and giving greater authority to the national government. Teachers' pay was determined not by negotiations but by a commission, modeled after wage setting in the National Health Service.

Other countries, such as China, Hungary, and Mexico, lack a free, democratic labor movement in the first place, meaning that teachers have little or no real voice in education decisionmaking. Teachers in other countries might be overwhelmed by governments' insensitivity to the needs and rights of teachers. Whatever the situation, the future may find the rights of teachers reduced and their salaries falling behind other professional employees. International labor groups, such as the International Labor Organization (ILO), seek to protect the rights of workers and have shown an interest in teachers around the world. As the ILO declared a decade ago: "Trade union rights are an essential part of human rights and fundamental liberties, and that the principles on which the freedom of association and the protection of trade union rights are based on, and enshrined in, the Universal Declaration of Human Rights, the International Treaties on civil, political, social, cultural and economic rights, and the statutes of the International Labour Organization."[29]

As nations experiment with new organizational structures and funding arrangements for their schools, teachers will face new concerns. As industrial employees have found their jobs "restructured," made more global, and becoming more technologically advanced, these workers discover that unionization is both less extensive and less effective—explaining in part why the percentage of U.S. workers who are members of unions is in steady decline (from 55 to 29 percent in the last four decades). What happens in those nations that experiment with school privatization (charter schools, vouchers, opting out, outsourcing, merger, direct funding of religious schools)? Will teachers unions likewise lose members—and find their members "selling" their services on the open market instead of bargaining collectively under the union banner? Will parents and their children go to the World Wide Web, download curricula, and teach their own children at home or with neighbors' children in small, "cottage-industry" style schools? If this happens, again the larger, more national and regional unions will find it difficult or impossible to organize and negotiate collectively.

Given the likelihood of a variety of changes nation by nation, at least four very different future courses of action emerge for teachers and their unions from this cross-national research:

—*Localism-Communitarianism.* Close the classroom door; work with students, their families, and communities; and leave the politics to politicians.

—*Nationalist-Syndicalism.* Continue to join "big government" and "big labor" and ensure that the teachers unions are visible, influential players in national decisionmaking.

—*Privatization-Free Agentry.* Sell services in the education marketplace, as vouchers, charter schools, grant-maintained schools, and other privatized forms of education take root.

—*Adaptation-Redefining Education.* Work within the system, altering the structure of schooling and engaging teachers in career development.[30]

---

29. International Federation of Free Teachers' Unions (1989, p. 50).
30. See Kerchner, Koppich, and Weeres (1997).

A description of each of these courses of action follows.

Action 1: Mind Their Own Business

At one extreme, teachers can stay local—returning to their classrooms, teaching kids, working with their communities and neighborhoods, and leaving the "big picture" to the politicians. Most teachers, when questioned, would say that unionization is a rather distant, abstract force that only interrupts their workday when members are called upon to attend a meeting, take a vote, or pay their union dues. (Even these payments are made painless and nearly invisible in some places, where union dues are automatically and involuntarily deducted from paychecks, under a plan called "agency shop.")

Teaching remains personal, local, professional, and restricted to the teachers' classroom, students, and school. But it was just this narrow, personal view that led to the need for unions in the first place since the teacher as lone operative lacked collective power, a unified voice, and meaningful clout. This quandary—how to live the life of a classroom teacher while still having a voice in collective, national affairs—is best captured by the United States and its National Education Association.

The NEA, of all of the teachers unions in the world, comes closest to institutionalizing the dream of teachers to have a real say in what happens to their organization. But the costs are enormous. How can an organization of 2.4-million members scattered across fifty states, 14,000 school districts, and in about 88,000 schools, hope to operate democratically yet efficiently? The NEA has tried over its long history to grant each local teachers' group the option to affiliate and, in the forty-four states that allow or support collective bargaining, the opportunity to unionize. Each local union then elects delegates to the state associations' governing boards, which in turn send representatives to the 10,000-member national Representative Assembly that votes as a collective on union policy (meeting in a convention hall or arena). To ensure that no single individual or faction seizes lifetime control of the union, the NEA's constitution sets term limits on its officers and requires that an ethnic minority teacher be elected president every eleven years or so.

Charles Kerchner, Julia Koppich, and Joseph Weeres focus on the difficulty that any large organization has in staying responsive to member needs and their work (teaching and learning). They explain: "Teacher unions organized teachers as people with jobs and essentially ignored the act of teaching and the process of learning. Above all, industrial union organization became job conscious. Unions were in the business to protect members' positions and to enhance the conditions under which they worked. . . . As a consequence, unions became highly attached to the centrality of the employment relationships . . . and were highly threatened by efforts to bring in resources from outside the bounds of the organization."[31]

Many of the fifteen nations analyzed in this study made little effort to separate teachers, as professionals, from other "civil servants" employed by governments to provide a wide range of public services. This dilemma, then, of having a meaningful, rewarding professional life while fulfilling the collective need for status, power, and support has generally swung toward the collective—and away from the individual. Yet, education remains a highly personal, interpersonal process, and teachers unions cannot hope to improve the learning of children by overlooking the culture of the teacher in the classroom.

Action 2: Join the National Power Structure

At the other extreme is a neocorporate or syndicalist view of the role of teachers, those joining big labor and big government, and sometimes sacrificing concerns for individual teachers' needs and rights to the big picture. One of the best critiques of the syndicalist view of national unions was Stephen Lawton's research on changes in Canadian labor relations, concentrating on the province of British Columbia. Lawton explains that "corporatist government is one in which nationwide [or province-wide] syndicates, or trusts of all employees in a given industry [such as education], negotiate with industry-wide unions of employees under the government's tutelage."[32] Since Canada leaves education to the provinces, these syndicates are typically provincial in scope, one representing the employer, the other the employees. British Columbia was the last province to grant collective bargaining rights to its public employees, starting in 1988. When British Columbia's conservative, probusiness Social Credit Party allowed teachers' associations in each of the province's school districts to decide whether to unionize, hoping by decentralizing the decision to weaken the main teachers' organization, the British Columbia Teachers Federation (BCTF), the tactic backfired.

31. Kerchner, Koppich, and Weeres (1997, p. 40); Kerchner and Mitchell (1988).
32. Lawton (1997, p. 21).

Not only did the BCTF organize and convince its members and teachers in every local district to vote to form a bargaining unit and to affiliate with the provincial union, but the teachers union also took control of the provincial body (or syndicate) representing teachers, the BC College of Teachers. Feeling their oats, the teachers also pressed for a "closed shop," meaning that teachers either joined the BCTF and paid their dues or these recalcitrants were removed from their jobs, even teachers with tenure and twenty years of experience. As Lawson noted, it would be hard to imagine teachers standing by and allowing management to remove tenured teachers for issues unrelated to their on-the-job behaviors; but here, teachers were inflicting such penalties on their own kind for not joining their teachers union.

The net effect of large-scale unionization in British Columbia and all across Canada (as well as other countries in this study) has been creeping corporatism, whereby syndicates at the provincial level assumed greater power and local school trustees and unions forfeited control. Lawton concludes his analysis of syndicalism in Canadian labor relations as follows:

> The adoption of provincial-wide collective bargaining in BC is part of a broader trend across Canada that includes the abolition of school boards in New Brunswick, elimination of traditional religiously based boards in Newfoundland, and the amalgamation of school districts and municipalities in several provinces, and the centralization of school finance in all but three provinces. BC innovation is part of an overall rearrangement of government in Canada that concentrates tremendous power in the provincial capitals. . . . Individuals and local agencies such as school boards [and local teachers] are becoming little more than spectators, while others decide how society and its schools should be run.[33]

Thus solitary teachers—traditionally cut off from real control and authority by their position in the school systems—now find that these large syndicates, organized to give voice and power to the unions, may also ignore individual teachers in their organized quest to promote unity and power. In addition to Canada, other nations are forming syndicates to unify and control labor relations in the public sector. A description of this mobilization in the various nations follows.

33. Lawton (1997, p. 24).

Australia's teachers unions are among the world's oldest and are the largest constituents of the state labor councils and the national Australian Council of Trade Unions. State policies have made possible such unified processes as mandatory arbitration of disputes, accessible to either the teachers union or school management during the bargaining.

England and Wales have seen various attempts to create teachers union syndicates to give unity and power to their six diverse educators' associations, the largest being the National Union of Teachers; others include the National Association of Schoolmasters/Union of Women Teachers and the Professional Association of Teachers, plus representation from school administrators under the Assistant Masters and Mistresses Association, Secondary Heads Association, and the National Association of Teachers in Further and Higher Education. These unions shared membership for a number of years on the Burnham Group, which bargained for employees with the national government. When the Thatcher government and the Burnham Group could not reach a settlement in the 1980s, a prolonged strike wore on, badly damaging labor-management relations and eventually forcing the Thatcher and later the Major governments to implement a more centralized form of decisionmaking. Syndicalism was not dead, only greatly weakened, as the government pursued forms of privatization of schools on the one hand, while concentrating greater power with the national government on the other.

France is the prototype of the syndicalist form of teacher labor relations, with teachers being an active, integral part of the national civil service and the trade union movement. France, with its highly centralized education system, single salary structure, and strong dependence on the Ministry of Education, has nearly 900,000 teachers, comprising about half the state employees in the nation. This group is organized into four major unions. As Guy Coq explained, "As far as school reform is concerned, the teachers unions are often accused of corporatism—the sacrifice of school improvement to the narrow self-interest of teachers and their collective organizations."[34]

Germany, much like Canada and the United States, has its teachers employed as civil servants by the state or province, called länder, in which they work. With three different unions, the determination of pay and conditions of work is strictly regulated and controlled, based on training, background, and the level of school in which teachers are employed.

34. Coq (1992, p. 110); Sabouret (1985).

With the liberalization of Greece under the government of Andreas Papandreou in the 1980s, the teachers were included in a unified pay scale for all civil servants, improving their salaries and benefits. While collective bargaining is not guaranteed, and Greece is not a partner to the International Labor Agreements (conventions) of the International Labor Organization, teachers are organized into unions that confer with the government on issues of work. Greek unions are not identified with a particular political party (union members ally with a range of parties, from communist to socialist and new democrats), leading to intense political activity within and between these federations. Hence Greek teachers are participants in virtually all government groups and councils, a complex relationship between schools, unions, teachers, and the government at various levels.

Hungary, with the breakup of the Soviet Union in 1989, watched as teachers joined a noncommunist ("conservative") teachers' association, the Democratic Teachers' Union, which in turn was supporting a new political party, the Association of Young Democrats (something of a misnomer since the oldest member of the Hungarian parliament is a "young democrat"). A leader of this new teachers' group, Zoltan Pokorny, has since become the Hungarian minister of education, under the banner of the Association of Young Democrats.

As Cortina explains, the Mexican education system was created in 1921 "to help build the new nation, to create a consciousness of nationality, to foster nationwide loyalty to the central government, and to homogenize the use of Spanish as the primary language." National development, solidarity, and allegiance made the single, national teachers union, SNTE, a critical link; the reward for participation was the promise that teachers, loyal to the SNTE and to the PRI, the national political party, might be promoted to positions of leadership and power in the national party.[35]

This position of public advocacy, not only for the education system but also for the major political party, led top national teachers union leaders to side with the government at times, against the best interests of students and schools. As Cortina found, "Beginning in the 1980s, successive administrations in the Ministry of Education initiated reforms to manage education in a more decentralized fashion and to improve the education and professional lives of teachers. Most of those reforms were blocked by the ruling group within the union (SNTE), the Vanguardia Revolucionaria,

35. Cortina (1998, p. 3).

which recognized that the decentralization of education would reduce the national power in the hands of the teachers union."[36] However, by 1992 laws were finally passed that attempted to break up the hegemony of the national government, national party, and national teachers union. Instead, the state educational administrators have greater control for the first time over teacher training, the retention and promotion of students, and access of students to preschool education.

Action 3: Sell Services in a Quasi-Public Education Marketplace

Political economists like to treat teachers as key producers, the largest group of public sector workers in the world. As providers of critical services, teachers could under other circumstances (for example, vouchers) "sell" their skills individually or collectively on the open market, much as do other entrepreneurs or even "free agents" in professional athletics. With a free market model of education, unions as constructed would have few if any roles to play—and presumably would lose membership. Already, there are clear signs that the labor movement in the private sector has fewer members and less power and control than during earlier industrial periods—as industry and the service economies become "restructured," more entrepreneurial, leaner, and more global in scope (meaning that unions in one nation have little chance of controlling the transfer of work and jobs around the nation and to other countries). As the means of production have shifted from large-scale corporations to smaller, more entrepreneurial companies, unions find it much more difficult to organize workers. It is no wonder that teachers unions in the United States, England, Israel, France, and Mexico, among others, resisted government attempts to decentralize and privatize education.

But, as education becomes privatized—and as parents receive government or private vouchers and can select from a range of public schools, charter schools, church schools, home schools, and even "virtual schools" run off the Internet—teachers could become free agents who could sell their services to the highest bidders. An analysis of teachers' pay, when compared with salaries for other occupations, is revealing as one indicator of the effect of markets on salaries. M. Orivel and R. Perrot, in their study of teacher career choices in France, determined that their country was "facing

36. Cortina (1998, p. 4).

a possible teacher shortage."[37] This paucity itself might drive up pay, letting supply and demand enhance or replace the role of unions and collective bargaining in determining salary levels.[38]

Pay differentials already exist within the teacher ranks, showing the impact of nonunion activity on salaries. Orivel and Perrot found that "in 1985, for example, the agreges [teachers with the elementary school qualification] in France earned F4,200 less per month than senior staff in other occupations; but a certified teacher (secondary teacher with standard qualifications) earned F20,000 more a year than a midlevel staff in the private sector."[39] Thus the effect of training and markets, if allowed to function, could raise teachers' salaries—another argument made by conservatives for a market-driven solution, rather than one bargained by unions in a more syndicalist mode.

France may be reflecting a worldwide trend toward teacher shortages, driving up demand and raising salaries and benefits. As the United Nations explained, the teacher shortage is "most acute in the United States, the United Kingdom, and France with Italy, Spain, Portugal and Greece not far behind." And since the 1980s, teacher salaries have substantially increased, which may or may not be sufficient to eliminate the shortage. They conclude: "The problem of potential or actual shortage of teachers is not peculiar to France. It is also acute in other countries but it must also be noted that where salaries of teachers relative to other professions are higher, as in Japan and Germany, the threat of shortages appears to be less immediate."[40]

Action 4: Work within the System for Reform

A fourth, more moderate course of action would be to follow the advice of Kerchner, Koppich, and Weeres in their book, *United Mind Workers*. They propose that the nature of teachers' work be redefined, while staying within the parameters of schooling as we know it. This book began with the assumption that the syndicalist, "big union" approach was stalling school reform, and that teachers and their unions must lead the way. The authors further explain:

37. Orivel and Perrot (1988, p. 67).
38. See "Business Opts for Choice," *Wall Street Journal* (February 25, 1991), p. 41.
39. Orivel and Perrot (1988, p. 68).
40. Orivel and Perrot (1988).

Most unions, and most management, were too mired in conventional wisdom to see the importance of teachers taking responsibility for their own work and the performance of colleagues. Even large-scale and seemingly permanent reforms bogged down when economic times turned rough, or a key leader departed. School boards seemed to have an unerring instinct for replacing reformist superintendents with enforcers of the conventional wisdom—as if school reform was an exercise in small-scale equilibrium.[41]

Kerchner, Koppich, and Weeres challenge the education system and the teachers unions of the United States, and by implication of the world, to take four bold steps, each of which is major but none of which destroys the public education system. These include: transforming unionism, improving the act of teaching, altering union-management agreements, and then institutionalizing the new kind of union. In other words, reconceptualize, improve, restructure, and make permanent.

This model emphasizes "career security" over job security, use of choice, career ladders, better pension systems, a redefinition of tenure, job ownership, and a link between certification and career development. In sum, a comprehensive, moderate solution for the future of teachers unions is workable, if a full, comprehensive, and integrated approach is taken. Or, this complex, subtle approach may be too slow, require too much coordination and control, and simply be too idealistic. A basic assumption—that teachers and their unions can lead reforms, rather than just follow changes in politics, the community, the wider society, and world—remains now to be tested in the twenty-first century. While these suggestions are aimed primarily at U.S. teachers and their unions, these ideas certainly apply to all countries where teachers struggle with how to grow as professionals, in high-quality schools, which work for students, while representing the economic and political needs of educators and their enterprise.

Teachers unions, then, share some characteristics with their private sector counterparts—that is, the need for a collective voice and the power to gain some financial advantages for members. But teachers unions are far less about the economics of schooling and much more about politics, lobbying, and organizing to enhance their resources, visibility, and involvement in the education process. The challenge worldwide for teachers

41. Kerchner, Koppich, and Weeres (1997, p. 4), citing Johnson (1984).

unions is how to meet the professional needs of their members without sacrificing their hard-earned power and status, and how to adjust to changes
in the way schooling is delivered, by trying to improve education opportunity while meeting the needs of teachers in whatever public or private
structure and funding system are imposed.

It is a delicate balancing act, on the one hand, between local autonomy,
mutual community support, and professional growth for teachers—that is,
teaching that "educates the worker while it educates the student"—and the
more syndicalist, nationalized, big union, big government, big everything
solution on the other.[42] In between lie wide fields of opportunity to harness
the collective power of teachers to meet the growing needs of children and
their families, produce better education results, enhance societies, and
improve unions all across the world.

References

Bedard, George, and Stephen Lawton. 1998. "The Battle over Ontario's Bill 160 and the
    Shape of Teacher Collective Bargaining." Occasional paper. Toronto: Ontario Institute
    for Studies in Education, University of Toronto (April 6).
Berube, Maurice R. 1988. *Teacher Politics: The Influence of Unions.* Greenwood Press.
Callahan, Raymond E. 1962. *Education and the Cult of Efficiency.* University of Chicago
    Press.
Conley, Sharon, and Bruce S. Cooper, eds. 1991. *The School as a Work Environment: Impli-
    cations for Reform.* Allyn and Bacon.
Cooper, Bruce S. 1988. "National Union Competition and the School Reform Movement:
    Should the NEA and AFT Merge?" Proceedings of the annual meeting of the Industrial
    Relations Research Association, pp. 70–79.
———.1992. *Labor Relations in Education: An International Perspective.* Greenwood Press.
———. 1998. "Merging the Teachers' Unions: Opportunity amid Complexity." *Education
    Week* (March 11): 52, 34; reprinted as "Viewpoint—Toward a More Perfect Union: An
    NEA-AFT Merger Would Create the Nation's Largest Labor Group. That's Good and
    Bad." *Teacher Magazine* (May–June 1998).
Cooper, Bruce S., and John Bussey. 1982. *Collective Bargaining, Strikes, and Financial Costs
    in Public Education: A Comparative Review.* Eugene, Ore.: ERIC Center for Education
    Management and University of Oregon.
Coq, Guy. 1992. "France." In *Labor Relations in Education: An International Perspective,*
    edited by Bruce S. Cooper, 93–114. Greenwood Press.
Cortina, Regina. 1992. "Mexico." In *Labor Relations in Education: An International Per-
    spective,* edited by Bruce S. Cooper, 223–40. Greenwood Press.

42. Kerchner, Koppich, and Weeres (1997, p. 211).

————. 1998. "The Training and Employment of Teachers in Mexico." In *Education and Development in Latin America,* edited by Laura Randall and Joan Anderson, pp. 29–43. Armonk, N.Y.: M. E. Sharpe, Inc.

Darvas, Peter. 1992. "Hungary." In *Labor Relations in Education: An International Perspective,* edited by Bruce S. Cooper, 137–56. Greenwood Press.

Eberts, Randall W., and Lawrence C. Pierce. 1980. *The Effects of Collective Bargaining in Public Schools.* University of Oregon Press.

Elboim-Dror, R. 1982. "Main Education Policy-Making Actors." In *Education Administration and Policy-Making: The Case of Israel,* edited by E. Ben-Barach and Y. Neumann, 34–54. Tel-Aviv: Unipress.

————. 1986. *Hebrew Education in Eretz Yisrael.* Vol. 1, 1854–1914. Jerusalem: Yad Ben-Zvi Institute Publications (in Hebrew).

Etzioni, Amitai, ed. 1969. *The Semi-Professions and Their Organization.* Free Press.

Gaziel, Haim. 1992. "Israel." In *Labor Relations in Education: An International Perspective,* edited by Bruce S. Cooper, 123–40. Greenwood Press.

Grimshaw, William J. 1979. *Union Rule in the Schools: Big-City Politics in Transformation.* Lexington Books.

International Federation of Free Teachers' Unions. 1989. *Agenda 5, 6, 9.* Amsterdam, Holland.

————. 1990–91. "Democracy, Education, and Trade Unionism." *Workers in Education* (December–January): 19.

International Labor Organization. 1984. *The Status of Teachers.* Geneva: ILO and UNESCO.

Jessup, Dorothy K. 1985. *Teachers, Unions, and Change: A Comparative Study.* Praeger.

Johnson, Susan M. 1984. *Teacher Unions in Schools.* Temple University Press.

Kerchner, Charles T., Julia E. Koppich, and Joseph Weeres. 1997. *United Mind Workers: Unions and Teaching in the Knowledge Society.* New York: Falmer Press.

Kerchner, Charles T., and Douglas E. Mitchell. 1988. *The Changing Idea of a Teachers' Union.* London and New York: Falmer Press.

Lawn, Martin, ed. 1985. *The Politics of Teacher Unionism: International Perspectives.* London: Croom Helm.

Lawson, John, and Harold Silver. 1978. *A Social History of Education in England.* London: Methuen.

Lawton, Stephen B. 1997. "Pressures for Change: Bargaining in British Columbia." *School Business Affairs* 63, 8 (August): 21–24.

LeClearcq, Jean Michel. 1984. *Education et Societé, au Japon.* Paris: Anthropos.

Lipset, Seymour Martin. 1956. *Union Democracy: The Internal Politics of the International Typographical Union.* Free Press.

————. 1962. "Introduction." In *Political Parties: A Sociological Study of the Oligarchic Tendencies of Modern Democracies,* edited by Robert Michels. Free Press.

Lortie, Dan C. 1969. "The Balance of Control and Autonomy in Elementary School Teaching." In *The Semi-Professions and their Organization,* edited by Amitai Etzioni, 21–54. Free Press.

————. 1975. *Schoolteacher: A Sociological Study.* University of Chicago Press.

Maeroff, Gene I. 1988. *The Empowerment of Teachers: Overcoming the Crisis of Confidence.* Teachers College Press.

McDonnell, Lorraine M., and Anthony Pascal. 1988. *Teacher Unions and Educational Reform.* Santa Monica, Calif.: RAND Corporation and the Center for Policy Research in Education, Rutgers University and University of Wisconsin-Madison.

Michels, Robert. 1959. *Political Parties: A Sociological Study of the Oligarchic Tendencies of Modern Democracies.* New York: Dover Publications.

Mills, Daniel Quinn. 1978. *Labor-Management Relations.* McGraw-Hill.

National Commission on Excellence in Education. 1983. *A Nation at Risk.* Government Printing Office.

Orivel, M., and R. Perrot. 1988. "Teacher Shortage and the Salary Structure." New York: UNESCO, United Nations Center for Education Research.

Ota, Haruo. 1985. "Political Teacher Unionism in Japan." In *The Politics of Teachers Unionism: International Perspectives,* edited by Martin Lawn, 103–40. London: Croom Helm.

Ravitch, D. 1974. *The Great School Wars: New York City, 1805–1973.* Basic Books.

Rosenholtz, S. J. 1985. *Teachers' Workplace: The Social Organization of Schools.* Longman.

Rosow, Jerome M., and Robert Zager. 1989. *Allies in Educational Reform: How Teachers, Unions, and Administrators Can Join Forces for Better Schools.* Jossey-Bass.

Sabouret, Jean Francois. 1985. *L'Empire du Concours.* Paris: Autrement.

Tyack, David B. 1974. *The One Best System: A History of American Urban Education.* Harvard University Press.

Urban, Wayne J. 1982. *Why Teachers Organized.* Wayne State University Press.

Wattenberg, Ruth. 1990. "Emerging from Dictatorship: Teachers from around the World and How We Can Help." *American Educator* (Fall): 11–14.

World Confederation of Organizations of the Teaching Profession. 1986. *Digest of Certain Conclusions Reached by the Joint ILO/Unesco Committee of Experts on the Application of Recommendations Concerning the Status of Teachers.* Morges, Switzerland.

9

CHARLES TAYLOR KERCHNER
JULIA E. KOPPICH

Organizing around Quality: The Frontiers of Teacher Unionism

I N A MINNEAPOLIS public school classroom, a teacher and students were
discussing what would constitute a good-quality writing project. The
teacher had written a rubric on the blackboard:

Not Finished Yet ◄──────────► Quality Work.

Down the columns were a series of characteristics about the project: its
content, sources of information, language use; and in the cells were approximations of quality work. Guided by their teacher, students produced specific examples of what would be a high-quality project and how they would
move their own work toward it.

This elementary school exercise provides a good starting point in an
exploration of building teacher unionism around academic quality. First,
the exercise itself is good pedagogy. The standards for a quality assignment
became public at the beginning of the writing process. Teachers and students provide examples, so quality became concrete rather than abstract.
And, the opposite of high quality was not low quality; it was "not finished
yet"—a description that honors the craft of revision and suggests that low-
quality work is unacceptable.

The authors would like to thank Cynthia Lopez-Ellwell for assistance in the preparation of this
chapter.

Beyond pedagogy, the lesson in that Minneapolis classroom is important because it exemplifies the relationship between teachers unions and education quality. Focusing on quality is a large systemic effort of the Minneapolis Public Schools (MPS) and the Minneapolis Federation of Teachers, Local 25, American Federation of Teachers (AFT), AFL-CIO. The quality rubric in the sixth-grade classroom is the tip of the structure that shows. It rests on an infrastructure of data-driven school accountability, teacher professional development, peer review, and a collective bargaining contract.

In symbolism and content, the teachers union contract drives the quest for quality. Several years ago union and district representatives realized that teachers and administrators seldom consult school district policy manuals, but they all *read* the contract. They rewrote the contract around a reform program designed to increase the quality of teaching in the district. Now, the clauses of the contract largely concern the content of teaching rather than the traditional wages and hours. For example, the contract contains more than thirty pages describing the teacher professional development program and how it works, while devoting three pages to pay rates.

Minneapolis is not the only district in which teachers unions have pulled at the levers of quality. This study focuses on five of the approximately twenty unions that are acknowledged to be in the forefront of educational reform: Minneapolis, Minnesota; Rochester, New York; Columbus, Ohio; Cincinnati, Ohio; and Seattle, Washington. The following sections illuminate three questions and answers about the current state of teachers union reform:

1. *Can teachers unions successfully organize around quality teaching and standards for students?* **The summary answer:** Unionization around teaching and learning quality is possible but difficult. The process holds political dangers for those unionists who try, and the results are by no means assured.

2. *Are there substantial barriers to the spread of reform unionism?* **The summary answer:** There is substantial resistance to unionism other than that built around industrial principles. Part of the resistance can be found in the culture of teaching itself and in the ideologies of teacher unionists and school administrators, who finds the existing division of labor comfortable. Part is in the organizational capacity of unions to engage in an educational quality agenda; they were designed for other purposes. And part is in an officially hostile public policy that allows but does not encourage reform.

3. *What statutory and structural choices would be necessary if a state were to decide to provide incentives for teachers to organize around quality?* **The summary answer:** No legislature has yet tackled the question of whether labor statutes should encourage unions to organize around educational quality. By focusing their rhetoric on demonizing unions, both public officials and policy analysts miss the larger issue of what kind of unionism is wanted. Teacher unionism in its current form is largely based on industrial organizational principles. Organizing unions around quality requires public policy based on craft, artistic, or professional principles. Organizing teachers around these principles requires changing statutes under which teachers work and allowing public policy to leverage change.

A History of "Accidental Policy"

Both national unions have officially put themselves in the quality education business. Both have endorsed peer review, training standards for teachers, and teacher work schedules that treat professional development as part of a teacher's job and not an add-on option. A small but increasing number of union locals are following this lead. However, in terms of labor policy, organizing teaching around quality is not the purpose for which unions were legitimated in statute. From a policy perspective, teachers union reform has been accidental, and virtually all the reforms have taken place in a hostile if somewhat benign legal climate. In order to answer the question of what kind of unionism is wanted, it must first be decided what kind of teachers are wanted.

By the time teachers entered into collective bargaining in the 1960s and 1970s, the word *unionism* largely meant industrial unionism. Older forms of worker organization—guilds, artisan associations, and craft unions—had largely been supplanted by a form of unionism designed to work within large hierarchies with an atomistic division of labor. In public education, industrial unionism was labor's answer to an education system constructed on the principles of scientific management, a system in which the content and pacing of work was not designed by teachers themselves but school administrators. As the history of education in the twentieth century clearly shows, schools were bureaucratized long before they were unionized.[1] It is somewhat ironic that teachers unions remain as one of the

1. Tyack (1974); Tyack and Hansot (1982).

strongest advocates for the very system whose managerial excesses and rigid rules they sought to tame with collective bargaining.

Part of the irony can be explained by the fact that schools, despite heavy borrowing from the scientific management movement, never were factories. Despite their bell schedules and thick policy documents, there is more than a little truth to the teacher lore "that I'm in charge when the classroom door is closed." In the industrial sense, schools were always incomplete bureaucracies. Although the assertion would horrify most teachers, schools are dramatically undersupervised by industrial standards. School organizations are almost always incapable of operating on a literal command-and-control basis. Still, the logic of industrial organization created a clear division between work creation and control and task execution. Under industrial bureaucracy, codified into industrial labor relations, managers asserted control over the content and design of teaching. In labor relations terms, these were management's reserved rights, not mandatory subjects of bargaining, and frequently law and custom excluded the content of teaching from the bargaining process altogether. Strictly interpreted, industrial organization would hold teachers responsible for the faithful reproduction of lesson plans and classroom routines developed elsewhere. That would be their obligation and sole responsibility. Invention, creativity, or spontaneity would not be required or expected.

The problem, of course, is that schools are utterly dependent on teachers *not* acting like industrial workers. Real teaching is a mixture of imperatives drawn from craft, artistic, professional, and industrial routines. If taken as an ideal type, each mode of work carries with it different demands on employers and unions. The guild and craft traditions, which preceded industrial organization, considered workers as members of communities. Even today craft unions wield control through apprenticeship and job placement programs. In most craft situations, development and enforcement of standards became part of what unions do. It is the case with white-collar unions, such as engineers. As Cobble reports, in the case of waitress unions, women assumed responsibility for "management" tasks such as hiring and discharge of employees, the mediation of on-the-job disputes, and the assurance of fair supervision. "In a sense workers in the culinary industry had instituted a form of self-management."[2]

The disjuncture between how teachers are organized has become increasingly apparent over the last fifteen years during which the overall

2. Kuhn (1970); Cobble (1991, p. 426).

institutional quality and capacity of public education has become a policy issue. Beginning with the National Commission on Education's 1983 report *A Nation at Risk*, the public policy discourse began to turn from criticism of the performance of public education to the *capacity* of public education.[3] Reforms from both the political left and right originate from a critique that holds that existing institutions are *incapable* of performing as they should.

Within this circumstance, teachers unions have attempted to fashion new ways of approaching teacher organization, although for reasons that will be discussed in a later section this response has been more muted and tentative than many would wish. Neither school districts nor teachers unions seem to fully realize the extent to which teaching needs to be rethought: what teachers do all day and all year, how they allocate their time, what decisions they make, and how they create and enact quality standards in school.

As was often the case, former AFT president Albert Shanker's voice was among the first heard raising the issue of reforming unionism as a way to change education. In a 1985 speech to the New York State United Teachers, he raised the idea of professional unionism.[4] (A similar speech was later delivered at the National Press Club in Washington.) Following Shanker's speech, the AFT began to pay increased attention to those union locals that were engaged in inventing new ways of organizing. Site management in Miami, peer review in Toledo, and career ladder pay plans in Rochester all became the object of attention within the union and in the education literature. The AFT also began to give explicit attention to organizing around quality by beginning a biannual teaching quality (QuEST) conference, which now rivals its biannual national convention in size and importance.

This attention has continued but much more tentatively than we believe necessary. The National Education Association's declaration of "new unionism" has been slow to take form. Merger plans with the AFT derailed in 1998 when the NEA representative assembly refused to ratify the leadership's plan. And although there are many small experiments with expanding the scope and substance of labor relations, there is yet to be anything approaching a sweeping vision. The AFT has strongly endorsed standards and made some hard calls on how to fix low-performing schools. But labor

3. Block (1990); Chubb and Moe (1990).
4. Shanker (1985).

relations in some of the nation's toughest urban school districts remain unproductive even as political forces gather to radically reform and restructure the districts.

Some reforms started in the 1980s and 1990s have stalled. Others prospered. In this historical and institutional context the three questions raised in this study emerge:
—Can teachers organize around quality?
—What are the barriers to doing so?
—What should be the policy response?
In exploring those questions we first turn to tangible examples of organizing around quality. These examples are grouped in three areas: standards for students and teachers, rewarding teachers for skills and knowledge, and teacher preparation and professional development.

Standards for Students and Teachers

Both unions have participated in efforts to create national standards through membership in the New Standards Project, the National Commission on Teaching and America's Future, and other bodies. The AFT has made standards the key to its quality schools strategy. Its Task Force on Redesigning Low Performing Schools has created an intervention strategy for low-performing schools that includes indicators of low performance as well as materials, procedures, and established schoolwide improvement strategies that can be used to respond.[5] At the same time, individual union locals provide compelling examples of enactment of standards, and they suggest why such activity is difficult.

Standards Become a Labor Issue in Cincinnati

The involvement of the Cincinnati Federation of Teachers (CFT) in standards setting presents an unexpected face to organizing around standards. Most descriptions of organizing around quality present an image of a rather domesticated Japanese-style union adding its weight to programs initiated by management. However, in Cincinnati the union's organizing around

---

5. Task Force on Redesigning Low Performing Schools (1998).

quality is often confrontational, making full use of the union's arsenal of organizing skills, political action, and bargaining.

For fifteen years CFT campaigned for tougher standards and against social promotion. Before a concerted union public relations and collective bargaining effort, principals often promoted students despite low performance or failing grades.[6] As a part of its desegregation efforts, the school district had created several highly visible and distinguished magnet schools, and these became an object of pride and a certain amount of self-congratulation. The union took it upon itself to publicly assert that all was not well in the remaining "neighborhood" schools. A key part in that campaign was the union's publicizing differences in curricular offerings in predominately white and predominately African American schools. Six of the junior high schools in the district did not offer algebra; five of them served African American communities.[7] After the union passed out flyers showing the report card of a student who was promoted over the teacher's objection after failing language arts, reading, spelling, math, and social science, the CFT began to gain editorial support:

> Teachers have an understandable interest in making as much money as they can, and the CFT has an interest in seeing as many teaching positions as possible in the Cincinnati public schools. But it speaks well of Cincinnati's teachers and their professional commitment that they see the improvement of educational standards as *the* most important issue on the bargaining agenda.[8]

By the 1985 collective bargaining contract, teachers had won the right to be consulted by parents and the principal if a grade was to be changed.[9]

The standards campaign continued, and in the early 1990s the school board passed much tougher graduation standards, including "no pass-no play" rules and limitations on access to extracurricular activities for students with poor grades. In applauding the move, the *Cincinnati Enquirer*

---

6. Mooney (1983).

7. Kemme (1984).

8. "Schools: The CFT Raises Some Basic Issues in Its Contract Negotiations," *Cincinnati Enquirer* (December 16, 1984), editorial.

9. Erardi (1985).

noted: "The board policy is a notable victory for, among others, the Cincinnati Federation of Teachers, which has been fighting for higher academic standards at a time when some professional educators and administrators were finding excuses for lowering them."[10]

The Cincinnati story continues. In 1999 and 2000 bargaining reached impasse in part over an attempt by the school superintendent to terminate peer review and other joint union-management committees. The dispute was submitted to a neutral fact finder whose report largely supported the teachers union. Fearing a strike during the time when the district was trying to pass a tax levy, the school board eventually supported a contract that continued much of what was in the existing contract. But even as the contractual dispute was settled, critics of the school board accused it of selling out to the teachers union. They promised to make the contract settlement a campaign issue in defeating the school tax election.[11]

The tortured path of labor relations in Cincinnati illustrates the difficulty and complexity of organizing around quality. When the district and teachers union negotiated a contract containing peer review and joint education reform committees in 1988 it was thought that a transition from conflict to cooperation had begun.[12] This has not been the case. Labor relations in the Cincinnati Public Schools (CPS) are now at least as conflictual as they were in the 1980s. The topics of conflict changed. Educational quality has become a labor issue mixed in with all the traditional topics about work rules and salary. In the recent negotiation traditional issues such as transfer, seniority, and salary were mixed with attention to standards, teacher recruitment, and professional development. Public contention over achievement and conflicts over privatization complicate bargaining.

Cincinnati, like most the state's big cities, was placed on "academic emergency" by the state department of education in 1999. Five state-sponsored charter schools were started in the district, draining more than 1,600 students from CPS. In addition to their bargaining conflicts, union president Tom Mooney and superintendent Steven Adamowski have been at

10. "Schools: New Academic Standards Send a Welcome Signal to Cincinnati," *Cincinnati Enquirer* (August, 16, 1991), editorial.

11. Dana DiFillippo, "CPA Endorses 3 Charter Schools," *Cincinnati Enquirer,* January 25, 2000; Phillip Pina, "CPS Vote Paves Way to Contract for Teachers," *Cincinnati Enquirer,* January 27, 2000.

12. Johnson (1989).

odds over the charter school movement, and particularly whether CPS should start its own charters. The superintendent sees charters as a way of breathing reform into the district and keeping students from leaving. Mooney opposes the district's opening of charters.[13]

National Board Certification

Along with presidents of both parties, the National School Boards Association, and virtually every professional and academic society, the NEA and AFT have endorsed the National Board for Professional Teaching Standards (NBPTS). Both unions have supported legislation to encourage teachers to become certified, and in many localities unions have bargained salary incentives for board certification. Numerous states and localities—often with private foundation support—have adopted fee supports, created salary supplements, allowed license portability, or made provision for board certification to count toward license renewal or continuing education units.

Collective bargaining allows schools to link monetary incentives to board certification. For example, the Los Angeles Unified School District and United Teachers Los Angeles bargained a 15 percent salary supplement for any board-certified teacher. In New York City, board certification qualifies a teacher for a salary differential of approximately $3,700. In Chicago, the union QuEST Center, with a grant from the John D. and Catherine T. MacArthur Foundation, is supporting twenty candidates for board certification. In Carbondale, Kansas, the Santa Fe Trail Unified School District 424 will pay the fee for three teachers and will provide release time for portfolio completion.

Board certification is important in its own right, but the influence of the board's methodology—teacher evaluation based on demonstrated practice rather than credit hours alone—is already having an influence in other domains. The same set of ideas that created national board assessments is starting to be applied to beginning teachers. Districts and unions are considering using the types of evaluative mechanisms and standards developed by the NBPTS in internal district teacher evaluations. The methodology of board certification and the process of peer review evaluation and renewal are beginning to support one another.

---

13. DiFillippo, "CPA Endorses 3 Charter Schools."

Peer Review Programs

Peer review is a powerful demonstration of how teachers create a knowledge of their own practice. In the thirty or so school districts that have enacted it, peer review brings higher standards to teaching. It significantly changes teaching by recognizing the importance of engagement and commitment as well as skill and technique. It recognizes a legitimate role for teachers in establishing and enforcing standards in their own occupation. For unions, it represents both a radical departure from established industrial norms and a rediscovery of traditional craft and guild union functions. Under peer review, the union's role balances protection of individual teachers with the protection of teaching. As Albert Fondy, president of the Pittsburgh Federation of Teachers, notes, "a union is not conceived with the primary mission of protecting the least competent of its members."[14]

Peer review started in 1981 when the Toledo, Ohio, schools and the Toledo Federation of Teachers added a one-sentence clause to the teachers' contract, in which the teachers agreed to police the ranks of their veterans in return for the right to review new teachers. Since then peer review has spread among progressive districts and both the AFT and NEA now support peer review, the latter having changed its position in a historic policy shift in 1997. Interest in peer review has increased in the wake of the NEA's policy change. In May 1998 a peer review conference sponsored by the Columbus, Ohio, local drew more than 500 participants from thirty states.[15] Among the districts with active peer review programs are: Seattle, Washington; Columbus, Ohio; Rochester, New York; Pittsburgh, Pennsylvania; Minneapolis, Minnesota; Hammond, Indiana; and Poway, California. In 1999 the California legislature followed Governor Gray Davis's initiative and mandated peer review statewide. Union and management support for the measure was lukewarm at best. It is still controversial in many quarters, but as Rochester Teachers Association president Adam Urbanski says, "Peer review is only controversial where it hasn't been tried."[16]

Most teacher assessment is what Columbus Education Association president John Grossman calls "dipstick" evaluation.[17] Such assessment is

---

14. Kerchner and Koppich (1993, p. 48).
15. Bradley (1998).
16. Kerchner and Koppich (1993).
17. Bradley (1998).

undertaken by school administrators to meet state mandates or community expectations of good practice. About 65 percent of the country's school districts use this type of evaluation.[18] Typically, evaluations involve short observations of teaching by a principal, a checklist of characteristics, and some kind of form for recording information. A conference may follow the observation, and teachers—through statute or contract—usually have the right to comment on the principal's assessment. The peer review systems we have seen differ in three important ways:

PEER REVIEW BRINGS HIGHER STANDARDS TO TEACHING. Although the sample size is too small to allow a broad statistical comparison, the historical evidence in such Ohio districts as Toledo and Columbus shows that more probationary and experienced teachers were dismissed under peer review than under the previous system of administrative review. Over sixteen years in Toledo, 52 experienced teachers out of a pool of about 2,600 were thought to have such serious performance problems that peer intervention was necessary. All but 10 have left the classroom. About 10 percent of Toledo's intern teachers are not rehired for a second year of teaching.

In Columbus, 178 teachers out of a teaching force of 4,800 have entered the district's intervention program during the last twelve years. More than 40 percent returned to teaching in what is called "good standing." The others resigned, retired, or were terminated. During the same period, 3,312 new teachers participated in the Columbus intern program, with 7 percent receiving unsatisfactory ratings.[19]

The more important contribution of peer review to standards comes through the much more extensive formative evaluation and assistance that a novice teacher receives during the peer review process. The resources that support peer review are a provision of collective bargaining. In every case we know of, the union bargained hard to allocate resources to the peer review program. In 1995 peer review became an issue that almost took teachers to strike in Toledo. In Rochester, the administrators' union sued the teachers union and the district over the peer assistance and review program, claiming that allowing teachers to evaluate one another violated the rights of administrators. Ultimately, the New York Supreme Court dismissed the suit.[20]

18. McGreal (1983, p. 9).
19. Bradley (1998).
20. O'Brien (1987).

PEER REVIEW RECOGNIZES THE IMPORTANCE OF ENGAGEMENT AND COMMITMENT, AS WELL AS SKILL AND TECHNIQUE. When supervising teachers spend time with classroom teachers, they are able to consider the teachers' classes and teaching practice as a whole rather than isolating details. Most evaluations by principals consist of one or two formal sessions during the year plus a few drop-ins. Principals also factor in parent complaints and the "buzz" around the school concerning new teachers. In contrast, we asked a supervising teacher in Poway, California (a 23,000-student district north of San Diego that has had a well-developed peer review program for a decade) about a new teacher whose contract was not renewed:

> Q. How many times would you say you were in this person's classroom?
> A. [laughter] Lots. From the first semester until we had the review board in the second semester, I put in approximately 70 hours. . . .
> Q. Did all the novices have your home phone number?
> A. You bet. Some of the best conversations were at night when [a teacher's] thinking, "Gosh, you know, *tomorrow*."
> Q. And they would call you up?
> A. Sure . . . maybe a couple of times a week.[21]

Engaging peer review does not mean that unions abandon their role of ensuring that teachers receive procedural due process. All peer review programs the authors are aware of include provision for a teacher who is reviewed negatively to appeal to the union for assistance and representation. In some peer review settings, a special union representative is designated, someone who has not been a part of the peer review process. However, in practice, the record established by the peer review process is so thorough, and the evidence is so complete, that aside from charges of discrimination or malfeasance, the evaluation record is generally compelling.

PEER REVIEW RECOGNIZES A ROLE FOR TEACHERS IN ESTABLISHING AND ENFORCING STANDARDS. Peer review forces teachers to reflect on their craft and to define what constitutes good teaching. As Miles Myers, former executive director of the National Council of Teachers of English

21. Kerchner and Koppich (1993).

has said, "Teachers have to be able to express good teaching in language that other teachers understand and accept."

Peer review is able to be tougher and still maintain standards of fairness because it is also much more extensive than traditional common law evaluations. The review plans used in Toledo, Ohio, and Poway, California, assign between ten and twenty novice teachers to supervising teachers. Assistance and evaluation is their full-time job. For new teachers, who must be granted tenure or terminated within two to three years, intensification means providing more help and giving novices a closer look at what expert teachers do.

Rewarding Teachers for Skills and Knowledge

The standard single salary schedule is one of the most ubiquitous organizational characteristics of public schools. In rich schools and poor, bargaining states and nonbargaining ones, teachers are paid according to the amount of education they have and number of years of service in the district.[22] Although unions are frequently credited or blamed for the situation, the salary schedule traces its origins to civil service and its spread to universal application to the post–World War II enrollment boom. It became necessary for school districts to attract women by paying them as much as male teachers, who had previously been paid more. While education and years of service may in some rough way equate to expertise, the system ignores any relationship between salary and effectiveness.

Nonetheless, departures from the standard single salary schedule have remained on the "undiscussable" list for most unions, and indeed for most schools. Unions fear the rise of managerial favoritism in setting salaries, as well as discontent among members who find themselves paid differently for reasons that are not easily explainable. Only a few unions have begun to look at alternatives. One of them is in Cincinnati, Ohio.

The Cincinnati Federation of Teachers negotiated a carefully crafted plan to link salary incentives and student achievement, but in May 1998 the rank-and-file issued a rebuff. Voting 1,160 to 804, the teachers rejected the plan, which in spirit they had approved by ratifying their contract in March 1997.[23] The plan is now under reconsideration.

22. Odden and Kelley (1996).
23. Archer (1998).

The rejection incident illustrates how difficult it is to gain acceptance of salary schedule changes, even when extensive efforts are made at communicating them and involving teachers fully in their development. For example, during the 1997–98 school year a forty-one-member committee, including twenty-one teachers, was convened to develop the "School Incentive Award." Committee minutes were posted on the district website and distributed to teachers at each school site.

In rejecting the award proposal, Cincinnati teachers also rejected bonuses of $1,400 for themselves and $700 for full-time civil service staff members. What did the teachers reject? Monetary bonuses were to be given to entire school staffs when students demonstrated improvement on designated indicators, including:

—Ohio proficiency tests (grades 4, 6, and 9; grade tests at 8, 10, and 12),
—Off-grade proficiency tests (grades 2, 5, and 7),
—Stanford 9 Achievement Test for the schools that used the test,
—student attendance,
—student dropout rate (grades 7–12),
—student dropback rate (grades K–12), and
—staff attendance.

Test data would be analyzed only for those students who had been enrolled at a given school for a minimum of two-thirds of the school days for the first three-quarters of the year. The indicators would accumulate points for the school; schools who had earned 75 percent of all possible points would be eligible for the award.

The Denver Public Schools and the Denver Teachers Association recently have captured attention for agreeing to a two-year pilot program that ties pay for all teachers in participating schools to performance. Each teacher in the twelve pilot schools will receive $500 for participating and up to $1,000 more if the majority of a teacher's students improved. Three assessment systems will be piloted. One group of schools will base its teacher rewards on the Iowa Test of Basic Skills, a second group on classroom work and tests, and a third on whether teachers have sought to improve their teaching by participating in specified staff development programs. At the end of the pilot period, a panel of teachers union and district officials will evaluate the results and recommend a permanent plan. During the pilot period, the conventional salary schedule remains in effect.[24]

24. Janofsky (1999).

Teacher Preparation and Professional Development

Almost all unions involve themselves in some kind of teacher professional development: some modest, some substantial and highly integrated with the district. One of the interesting aspects of union involvement in professional development is that often the union rather than the school district leadership provides the continuity to keep a project alive. For example, during the late 1980s and early 1990s Dade County Public Schools witnessed five changes of superintendents, along with rapid demographic changes in its student body, a recession, and a devastating hurricane. The set of staff development programs negotiated with the United Teachers of Dade survived these tough times (some with substantial modification) and continue today because they had both an anchor in negotiated agreements and continuing union leadership.[25]

If done well, the union connection to professional development creates a powerful systemic effect connecting professional development to training and induction, assessment of schools and teachers, the curriculum, and the salary schedule. The Minneapolis and New York City public schools offer particularly good examples of a long-term working relationship that has increasingly focused on student standards and achievement.

The Minneapolis process illustrates effects of gradually building and deepening the relationship between management and labor. Begun in 1984 with a joint Labor/Management Task Force on Teacher Professionalism, the process spawned a mentor teacher program and five years later a new teacher evaluation process. A pilot project started with 400 teachers in 1991 and gradually expanded to include the whole district by 1996–97. The Minneapolis evaluation system development coincided with 1995 legislation, Minnesota State Law 125.17, which was drafted and supported by the union. This law requires all teachers to have a peer review plan whose implementation is controlled by teachers.

The professional development program, which is administered by a joint district-union panel, links professional education to how teachers gain tenure in the district, their pay, and teacher support and evaluation. A teacher-administrator Career-in-Teaching Panel reviews and assesses the program and makes recommendations regarding staffing and operations. Most of the day-to-day work is done by mentor teachers selected from the ranks of MPS lead teachers. They serve for three years before returning to

25. Phillips (1993).

the classroom and work with teachers who are served by the program as well as provide other professional development coaching and training to teachers in the district.

In Minneapolis there has been a concerted effort to systemically link professional development and school improvement using the teachers' collective bargaining contract as one of the primary vehicles. To Minneapolis Federation of Teachers president Louise Sundin the connection seems logical. "Teachers pay attention to the contract. Policy manual and guides are never consulted by either teachers or managers. The contract is." As a result, the contract combines traditional subjects of bargaining—wages and work rules—with long sections on professional development and school improvement. It includes a preamble that joins the union to the school district's adopted mission statement: "We exist to ensure that all students learn." And it also pledges the union to support a unified effort to overcome "the seemingly overwhelming factors of poverty, racism, and disillusionment, to arrive at an environment where teachers can teach successfully. . . . Therefore, we cannot afford to waste energy or resources distracting ourselves with petty power struggles."[26]

Through the contract and joint committees, the union links to the school improvement and accountability program. For example, each school issues a report on student progress toward passing the Minnesota Basic Skills Test. Article VI of the 1997–99 contract, titled "schools as centers of performance," covers the school improvement process and its governing philosophy of site-based management. That section of the contract also incorporates the district accountability framework through which teachers and principals take the primary role in increasing student achievement and staff development.[27] As a part of this system, each school improvement plan has specific goals and specified means of measuring progress. For example, one of the district goals is to see that all students read well by the third grade. At the Sheridan Global Arts and Communications School, a 750-student elementary magnet, tests revealed that few students (about 11 percent) came to first grade with the language skills needed to learn how to read; they had no book awareness and often no experience with books. One teacher told of students who were unclear about where the front of the book was or did not know the print runs from left to right, top to bottom. Interestingly, teachers at Sheridan described the situation without pointing fingers at children

26. Minneapolis Public Schools and Minneapolis Federation of Teachers (1997, pp. 2, 4).
27. Minneapolis Public Schools and Minneapolis Federation of Teachers (1997, p. 40).

or their families. The school staff members accepted the need to understand and work with the set of situations they were given.

Thus the first element of the school's improvement plan was to increase the percentage of readers. In pursuit of this goal, the school created a plan of work, allocating both budget and responsibility, and tied each element to indicators of success. The reading analysis they developed involved grouping, not tracking, and moving students up and through the levels. All books are color coded so teachers and students can try their ability at the next level. Students check with teachers to move between levels.

As was the case with the opening illustration about a quality rubric in a sixth-grade classroom, the Sheridan School improvement plan illustrates the systemic way in which unionism can link classroom and policy. The Sheridan School was able to focus on reading quality because the union and district had negotiated a succession of contracts and other working documents that made resources available for the school to recognize and respond to its reading problem.

In New York City, the United Federation of Teachers (UFT) and the school system collaborate in creating staff development that is embedded in the schools and in the work days of teachers. More than 220 teacher specialists staff professional development teacher centers in schools. Through the centers, these teachers deliver classroom coaching and mentoring and direct assistance with school-adopted interventions, such as Success for All. A substantial number of the teacher specialists have received intensive workshop training in the New Standards Project, whose work has been adopted by the school district. They are the means of transmission for turning the New Standards Project from rhetoric to reality.

Embedded staff development was spurred by the increased attention being given to standards and accountability. Some ninety-seven New York City schools are on the state chancellor's list of schools on academic probation. Both the union and the district needed a response to schools already named and to those that might be. Providing high-quality professional development in schools was one of the responses, one that the UFT endorses and a program it operates. Embedded staff development is particularly well developed in Community School District 2, which includes a widely diverse economic swath in central Manhattan.

UFT staff members point to a paradigm shift within the union to focus on outcomes and instruction. Interestingly, union staff teachers appear to be treating professional development as an entitlement under the contract rather than a mandated duty.

Barriers to Organizing around Quality

Just as one can observe and enumerate examples of union organizing around educational quality and student achievement, any observer would be forced to note that teachers union organizing outside of its industrial origins has not spread rapidly. Both national unions exhibit tentativeness about how departures from industrial unionism should proceed. In the late 1980s the AFT promoted site-based management and school decentralization as the keystones of organizational reform only to abandon the effort in favor of a strong emphasis on standards and adoption of a limited number of coherent reform strategies. The NEA's new unionism was supposed to ignite a bubbling pot of locally initiated reforms, but the evidence from the first years illustrates the difficulties of moving forward. AFT and NEA locals associated with the Teacher Union Reform Network (TURN) have undertaken many of the boldest reforms, including those described in this chapter. But TURN comprises fewer than twenty-five locals, and even its members struggle with how far and how fast to go. (For current information about teachers union reform efforts check the authors' website, *www. mindworkers.com,* or the TURN site, *www.turnexchange.net.*) In sum, union reform appears to have little of the momentum that characterized the growth of collective bargaining in the 1960s and 1970s. Without a driving force behind it, the new unionism is likely to remain not only new, but novel.

A review of our work, and examination of data from selected districts, suggests that union reform faces four fundamental barriers:

1. existing cultures of teachers and school administrators,
2. the organization of unions themselves,
3. the array of political forces in education, and
4. the ways in which culture, organizational capacity, and educational politics are embedded in public policy.

Each of the four will be discussed in the sections that follow. These discussions lead to a concluding recommendation for rewriting labor law to encourage organizing around quality.

1. Alien Cultures

Much has been made of the recalcitrance of unions, and indeed there is a delicious irony in the fact that teachers unions, which organized in opposition to the authority system of public education, should be the fiercest defender of the system against alternative ways of delivering schooling. However, for the most part union leaders are reflecting their members' views. Unlike many policy activists, teachers do not believe that public education is facing a large institutional change or that schooling needs to change in major ways. We are told that polls done by the unions themselves show that teachers want help with problems of student achievement, but that they do not particularly associate their unions with this function. Indeed, teachers who work at charter schools seem disassociated from the union and public education altogether.[28] Younger teachers who see a need for change often do not associate reform with their union. Older teachers, who are often on union representative councils, see relatively less need for change and their beliefs percolate upward in the unions. Teachers from small towns and comfortable suburbs outweigh and outvote the cities and poverty belts, where public education faces its most visible challenges.

In addition, union staff and school administrators, although often opponents at the bargaining table, are frequently united in their embrace of industrial unionism. By word and deed, most school administrators believe that a union's voice needs to be made as quiet as possible and the scope of negotiations restricted to teachers' economic interests. Although the American Association of School Administrators has sponsored some efforts in "joint team" training, unions are not generally thought of as a partner in educational reform. A majority of union staff probably believes the same. It is not uncommon to hear comments such as, "We just want to represent teachers; we've no interest in running the district. We've got plenty to do as it is keeping an eye on those principals who won't live by the contract."

Moreover, there is a belief that unions cannot organize around reform. Despite polls and focus groups showing that teachers are frustrated by their lack of success in the classroom, union staff and officers report great difficulty getting teachers to support reform ideas and to work actively to advance them. The emotional pull, the elemental anger, that allowed teachers to organize against school administrators is harder to tap in getting teachers to organize around quality. The assertion that taking charge of quality is a union's role is dulled by a history of highly individualized and restricted view of teaching, what one observer called "shallow professionalism." In this occupational world view the union is a mechanism to get

28. Koppich, Holmes, et al. (1998).

administrators to leave teachers alone, insulating them behind the closed classroom door. Within this belief system, messages that teachers should organize to enforce standards in schools, should be responsible for weeding out bad teachers, and should take charge of reform are not always well received.[29]

More than a decade ago Kerchner and Mitchell observed what they called *generational* behavior in teachers unions—different eras of ideological belief, each separated by revolutionary struggles for control of teachers union locals and corresponding turnovers in school administrators.[30] Teachers union officers and staff who lead change often face substantial opposition from their members and contenders for their positions. Union staffs are divided between those who support a new identity and those who oppose it. At issue are both changes in unionism, a belief system, and unionization, a way of getting organized. Embrace of the educational quality agenda represents a generational change that has not yet played out as either belief or organizational reality.

2. Organizational Capacity

Even if unions want to get organized around craft, artistic, or professional work motifs, it is still an open question whether they can pull it off. Again, contrary to the ways in which unions are portrayed, unions have small staffs and generally modest budgets. A recent field visit to a mid-sized city union revealed a picture of a union office with a professional staff of seven people, compared with a school district housed in a central office building of seven stories. Clearly, questions of joint operations between unions and school districts are compromised by the union's organizational capacity.

The capacity question is not simply a matter of staff; it is what the staff knows how to do. Most union staff gained their positions because they were good organizers or good advocates, not because they were especially skilled at day-to-day operations. They are generally better at rocking boats than steering them. Organizing—a core union skill—means motivating people to action, usually for a short period of time, as in a political campaign, a strike, a representation election, or some other episodic event. Only recently has the term *organizing* begun to be used in union circles to

---

29. National Foundation for the Improvement of Education (1996); Kerchner and Koppich (1993).
    30. Kerchner and Mitchell (1988).

mean organizing a teacher's daily work routines and schedule to increase educational quality or support reforms.

Unions are less well organized for the "steady work" of education—creating and spreading a curriculum, professional development, or the actual operation of schools. Their core purpose is to represent people doing the work of schooling, not getting the work itself done.

Much of the reforms of the 1980s involved unions taking what we called *joint custody of reform.*[31] In many cases, these efforts stretched the unions beyond their reasonable capacity to deliver. The problem was not in the ability to reach a collective bargaining agreement that dealt with reform. Rather, the problem was in converting the agreement into action; the details of implementation seem to swamp organizations. Ironically, these implementation problems also seem to swamp school districts. But school districts have difficulty delivering on reform for different reasons than unions do. School districts, particularly urban ones where most of the inventive locals operate, suffer from high degrees of instability at the top. Superintendents turn over rapidly. Fiscal relationships are precarious. And there are frequent interventions from the outside. In the political realm, the union is often the most stable player. One union executive recently complained of the difficulty of carrying on reform while the administrative ranks keep changing. He reeled off the long list of associate superintendents and other administrators who had moved through his district in the last decade, saying, "It's like teaching a parade."

3. Political Forces

Union reform is also made difficult by the array of forces in educational politics. While it is true that teachers unions are formidable friends or enemies in political battles, they are much less monolithic and much more vulnerable than is commonly believed.

The failure of the NEA-AFT merger in July 1998 provides an indication of just how fractious the internal politics can be. There is, for example, no shared understanding of whether teachers unions should be associated with organized labor, either formally through membership in the AFL-CIO, as is the AFT, or through some political and social coalition. There is no consensus about the "new unionism" agenda proclaimed by NEA president Bob Chase. And there is no unified national agenda on educational reform.

31. Kerchner and Koppich (1993).

Internal fractiousness affects the unions' ability to respond to an increasingly harsh external political environment. In thirty-seven states, unions face Republican governors, many of whom were raised in a political culture in which little good was said about public education and nothing at all good was said about unions. Unlike Republican officeholders in the post–World War II generation, contemporary incumbents do not see organized labor as serving an institutional function for either the country or their states. Some governors, such as Tommy G. Thompson (R-Wis.) and John Engler (R-Mich.), have pointedly positioned themselves as opponents of teachers unions.[32]

Within the cities, unions face additional political pressure. Big-city mayors have become educational activists. Some, such as Milwaukee mayor John O. Norquist, who set up charter schools under city rather than school district control, explicitly say that they cannot attract the middle class back to the city unless the schools perform better. "People were leaving for the suburbs because of the quality of public schools, and that's not acceptable."[33] Other mayors simply look covetously at the slice of local tax revenues going to schools. In these local political situations, teachers unions and public schools have lost some allies. African American politicians, traditionally supporters of public school reforms, have become increasingly doubtful of the system's ability to right itself and increasingly prone to look at quasi-market alternatives.

In addition to weakness among public officials and political parties, unions are disadvantaged by the rise in popularity of populist politics, on both the right and left. Community control of schools, which can have either right- or left-wing origins, is as much an enemy of the status quo as educational vouchers.

In this context, unions have simply lost the momentum of change. One of the great change forces in public education over the past half century, unions are largely reduced to fighting against changes supported by others rather than advocating for and organizing around a set of educational ideas. To argue for a new or changed institution of public education is much different than it was to organize teachers within the existing institution. Until unions have an agenda, it will not be possible for them to develop policy alternatives.

---

32. See chapter 6 in this volume for more on this topic.
33. White (1999, p. 34).

4. Teaching Law and Policy

If the country wants to encourage teachers to move away from industrial definitions of their work, and it wants to capture the energy of teachers behind a systemic educational quality agenda, then the incentives inherent in labor law need to be restructured. Although teachers unions, like other labor organizations, started as social movements, they gained status and influence because they gained a statutory anchor. Labor law legitimates, protects, and spreads the work of organizers. In teacher labor relations, it was only after states began to adopt statutes modeled on the federal National Labor Relations Act (NLRA) that collective bargaining expanded rapidly across the country. Statutes could be copied by one state from another. The introduction of a statute provided an orderly way for a transition into collective bargaining. It is not accidental, for example, that the educational labor relations statute in California bears a strong resemblance to that in Indiana. Statutory borrowing from one state to another generated a common ethos and indeed a common handbook of law and practice, Wollett and Chanin's *The Law and Practice of Teacher Negotiations*, which served as the touchstone for the institutional patterning of the NEA.[34] Collective bargaining was able to spread from place to place relatively easily because each school district and each union did not have to invent it anew. While teachers had to go through a psychological and political revolution that we have called *generational change,* the behaviors and structures of collective bargaining could be copied from other districts.[35] Without a similar patterning effect, building teachers unions around quality and educational reforms—what we have called *unionism for the knowledge society*—is not likely to spread rapidly.

A New Labor Relations Statute for Educators

It is both good news and bad that the educational reforms of the past decade have been accomplished without major changes in labor relations statutes. It is true, as traditionalists argue, that the current law is intended to be organic and flexible. That the experiments of the last decade or so

---

34. Wollett and Chanin (1974).
35. Kerchner and Mitchell (1988); DiMaggio and Powell (1983).

were possible is evidence that changes in law are not necessary in order to experiment with changing labor relations. However, a closer look reveals a legal structure designed to preserve industrial-style labor relations rather than allow it to change easily. First, current statutes are subject to interpretation that would chill any substantive workplace reforms of the sorts we have described and reduce educational reform to narrow managerialism resulting in employee participation within an entirely management-controlled environment. Second, the current statutes have no incentives for schools and districts to change. Labor law as we know it is built around large hierarchies and centralized control. If schools are to change, the institutional incentives for change need to be altered, and the labor code is one of these incentives.

There are seven substantive mismatches between the existing laws and educational reform:

—*Coverage.* Which workers are eligible for protection under labor statutes?

—*Bargaining unit.* Which employees should be grouped together to be represented by unions?

—*Cooperation.* Under what legal aegis can unions and employers develop joint working arrangements?

—*Scope of bargaining.* What issues are employees and unions supposed to discuss?

—*Peer review.* How can employees take on the professional responsibility of judging the quality of work performed by their colleagues?

—*Union as employment agent.* How can unions facilitate workers who have nontraditional jobs, nonemployment contractual relations, or relations with individual schools rather than districts?

—*Dispute resolution.* How can workers and managers learn to solve workplace problems peacefully, and what recourse will the system have when they fail?

Which Workers Are Covered?

Both employed professionals and independent contractors have precarious status under existing labor law.

Professionals and others whose work definition includes making organizational decisions run afoul of the legal tradition that excludes managers from protections under labor law. The NLRA posits a fundamental dividing line between labor and management. Legislative history and court decisions interpreting the law assert that collective bargaining by people on the management side of that line would create intolerable divided loyalties. Employees affiliated with management would be torn between their responsibilities to their employers and their solidarity with other employees in the union movement. These conflicts could impair the job performance and threaten the organization.[36]

The tradition of denying supervisors bargaining rights causes potential problems when the work of teachers takes on decisions that traditionally were the province of managers. The 1980 U.S. Supreme Court decision in *National Labor Relations Board* v. *Yeshiva University,* 444 U.S. 672, reinforced the separation of workers and managers in higher education, as did the recent case involving nurses.[37] The 1947 Taft-Hartley amendments to the NLRA specifically excluded supervisors from coverage under the law, specifying (in section 2[11]) that supervisors are those who have the authority to hire, transfer, suspend, lay off, recall, promote, discharge, assign, reward, or discipline other employees. Faculty members at Yeshiva were denied collective bargaining rights because their faculty senate and its committees made substantive decisions at their university. Thus they were considered "supervisors" under the law and ineligible for bargaining rights. Although this federal legal doctrine has never been applied to a state case governing public school teachers, it stands as a symbolic barrier, a monument that the law did not intend workers and management to share decisional power. "In the end the *Yeshiva* case is troubling because it is at war with the idea of consensus between professional employees and their administrators."[38] This legal status is troubling not only to teachers but also to other professional employees.

A second legal issue arises among independent contractors—persons who may work at an organization but are not considered employed by it. With the use of contracting-out mechanisms and part-time contingent labor workers, and even the use of professional service contracts, inclusion of the independent contractor status within the protection of labor laws is of the utmost importance.

When it passed the NLRA in 1935, Congress had in mind protecting workers who moved from workplace to workplace. The scope of protection was not to be limited to single enterprises. The Supreme Court even

36. Rabban (1989, p. 1778)
37. *National Labor Relations Board* v. *Health Care and Retirement Corporation of America* (1994).
38. Schlossberg and Fetter (1986, p. 15).

extended the law's protection to newspaper boys—coverage that outraged publishers and was subsequently removed by amendments in 1947. Over time, however, coverage of the labor law has come to be associated with current employment.[39]

The concept of a broadened scope of coverage gains importance if teachers are no longer employed by a single school district and if their social and economic security does not rest on continued employment. This would be the case if the numbers of charter schools grew considerably or if large numbers of teachers became independent contractors under arrangements being pioneered by the Association of Educators in Private Practice.

The Bargaining Unit

Bargaining unit provisions determine which workers are grouped together for the purposes of negotiation and representation. The goal is to form what the law calls a community of interest among workers, and thus groups are formed according to the type of work they do. Almost always, teachers and professionals are divided into separate units. Classroom aides, janitors, cooks, secretaries, and school security workers usually have their own bargaining units. In larger districts they tend to be separated one from another; in smaller ones they are often combined. Sometimes credentialed or licensed workers other than teachers are placed in separate units, too. Thus nurses, counselors, and librarians often bargain separately from teachers.

This arrangement makes a number of structural reforms difficult. For example, a school site labor agreement called an *educational compact* that explicitly ties educational plans to resource distribution is advocated in *United Mind Workers*.[40] Such agreements would need to be the product of the entire community of interest: everyone who works for money in schools, and students and parents who work but do not draw salaries. It also advocates a staffing scheme that is a career ladder with teaching at the top that allows flexibility and differentiation in staffing. In order for such staffing to be feasible, employees would have to bargain together or at least have areas of joint responsibility. Otherwise, every occupational boundary would become a battleground, as was historically the case with the building trades and which can now be seen in health care.

39. Pleasure and Greenfield (1985, p. 184).
40. Kerchner, Koppich, and Weeres (1997).

The question of teacher-as-free-agent also arises under charter school and other autonomous school arrangements.

Cooperation and Joint Enterprises

Cooperation between labor and management is still legally suspicious. Although NLRA author Senator Robert Wagner (D-N.Y.) espoused cooperation among workers, the law for which he is remembered, and the state statutes derived from it, nearly universally place barriers in the way of a close working relationship between unions and management. The framers of the law were concerned with so-called company unions, organizations that looked like unions but were dominated by management and formed to forestall worker organization by independent unions.

Section 8(a)(2) of the NLRA provides that it shall be an unfair labor practice for an employer to:

> dominate or interfere with the formation or administration of any labor organization or contribute financial or other support to it: Provided, that . . . an employer shall not be prohibited from permitting employees to confer with him during working hours without loss of pay.

Employee organizations (Section 2[5]) included virtually any kind of employee representation committee or organization that deals with wages or working conditions.

Currently, however, there is a felt need to form substantive joint enterprises, such as professional practice committees and professional development schools, without violating the employer assistance or domination prohibition. While recent lower court decisions have seemed to recognize that changing conditions strengthen the case for cooperative employer-employee relations, the Supreme Court has yet to clarify the situation.

Development of a legal structure more conducive to the implementation of professional values requires changes in the concept of company domination. Collegial committees or actual joint operations *need* support from employers. Teachers should be able to form committees that advise and actually make policy, and school authorities should be able to assist those committees with staff support and budgets without violating the labor statute.

We agree with David Rabban's suggestion that "the definition of company domination that best promotes professional values should be limited to actual employer interference with the independent decision making of employee committees, whether or not this interference derives from anti-union animus. Unless committees of professional employees are able to reach their own conclusions, they cannot provide the employer with the expert advice that justifies their existence."[41]

The Scope of Bargaining

Industrial style bargaining evokes a legal fiction: that wages and the work rules of teachers can be separated from educational policy. While many critics of collective bargaining have taken pains to show that unions have encroached on the educational policy arena, they miss the point. Even the narrowest constriction of the scope of bargaining—wages, classification of workers, benefits, and hours of work—effectively encumbers virtually all the operating budget of a labor-intensive organization such as a school system. Moreover, the scope of bargaining has a tendency to expand over time as the parties to labor agreements use that vehicle to solve personnel problems and settle disputes. This is most often done without reference to the educational consequences of the agreement, thus creating what we have called "accidental policy making."[42] It is the worst of all worlds, one which preserves the legal position that educational policy remained in the hands of legislatures and school boards while operating in an environment where professional-level employees effectively controlled the budgetary expenditures and time allocation. Narrow scope bargaining, as embodied in the NLRA framework and recent state statutes, makes it impossible to solve the problem of professional judgment and public accountability.

However, simply broadening the scope to mandate bargaining on virtually any issue would be to introduce intolerable inflexibility into the process. The practice of union locals that attempt to use collective bargaining for educational reform varies widely. Some districts, such as Minneapolis, attempt to make the contract become the district's reform plan, and they craft a document that is as much intended for advice and direction as it is to withstand attack during legal interpretation. The document becomes more organic and less legalistic. Other locals deliberately

41. Rabban (1989, p. 1755).
42. Kerchner and Mitchell (1988).

try to use other vehicles for educational quality, professional development, and educational policy questions. In *United Mind Workers*, we advocate a school site agreement called an Enterprise Compact, somewhat similar to that being used in some manufacturing settings in which there are specific resource allocation decisions made on the basis of continuing improvement.[43] The agreement becomes a means for creating joint custody of reform. No state has yet legislated an expectation that school districts and unions should use collective bargaining as a means of educational reform.

Peer Review

Peer review challenges both the ideology and the practice of current labor relations in rather obvious ways. It also is legally suspect. The courts have held that by achieving the status of exclusive representative for a group of employees, unions also take on a duty to "exercise fairly the power conferred upon it in behalf of all those for whom it acts, without hostile discrimination among them."[44]

This duty is felt in several circumstances, but the one most associated with peer review is the representation requirement when employees are disciplined or discharged. The courts have held that a union has discretion in deciding how far to press a grievance brought by a member in these cases, so long as it does not discriminate against or among groups of members.[45] Thus not every grievance needs be carried to arbitration or into the courts. But in peer review cases, the union approves of and participates in a process in which members judge other members, and unions have generally agreed that they will not challenge the substance of peer review rulings. While the existing peer review experiments have produced no legal challenges from teachers who were judged to be incompetent, the status of unions remains unclear, and a statute that anticipated workers serving in a professional peer review situation should be honored.

Peer review also challenges sections of education statutes that reserve the managers' right to evaluate employees. Principals in Rochester, New York, unsuccessfully challenged the teachers union's introduction of peer review on this ground. In California districts that adopted peer review, administrators sign the final recommendations, thus complying with the

---

43. Kerchner, Koppich, and Weeres (1997); Bluestone and Bluestone (1992).
44. *Steele* v. *Louisville and N.R.R.*, 323 US 192, pp. 202–03.
45. Morris (1971).

letter of the law. A recent analysis of peer review by union attorneys suggests contractual language that would assure that teachers serving on peer review panels or as supervising teachers would not compromise their status as bargaining unit members.[46]

Unions as Agents of Employment

Craft unions flourished in the nineteenth century because labor organizations were able to control entire fields of work through a combination of solidarity, coercion, and licensure. The modern professions followed in the footsteps of the guilds by regulating entry to work through education and apprenticeship and setting the standards of practice. Membership in medical or bar associations became a matter of social expectation and often a requirement of forming a successful practice.

Thus the practicality of a form of unionism that extends beyond one employer depends on the legitimated right of unions to undertake activities that create representation throughout a field of employment. Current law discourages such activity.

Dispute Resolution

While one hopes that organizing around quality will be cooperative in the sense that it forms a community of professionals and broader community support, any system of employment relations that does not anticipate disputes is doomed from the outset. For labor relations, the question is always how to balance workers' rights to voice their interests in ways that do not lead to unreasonable disturbances in the work of schools or overly costly, protracted, and cumbersome dispute resolution techniques.

Any autonomous school with high levels of faculty involvement—such as some charter schools—might anticipate that the range and nature of conflict will be different, not that the level of conflict will necessarily be higher or lower.

Conventional labor law differentiates disputes over *rights* from those over *interests*. Rights disputes usually take the form of grievances, typically a employee's charge that management failed to do what was required under the contract. Most often, grievances arise when the contract is unclear, for example about which employees are to have preference in transfers to a

46. AFT-NEA (1998).

different school or whether a principal's called staff meeting was allowable under the contract. Rights disputes are subject to a contractually required step-by-step dispute resolution process familiar to most educators. The endpoint in this process is frequently binding arbitration. In contrast, interest disputes arise during collective bargaining or union organizing when agreements cannot be reached over the terms of a contract or whether a union will be recognized. These disputes are the most difficult and frequently explosive, leading to overt conflict and direct action through strikes and other means.

In union engagement in educational quality, the line between rights and interests is less clear than in conventional systems. In more autonomous schools, teachers and administrators will carry with them the rights to set work parameters and also the responsibility to make the school function smoothly. The ability to engage in conflict as if it is someone else's responsibility to operate the school will vanish, and neither labor nor management will be able to leave disputes unsettled without consequences.

The experiences of schools that have experimented with highly participatory school site management or decisionmaking programs illustrate the need for high levels of dispute resolution training and skills. Where the primary skill of labor activists in the industrial setting is to rally workers around clearly (if sometimes artificially) articulated divisions with management, the dominant skill in the knowledge era is to form communities of interest. If the experience of labor relations reform efforts over the last decade are any guide, a great deal of training, expertise, and support will be necessary to increase skill in process, problem solving, and dispute resolution skills. Teachers and administrators in Glenview, Illinois, for example, invested heavily in meeting process skills, and those in Pittsburgh, Pennsylvania, in consensus decisionmaking.[47] Interestingly, the origins of emphasizing dispute resolution had less to do with labor-management relationships and much more to do with controlling the conflict between students that was preventing school reform programs from going forward. Teachers then found that they needed the medicine they were giving the children.

Additionally, any dispute resolution system must come to grips with the right to strike. Striking remains controversial in the public sector: a blasphemy to detractors and ideological bedrock for unionists. Increasingly, however, strikes are seen as of dubious utility, a right that is needed but frequently not useful.

---

47. Kerchner (1991); Smylie (1991); Smylie, Brownlee-Conyers, and Crowson (1991).

Connecting the right to strike and educational issues is uncharted territory. Except under extreme circumstances, we do not believe that the right
to strike should be extended to individual schools when the economic and
security aspects of their employment are still contained in a master contract
with a school district or some other regional authority. It is interesting to
note that strike and the threat of strike over educational issues have been
relatively common in school districts that have organized around quality.
Rochester, Cincinnati, Toledo, and Poway have all had protracted disagreements over educational issues that were taken to the verge of strike.

Conclusion: Making Policy Choices

The "teachers union problem" is seldom discussed in polite social conver-
sation much less substantive policy arenas. Critics paint unions as the problem that needs to be fixed, most usually by elimination. Unions see themselves as political influentials who are not a problem, just a force to be dealt
with. Serious policy discussion about unions disappears into a black hole,
underdiscussed and underresearched.[48] Thus it is timely to inquire into the
public policy dimensions of teacher unionism, particularly into the extent
to which policy options can be crafted that support educational quality.

We have a choice. We can continue to ignore labor relations in public
policy discussions about education reform, or we can attempt to grasp the
issues. It is possible to fashion a labor policy that encourages organizing
around principles other than industrial unionism by creating both belief
and practice that recognize the energy and power in unions in useful ways.
But it is also possible—either by design or by accident—to create the labor
policy agenda in such ways that virtually every proposal that is made
becomes an attack on unions. For example, there are vastly different kinds
of charter school legislation. Some strip union representation capacity; others provide a role for unions. There are different ways of reconstituting
failing schools. Some scapegoat teachers and their jobs; others combine
school reorganization with resources and professional development so that
teachers and administrators actually have a chance to make schools better.

We believe policy scholars possess an important historic opportunity to
shape alternatives for how teachers work and how schools are organized.

48. Bradley (1996).

The policy key is what is called "the law of work," not just labor statutes but also educational and government codes that effectively define what teachers do all day. Teachers and others who "think for a living" need something other than an industrial-style workplace.[49] By ignoring labor relations policy, school reform has been tied to either an unsatisfactory present or an antiquated past. Few would argue, particularly those who favor the radical restructuring of education, that the current system of school governance will deliver the education system that can educate the vast majority of Americans to high academic standards.

But absent a serious discussion of policy options for teacher work, what matters most has been ignored. Of all the factors under a school's control, good teaching contributes most heavily to student achievement.[50] The magnitude of differences between good and bad teachers dwarfs other factors. Thus the set of rules that determines who is allowed to teach, what teachers are expected to do, what education and support they get, and who is allowed to remain a teacher becomes a public policy issue of the first magnitude.

References

AFT-NEA. 1998. *Peer Assistance and Review: An AFT/NEA Handbook.* Washington, D.C.

Archer, Jeff. 1998. "Cincinnati Teachers Rebuff Bonus-Pay Design." *Education Week* (May 27).

Block, Fred. 1990. *Postindustrial Possibilities: A Critique of Economic Discourse.* University of California Press.

Bluestone, Barry, and Irving Bluestone. 1992. *Negotiating the Future: A Labor Perspective on American Business.* Basic Books.

Bradley, Ann. 1996. "Education's Dark Continent." *Education Week* (December 4).

———. 1998. "Peer-Review Programs Catch Hold as Unions, Districts Work Together." *Education Week* (June 3), electronic edition.

Chubb, John E., and Terry M. Moe. 1990. *Politics, Markets and America's Schools.* Brookings.

Cobble, Dorothy Sue. 1991. "Organizing the Postindustrial Work Force: Lessons from the History of Waitress Unionism." *Industrial and Labor Relations Review* 44 (3): 419–36.

DiMaggio, Paul J., and Walter W. Powell. 1983. "The Iron Cage Revisited: Institutional Isomorphism and Collective Rationality in Organizational Fields." *American Sociological Review* 48 (1): 147–60.

49. Kerchner, Koppich, and Weeres (1997); Marshall and Tucker (1982).
50. Sanders (1998).

Erardi, John. 1985. "Teachers Win on Big Items: Accord on Class Size, Pay Holds Off Strike." *Cincinnati Enquirer* (February 22).

Janofsky, Michael. 1999. "For Denver Teachers, a Pay-for-Performance Plan." *New York Times* (September 10).

Johnson, Susan Moore. 1989. "Bargaining for Better Schools: Reshaping Education in the Cincinnati Public Schools." In *Allies in Education Reform: How Teachers, Unions and Administrators Can Join Forces to Better Schools,* edited by Jerome M. Rosow and Robert Zager, 124-45. Jossey-Bass.

Kemme, Steve. 1984 "Black Schools Have Weaker Curricula." *Cincinnati Enquirer* (December 4).

Kerchner, Charles T. 1991. "Louisville: Staff Development Drives a Decade of Reform." Project report, Project VISION, Claremont Graduate School, Claremont, Calif.

Kerchner, Charles T., and Julia E. Koppich. 1993. *A Union of Professionals: Labor Relations and Educational Reform.* Teacher's College Press.

Kerchner, Charles T., Julia E. Koppich, and J. G. Weeres. 1997. *United Mind Workers: Unions and Teaching in the Knowledge Society.* Jossey-Bass.

Kerchner, Charles T., and Douglas E. Mitchell. 1986. "Teaching Reform and Union Reform." *Elementary School Journal* 4 (4): 449–70.

———. 1988. *The Changing Idea of a Teachers' Union.* New York and London: Falmer Press.

Koppich, Julia E., P. Holmes, et al. 1998. *New Rules, New Roles? The Professional Work Lives of Charter School Teachers.* Washington, D.C.: National Education Association.

Kuhn, Thomas S. 1970. *The Structure of Scientific Revolutions.* University of Chicago Press.

Marshall, Ray, and Marc Tucker. 1992. *Thinking for a Living: Education and the Wealth of Nations.* Basic Books.

McGreal, Thomas. 1983. *Successful Teacher Evaluation.* Alexandria, Va.: Association for Supervision and Curriculum Development.

Minneapolis Public Schools and Minneapolis Federation of Teachers. 1997. *Teacher Contract, Agreements and Policies, June 1997–June 30, 1999.* Minneapolis Public Schools.

Mooney, Tom. 1983. "Don't Blame the Teachers." *Cincinnati Enquirer* (December 12).

Morris, Charles J., ed. 1971. *The Developing Labor Law.* Washington, D.C.: Bureau of National Affairs.

National Commission on Excellence in Education. 1983. *A Nation at Risk: The Imperative for Educational Reform; A Report to the Secretary of Education.* ED 226006. U.S. Department of Education.

National Foundation for the Improvement of Education (NFIE). 1996. *Teachers Take Charge of Their Learning: Transforming Professional Development for Student Success.* Washington, D.C.

Odden, Alan, and Carolyn Kelley. 1996. *Paying Teachers for What They Know and Do: New and Smarter Compensation Strategies for Improving Schools.* Thousand Oaks, Calif.: Corwin.

O'Brien, John. 1987. "Mentor Teacher Plan Wins." *Democrat and Chronicle* (June 19).

Peterson, Paul E. 1976. *School Politics Chicago Style.* University of Chicago Press.

Phillips, La Rae. 1993. "Miami: After the Hype." In *A Union of Professionals: Labor Relations and Educational Reform,* edited by C.T. Kerchner and J. E. Koppich, pp. 116–35. Teachers College Press.

Pleasure, Robert J., and Patricia A. Greenfield. 1995. "From Servants to Workers: A Modern Law of Work in the United States." In *Proceedings of the Forty-Seventh Annual Meeting,* edited by Paula Voos. Madison, Wis.: Industrial Relations Research Association.

Rabban, David M. 1989. "Distinguishing Excluded Managers from Covered Professionals under the NLRA." *Columbia Law Review* 89 (8): 1775–860.

Sanders, William L. 1998. "Value-Added Assessment." *School Administrator* 55 (11): 24–27.

Schlossberg, Stephen I., and Steven M. Fetter. 1986. *U.S. Labor Law and the Future of Labor-Management Cooperation* (Bureau of Labor Management Relations Report no. 104). Washington, D.C.: Government Printing Office.

Shanker, Albert. 1985. *The Making of a Profession.* Washington, D.C.: American Federation of Teachers.

Smylie, M. 1991. "Glenview, Illinois: From Contract to Constitution." Project report, Claremont Graduate School, Claremont Project VISION.

Smylie, Mark A., Jean Brownlee-Conyers, and R. L. Crowson. 1991. "When Teachers Make District Level Decisions: A Case Study." Paper presented at the annual meeting of the American Educational Research Association, Chicago, Ill.

Task Force on Redesigning Low Performing Schools, American Federation of Teachers. 1988. Electronic document (http://www.aft.org/edissues/rsa).

Tyack, David B. 1974. *The One Best System: A History of American Urban Education.* Harvard University Press.

Tyack, David, and Elizabeth Hansot. 1982. *Managers of Virtue: Public School Leadership in America, 1820–1980.* Basic Books.

White, Kerry A. 1999. "Ahead of the Curve." *Education Week* 18 (January 13): 32–35.

Wollett, Donald H., and Robert H. Chanin. 1974. *The Law and Practice of Teacher Negotiations.* Washington, D.C.: Bureau of National Affairs.

Contributors

Dale Ballou is professor of economics at the University of Massachusetts at Amherst, where he has been researching the economics of education reform.

William Lowe Boyd is distinguished professor of education at Pennsylvania State University, University Park.

James G. Cibulka is professor of education policy, planning, and administration at the University of Maryland, College Park, and associate dean in the College of Education.

Bruce S. Cooper is professor and vice chair in the Division of Administration, Policy, and Urban Education, Fordham University Graduate School of Education, New York.

Howard L. Fuller is professor of education at Marquette University, where he founded and directs the Institute for the Transformation of Learning. He was superintendent of the Milwaukee Public Schools from 1991 to 1995 and was secretary of the Wisconsin Department of Employment Relations.

Michael E. Hartmann, an attorney, is coordinator of civic renewal for the Lynde and Harry Bradley Foundation. He previously was director of research for the Wisconsin Policy Research Institute.

Susan Moore Johnson is the Carl H. Phorzheimer Jr. Professor of Teaching and Learning at the Harvard Graduate School of Education, where she served as academic dean from 1993 to 1999.

Susan M Kardos, a former middle school teacher, is currently an advanced doctoral student in administration, planning, and social policy at the Harvard Graduate School of Education.

Charles Taylor Kerchner is the Hollis P. Allen Professor of Education at Claremont Graduate University and a frequent collaborator with Julia Koppich.

Julia E. Koppich is president of Julia Koppich and Associates, a consulting firm specializing in educational policy and reform.

Tom Loveless, formerly a public school teacher and a professor at Harvard University, is director of the Brown Center on Education Policy at the Brookings Institution.

George A. Mitchell is a partner in the Mitchell Group, a public policy consultancy, and is assisting Howard Fuller in expanding the research capacity of the Institute for the Transformation of Learning.

David N. Plank is professor in the College of Education at Michigan State University, where he specializes in the areas of educational policy and finance.

Michael Podgursky is professor of economics at the University of Missouri, Columbia, and frequently collaborates with Dale Ballou.

Joe A. Stone is W. E. Miner Professor of Economics and dean of the College of Arts and Sciences at the University of Oregon.

Gary Sykes is professor of administration and teacher education at the Michigan State University College of Education.

Maris A. Vinovskis is the Bentley Professor of History, a senior research scientist at the Institute for Social Research, and a faculty member of the School of Public Policy at the University of Michigan.

Index

Accreditation. *See* Teacher education programs
Adamowski, Steven, 288–89
Administrators. *See* School administrators
Allen v. *Alabama,* 81
American Association of Colleges of Teacher Education (AACTE), 72
American Association of School Administrators, 299
American Educational Research Association (AERA), 215–17
American Federation of Labor-Congress of Industrial Organizations (AFL-CIO), 265, 282
American Federation of Teachers (AFT): AFL-CIO affiliation, 265, 301; bargaining power, 107, 118–19; Commission on Educational Reconstruction, 218; educational research, 5, 211–12, 214, 217–22, 225–28, 230, 231–34; Education for Democracy Project, 220; education standards, 3, 5, 106, 151–52, 222, 225–26, 231–32, 282, 285, 286; membership, 99; Minneapolis, 282; organizational structure, 170; peer review of teacher performance, 290; QuEST initiative, 285, 289; reform of unionism, 26, 285, 298; relations with NEA, 169, 171, 193, 217–20, 233, 260–61, 285, 301; teacher professionalism, 70–76, 79, 193. *See also* Shanker, Albert
American Medical Association (AMA), 77, 79, 82
Argys, Laura M., 54, 60–62, 64
Arizona, charter schools, 168, 179
Arkansas, labor relations policies, 260
Association of Educators in Private Practice, 306
Australia: collective bargaining rights for teachers, 247–48, 249, 252; school funding and political jurisdictions, 243, 245; teachers unions, 244, 245, 247, 265, 273
Avila Camacho, Manuel, 254